THE POLITICAL AND LEGAL FRAMEWORK OF TRADE RELATIONS BETWEEN THE EUROPEAN COMMUNITY AND EASTERN EUROPE

The Political and Legal Framework of Trade Relations Between the European Community and Eastern Europe

Edited by

MARC MARESCEAU

Professor of EEC Law at the Universities of Ghent and Brussels

EUROPEAN INSTITUTE — UNIVERSITY OF GHENT

MARTINUS NIJHOFF PUBLISHERS

DORDRECHT — BOSTON — LONDON

Library of Congress Cataloguing-in-Publication Data

The Political and legal framework of trade relations between the
  European community and eastern Europe / edited by Marc Maresceau.
      p.   cm.
  Includes bibliographical references and index.
  ISBN 0-7923-0046-7
    1. European Economic Community--Europe, Eastern--Congresses.
  2. Foreign trade regulation--European Economic Community countries-
  -Congresses.   3. Foreign trade regulation--Europe, Eastern-
  -Congresses.   4. Europe--Foreign economic relations--Europe,
  Eastern--Congresses.   5. Europe, Eastern--Foreign economic
  relations--Europe--Congresses.   I. Maresceau, Marc.
  KJE5113.A85   1987
  341.7'54--dc19   88-38800

ISBN 0—7923—0046—7

Published by Martinus Nijhoff Publishers,
P.O. Box 163, 3300 AD Dordrecht, The Netherlands

Sold and distributed in the U.S.A. and Canada
by Kluwer Academic Publishers,
101 Philip Drive, Norwell, MA 02061, U.S.A.

In all other countries, sold and distributed
by Kluwer Academic Publishers Group,
P.O. Box 322, 3300 AH Dordrecht, The Netherlands.

printed on acid free paper

Printed in The Netherlands

Table of contents

vi

viii

Abbreviations

AJIL	American Journal of International Law
ASEAN	Association of South East Asian States
AWD	Aussenwirtschaftsdienst des Betriebs-Beraters
BIS	Bank for International Settlements
BISD	Basic Instruments and Selected Documents (GATT)
BLEU	Belgo-Luxembourg Economic Union
Bull EC	Bulletin of the European Communities
CAP	Common Agricultural Policy
CMEA	Council for Mutual Economic Assistance
CMLRev	Common Market Law Review
COCOM	Coordinating Committee for Multilateral Export Controls
COMECON	Council for Mutual Economic Assistance
CPSU	Communist Party of the Soviet Union
CSCE	Conference on Security and Cooperation in Europe
ECE	Economic Commission for Europe
ECR	European Court Reports
ECJ	European Court of Justice
ECSC	European Coal and Steel Community
ECU	European Currency Unit
EEC	European Economic Community
EEe	Eastern European enterprise
EFTA	European Free Trade Association
EP	European Parliament
Fed Reg	Federal Regulation
FTO	Foreign Trade Organisation
GATT	General Agreement on Tariffs and Trade
GDP	Gross Domestic Product
GSP	General System of Preferences
ICLQ	International and Comparative Law Quarterly
IEA	International Energy Agency

IMF	International Monetary Fund
J Pol Econ	Journal of Politics and Economics
JWTL	Journal of World Trade Law
LIBOR	London Inter Bank Offered Rate
MFN	Most Favoured Nation
NIC's	Newly Industrialised Countries
NME	Non-Market Economy Country
NMP	Net Material Product
OECD	Organisation for Economic Cooperation and Development
OJ	Official Journal of the European Communities
Pc	Per cent
QRs	Quantitative Restrictions
SEW	Sociaal-economische Wetgeving
SITC	Standard International Trade Classification
UNCTAD	United Nations Conference on Trade and Development

Preface

Bernard Shaw's view that "we must trade and travel and come to know one another all over the habitable globe"[1] seems hardly to have inspired the relations between Western and Eastern Europe in the second half of the XXth century. Stagnation, mistrust and hostility have for too long been the main characteristics of these relationships. Certainly, from an editorial point of view, a Manichean approach presented a comfortable position: a text on the relations between the European Community and Eastern Europe could be used for decades.

This volume on the political and legal framework of trade relations between the European Community and Eastern Europe may be an indication that things are fundamentally changing. Basically, it contains the reports of a colloquium organised by the Department of European Community Law of the University of Ghent on 17—18 December 1987. This meeting in Ghent was in many respects a unique event. One seldom finds on the same platform so many prominent speakers from Western and Eastern Europe brought together on a multidisciplinary basis. Such an approach was indeed indispensable because of the very nature of the object of the meeting which was, why should we conceal it, a very complex, delicate and sensitive one embracing political, legal and economic issues all at once. This also explains why this volume contains contributions from "practitioners in the field" consisting of top level politicians, diplomats and officials or prominent businessmen, together with reflections from distinguished academics.

It was certainly a mere coincidence that the Ghent Colloquium happened to take place just one week after the arms reduction agreement between President Reagan and Secretary General Gorbachev but this event illustrated perhaps even more the necessity of such a meeting. It is not easy to explain why an agreement on nuclear arms in Europe can be reached between the USA and the USSR while at the same time Europeans among themselves have thus far been unable to agree on basic frameworks for their mutual relations. Clearly, the lack of normalisation of

M. Maresceau (ed.), The Political and Legal Framework of Trade Relations Between the European Community and Eastern Europe. ISBN 0–7923–0046–7.
© 1989 by Kluwer Academic Publishers, Dordrecht – Printed in the Netherlands.

trade relations was and is detrimental to Europe as a whole. It is therefore undoubtedly a positive sign that more and more people at various levels in Western and Eastern Europe seem to realise this. Times have indeed rarely been so propitious for a sincere reappraisal of the situation. Besides the improvement of the general political climate between East and West there are in Western Europe strong calls, particularly from the business community, for substantial trade improvement with Eastern Europe. Moreover, in many Eastern European countries structural economic reforms are taking place and last but not least the new policies introduced by the Soviet leadership are all important factors to be brought into the discussion. Without doubt Secretary General Gorbachev's words that "we must tackle problems in a spirit of cooperation rather than animosity"[2] are also particularly relevant to the trade relations between Western and Eastern Europe. Of course, there are still many problems to be overcome, approaches and aims may be different and realism in the development of future relations is needed. Moreover, all structural economic reforms need time to produce results and a normalisation of mutual relations between the EEC and Eastern Europe cannot, on its own, provide an immediate boost in existing trade patterns. It is clear, however, that in this new climate a dynamic form of trade relations between the EEC and Eastern Europe can be developed.

This book — of which a Russian edition under the supervision of Dr. Y. Borko, Head of Department of the Institute of Scientific Information for Social Sciences, Academy of Sciences of the USSR, is also forthcoming — does not simply reproduce the written reports of the colloquium but its layout does largely correspond to the structure of the meeting of 17—18 December 1987. The first part covers the general framework of trade relations between the European Community and Eastern Europe while the second part focuses on the position of Western European enterprises in Eastern Europe. The third part deals with specific East-West European trade issues. The texts of the concluding speeches at the colloquium by Mr. Sychev, Secretary of the Council for Mutual Economic Assistance, and Mr. De Clercq, Member of the Commission of the European Communities responsible for External Relations, form the last part of this book. They have been included in the form they were presented, but most of the other reports were revised by the rapporteurs at the beginning of 1988 for the purpose of this publication. However, even since then, important events have taken place. On 25 June 1988 the EEC and the CMEA adopted the Joint Declaration on the establishment of official relations between both organisations.[3] On 30 June 1988 the EEC and Hungary initialled the text of an agreement on trade and commercial and economic cooperation.[4] These recent evolutions have, as much as possible, been incorporated in an introduction and in an addendum the text of the Joint Declaration and the Agreement EEC — Hungary is included.[5]

This book is a direct result of the colloquium of 17—18 December. I would therefore like to express my sincere gratitude to the institutions that made this colloquium possible. Substantial support was received from the Commission of the European Communities, the Belgian National Fund for Scientific Research (N.F.W.O.), the Belgian Ministry of Education and the University of Ghent. A generous contribution to the colloquium was made by the Generale Bank while the City of Ghent also played an important role in providing the necessary backing.

I owe a special debt of gratitude to Mr. De Clercq, the Commissioner for External Relations, who gave active moral support to this initiative from the moment the organisation of the colloquium was not much more than an extravagant idea in the organiser's mind and to Mr. Delors, the President of the Commission, who very kindly accepted the patronage of the colloquium. Mrs. Coninsx, a member of Mr. De Clercq's Cabinet, also provided many invaluable suggestions for which I am most grateful.

All the speakers and rapporteurs from Western and Eastern Europe who have contributed to this book deserve a special mention. Their willingness to collaborate on this initiative and their friendship resulted in a very stimulating joint venture.

Finally, I must express my sincere gratitude to all the members of my staff and to the many freelance collaborators who joined us in this undertaking. They contributed considerably to the success of the Ghent Colloquium and all experienced that organising a colloquium is a difficult but nonetheless fascinating adventure. A special word of thanks goes to Mrs. Van den Spiegel who from the very beginning was involved in this initiative and without whom the organisation of the colloquium — and therefore also the publication of this book — would never have been possible. I also have a special debt to Miss Van den Bossche and Mr. Sarre, both Research fellows with the Belgian Fund for Joint Basic Research (F.K.F.O.) at the University of Ghent, who took upon themselves a substantial amount of the editorial work.

Ghent, 10 August 1988
Marc Maresceau

Notes

1. B. Shaw, *The Intelligent Women's Guide to Socialism and Capitalism*, London, Constable and Company Ltd., 1928, p. 157.
2. M. Gorbachev, *Perestroika. New thinking for our country and the world*, London, Collins, 1987, p. 9.
3. See addendum I.
4. Since the completion of this volume the Agreement between the EEC and Hungary has

been signed and published in the *Official Journal of the European Communities* (L 327/1, 1988), see addendum II.

5. An agreement between the EEC and Czechoslovakia was initialled and concluded after the setting of this book by the publisher. After proof-reading it was still possible to include the text of the Agreement on trade in industrial products signed on 19 December 1988, see addendum III.

PART ONE

General framework of trade relations
European Community-Eastern Europe

A general survey of the current legal framework of trade relations between the European Community and Eastern Europe

MARC MARESCEAU

Professor; Director Department of European Community Law, University of Ghent

I. Introduction

The legal basis for the development of a common commercial policy by the European Community is laid down in Art. 110 ff., in particular Art. 113, of the EEC Treaty. Art. 113 provides that "after the transitional period the common commercial policy shall be based on uniform principles, particularly with regard to changes in tariff rates, the conclusion of tariff and trade agreements, the achievement of uniformity in measures of liberalisation, export policy and measures to protect trade such as those to be taken in case of dumping or subsidies". Just before the end of the transitional period, that is to say in December 1969, the Council of Ministers enacted a Regulation in which it stated that the common commercial policy should also apply towards State-trading countries, but recognised at the same time the somewhat specific nature of this relationship.[1] In practice, this meant that the transitional period was extended in such a way that bilateral trade agreements between the individual Member States of the European Community and Eastern European countries were further maintained. However, those bilateral agreements were due to expire by the end of 1974 or had otherwise to be denounced by that date.[2]

Before this deadline arrived contacts took place between the CMEA and the Commission but they did not lead to concrete results (Maslen, *infra* pp. 85—86) while no bilateral trade agreements between the EEC and Eastern European countries were concluded to replace the existing bilateral agreements between the Member States of the Community and Eastern European countries.[3] This explains why, since the end of 1974, the legal framework of trade relations between the EEC and Eastern Europe has to a large extent been determined by unilateral or autonomous commercial policy measures. However, it would be wrong to describe,

M. Maresceau (ed.), The Political and Legal Framework of Trade Relations Between the European Community and Eastern Europe. ISBN 0–7923–0046–7.
© *1989 by Kluwer Academic Publishers, Dordrecht – Printed in the Netherlands.*

from the point of view of European Community law, the framework of trade relations EEC-Eastern Europe only in terms of unilateral Community measures. With Romania a bilateral agreement on trade in industrial products was concluded in 1980. Sectoral agreements between the EEC and a great number of Eastern European countries have also been signed. In addition, several Eastern European countries are at present Contracting Parties to GATT. The GATT and/or their respective Protocols of Accession to GATT therefore affect the relations of those countries with the EEC. Moreover, important recent evolutions need to be added to this general picture. On 25 June 1988 a Joint Declaration EEC-CMEA was signed which, although not directly dealing with trade, will have a considerable impact on the normalisation of relations between the EEC and Eastern Europe as a whole, while on 30 June 1988 a trade and cooperation agreement EEC-Hungary was initialled which is due to be signed on 26 September 1988.[3 bis]

The main purpose of this survey, which by no means pretends to be an exhaustive analysis, is to present a comprehensive basic legal structure of the trade relations between the EEC and Eastern Europe.[4] This should help the reader to put the contributions of the various authors contained in this book in a broader EEC law perspective. In this short survey an attempt has also been made to include some substantial new evolutions which have occurred since the contributions to this book were submitted.

II. Inter-institutional relations EEC-CMEA

The difficulties on the road towards an EEC-CMEA agreement have been highlighted in the text by Mr. Maslen (*infra* pp. 85—92) and the expectations of Mr. De Clercq (*infra* pp. 315—318) and Mr. Sychev (*infra* pp. 311—313) expressed at the Ghent Colloquium on 18 December 1987 have finally materialised in the signature of the Joint Declaration on 25 June 1988.[5]

While the text of the Declaration is kept short — it hardly covers one page in the *Official Journal of the European Communities* — its repercussions may be considerable. First, the Joint Declaration aims at establishing official relations between the EEC and CMEA. This, of course, has great political significance: after years of deadlock and obstruction it demonstrates a willingness by both parties to turn a page in each other's mutual history. Practically speaking, it implies a recognition of the EEC by the individual members of CMEA and as a result of this all Eastern European countries — except up to now Romania — have asked for an accreditation of Ambassadors to the European Communities. However, at this stage, the Joint Declaration does not imply that the EEC as such will be accredited to the CMEA nor *vice versa*.

Secondly, the Parties to the Joint Declaration agree "(to)develop co-operation in areas which fall within their respective spheres of competence and where there is a common interest". Under the present CMEA rules, commercial policy is not within the CMEA's "sphere of competence" and is therefore excluded as an immediate area of cooperation. The Community has also on various occasions taken the point of view that trade, rather than to be covered by an agreement or a declaration between the EEC-CMEA, had to be brought within the framework of direct relations between the EEC and individual Member States of the CMEA (De Clercq, *infra* p. 317 and Maslen, *infra* p. 89). In this respect it should be noted that the Council Decision of 22 June 1988 on the conclusion of the Joint Declaration, by stipulating that "whereas, for the attainment of the objectives of the Community in the sphere of external relations . . . the Treaty has not provided the necessary powers, other than those of Article 235", implicitly assumes that the Joint Declaration cannot be brought within the scope of Art. 110 ff. EEC Treaty.

The domains of potential cooperation are not indicated in so many words in the Declaration. They are to be determined together with the future forms and methods of cooperation in later contacts between the two organisations. In the past, areas such as statistics, economic planning and forecasting, norms and standards and environment have been mentioned.[6] The CMEA is particularly interested in scientific and technological cooperation (Sychev, *infra* pp. 312—313 and Ougarov, *infra*, pp. 99—100). The way in which institutional cooperation will be developed in the future will also be determined by the evolution within CMEA itself.[7]

Finally, the long-standing bone of contention known as the "Berlin territorial clause" — which has delayed the signature of the Declaration and which had become a *conditio sine qua non* for a political agreement between the EEC and CMEA — has been settled. The Declaration explicitly stipulates that for the Community the territorial scope of the Declaration covers "the territories in which the Treaty establishing the European Economic Community is applied and under the conditions laid down in that Treaty". A unilateral declaration by CMEA makes it clear that the Joint Declaration does not affect the Four Powers Agreement on Berlin of 3 September 1971.[8]

III. Trade relations and economic cooperation EEC-Eastern Europe

Broadly speaking, the framework of trade relations EEC-Eastern European countries can be divided up into bilateral and multilateral relationships on the one hand and autonomous Community rules and mechanisms on the other.

A. *Bilateral agreements*

1. *General trade and/or economic cooperation agreements.* To date the EEC has concluded a general trade agreement with Romania and at the moment of writing this survey a trade and commercial and economic cooperation agreement with Hungary was initialled and is due to be signed in September. Agreements with other Eastern European countries will also be negotiated in the near future (Benavides, *infra* p. 22).

a. *Romania.* The Agreement with Romania signed in 1980[9] is of a non-preferential nature and covers trade in industrial products (Dijmărescu, *infra* p. 40). There have been suggestions to broaden the scope of the existing agreement by replacing it by a "trade and cooperation agreement" but such a move has so far proved to be difficult. It appears that the Community for economic as well as for political reasons is dissatisfied with the current state of affairs in its relations with Romania. Due to a drastic attempt to reduce her foreign debt Romania has considerably decreased her imports. This has inevitably hit the Community's exports to Romania[10] so that, for the moment, the prospects for improved trading conditions between the EEC and Romania or for a broader framework agreement are not very promising.

b. *Hungary.* A very important agreement was initialled on 30 June 1988 between the EEC and Hungary.[10 bis] It covers, as its title indicates, "trade and *commercial* and economic cooperation".[11] After the Trade and Economic Cooperation Agreement with the People's Republic of China, the Agreement with Hungary is the second "cooperation agreement" with a socialist country, exceeding the former in extent and scope. The trade and cooperation agreement with Hungary is indeed the first agreement of its kind with a European socialist country.

The various aspects of the relations EEC-Hungary are further analysed in detail (Balázs, *infra* pp. 55—74). Suffice it here to highlight the main characteristics of this agreement. The Preamble of the Agreement refers to "the favourable implications for trade and economic relations between the Contracting Parties of their respective economic situations and policies" and to the principles of equality, non-discrimination, mutual benefit and reciprocity as objectives for cooperation. The Agreement, in its trade chapter, starts by making a reference to the application of the most-favoured nation principle in accordance with GATT (Art. 1). *Ratione materiae*, the Agreement is applicable to all products except those covered by existing bilateral sectoral agreements and arrangements such as agricultural products and textiles (Art. 3). Also products covered by the European Coal and Steel Community Treaty are excluded from the scope of application of the Agreement.[12] Most importantly, the Agreement contains an explicit commitment on the part of the Community to eliminate existing quantitative restrictions on imports into the Community of products originating in Hungary. The procedure and time-limits for the abolition of quantitative restrictions are laid down in an additional Protocol.[13] For non-sensitive products the Community undertakes to abolish existing quantitative restrictions within one year after the entry into force of the agreement. For another category of products the deadline for the elimination of quotas is 31 December 1992. Finally, for a limited number of very sensitive products (e.g. textiles, wood, glass, leather products, colour TV sets) the deadline for the abolition of existing quotas is 31 December 1995. Hungary, for her part, explicitly agrees *inter alia* not to apply discriminatory measures and procedures in areas such as business facilities, import licensing, administration of global quotas for consumer goods, and the awarding of contracts as a result of World Bank or other international tenders. Moreover, Hungary guarantees legal protection of intellectual property rights for both products and processes in accordance with international conventions to which Hungary is a party (see Annex relating to Art. 10 of the Agreement). The Agreement also contains a detailed safeguard mechanism consisting of a consultation procedure as well as a procedure to introduce import restrictions (Art. 7). It should be noted that for certain categories of certain products and under certain conditions a specific safeguard mechanism can be applied until 31 December 1998. In this case resort to GATT in order to solve disputes is only allowed once the specific safeguard procedure provided for in the Protocol to the Agreement has been fully implemented.

Furthermore, the agreement stipulates that countertrade practices may create trade distortions, therefore remaining exceptional mechanisms for mutual trade. Countertrade cannot be imposed by the Contracting Parties on their respective companies but where firms or companies resort to countertrade the Contracting Parties will encourage them to provide all relevant information to facilitate the transaction (Art. 10, sub 3). Lastly, the Contracting Parties will encourage the adoption of arbitration as a means for the settlement of disputes arising out of commercial and cooperation transactions concluded by firms, enterprises and economic organisations (Art. 9).

The second part of the Agreement deals with economic cooperation. The main cooperation objectives are *inter alia* "-to reinforce and diversify economic links between the Contracting Parties; -to contribute to the development of their respective economies and standards of living; -to open up new sources of supply and new markets; -to encourage cooperation between economic operators, with a view to promoting joint ventures, licensing agreements, and other forms of industrial cooperation to develop their respective industries; -to encourage scientific and technological progress". To this end the Contracting Parties agree to encourage the adoption of measures aimed at creating favourable conditions for the facilitation of exchanges of commercial and economic information, for the development of a favourable investment climate, joint ventures and licensing agreements. The provisions of the Agreement EEC-Hungary replace the provisions of agreements concluded between the Member States of the Community and Hungary "to the extent to which the latter provisions are either incompatible with or identical to the former" (Art. 14(2)). But as it is the rule with all cooperation agreements concluded by the Community with third countries, the Agreement EEC-Hungary also continues to allow Member States to undertake bilateral activities with Hungary in the area of economic cooperation and to conclude, where appropriate, new economic cooperation agreements (Art. 12). Finally, a joint committee is set up to ensure the proper functioning of the Agreement.

It is obvious that this agreement, which is the result of long and exhausting negotiations, constitutes an important milestone in the relations between the EEC and Eastern Europe. It contains clear commitments for both Contracting Parties. The formulation of the terms of the Agreement, at least as far as the trade aspect is concerned, is such that for the Contracting Parties precise and legally binding obligations are created. From the point of view of Community law there can be no doubt about the fact that these obligations are enforceable in the legal order of the European Community. The deadlines of the implementation periods are well determined and non-respect by the Community or by Member States could lead to legal actions before the European Court of Justice or before domestic courts. It should also be mentioned that Hungary has committed itself to clearly defined legal obligations which can considerably stimulate and increase Western European business operations. The Agreement EEC-Hungary is probably the Community bilateral agreement containing a record number of references to GATT.[14] Already Art.1 of the Agreement makes a general reference to the MFN principle. It is also interesting to note in this respect that the Community's undertaking to abolish the existing quantitative restrictions has been put in a GATT perspective, particularly by referring to Art. 4 (a) of the Protocol of Accession of Hungary to GATT. Moreover, the safeguard procedure incorporated in the EEC-Hungary Agreement (Art. 7) is largely inspired by the procedure of Art. 5 of the Protocol of Accession of Hungary to GATT. In case of disagreement between the EEC and Hungary concerning the interpretation of the safeguard mechanism contained in the bilateral Agreement either party may refer the question to the Contracting Parties of the GATT in accordance with Art. 5 of Hungary's Protocol of Accession.

c. *Czechoslovakia*. Negotiations for a trade agreement with Czechoslovakia were virtually completed at the moment of writing this introduction (Cernohuby, *infra* p. 53). This agreement — limited in scope — is the result of a pragmatic approach by both parties and is intended to cover trade in industrial products. However, some last minute difficulties arose when Czechoslovakia — probably on the basis of what had been agreed upon in the Agreement EEC-Hungary — asked for a clear deadline on the elimination of quantitative restrictions by the Community.[15] Negotiations will be resumed in the second half of 1988.[15 bis]

d. *USSR, Poland, Bulgaria, GDR*. The Commission has, for the moment, no mandate to negotiate agreements with the USSR, Poland, Bulgaria and the GDR and so far only exploratory talks with those countries have been held.

Poland and Bulgaria have already expressed their interest in concluding a trade and cooperation agreement with the Community while the German Democratic Republic is interested in concluding a trade agreement on condition, however, that this does not interfere with the existing protocol on German internal trade.[16]

In March 1988 the USSR submitted to the Commission her thoughts on possible future relations with the Community.[17] They include an ambitious programme for an agreement or agreements covering industrial investment, as well as technological and sectoral cooperation. According to Mr. Ivanov, Vice-President of the State Commission for External Economic Relations of the Council of Ministers of the USSR, the possible agreements with the Community should be innovative in a sense "that one should be aware that, with perestroika under way, an access to the future Soviet markets will be feasible not through old-fashioned merchant exchange, diminishing nowadays in its volume and attraction, but predominantly through new types of business arrangements, conducive to industrial, investment and technological cooperation".[18] The Ivanov-proposal includes vast areas for cooperation such as investment, coproduction, financing, currency, Ecu, research and development, intellectual property, energy, transportation, agriculture, fishing, standardisation, environment, textiles, nuclear safety, statistics, competition, relations with third countries, conditions for businessmen, and institutional arrangements.

This proposal certainly constitutes a serious challenge for the Community. In March 1988 a first exploratory meeting took place in Brussels and the reaction of the Commission was cautious. The Commission has indicated that in the past the Community's practice has been first to conclude a trade agreement and if possible afterwards to broaden its scope towards a trade and economic cooperation agreement. It is true, of course, that the USSR may be less inclined to conclude a classical trade agreement since most of the products exported by the USSR to the Community happen to be imported duty free or at a low tariff (oil, gas, raw materials). However, there are indications that the Commission is now willing to favourably consider future discussions on the prospects of a cooperation agreement if certain conditions are met.[19] Without doubt, those conditions will *inter alia* imply that future agreements should not be a one-way operation and, particularly, in the area of business facilities the EEC may wish to obtain clear commitments from the USSR.[20]

2. *Sectoral agreements.* The Community has concluded a number of sectoral agreements with Eastern European countries such as Romania, Poland, Hungary, Czechoslovakia and Bulgaria.[21] These agreements cover the following areas: textiles, iron and steel and agricultural products such as sheep- and goatmeat. The basic characteristic of all these agreements is a voluntary restraint undertaking by the Eastern European contracting party. In a few sectors, such as e.g. iron and steel, the Eastern European countries have agreed not to sell below certain minimum prices. The conclusion by the Community of sectoral agreements with Eastern European countries has not prevented some Member States from asking the Community for authorisations under Art. 115 EEC Treaty to limit indirect imports within the Community.[22]

B. *Multilateral framework*

A number of Eastern European countries are members of GATT. Czechoslovakia was a founding member of GATT and remained a GATT Contracting Party even after the change in her political régime. Poland, Romania and Hungary acceded to GATT, all on different terms of accession (Martonyi, *infra* pp. 271–272). It appears that there is a general and long-standing complaint by those countries as far as the EEC is concerned. They all consider themselves to be victims of discriminatory quantitative restrictions by the Community. Although the problem of quantitative restrictions was examined at length when the terms of accession of Poland, Romania and Hungary were discussed, it was understood — at least by the Eastern European Contracting Parties — that the Community's quantitative restrictions would gradually by eliminated.[23] It should be recalled that, as far as Hungary is concerned, the bilateral agreement with the Community provides that all existing quantitative restrictions be eliminated by 1995.

C. *The Community import régime*

1. *General rules on imports into the Community also affecting imports from Eastern Europe*

a. *Direct imports.* A number of general rules on imports into the Community are also relevant for imports of goods originating in Eastern Europe. Of course, such goods are, just as any other goods originating in third countries, subject to the tariffs of the Common Customs Tariff. As a consequence of bilateral or multilateral agreements and unilateral Community measures, those tariffs can be abolished or decreased. The Community's competence to increase the level of an existing customs tariff is limited as a result of international obligations and Member States of the Community have totally lost their competence to change of their own motion the Common Customs Tariff.

Since the Community does not determine the customs duty in function of the origin of a product but on the basis of its classification in the Common Customs Tariff, tariffs applicable to goods originating in Eastern Europe are in principle the same as compared to those applicable to identical or similar products originating in other third countries. Only if the Community has concluded specific agreements such as association or free trade agreements — as, for example, with the EFTA-countries — or if goods originate in developing countries, is preferential customs treatment based on the origin of the imported goods applicable.[24]

Customs duties are not the only levies which may be imposed on imported products. Other duties known as "charges having equivalent effect" as customs duties may also be levied. It results from the case-law of the European Court of Justice that Member States of the Community are prevented from unilaterally imposing such charges on direct imports from non-EEC countries. In the *Diamantarbeiders v. Indiamex* case[25] the European Court held that the Common Customs Tariff, as such, did not include "charges having equivalent effect" but it derived from the objectives of the Common Customs Tariff the principle that Member States are prohibited from amending, by means of charges supplementing such duties, the level of protection as defined by the Common Customs Tariff. According to the Court, "since the adoption of (the) common commercial

policy falls within the exclusive jurisdiction of the Community, the equal-
isation of charges other than customs duties as such for all the Member
States or their elimination is dependent upon an intervention by the
Community".

In this context it should also be remembered that under Community
law currently in force, taxation on direct imports from non-EEC countries
is still largely a matter in the hands of the Member States. However, as far
as this point is concerned, Member States are bound by international
obligations resulting from GATT or from bilateral agreements concluded
by the European Community.

The non-respect of the non-discrimination principle in the area of
taxation, as accepted by the Contracting Parties to GATT, should be
assimilated to a violation of a Community law obligation[26] and could,
therefore, lead to proceedings ex Art. 169 EEC Treaty before the
European Court of Justice.[27] Moreover, in a number of bilateral agreements concluded between the European Community and third countries
discriminatory tax treatment is prohibited. A clear example of such a
prohibition is Art. 3, sub c, of the Trade and Economic Cooperation
Agreement between the EEC and the People's Republic of China where
MFN-treatment is made applicable to all matters regarding taxes levied
directly or indirectly on Chinese products imported directly or indirectly
into the Community.[28] Obviously, such a clause may be relevant for
countries — such as China — which are not members of GATT but its
significance must not be overestimated. There where no multilateral or
bilateral agreements provide for the elimination of discriminatory tax
treatment on direct imports from third countries Member States cannot
with impunity hit imports from third countries by means of discriminatory
taxes. In the hypothesis that Member States are allowed to impose such
taxes — a point of view which is not so apparent since this could seriously
interfere with the common commercial policy of the Community[29] —
trade deflection could occur. This would mean that goods subject to
higher taxes in a Member State could be imported in another Member
State with a lower tax rate and then be exported to the Member State with
the higher tax burden. The application of the *Cooperativa Cofrutta*
judgment of the European Court of Justice (see *infra* p. 13) could take
away the protectionist effect of the discriminatory tax burden imposed by
the latter Member State.

b. *Indirect imports.* Goods originating in non-EEC countries, including
Eastern European countries, and duly imported in a Member State of the
Community — that is to say that all customs formalities in that Member

State have been fulfilled — can be exported from the importing Member State to all other Member States of the Community in accordance with Art. 9 and 10 EEC Treaty. This means that those exports cannot be subjected to customs duties or any other financial charges, quantitative restrictions or non-tariff barriers. They are, as the European Court of Justice has clearly indicated in the *Donckerwolcke* case,[30] entitled to free circulation in the Community and assimilated to products originating in a Member State. Of course, the derogations to the principle of free movement in intra-Community trade of goods applicable to goods originating in a Member State (Art. 36 EEC Treaty) are also applicable to goods originating in third countries and brought into free circulation. Besides this exception there is, however, also a second type of derogation which is exclusively applicable to products originating in third countries and brought into free circulation in a Member State. This exception is laid down in Art. 115 EEC Treaty allowing Member States on the basis of an authorisation from the Commission to take specific safeguard measures in the absence of a Community common commercial policy. Thus far a wide use has been made of this procedure also in relation to imports of products originating in Eastern Europe.[31] Particularly France and Italy have asked the Commission for safeguard authorisations under Art. 115 EEC Treaty mainly for textile products and certain industrial goods.

As far as taxes imposed on goods originating in third countries and brought into free circulation are concerned, the *Cooperativa Cofrutta* ruling of the European Court of Justice[32] provides a clear answer. In that case the European Court held that Article 95 EEC Treaty — which stipulates that no Member State shall impose, directly or indirectly, on products of other Member States any internal taxation in excess of that imposed on similar domestic products — is applicable to products originating in third countries and brought into free circulation in a Member State. The Court's reasoning was based on the inherent link between Art. 9 and 95 EEC Treaty and on the assimilation-reasoning as expressed in the *Donckerwolcke* case. The purpose of Art. 95, according to the Court, "is to ensure free movement of goods between the Member States in normal conditions of competition by the elimination of all forms of protection which result from the internal taxation which discriminates against products from other Member States".

2. Specific Community regulations covering imports from Eastern Europe.
It has already been mentioned that the existing trade policy of the Member States of the Community vis-à-vis Eastern European countries was to be replaced by the Community's common commercial policy by the

end of 1974. At the moment the main unilateral legal instrument governing trade relations with Eastern Europe is Community Regulation 1765/82 dealing with imports from State-trading countries.[33] The concept "State-trading country" includes *inter alia* all Eastern European CMEA member states.[34] The basic idea of this import régime is that products covered by the Annex to the Regulation are not subject to quantitative restrictions. The Annex forms the so-called common liberalisation list (exhaustive list). However, many products which in one way or another are considered to be sensitive for one or more Member States are not included in the Annex to Regulation 1765/82. Those products are covered by Community Regulation 3420/83 of 14 November 1983 on import arrangements for products originating in State-trading countries not liberalised at Community level.[35] This Regulation requires the Council to lay down before the 1st of December of every year the quotas which Member States are authorised to maintain the following year concerning the import of products originating in State-trading countries covered by the Regulation.[36] This regulation consolidates so to speak the quotas applied by Member States through their existing bilateral agreements with various Eastern European countries.[37] The main rule of this Regulation is that those products are subject of quantitative import restrictions in the Member States as indicated in the Annex. The goods mentioned in the Annex can only be put into free circulation in the Community subject to the granting of an import authorisation. It is precisely these "discriminatory quantitative restrictions", to use Eastern European terminology, that are strongly resented by the Eastern European countries. From a Community point of view a serious implication of this Regulation is that for the products covered it leads to a splitting up of the common market. This in turn may lead to applications of Art. 115 EEC Treaty in order to avoid trade deflection. Another interesting question, of course, and one which at this moment has not yet been solved, concerns the conditions under which these specific national quantitative restrictions can be replaced after 1992.[38] Of course, the Regulation in question will also need to be adapted as a result of commitments undertaken by the Community such as, for example, in the Agreement with Hungary.

In addition, it should be mentioned that the two basic import regulations lay down detailed investigation procedures. These procedures must be followed before a Member State is entitled to take any surveillance or safeguard measures. So far, there have been few applications of such measures regarding imports from Eastern Europe.

Finally, non-tariff barriers known in EEC terminology as "measures having an effect equivalent to quantitative restrictions" are not covered by the Community Regulations on imports. Elimination of such measures is sometimes provided in multilateral agreements such as GATT or the Lomé Conventions and in bilateral agreements concluded by the Community (e.g. with the EFTA-countries). The case-law of the European Court demonstrates, however, that one should be careful when dealing with the concept of "measures having equivalent effect" in Community law. In the *Polydor v. Harlequin*[39] case the Court made it clear that the contents of the notion "measures having equivalent effect" used in an intra-Community context (Art. 30 EEC Treaty) did not necessarily have the same meaning as that in a European Community-third country context since the objec-tive of the EEC Treaty on the one hand, and that of an agreement between the EEC and a third country on the other, is not identical.

3. *Anti-dumping measures.* Although the Community anti-dumping mechanism laid down in Community regulations is the result of multi-lateral agreements (GATT and Tokyo Round) the application to concrete cases is based on a unilateral Community decision. Dumping is defined in the Community regulations as selling below normal value. A Community anti-dumping proceeding is initiated by the Commission after a complaint by a Community industry. The dumping must cause injury to the Com-munity industry before the anti-dumping mechanism can be triggered. Since the coming into force of the basic Community anti-dumping Regula-tion of 1979, which was replaced by a new Regulation in 1984, there has been a substantial increase in anti-dumping procedures in the Community with a considerable number of anti-dumping procedures being initiated against imports from State-trading countries. Prof. Jacobs has clearly demonstrated (*infra* p. 299) in this context that one of the main issues is the determination of "normal value". What is indeed the "normal value" of a product produced in an Eastern European country? The Community anti-dumping Regulation departs from the assumption that there is no such notion as "normal value" in a State-trading country. Thus, the normal value will be determined on the basis of (a) the price at which the like product of a market economy third country is actually sold for consump-tion on the domestic market of that country or to other countries, or (b) the constructed value of the like product in a market economy third country.

These points of reference used for the determination of normal value have sometimes been criticised and challenged by exporters from State-trading countries. The application of the Community anti-dumping mechanism implies that in last resort a genuine competitive advantage of a State-trading country vis-à-vis a market economy country cannot be taken into consideration. Although in the past most anti-dumping procedures initiated against imports from Eastern Europe have led to price undertakings from the exporters, there are now a few new cases pending before the European Court of Justice (Jacobs, *infra* pp. 300 and 302). It is perhaps also interesting to note in this respect that in 1983 a Soviet import-export firm — Raznoimport — did not hesitate to challenge directly, in other words not through a Community importer, an anti-dumping procedure before the Court of Justice.[40] A few cases, also involving imports of Soviet products, are now pending before the Court. Reference can be made, for example, to the *Deep freezers* case[41] or to the *Enital* case.[42] The latter may be of particular interest in the light of the existing case-law of the European Court on admissibility of actions brought by an importer under Art. 173(2) EEC Treaty. So far, the Court has always rejected such an action holding that importers do not satisfy the admissibility test of Art. 173(2) EEC Treaty, in other words because they, as opposed to the exporter, are not "directly and individually concerned" by the anti-dumping Regulation. However, there has been one exception in the Court's approach namely where the importer is a subsidiary of the exporter.[43] In the *Enital* case Energomachexport, a Soviet firm, is one of the shareholders of the Italian applicant.

4. *Application of Community anti-trust provisions.* The anti-trust provisions of the EEC, on the basis of the effects doctrine,[44] are also applicable to Eastern European companies, firms or entities involved in anti-competitive practices affecting competition within the Community. This is the clear message we find in the Commission anti-trust decision on *Aluminium imports from Eastern Europe.*[45] In this decision it appeared that foreign trade organisations from the USSR, Poland, Hungary, Czechoslovakia and the GDR had agreed to sell aluminium only to a group of Western primary aluminium producers. In return for this the Eastern European foreign trade organisations agreed not to sell to other potential Western purchasers. The main purpose of the agreement from the point of view of the Western contracting parties was, of course, to maintain prices, particularly in the EEC. In its decision the Commission held that the said arrangements constituted infringements of Art. 85(1) EEC Treaty. The Commission explicitly stated that, although the Eastern European trade organisations were State enterprises, they did not benefit from sovereign immunity. Here, according to the Commission, one did not deal with "acts of government" but with "acts of trade".[46] Trade activities of such companies, therefore, come within the scope of the EEC anti-trust provisions, "even if the foreign trade organisations were indistinguishable under Socialist law from the State" and "whatever their precise status may be under the domestic law of their country of origin". The economic reforms in Eastern Europe whereby more autonomy is granted to individ-

ual enterprises could lead to a potential increase in the application of EEC anti-trust law.

5. *General system of preferences.* The Community General System of Preferences applicable to developing countries has also been extended to some State-trading countries such as, for example, the People's Republic of China. So far, Romania is the only Eastern country benefitting from GSP.[47]

D. *Community rules on exports affecting trade with Eastern Europe*

The Community rules governing exports are laid down in Regulation 2603/69 of 20 December 1969.[48] The leading principle is that exports are free and therefore not subject to quantitative restrictions. There are, however, exceptions to this principle. A main exception is Art. 10 of the regulation, as amended by Regulation 1934/82, which allows Member States to impose quantitative restrictions for the products listed in the Annex to the Regulation. Quantitative restrictions may be imposed until such time as the Council has established common rules. The Court of Justice has recognised for the products concerned that these provisions constitute a specific authorisation permitting the Member States to impose quantitative restrictions on exports.[49] Since the list covers essentially petroleum products this derogation is rather irrelevant as far as exports to Eastern Europe are concerned. Art. 11 of Regulation 2603/69 also allows Member States to apply restrictions to exports on the grounds of public morality, public policy, public security, or for the protection of public health or national treasures. The reference to "public security" in Art. 11 of Regulation 2603/69 does not give Member States "carte blanche" to introduce export controls for strategic and security purposes. Regulation 2603/69 and in particular Art. 11 has to be seen in the light of EEC Treaty provisions and in particular Art. 223 or 224 EEC Treaty. It would seem that from a strictly legal point of view national export controls, as a derogation from the common commercial policy, should be given a narrow interpretation.[50] However, practice demonstrates that companies established in the Community have only very exceptionally used judicial means to challenge export controls imposed as a consequence of the application of COCOM rules or as a result of the extraterritorial application of US law.[51]

It is not totally unlikely that the further improvement of the general political and trade climate between East and West could affect current approaches to export controls and there is increasing pressure from the Western European business community for changes in this respect. No doubt it is also time to introduce the EEC law dimension into the analysis of the export control issue (Steenbergen, *infra* pp. 255—267).

Notes

1. See Council Regulation 109/70 of 19 December 1969, *O.J.*, L 19/1, 1969.
2. J. Maslen, "The European Community's Relations with the State-trading Countries, 1981—1983", *Yearbook of European Law 1983*, pp. 323—346; same author, "The European Community's Relations with the State-Trading Countries of Europe, 1984—1986", *Yearbook of European Law 1986*, pp. 335—356; see also M.-A. Coninsx, "Oost-West relaties, gezien vanuit economisch en handelsperspectief", in *Vlaanderen, Belgie en Europa in de wereld*, LSC Documenten, No. 2, 1987, pp. 17—32; J. Pinder, "The EC and Eastern Europe under Gorbachev. How normal could relations become?", paper at NATO Colloquium 1988: *The Economies of Eastern Europe under Gorbachev's influence* (mimeo).
3. Sometimes Member States of the Community conclude "cooperation agreements" with Eastern European countries which interfere with Community commercial policy. On this problem, see J. Maslen, *op. cit., Yearbook of European Law 1983*, p. 330.
3 bis. On 26 September 1988 the Agreement was signed (*OJ.*, L 327/1 1988, for text see addendum II p. 321). On 19 December 1988 on agreement between the EEC and Czechoslovakia on trade in industrial products was also signed (*O.J.*, C 7/3 1988, for text see addendum III, p. 333).
4. This introduction does not cover the general EEC law issues involved in the decision-making process as far as the external relations of the European Community are concerned. Thus the relationships Member States — Commission — Council and the issue of the legal basis for concluding agreements with third countries are not included. In this respect for some comments with regard in particular to the relations with Eastern Europe, see Balázs, *infra* p. 68.
5. See *O.J.*, L 157/35, 1988, for text see addendum I, p. 319.
6. See *Report on relations between the European Economic Community and the Council for Mutual Economic Assistance and the Eastern European member States of the CMEA*, Rapporteur Seeler, European Parliament, Working Documents, 1986—1987, Doc. A2-187/86, p. 18.
7. At the Praque CMEA Summit of July 1988 possible reforms of the CMEA's institutional structures were discussed. For a recent short analysis of CMEA's problems see Maximova, "Le CAEM dans la voie d'une renovation fondamentale", *URSS – USSR, Bulletin quotidien*, Agence Novosti, 28 July 1988; on CMEA reforms in general, see L. Csaba, "Le CAEM sous le signe de la restructuration", *Le Courrier de Pays de l'Est*, 1986, p. 3.
8. The text of the unilateral declaration made by CMEA was not published in the *Official Journal of the European Communities*. The unilateral declaration was made by means of a "note verbale", see *Le Soir*, 10 June 1988.
9. For text, see *O.J.*, L 352/1, 1980.
10. See declaration made by Mr. De Clercq before the Political Committee of the European Parliament, *Agence Europe*, 26 March 1988.
10 bis. See note 3 bis.
11. Italics added. Up to now it is the first time that this rather cumbersome title "Agreement on Trade and Commercial and Economic Cooperation" has been used for agreements with third States. Probably because of the strong emphasis on "business facilities" the adjective "commercial" has been added next to the adjective "economic"

although, of course, in a broad interpretation of the expression "economic cooperation" commercial cooperation could also be implied. Be it as it may, this explicit reference to "*commercial* cooperation" suggests probably more than just a terminological fancy. It could well be that precisely this form of cooperation will become an expanding domain in future developments of bilateral agreements, particularly with other Eastern countries.

12. The Agreement European Community-Hungary does not cover ECSC products. A separate agreement — following the procedures laid down in the ECSC Treaty — is to be concluded. Hungary would like to conclude such an agreement with the Community which should include the main principles of the Agreement EEC-Hungary.

13. See Protocol on the abolition of quantitative restrictions referred to in Article 4.

14. The Agreement contains more than 10 explicit references to GATT or Hungary's Protocol of Accession to GATT.

15. *Agence Europe*, 21 July 1988.

15 bis. See note 3 bis.

16. *Agence Europe*, 25 July 1988.

17. *Agence Europe*, 4 March 1988.

18. *Agence Europe*, 11 March 1988.

19. *Agence Europe*, 25 July 1988.

20. It appears that, as a principle, this point could be agreed upon, see declaration of Mr. Ivanov as summarised in *Financial Times*, 4—5 June 1988: "Russia seeks to relax trade rules". Mr. Ivanov further suggested that an agreement EEC-USSR should contain, besides the legally binding commitments covering trade and industrial cooperation, also the intention to cooperate in other areas and a list of problems — such as anti-dumping — for which consultations could be held.

21. See J. Maslen, *op. cit.*, *Yearbook of European Law 1983*, pp. 330—333 and *Yearbook of European Law 1986*, p. 348.

22. See F. Sarre, "Art. 115 EEC Treaty and Trade with Eastern Europe" *Intereconomics*, 1988, pp. 233—240.

23. See, as far as Hungary is concerned, *Hungary and the European Communities. Facts, Trends, Prospects*, (Ed.) Hamori and Inotai, Budapest, Hungarian Scientific Council for World Economy, 1987, p. 10 ff.

24. See in general E. L. M. Völker, "The Major Instruments of the Common Commercial Policy of the EEC", in *Protectionism and the European Community*, Deventer, Kluwer, 1987, 2nd ed., p. 27.

25. See Case 38/73, [1973] *ECR* 1609.

26. On this point see M. Maresceau, "The GATT in the Case-law of the European Court of Justice", in *The European Community and GATT*, Deventer, 1986, p. 110, but see the *Poitiers*-measures at p. 113.

27. See J. Bourgeois, "Les engagements internationaux de la Communauté et leurs implications sur le plan interne", in *Relations extérieures de la Communauté européenne et marché intérieur: aspects juridiques et fonctionnels*, College of Europe, vol. 45, 1988, p. 178.

28. For the text of the Agreement EEC-China, see *O.J.*, L 250/2, 1985.

29. So far the European Court has not yet examined explicitly this question from a common commercial policy perspective. In the *Tivoli* case the Court only held that Art. 95 EEC Treaty was not applicable to direct imports from non-EEC Member States into a Member State of the Community, Case 20/68, [1968] *ECR* 199.

30. Case 41/76, [1976] *ECR* 1921.

31. See F. Sarre, at note *22*.

32. Case 193/85, 7 May 1987, not yet published.

33. *O.J.*, L 195/1, 1982.
34. See the Annex to the Regulation on common rules for imports from State-trading countries (mentioned at note 33) which enumerates those countries which are, for the purpose of this Regulation, considered to be State-trading countries. As far as Eastern Europe is concerned the Annex covers Bulgaria, Poland, Romania, Czechoslovakia, the German Democratic Republic and the USSR.
35. *O.J.*, L 346/6, 1983.
36. The national quotas applicable for 1988 are to be found in Council Decision 87/60, *O.J.*, L 31/67, 1987 amended by Council Decision 88/83, *O.J.*, L 43/1, 1988.
37. As a result of this regulation Member States can no longer maintain a national import policy with regard to imports from Eastern Europe, cfr. J. Bourgeois, "The Common Commercial Policy-Scope and Nature of the Powers", in *Protectionism and the European Community*, Deventer, Kluwer 1987, 2nd ed., p. 9.
38. On this point see Ambassador M.H. Froment-Meurice, *La dimension extérieure du Marché intérieur*, 31 March 1988; on the impact of the Internal Market on the application of Art. 115 EEC Treaty, see A. Mattera, "L'achèvement du marché intérieur", in *Relations extérieures de la Communauté européenne et marché intérieur: aspects juridiques et fonctionnels*, College of Europe, 1988, vol. 45, p. 213
39. Case 270/80, [1982] *ECR* 329.
40. Case 120/83, [1983] *ECR* 2573.
41. Case 77/87 (*Technointorg v. Council*). Since the completion of this book the court gave judgment in this case on 5 October 1988 in which it rejected the action brought by Technointorg.
42. Case 304/86.
43. Case 118/77, *Import Standard Office v. Council*, [1979] *ECR* 1277.
44. The Commission of the European Communities assumes that the EEC anti-trust provisions apply to companies established in or outside the territory of the Community as soon as agreements or restrictive practices have or may have an effect on trade between Member States. This approach was followed by the European court of Justice in the *Woodpulp* case, see case 89/85, 104/85, 114/85, 116/85, 117/85, 125/85, 126/85, 127/85, 128/85 and 129/85.
45. Decision of 19 December 1984, *O.J.*, L 92/1, 1985.
46. See previous note at p. 37.
47. Romania was included among the GSP beneficiaries from 1 January 1974, see *Seventh General Report on the Activities of the European Communities*, 1973, p. 443. Bulgaria's application to be included in the Community's GSP did not receive a positive reply.
48. *O.J.*, L 324/25, 1969.
49. Case 174/84, *Bulk Oil v. Sun International*, [1986] *ECR* 559.
50. P. J. Kuyper, "De Amerikaanse uitvoerbeperkingen in een nieuw jasje: een verbetering?," *SEW*, 1987, pp. 20—22.
51. But see judgment of 17 September 1982, President of the District Court at The Hague. In this case the President refused to apply the trade embargo imposed unilaterally by the American authorities after the Pipeline dispute. Invoking "the Universally accepted rule of international law that in general it is not permissible for a State to exercise jurisdiction over acts performed outside its borders", the President of the Court concluded, by rejecting in this case the application of exceptions to this general rule, that "it cannot ... be seen how the export to Russia of goods not originating in the United States by a non-American exporter could have any direct and illicit effects within the United States", text in *International Legal Materials*, 1983, pp. 66—74.

Bilateral relations between the European Community and Eastern European countries: the problems and prospects of trade relations

PABLO BENAVIDES

Director for Relations with Eastern European and EFTA countries, Commission of the European Communities

East-West relations in December 1987, a period when so many extraordinary events are taking place around us, is an exciting subject even if we limit the analysis of this issue to some very specific aspects of it.

We are now facing the third historical phase in these relations: the first one was that of the building-up of the very preliminary works of the Community; it was marked by a policy of undiscriminated and overall hostility by Eastern Europe towards the Community, both in multilateral activities and fora and in bilateral contacts. Until the signing of the Treaty of Rome in 1972, the Eastern European countries did not accept the existence of the European Community. The European Community was considered to be a reflection of the purest and hardest capitalism and an economic extension of NATO. The second period, which started in 1972, could be defined as the period of the failed/unsuccessful recognition of realities. This recognition unfortunately never took place and a real opportunity was lost. However, a number of important events occurred: several Eastern European countries — Hungary, Poland, Romania — joined the GATT and the implementation of the EEC Common Commercial Policy required an homogeneous treatment by the Community of the Eastern European countries and the simultaneous termination of the trade agreements signed by the Member States. This should have meant the replacement of this intricate network of bilateral agreements by Community-wide agreements. The lack of reaction from Eastern European countries to the Community proposals led the Community to denounce these agreements and to adopt the present autonomous commercial régime.

We are now witnessing the third period in the history of our relations. It could be called the "Gorbachev period", even though its starting point would have to be found before Mr. Gorbachev came to power. At any

M. Maresceau (ed.), The Political and Legal Framework of Trade Relations Between the European Community and Eastern Europe. ISBN 0–7923–0046–7.
© 1989 by Kluwer Academic Publishers, Dordrecht – Printed in the Netherlands.

rate, this era is put under the sign of non-contention, "rapprochement" and, hopefully, cooperation between the Eastern European countries and the EEC.

This period started about 1983 when Hungary and Czechoslovakia first made approaches to the Community about concluding trade agreements with the EEC. Only Romania had until then signed in 1980 a non-sectoral agreement with the Community on trade in industrial goods. We could, of course, add to that some arrangements on specific products such as textiles, steel or some agricultural products. But the agreements presently under negotiation concerning Czechoslovakia, Romania and Hungary or those under preparation after several rounds of exploratory talks with Bulgaria and Poland, are but one aspect of the overall new approach in our relations with Eastern European countries. This approach is a response to the old Community's will and the more recent interest of those countries to have mutual normal relations. "Normalisation" has been the key word to define this approach.

Much has been said about this normalisation; sometimes with no real foundation. What do we mean by "normalisation"? This term means that the Community should not deal with those countries through any sort of go-between. It means that the EEC will have the same kind of relations with them as it has with all other countries in the world: to be able to discuss any sort of problems with them, to negotiate agreements, to accredit missions to the Community and, above and before all, of course, to put an end to the "guerrilla" of some of those countries to hinder Community participation in international organisations and conventions.

The analysis of the economic and trade relations between Eastern European countries and the EEC proves that for the last two years the exchanges between the CMEA member countries and the Community have faced similar problems and have suffered from the same troubles as the rest of world exchanges. The sinking prices of oil and energy, together with the increase of those of industrial goods, have played a major role in the deterioration of the terms of trade between the Community and the Soviet Union. The structure of Soviet exports has accelerated this deterioration, which in 1986 reached some 40 p.c. and almost 30 p.c. during the first half of this year (1987). The price of cereals which have been imported in the USSR in rather important quantities in the last year has somewhat alleviated this impact on the terms of trade. The reaction of the Soviet Union has been an increase of the volume of her exports mainly of energy products and raw materials. Concerning the other Eastern European countries, the alignment of world prices to their commerce has been less detrimental. Their terms of trade have deteriorated by 12 p.c. in 1986 and by 4 p.c. in the first half of this year (1987). Their exports have slightly increased, whereas imports from the Community have been diminishing in the last two years.

What are the prospects for the near future? An improvement of the terms of trade and some increase in the volume of exports, notably as concerns the Soviet Union, should slightly encourage the imports from the Community. The expansion of some national economies in Eastern Europe should also contribute to promoting imports of EEC products.

Nevertheless, this is not the main purpose of these lines. What we are bound to describe is the new framework of our relations. This does not necessarily mean that this new context will determine a dramatic and spectacular change in our mutual exchanges, though when one looks at the present level of our exchanges, at the investments of each party in the other's territory or at the reciprocal contacts between our businessmen or our economic operators, a deep feeling of frustation can hardly be avoided. Such geographically close neighbours have been rather poor economic partners. Trade exchanges of the EEC with Eastern European countries reach just 7 p.c. of our global exchanges. Very few investors have up until now dared try a joint venture in Eastern Europe. And trade or economic relations are for quite a number of reasons the *"domaine réservé"* of some large well-known companies, but seldom of small and medium-size firms.

What do the Eastern European countries expect from the Community in the future? What are — on the other hand — the expectations of the EEC as concerns its relations with that geographical area?

Since 1985 most of the Eastern European countries have shown a clear interest in negotiating agreements which could provide them with a legal framework for their economic relations with the EEC. The approach of those countries is quite generally in favour of trade and economic cooperation agreements thus both covering trade questions and opening new prospects for cooperation in fields of mutual interest. The sectoral arrangements or the merely autonomous régime which is applied by the Community can no longer be the most proper way for our relations, but the EEC approach remains a step-by-step one. This does not exclude the possibility of cooperation on bilateral pragmatical terms both with the Community and its Member States but does not necessarily either preclude a cooperation section in a first stage of our agreements.

As concerns trade questions, the Eastern European countries have focused their main efforts on reaching larger and freer access to the EEC market, both for industrial and agricultural goods. A crucial issue of their request is the elimination of the quantitative restrictions which have been maintained by the Community specifically on imports from those countries. This sensitivity does not only refer to economic risks; no doubt some of these quantitative restrictions apply to products or sectors which could be seriously damaged by too aggressive competition from Eastern European producers. But we should not forget that the present legal treatment of these imports stems from two different situations of countries according to their status of Contracting Parties of the GATT and from the obligations accepted by them in their Protocols of Accession to the GATT. A larger and freer access to the EEC market could be envisaged, provided that Eastern European countries were able to reciprocate in the same field of trade exchanges.

Nobody could deny that the present level of our exchanges is far from satisfactory and that the forecast for the future remains rather gloomy. The Community, unfortunately, harbours no great expectations in this respect. We would very much welcome a great improvement in our exchanges with Eastern European countries in terms of volume, of diversification, of quality, of regularity, of supply and servicing. Practices such as compensation trade or bureaucratic hindrances are not conducive to this improvement which the Community, together with Eastern European countries, are aiming at. We hope that the process of economic reforms under way regarding external trade policy will have an encouraging and dynamic effect on our mutual exchanges.

The new legal framework of our relations, in the view of Eastern European countries, should look further than just trade. It should provide the basis for economic cooperation which would, among others, take the form of joint ventures. Foreign capital from EEC countries would be welcome in those countries and quite a number of measures have been taken recently to foster and encourage this movement. Nothing prevents the Community from sharing this will and our current negotiations with some of those countries as well as in the bilateral agreements of EEC Member States seek improvements in conditions for this or other forms of industrial cooperation.

Nevertheless, this interest, although shared by both sides, will have to overcome the divergence of final aims which will be to gain access to our respective markets and to find the appropriate surroundings in terms of what is known under the generic denomination of business facilities. Foreign investors need to be attracted in any market through clear and transparent information on the statistical, legal or social data in the macroe-conomic context, as well as on the sector concerned or on the partner firm. Nobody can be asked, when their own money is at stake, to take blind risks. Has this been the reason why joint ventures in Eastern Europe, at the end of 1986, represented an investment of not more than 200 million Dollars or why the experience tested in some Eastern European countries since the 70s has not come up to expectations?

Those countries should also think seriously of encouraging investments in the EEC in order to provide their trade with a firm and solid basis. Trade is no longer an erratic or sporadic action, but is made mainly through well-established companies having perfect knowledge of the market they are supposed to supply. If the Eastern European countries wish to lay the foundations of a promising evolution of their exchanges with the EEC they cannot avoid adapting their trade methods to those which are usually put into practice in the Community market.

These few lines did not intend to describe the past of our relations, nor to provide a flow of statistics, nor even to draw a picture of what the negotiations between the Community and the Eastern European countries are at present. Their unique purpose was to raise some of the questions which our relations are facing in this new era. Our respective targets do not basically differ; the ways may, perhaps, diverge in the short term. As concerns the Community, our role as we see it, is to encourage a new opening-up in our relations with Eastern European countries, not by interfering in their economic, and even less in their political system, but by affording the possibility of discussing and cooperating together, by building new frameworks in the form of agreements and joint bodies in which to meet, by providing our economic operators with a context as transparent as possible so that mutual confidence can improve and enlarge these relations to the high level our peoples deserve.

Annex

*Development of trade balances between the European Community and
its individual Member States, with East European Countries, 1984—1987*

Trade balances (X—M) of the EEC (12)
with Eastern European countries 1984—1987 (Mi ECU) — February 1988.

EEC 12

BALANCE [1] WITH	1984	1985	1986	1986 Jan—June	1987 Jan—June
BULGARIA	696.7	1052.9	923.5	493.9	350.1
CSSR	−489.4	−305.8	−164.1	−228.1	−98.0
GDR*	−783.7	−884.2	553.3	−316.9	−229.2
HUNGARY	321.9	472.6	561.9	358.8	226.3
POLAND	−1029.1	−839.2	−558.9	−352.0	−275.4
ROMANIA	−2001.5	−1753.3	−1495.9	−769.3	−785.4
EASTERN EUROPE (6)	−3285.1	−2257.1	−1286.9	−813.5	−811.8
USSR	−10478.0	−8201.2	3283.3	−1646.3	−1319.8
EASTERN EUROPE (7)	−13763.1	−10458.3	−4570.2	−2459.8	−2131.6

[1] Positive balance = surplus with East European country; negative balance = deficit with East European country
* excluding inner-German trade
Source: *EUROSTAT. Data Bank Cronos.*, 12 Jan 1988, Brussels.

Trade balances (X—M) of the EEC (12)
with Eastern European countries 1984—1987 (Mi ECU) — February 1988.

GERMANY

BALANCE[1] WITH	1984	1985	1986	1986 Jan—June	1987 Jan—June
BULGARIA	410.9	531.7	600.0	265.2	232.9
CSSR	−111.5	−61.8	63.6	−65.8	19.6
GDR*	0	0	0	0	0
HUNGARY	309.6	375.9	434.0	252.1	189.6
POLAND	−174.4	−94.0	−50.8	−43.7	8.1
ROMANIA	−253.2	−280.6	−400.6	−194.5	−178.0
EASTERN EUROPE (6)	181.4	471.4	646.2	212.9	272.2
USSR	−1366.7	−1132.4	185.3	−152.0	323.0
EASTERN EUROPE (7)	−1185.3	−661.0	831.5	60.9	595.2

[1] Positive balance = surplus with East European country; negative balance = deficit with East European country
* excluding inner-German trade
Source: *EUROSTAT. Data Bank Cronos.*, 12 Jan 1988, Brussels.

Trade balances (X—M) of the EEC (12)
with Eastern European countries 1984—1987 (Mi ECU) — February 1988.

FRANCE

BALANCE[1] WITH	1984	1985	1986	1986 Jan—June	1987 Jan—June
BULGARIA	63.8	139.0	60.1	46.1	19.2
CSSR	−48.1	−25.8	−25.8	25.3	8.9
GDR	−66.8	−115.1	−56.7	42.3	30.5
HUNGARY	−12.6	32.4	13.7	20.6	−1.9
POLAND	−68.2	−110.7	−36.5	−17.9	−26.1
ROMANIA	−155.3	−217.2	−335.7	−178.6	−175.9
EASTERN EUROPE (6)	−287.1	−297.4	−403.1	−197.6	−224.0
USSR	−295.4	−424.0	−681.1	−280.9	−167.5
EASTERN EUROPE (7)	−582.5	−721.4	−1084.2	−478.5	−391.5

[1] Positive balance = surplus with East European country; negative balance = deficit with East European country

Source: *EUROSTAT. Data Bank Cronos.*, 12 Jan 1988, Brussels.

Trade balances (X—M) of the EEC (12)
with Eastern European countries 1984—1987 (Mi ECU) — February 1988.

ITALY

BALANCE[1] WITH	1984	1985	1986	1986 Jan—June	1987 Jan—June
BULGARIA	74.3	109.3	99.8	52.4	26.6
CSSR	−122.1	−54.0	−63.9	−45.8	−37.6
GDR	22.8	−31.8	0.6	15.2	13.0
HUNGARY	−125.8	−92.9	56.90	−16.0	34.8
POLAND	−189.9	−77.4	−77.2	−56.3	−51.5
ROMANIA	−1115.6	−983.3	−487.6	−305.7	−252.6
EASTERN EUROPE (6)	−1456.4	−1130.2	−585.3	−386.2	−362.8
USSR	−3120.9	−1916.0	−719.3	−457.4	−340.1
EASTERN EUROPE (7)	−4577.3	−3046.2	−1304.6	−843.6	−702.9

[1] Positive balance = surplus with East European country; negative balance = deficit with East European country
Source: *EUROSTAT. Data Bank Cronos.*, 12 Jan 1988, Brussels.

Trade balances (X—M) of the EEC (12)
with Eastern European countries 1984—1987 (Mi ECU) — February 1988.

BELG-LUX

BALANCE [1] WITH	1984	1985	1986	1986 Jan—June	1987 Jan—June
BULGARIA	36.1	54.0	34.1	20.6	19.8
CSSR	3.8	8.7	15.2	5.1	3.2
GDR	−75.7	−132.7	−56.5	−29.6	−35.9
HUNGARY	55.9	62.3	55.2	33.1	23.9
POLAND	−44.5	−28.1	−18.8	−15.5	−21.8
ROMANIA	19.1	13.8	−1.4	13.6	−16.7
EASTERN EUROPE (6)	−5.3	−21.9	27.9	27.5	−27.4
USSR	−1764.4	−657.4	−588.3	−204.9	−267.9
EASTERN EUROPE (7)	−1769.7	−679.3	−560.4	−177.4	−295.3

[1] Positive balance = surplus with East European country; negative balance = deficit with East European country
Source: *EUROSTAT. Data Bank Cronos.*, 12 Jan 1988, Brussels.

Trade balances (X—M) of the EEC (12)
with Eastern European countries 1984—1987 (Mi ECU) — February 1988.

NETHERLANDS

BALANCE[1] WITH	1984	1985	1986	1986 Jan—June	1987 Jan—June
BULGARIA	25.9	13.9	23.4	16.2	7.6
CSSR	−53.4	−30.0	−41.8	−26.1	−8.9
GDR	−84.7	−148.5	−76.2	40.5	−16.2
HUNGARY	39.7	47.8	66.0	38.0	35.8
POLAND	−50.5	−45.7	9.6	5.3	7.6
ROMANIA	−172.0	−167.1	−175.0	−89.7	−56.3
EASTERN EUROPE (6)	−295.2	−329.5	−193.9	−96.7	−45.6
USSR	−2788.9	−3042.8	−891.0	−577.5	−406.7
EASTERN EUROPE (7)	−3084.1	−3372.3	−1084.9	674.2	−452.3

[1] Positive balance = surplus with East European country; negative balance = deficit with East European country
Source: *EUROSTAT. Data Bank Cronos.*, 12 Jan 1988, Brussels.

Trade balances (X—M) of the EEC (12)
with Eastern European countries 1984—1987 (Mi ECU) — February 1988.

UN-KINGDOM

BALANCE[1] WITH	1984	1985	1986	1986 Jan—June	1987 Jan—June
BULGARIA	61.6	146.2	64.3	61.5	34.5
CSSR	−81.11	−52.2	−43.1	−36.6	−32.7
GDR	−283.3	−270.7	−200.8	−107.2	−67.3
HUNGARY	37.6	28.2	29.9	15.8	9.0
POLAND	−155.9	−205.1	−195.1	−125.1	−60.8
ROMANIA	−260.7	−43.4	−13.8	1.8	−41.5
EASTERN EUROPE (6)	−681.6	−397.0	−358.4	−193.5	−158.8
USSR	−314.4	−517.7	−351.2	16.3	−224.7
EASTERN EUROPE (7)	−996.0	−914.7	−709.6	−177.2	−383.5

[1] Positive balance = surplus with East European country; negative balance = deficit with East European country

Source: *EUROSTAT. Data Bank Cronos.*, 12 Jan 1988, Brussels.

Trade balances (X—M) of the EEC (12)
with Eastern European countries 1984—1987 (Mi ECU) — February 1988.

IRELAND

BALANCE [1] WITH	1984	1985	1986	1986 Jan—June	1987 Jan—June
BULGARIA	1.6	6.5	6.0	2.6	1.6
CSSR	−8.9	−8.8	−3.9	−2.8	0.7
GDR	−8.3	−9.7	−12.4	−7.7	−2.7
HUNGARY	4.0	7.1	7.7	3.6	4.7
POLAND	−55.9	−67.6	−55.5	−33.8	−24.4
ROMANIA	−4.9	−2.8	−21.7	−2.0	−20.0
EASTERN EUROPE (6)	−71.4	−75.3	−79.9	−40.2	−40.1
USSR	−33.1	−13.2	14.2	8.3	−2.8
EASTERN EUROPE (7)	−104.5	−88.5	−65.7	−31.9	−42.9

[1] Positive balance = surplus with East European country; negative balance = deficit with East European country

Source: *EUROSTAT. Data Bank Cronos.*, 12 Jan 1988, Brussels.

Trade balances (X—M) of the EEC (12)
with Eastern European countries 1984—1987 (Mi ECU) — February 1988.

DENMARK

BALANCE[1] WITH	1984	1985	1986	1986 Jan—June	1987 Jan—June
BULGARIA	11.9	9.9	9.1	3.1	2.6
CSSR	−42.4	−50.3	−27.4	−15.8	−9.7
GDR	−185.7	−188.1	−136.4	−76.2	−48.9
HUNGARY	−5.6	−5.2	−2.5	−1.0	2.5
POLAND	−147.0	−111.4	−82.0	−43.3	−59.6
ROMANIA	−18.0	−19.7	−19.3	−16.3	−5.1
EASTERN EUROPE (6)	−386.7	−364.8	−258.6	−149.7	−118.2
USSR	−266.9	−194.4	−15.8	38.3	−23.3
EASTERN EUROPE (7)	−653.6	−559.2	−274.4	−111.4	−141.5

[1] Positive balance = surplus with East European country; negative balance = deficit with East European country
Source: *EUROSTAT. Data Bank Cronos.*, 12 Jan 1988, Brussels.

Trade balances (X—M) of the EEC (12)
with Eastern European countries 1984—1987 (Mi ECU) — February 1988.

SPAIN

BALANCE [1] WITH	1984	1985	1986	1986 Jan—June	1987 Jan—June
BULGARIA	16.7	24.5	3.0	11.3	17.0
CSSR	4.6	−6.5	−3.0	−2.8	−8.3
GDR	14.8	78.3	14.2	20.0	−5.6
HUNGARY	23.8	36.9	29.6	21.1	4.1
POLAND	−111.6	−76.5	−24.7	−12.4	−22.3
ROMANIA	−27.1	−40.2	−18.4	−3.5	−22.1
EASTERN EUROPE (6)	−78.7	16.5	0.6	33.7	−37.3
USSR	−26.2	187.6	−26.0	34.7	−156.6
EASTERN EUROPE (7)	−104.9	204.1	−25.4	68.4	−193.9

[1] Positive balance = surplus with East European country; negative balance = deficit with East European country
Source: *EUROSTAT. Data Bank Cronos.*, 12 Jan 1988, Brussels.

Trade balances (X—M) of the EEC (12)
with Eastern European countries 1984—1987 (Mi ECU) — February 1988.

GREECE

BALANCE[1] WITH	1984	1985	1986	1986 Jan—June	1987 Jan—June
BULGARIA	−10.1	14.4	25.1	15.5	−15.6
CSSR	−25.3	−21.8	−24.3	−9.0	−11.3
GDR	−98.5	−38.1	−14.4	−7.6	−2.1
HUNGARY	−8.9	−22.4	−16.3	−8.5	−9.2
POLAND	−23.5	−4.5	−18.1	−3.7	−7.6
ROMANIA	−25.3	−22.4	−6.4	4.9	−14.5
EASTERN EUROPE (6)	−191.8	−94.9	−54.6	−8.4	−60.3
USSR	−493.2	−509.8	−210.7	−65.4	−69.8
EASTERN EUROPE (7)	−685.0	−604.7	−265.3	−73.8	−130.1

[1] Positive balance = surplus with East European country; negative balance = deficit with East European country
Source: *EUROSTAT. Data Bank Cronos.*, 12 Jan 1988, Brussels.

Trade balances (X—M) of the EEC (12)
with Eastern European countries 1984—1987 (Mi ECU) — February 1988.

PORTUGAL

BALANCE [1] WITH	1984	1985	1986	1986 Jan—June	1987 Jan—June
BULGARIA	4	3.5	−1.6	−0.6	4.0
CSSR	−4.9	−3.5	−7.5	−3.4	−4.2
GDR	−18.3	−27.7	−14.7	−10.8	−7.0
HUNGARY	3.2	2.6	1.6	0.6	2.5
POLAND	−7.9	−18.3	−9.8	−5.6	−1.9
ROMANIA	11.5	9.5	4.1	4.5	−2.9
EASTERN EUROPE (6)	−12.3	−33.8	−27.8	−15.3	−9.5
USSR	−8.0	18.7	0.6	−5.6	16.7
EASTERN EUROPE (7)	−20.3	−15.1	−27.2	−20.9	7.2

[1] Positive balance = surplus with East European country; negative balance = deficit with East European country
* excluding inner-German trade
Source: *EUROSTAT. Data Bank Cronos.*, 12 Jan 1988, Brussels.

Trade relations between Romania and the European Community

EUGEN DIJMĂRESCU

Head of Department, Institute for World Economy, Bucharest

I. Introduction

Romania's economic ties with the EEC, and its 12 Member States, bear witness to Romania's foreign policy aimed at promoting balanced relations with all other countries in the world, irrespective of their social and economic system. This posture, widely supported by the developments in today's world, is based on the reality of the contribution which trade and cooperation among all countries in Europe make to the fostering of peaceful coexistence and to the promotion of peace and cooperation throughout the world.

The significance which Romania attaches to trade with the Community's Member States is clearly shown by the rise of its share within the overall trade exchanges with European market economies, namely from 63.3 p.c. in 1960 to 87.9 p.c. in 1986.[1] During the 1980s, the EEC accounted for 15 to 20 p.c. of Romania's overall foreign trade.

A thorough analysis of developments within the Community and their consequences for third countries is the background of Romania's approach to the development of her economic relations with the EEC — from the enactment of Art. 113 EEC Treaty through to the most recent European Single Act. Already in 1973 President Nicolae Ceausescu stated: "Romania believes that developments within the EEC are objective by their nature and they have a certain significance for the development of productive forces, for overall progress"[2] and a year later he mentioned that "the Common Market is one of today's realities which may not be ignored."[3] Like in any other case, Romania is closely linking the policy towards the EEC to her goals of economic growth, on the basis of principles such as full respect of national independence, national sovereignty, territorial integrity, non-interference in domestic affairs, equality of rights and mutual benefit.

M. Maresceau (ed.), The Political and Legal Framework of Trade Relations Between the European Community and Eastern Europe. ISBN 0–7923–0046–7.
© *1989 by Kluwer Academic Publishers, Dordrecht – Printed in the Netherlands.*

II. The legal and institutional framework of economic relations between Romania and the EEC

The tradition of Romania's economic ties with the EEC Member States — along the various stages of implementation of the Treaty of Rome — led to the setting-up of institutionalised relations not only with each Member of the Community, but also with the European Economic Community as an entity. Starting from the true necessity of building up a foreign economic policy based on acknowledgement of objective economic and political realities — without which the opportunities of international comprehension and cooperation would be undermined — Romania was, among the CMEA member countries, the first to set up institutional links with the EEC. Indeed, on 28 July 1980, Romania and the EEC signed in Bucharest a non-preferential agreement on trade in industrial products and at the same time an agreement on the setting-up of a Joint Committee between the two parties was concluded, the first to be established by the Community with an Eastern European country.[4] But even before then, an agreement on trade in textiles had *de facto* been in operation since 1978 — *de jure* since 1980[5] — as well as an arrangement on trade in steel products signed in 1978.

The Agreement concluded between Romania and the EEC on trade in industrial products has been in force since 1 January 1981. It does not apply to textile products which are covered by a separate agreement nor to ECSC items (Article 1, para. 2). The Agreement is supplemented by a Protocol related to the implementation of Article 4, providing for the suspension by the Community of quantitative restrictions on imports of specific products originating in Romania. The progress made in this area amounts to a degree of liberalisation for somewhat 94 p.c. of the EEC tariff headings, but — as will be seen later on — it does not match Romania's volume of exports since the pattern of those exports is to a great extent made up of non-liberalised items.

Concluded for a period of 5 years, the Agreement continues to govern bilateral trade by virtue of tacit renewal (Art. 13). Its management is ensured by the already mentioned Joint Committee Romania-EEC. This Committee has the power to manage the implementation of the Agreement and arrangements for trade between the two parties (Article 1), including those concluded previously, as well as to deal with other matters of mutual interest. The Agreement on the establishment of the Joint Committee also provides for the two parties to apply the treatment of the most-favoured nation to their trade, in compliance with their membership of GATT.

The decision of the Community, taken in 1974 and applied since the beginning of 1975, which granted Romania the benefit of the GSP treatment, according to her level of development, made an important contribution to the creation of a favourable framework.[6] As a matter of fact, the EEC Council endorsed this decision in 1980, since the Preamble of the agreement on the setting-up of the Joint Committee between Romania and the EEC acknowledges Romania's status as developing country and member of the "Group of 77".

Within this legal and institutional framework, Romania's economic relations with the EEC and its Member States have made important progress, mainly with regard to her exports to the EEC (see Tables 1 and 2).

III. The conduct of trade and cooperation between Romania and the EEC

The way the two parties have conducted their trade and cooperation has not been easy (see Table 1). The volume of trade went up and down, reflecting economic conditions in Romania and the EEC, and the crisis in the world economy (see further). Nevertheless, through an open dialogue

Table 1. Romania's trade with the EEC — 12 (millions of ECU)

	Exports	Imports
1958	72	56
1960	111	105
1965	224	256
1970	462	500
1975	989	1,105
1977	1,088	1.276
1978	1.179	1,513
1979	1,662	1,864
1980	1,826	1,772
1981	1,963	1,765
1982	1,891	1,103
1983	1,905	914
1984	3,060	1,058
1985	2,910	1,157
1986	2,483	987

Sources: *Eurostat, External Trade, Statistical Yearbook* 1987, series 6 A.

Table 2. Romania's trade with the Member States of the
EEC in 1986 (1000 ECU)

	Exports to	Imports from
Belgium & Luxemburg	49,434	48,010
Denmark	30.546	11,239
F.R. of Germany	750,739	350,112
Greece	54,807	48,355
Spain	47,827	29,384
France	515,239	159,549
Ireland	24,533	2,769
Italy	647,115	159,484
The Netherlands	222,103	47,139
Portugal	4,964	9,135
United Kingdom	135,464	121,718

Sources: *Eurostat, External Trade, Statistical Yearbook*
1987, series 6 A.

a better knowledge and a better comprehension of each other's preoccupations and priorities has been achieved. Proceeding along the same lines,
the potential of everyone will be better realised and the volume of trade
and cooperation will increase and diversify. This seems to be the natural
way, stemming from the deepening of interdependencies between the
national economies. Hence, a brief review of mutual relations will help to
better understand the intentions for the future.

The first finding is that Romania's trade with the EEC Member
States, like the evolution of the whole of her foreign trade, mirrors the
developments inside the national economy, as well as those of the world
economy. Therefore, trade with the EEC, although reflecting the general
trends in Romania's foreign exchanges, has primarily been determined by
the specific problem of the settlement of payments in convertible
currency. Although the last remark restates a well-known truth, *stricto
sensu* it has economic significance as long as equality in a contract
requires every party to possess the agreed means of payment. As a
country without convertible currency, Romania is forced to a dual balance
of payments: one for operations in convertible currencies, the other for
transactions made with other currencies. Therefore, in order to buy with
convertible currencies, Romania should first earn those sums through
exports or borrow them. But since the actual policy of Romania is to pay
off her foreign debt, resorting to credits is precluded. Therefore, exports
remain the only source of foreign income for financing imports.

As a general remark, empirically proved, the dynamics of trade between Romania and the EEC were higher at a time when the whole economy grew faster and less sustained when the worldwide economic crisis blew up and hit both international trade and every national economy, irrespective of social and economic system or development level. For instance, during the extensive development of the Romanian economy, along with various forms of trade, the relations with EEC Member States have been marked by different industrial, technical and scientific forms of cooperation with Community firms, which contributed to the development of certain branches of Romanian industry. Noteworthy are — among many others — those in civil aircraft (helicopters with SNIAS and Aérospatiale, France and medium couriers with British Aerospace, jet engines with Rolls-Royce, United Kingdom), trucks and cars (with MAN, Federal Republic of Germany, Renault and Citroën, France), tractors (with FIAT, Italy), heavy motors (with Renk Augsburg, Federal Republic of Germany), electrical appliances (refrigerators with Thomson, France, washing machines with San Giorgio, Italy), machine-tools (with Indiamka, Belgium), ceramic materials (with Technoceram, Italy), compressors (with Odorice, Italy), acrylic fibres (with Romalfa, Italy), etc.[7]

Governed by the Romanian law on joint ventures, enacted in 1972 — which has as a prime feature the fact that joint ventures set up in Romania are self-conducting according to their statute and form of incorporation — joint ventures have been established in Romania to manufacture and sell acrylic fibres (Rifil S.p.a. in Savinesti) with Romalfa, Italy, heavy motors for ships (Resita-Renk A. G. in Resita) with Renk Augsburg, Federal Republic of Germany and Axel cars (Oltcit S. A. in Craiova) with Citroën, France. Another manufacturing joint venture is RomControl-Data in Bucharest, with Control Data Corporation, U.S.A., which produces peripheral equipment for computers.

Along with several trading joint ventures opened by Romanian foreign trade companies in most of the Member States of the EEC, joint banks have been set up by the Romanian Bank for Foreign Trade together with Western banks in France, the United Kingdom, Italy and the Federal Republic of Germany. Simultaneously, the Société Générale of France and the Frabo-Bank A. G. of the Federal Republic of Germany have opened branches in Bucharest. The first Western bank which opened an office in Bucharest was Manufacturers Hanover Trust of New York.[8]

The second finding is that, within the tendency of growth and diversi-fication of bilateral exchanges, two stages may be considered, related to the ratio between imports and exports. Until 1980 the value of Romanian imports from the Community has generally been higher than the value of exports. This situation was due to the intensity of investments in Romania during her extensive economic development, which made necessary the import of industrial machinery and equipment required by the broad process of erecting industrial capacities throughout the whole country, meant to ensure the harmonious development of every county. For instance, the share of industrial equipment in Romania's overall imports was 39.9 p.c. in 1965, 34.7 p.c. in 1975, but dropped to 29.1 p.c. in 1986.[9] Important trade deficits in convertible currencies were thus accumulated, which together with banking and governmental credits drawn for the same purpose — from the EEC Member States, from other industrialised countries and international financial institutions — resulted in Romania's foreign debt at a time when foreign oil prices and interest rates had risen sharply. The promotion of a policy for balanced trade, the worsening of international terms of borrowing and the political decision of Romania to pay off her foreign debt, made it necessary, since the beginning of the 1980s, to annually achieve trade surpluses in convertible currencies. A reduction of imports was implied, especially since the targeted growth of exports meant to cover both imports and the service of foreign debt and its interest was not reached.

In relation to the remarks mentioned above, some additional comments may be made.

1. Imports or exports should be looked at from both sides. For instance, not only the Romanian imports from the EEC have declined between 1981—1986, but the evolution of exports to the EEC shows that for every year during the same period the dollar value of Romanian exports was smaller than the amount for 1980. This situation does not in any way satisfy the Romanians, whose trade policy continues to be guided by the principle of mutual development of exchanges with all countries (see Table 3).

The conversion into US Dollars of the amount of Romanian exports to

Table 3. The comparative evolution of Romanian exports to the EEC, in ECU and dollar terms at the annual average exchange rate (millions ECU)

	1980	1981	1982	1983	1984	1985	1986
ECU	1826	1963	1891	1905	3060	2910	2483
US Dollars	2583	2199	1853	1695	2417	2212	2433

Sources: Computed from *Eurostat, External Trade, Statistical Yearbook*, series 6 A, 1987.

the EEC, although less important for the Community, has a great significance for Romania, since her convertible balance of payments is always
expressed in US Dollars.

Romania was and is not indifferent to the export offer of Community
firms. Industry, which has become the main branch of the Romanian
economy and efforts made by Romania to keep it in line with technological progress, require the import of equipment which is not manufactured locally. Since the equipment should be paid for, this cannot
be achieved without earnings derived from exports. In other words,
Romania's possibilities of buying from the Community are dependent on
her opportunities to export to those markets. This conclusion is the logical
result of the economic and financial conditions prevailing today in the
world market.

2. Despite the progress made — since the agreements signed in 1980 —
in liberalising the access-level of Romanian exports to the Community
markets, when they are looked at in close connection with the pattern of
Romania's offers for export, the achievements are still far from being
satisfactory. Therefore, Romania is highly concerned with quantitative
restrictions still damaging her exports of industrial products to the EEC
markets. The maintenance of small quotas and ceilings opened for
important Romanian exports to some of the EEC markets (such as T.V.
sets, fertilisers, electrical motors, furniture, semi-conductors, transformers,
plastics, tires, excavators, tractors, aluminium products, textiles and
footwear), or the practice of quota-retention for the export of steel
products, seldom make the volume of trade to be satisfactory both for
importers and exporters.[10]

Reducing barriers that hinder the access of Romanian industrial goods
to the Common Market, a more flexible administration of agreements on
trade in textiles and steel, a more attentive mastering of anti-dumping
procedures — in order to avoid them when real dumping does not occur
(as happened in the case of some chemical products exported by Romania
to the EEC) — as well as the specific settlement of various disputes that
might occur in trading agricultural products, are some of the issues of
concern for Romania, when — within the existing institutional framework
— the opportunities for further expansion of economic relations with the
European Economic Community are examined.

3. Romania has a "trade surplus" with the EEC (see Table 4). Although
what is mentioned above sheds more light on the issue, some specific
elements might help to obtain full clarification. If an attentive computation

Table 4. Breakdown by SITC sections of Romania's trade with the EEC in 1986 (1000 ECU)

SITC		Exports	Imports
0 + 1.	Food, beverages and tobacco	102,024	120,896
2.	Crude materials	89,618	48,925
3.	Fuel products	812,783	44,502
4 + 5.	Oils, fats and waxes, chemicals	157,392	172,837
6.	Manufactured goods classified by material	429,577	282,318
7.	Machinery and transport equipment	178,909	166,804
8 + 9.	Miscellaneous manufactured articles and goods not classified elsewhere	712,470	148,700

Sources: *Eurostat, External Trade, Statistical Yearbook* 1987, series 6 A.

is made, it emerges that Romania's surpluses of the last years do not yet compensate for the trade deficit incurred between 1958—1980 and for the sum of credits (including interest) received from the EEC Member States over the same period. Therefore, how can anyone speak about a mutual development of trade before eliminating the financial disequilibria which have lasted for so long?

On the other hand, when the volume and pattern of trade are analysed together, it can easily be seen that the surpluses of the last years are mainly due to one and the same merchandise, namely oil products, which often account for more than 35 p.c. of Romanian exports to the EEC. Instead, for important goods, such as machinery and equipment, transport equipment, chemicals and other industrialised products (except for consumer goods), the Community's exports to Romania continue to exceed the import volume.

Finally, it should not be forgotten that, no matter what the size of Romania's trade surplus, this amount has, under various forms, returned every year to the Community Member States, as payments for imports, services, foreign debt and interest. These facts are already known by commercial and financial creditors who have noted a reduction by half of Romania's foreign debt over a relatively short period.

IV. The way ahead

The OECD/BIS report of Statistics on External Indebtedness, including bank and trade-related external claims, shows that in June 1987 the total amount of Romania's external debt has dropped to 3.436 million US Dollars.[11]

As it is well known, Romania has for some years adopted a policy aimed at achieving a surplus of her trade balance, in order to get a positive balance of current accounts and pay for her foreign debt. Serious efforts are being made towards this goal, opening opportunities for full payment of the debt. Hence, the required prerequisites to speed up economic ties with other countries — the EEC included — are gathered. According to this aim, Romania has submitted to the Community a proposal for raising the status of their economic relations, through the signing of an agreement on economic and commercial cooperation, able to give new impetus to trade and cooperation.[12] Romania wishes that negotiations opened in 1987 be supported by the willingness of all parties to reach a formula capable of providing ways and means to give such an agreement the economic substance which corresponds to the nature of the new legal framework. Making clear Romania's stance, President Nicolae Ceausescu stated: "We declare ourselves to be in favour of a broad cooperation with the EEC Member States and with the EEC as an entity and we are ready to conclude a general agreement and to establish diplomatic relations. At the same time, we believe the establishment of direct relations necessary between the EEC and CMEA, according to everyone's competences".[13] Romania sees the new agreement not only as a sum of those agreements already existing, but as a development, with a wider scope in various areas of trade and cooperation. The Romanian economic organisations, both the manufacturing ones and those involved in exports and imports, look trustfully forward, since actions undertaken by Romania go hand in hand with the logic of history. For instance, the text of the new agreement, providing incentives for industrial cooperation would help arouse the interest of partners and increase the flows of trade generated by cooperation.

Opportunities opened in Romania in various fields to Community partners, are derived from the long-term economic targets of the modernisation programme of industrial capacities and the structural adjustment of the economic branches. The 1986—1990 Five-year Plan provides for an increase of national income by 9.9—10.6 p.c. on a yearly average, 13.3—14.2 p.c. for the net industrial output, 8.5—9 p.c. for the net agricultural production, a rise of about 8.8 p.c. of the foreign trade over the whole period compared with the period 1981—1985 and about 3.6 p.c. for investments.[14] In order to reach those targets, the Law enacting the Five-year Plan provides that scientific research, technological development and promotion of technical progress plays an essential role in modernising all branches of the national economy. In fact, 90 p.c. of the total amount of investments is dedicated to the development and up-dating of the economy. It is assumed that by 1990 some 46 p.c. of the products manufactured by industry will be new or modernised, via an accelerated process of automation, promotion of electronics and robots throughout the basic branches of the economy. Simultaneously, attention is paid to diminishing the weight and specific consumption of manufactured items, and to the rise of efficiency in all areas of economic activity. Implementation of those programmes, in accordance with the requirements of contemporary scientific and technological changes, cannot be achieved without broad participation in the international division of labour. Hence, within the framework opened by existing agreements between Romania and the EEC and its Member States, the specialised Romanian enterprises are ready to examine with all due attention the proposals of Community firms.

As a member of CMEA, and starting from her traditional economic ties with the Member States of the Community, Romania fully supports the holding of talks between the CMEA and the EEC concerning the establishment of direct links, in compliance with competences provided by the statutes of each organisation. This will help the establishment of institutionalised trade relations between other member countries of the CMEA and the EEC, opening new horizons for Pan-European trade and cooperation, for the strengthening of security of European soil, freed from the burden of nuclear arms, and for the peace of the world.

Notes

1. Anuarul statistic al R. S. România (Statistical Yearbook of the S. R. of Romania) 1961 and GATT — Statistiques du commerce extérieur de la Roumanie, doc. L/6237, 1987.
2. Nicolae Ceauşescu, *România pe drumul construirii societăţii socialiste multilateral dezvoltate* (Romania on the path of building-up the many-sided developed socialist society), vol. 8, Editura politică, Bucharest, 1973, pp. 410—411.
3. Ibid, vol. 9, 1974, p. 30.
4. *O.J.*, L 352, 1980.
5. Commission des Communautés Européennes — Accords et autres engagements bilatéraux qui lient les Communautés à des pays tiers, Brussels, January 1984, p. 50.
6. E. Dijmărescu, *Preferinţe vamale în comerţul internaţional* (Tariff preferences in international trade), Editura ştiinţifică şi enciclopedică, Bucharest, 1980.

7. A. Puiu (Ed.), *România în circuitul economic mondial; Priorități în comerțul nostru exterior* (Romania in world-wide economic circuit; Priorities of our foreign trade), Academy of Economic Studies, Bucharest, 1983.
8. I. Cetățeanu (Ed.), *Spre o nouă ordine în comerțul internațional* (Towards a new order in international trade), Editura Scrisul românesc, Craiova, 1985.
9. Anuarul statistic al R.S. România (Statistical Yearbook of the S.R. of Romania) 1987.
10. M. Petrescu (Ed.), *Acordul General pentru Tarife și Comerț* (General Agreement on Tariffs and Trade), Editura științifică și enciclopedică, Bucharest, 1987.
11. OECD/BIS, Statistics on External Indebtness: Bank and Trade related non-bank external claims on individual borrowing countries and territories at end-June 1987, Paris and Basle, January 1988.
12. *Bull. EC.*, 12—1986.
13. Nicolae Ceaușescu, vol. 29, 1987, p. 691.
14. Legea planului național unic de dezvoltare economică și socială a Republicii Socialiste România în cincinalul 1986—1990 (Law of the National Plan of Economic and Social Development of the Socialist Republic of Romania over the Five-year period 1986—1990).

Trade relations between Czechoslovakia and the European Community

MILAN ČERNOHUBÝ
Director General Ministry of Foreign Trade, Prague

It should be emphasised at the outset that the strategic targets of the Czechoslovak economy, linked with an extensive restructuring of the economic mechanism, are aimed at the establishment of an efficient export structure and increased participation in the international division of labour. The main streams of this development are defined in the first place by the intensification of cooperation with CMEA countries which, on the other hand, does not exclude or diminish our efforts to strengthen and expand our cooperation with other countries including the developed industrial countries of the West. Among them, the role of the European Community is particularly important, with the share of more than 60 p.c. in the total Czechoslovak trade turnover with OECD countries. This is hardly surprising if we take into consideration geographical factors, traditions in trade, similar industrial structures as well as some other factors positively influencing trade flows between Czechoslovakia and most of the EEC Member States.

All these factors, or at least some of them, have had a positive influence on the development of Czechoslovak trade with the European Community in the last few years which has registered the fastest growth among all OECD countries. This trend in trade exchanges has continued also during 1987, particularly as far as Czechoslovak imports from the European Community are concerned which — based on a comparison of statistics for the period January-September 1986/87 — have grown by 17 p.c. This is well above the average of total Czechoslovak imports, both from East and West.

In spite of this generally positive development, however, we are still far from satisfied, especially if we take into consideration the total share of the European Community in Czechoslovak foreign trade which remains on the level of about 10 p.c. Also the slowing down of Czechoslovak exports to the European Community in 1986 and the first three quarters of 1987 is something that calls for attention. This state of affairs does not

M. Maresceau (ed.), The Political and Legal Framework of Trade Relations Between the European Community and Eastern Europe. ISBN 0–7923–0046–7.
© *1989 by Kluwer Academic Publishers, Dordrecht – Printed in the Netherlands.*

reflect actual potentials existing on both sides and I am convinced that it is unsatisfactory for both sides.

However, our trade prospects with the European Community need to be approached realistically without either exaggerating or minimising the opportunities available. In our view any substantial progress is subject to improved mutual confidence and a better understanding. We, in Czechoslovakia believe that the time for a move in this direction has already come. This is not only because of negotiations initiated between the European Community and some socialist countries — Czechoslovakia among them — but more significantly, because of a constructive dialogue between the world's two biggest economic integration groupings, the Council of Mutual Economic Assistance and the European Community, which has broader than purely economic aspects and which could contribute, in case of its successful accomplishment, to increased confidence in Europe. The favourable impact of such a situation on the possible development of East-West trade does not need any comment.

But before any step forward is made, problems impeding this generally desirable objective should be identified and analysed. What are these problems as we see them from our side?

First of all, since 1975 when the provisions of the Treaty of Rome on common commercial policy became fully applicable, Czechoslovakia has had no bilateral agreements regulating relations with the European Community or its Member States in the field of trade policy. The only legal instrument providing for mutually applicable most-favoured-nation treatment therefore remains the General Agreement on Tariffs and Trade (GATT). Such a situation makes the dialogue between the two sides in no way easy.

Certain exceptions are presented by the so-called sectoral arrangements concluded in some sensitive sectors, namely in steel, textiles and some agricultural products, which are based on voluntary self-restraint commitments. In principle, we have reservations against these kinds of arrangements because they limit free access of products to the market and their compatibility with the spirit of GATT is questionable. On the other hand, we cannot close our eyes to the serious structural problems prevailing in these sectors of production and therefore we accept these arrangements, if only as a temporary exception to the principle of free trade. With these reservations, our assessment of their practical importance is positive. They provide both sides with a certain degree of certainty, enable an exchange of views on relevant problems in trade with the respective commodities and in such a way prevent possible misunderstandings.

Such consultation provides a convenient but only limited institutional framework which does not enable us to tackle the most controversial element in the trade policy of the European Community towards socialist countries, i.e. the system of autonomous quotas imposed on various products, quotas applied not on a general but selective basis and therefore clearly discriminatory. These quotas are mostly applied to a wide assortment of our industrial consumer goods, some chemicals, agricultural products and exceptionally — in Italy, Spain and Portugal — even to certain engineering products. The importance of these import restrictions is sometimes played down by pointing out that they cover only a small part of overall Czechoslovak exports. Such an argument, however, misses the point because it fails to take into consideration the fact that these quotas adversely affect products which are quite often of vital importance to many Czechoslovak exporters whose economic results depend on their export activities in given products. If these products are under quantitative restrictions, then the companies are seriously damaged.

In our view the system of autonomous quotas is incompatible with the principles of GATT where Czechoslovakia is a founding Contracting Party whose status has never been modified. We believe therefore, that we are entitled to full and unconditional MFN-treatment.

We explained this approach during the first round of official negotiations on the Agreement on trade in industrial products held in July 1987 in Brussels and consequently during further official and expert meetings. It seems that our reasoning has met with understanding on the side of our partners. That is encouraging, in spite of the fact that important negotiation on the economic package of the agreement is still before us.

On our part we believe that a constructive approach towards the problems which have accumulated in the past would not only clear the way to increased mutual confidence, but at the same time would be reflected in a faster and more dynamic exchange of goods and a more diversified pattern of trade both on the side of exports as well as imports.

Speaking about the general approach to relations with the European Community, the Czechoslovak side gives preference to a pragmatic, step-by-step approach. Before opening negotiations on an overall trade and industrial cooperation agreement we consider it necessary to assess — very carefully — experience gathered from all existing arrangements and only after that, with all necessary knowledge at hand, decide on further steps. This is, among other things, the reason why we attach such importance to our present negotiations on the Agreement on trade in industrial products. We do not request any preferences, but on the other hand, insist on removing all discriminatory practices applied against Czechoslovak exports contrary to the principles of non-discrimination as codified in GATT.

Such is a brief analysis of our trade relations with the European

Community. I, personally, have been responsible for Czechoslovak trade and economic relations with the European Community since 1983, presided on the Czechoslovak side for most of the negotiations, participated in some others and during this short period of time have seen ups and downs in our relations. Therefore, I personally appreciate the latest positive developments in progress along both bilateral and multilateral lines. In spite of some existing difficulties, I am pleased to find a constructive approach on the side of our partners, both the Commission of the EEC and many of the Member States coupled with a generally better atmosphere and mutual desire to improve the present state of things. We, on our part, will try to develop the dialogue in a positive direction and bring it to a successful conclusion, beneficial for both sides. All these facts make me optimistic for the future.

Trade relations between Hungary and the European Community

PÉTER BALÁZS

Deputy of the Secretariat for Foreign Economic Relations of the Government of the People's Republic of Hungary; Associate Professor, University of Budapest

I. Characteristics and trends of trade

The EEC is an outstanding trading partner for Hungary. The Community — as a whole — takes second place in the range of Hungary's trading partners after the Soviet Union. Taken individually, half of the EEC's Member States play an important — some of them even a determinant — role in Hungary's foreign economic relations (see Table 1).

Trade between Hungary and the EEC has shown, since the formation of the Community, a generally increasing trend (see Table 2). However,

Table 1. Trading partners of Hungary in 1986.

Country	Hungarian exports			Hungarian imports		
	MIO	HUF	%	MIO	HUF	%
Total	420	303	100,0	439	691	100,0
USSR	140	850	33,5	136	684	31,1
EC /12/	75	424	18,0	99	388	22,6
FRG	35	518	8,5	55	502	12,6
Austria	32	903	7,8	38	740	8,8
GDR	26	243	6,2	31	741	7,2
CSSR	24	166	5,8	22	137	5,0
Poland	16	299	3,9	19	373	4,4
Switzerland	13	742	3,3	13	988	3,2
Italy	13	253	3,2	11	228	2,6
Yugoslavia	11	263	2,7	10	363	2,4
Great Britain	8	157	1,9	10	126	2,3
Romania	8	267	2,0	7	934	1,8
China	7	478	1,8	7	607	1,7
USA	9	650	2,3	4	985	1,1
France	7	001	1,7	7	367	1,7

Source: Külkereskedelmi statisztikai évkönyv 1986. 1 USD = cca 47 HUF.

M. Maresceau (ed.), The Political and Legal Framework of Trade Relations Between the European Community and Eastern Europe. ISBN 0–7923–0046–7.

we have to bear in mind that not only exports and imports were growing, but the number of the EEC's Member States as well.

The share of the six EEC Member States in Hungary's foreign trade was about 14—15 p.c. in 1958. The share of the "Nine" had increased above 20 p.c. by the beginning of the 1980s. At present the share of the EEC in Hungarian exports is 17—18 p.c., in imports about 22 p.c. (see Table 3).

Hungary's share of the EEC's external trade was about 0.3 p.c. by the late 1950s, it had more than doubled by the early 1970s. In the East European region Hungary has been an increasingly important export market for the Community with actually 0.7 p.c. of the total external exports of the EEC. The share of Hungarian exports in the Community's external imports is slightly more than 0.5 p.c. (see Table 4).

Table 2. Trade between the EC and the European CMEA countries (in Mio Ecu).

Country	1970	1971	1972	1973	1974	1975	1976	1977	1978	1979
					Imports					
USSR	1543	1597	1683	2310	3626	3899	5679	6300	6671	8568
GDR	225	241	284	327	482	494	615	631	724	765
Poland	667	756	885	1149	1493	1624	2008	2173	2310	2485
Czechoslovakia	466	528	575	696	816	851	1017	1105	1131	1325
Hungary	366	397	514	647	713	702	870	1043	1058	1307
Romania	449	490	562	684	861	892	1150	1055	1131	1616
Bulgaria	185	184	186	228	238	204	294	308	331	463
					Exports					
USSR	1410	1349	1573	2195	3405	4989	5239	5942	5705	6353
GDR	211	248	317	312	448	479	583	507	565	779
Poland	189	676	986	1658	2479	2677	2876	2586	2546	2523
Czechoslovakia	551	646	648	759	1030	1045	1262	1275	1256	1312
Hungary	406	503	543	642	1081	968	1071	1361	1572	1506
Romania	487	526	628	776	1127	1708	1143	1233	1471	1781
Bulgaria	224	223	219	284	507	678	604	579	578	643
					Trade balance					
USSR	−133	−248	−110	−115	−221	1090	−440	−358	−966	−2215
GDR	−14	7	33	−15	−34	−15	−32	−124	−159	14
Poland	−81	−80	101	509	986	1053	868	413	236	38
Czechoslovakia	85	118	73	63	214	194	245	170	125	−13
Hungary	40	106	29	−5	368	266	201	318	514	199
Romania	38	36	66	92	266	178	−7	178	340	165
Bulgaria	39	39	33	56	269	474	30	271	247	180

Source: Eurostat spec. no. 1958—1983 and 3/1988.

Table 2. Trade between the EC and the European CMEA countries (in Mio Ecu).

Country	1980	1981	1982	1983	1984	1985	1986
				Imports			
USSR	11214	13541	17045	18615	22960	20710	13158
GDR	911	1158	1293	1414	1721	1832	1626
Poland	2723	2062	2256	2415	3457	3572	2948
Czechoslovakia	1505	1564	1751	1873	2158	2272	2108
Hungary	1415	1461	1534	1662	1884	2014	1888
Romania	1767	1829	1770	1819	3060	2910	2483
Bulgaria	478	555	589	529	556	586	549
				Exports			
USSR	7583	7886	8984	12022	12482	12509	9875
GDR	842	1048	710	792	937	947	1073
Poland	2841	2307	2051	2074	2428	2733	2389
Czechoslovakia	1368	1385	1399	1451	1668	1966	1944
Hungary	1592	1959	1962	1957	2206	2486	2450
Romania	1708	1699	1060	885	1058	1157	987
Bulgaria	774	963	1023	1095	1253	1639	1472
				Trade balance			
USSR	−3631	−5655	−8061	−6593	−10478	−8201	−3283
GDR	−69	−110	−583	−622	−784	−885	−553
Poland	118	245	−205	−341	−1029	−839	−559
Czechoslovakia	−137	−179	−352	−422	−490	−306	−164
Hungary	177	498	428	295	322	472	562
Romania	−59	−130	−710	−934	−2002	−1753	−1496
Bulgaria	296	408	434	566	697	1053	923

Source: Eurostat spec. no. 1958—1983 and 3/1988.

Table 3. Share of the EC from the total foreign trade of Hungary (in %).

	1960	1970	1975	1980	1985	1986
EC imports	13.7	16.7	13.0	20.6	16.0	17.4
EC exports	15.2	17.0	16.3	22.9	21.5	22.5

Source: UNCTAD Statistics.

The two sides of trade developed in a harmonious way until 1973, even if there was some regular export surplus in favour of the EEC. From 1974, we witnessed a split between the evolution of exports and imports

Table 4. Share of Hungary from the total external trade of the EC (in %).

	1960	1970	1975	1980	1985	1986
Hungarian exports	0.35	0.61	0.56	0.52	0.50	0.56
Hungarian imports	0.51	0.74	0.82	0.73	0.66	0.72

Source: UNCTAD Statistics.

which resulted in a deficit for Hungary of about 400 mio USD per year (see Table 1 and Figure 1).

One of the main reasons for this was the limitation of imports of food and agricultural products by the extension of the Common Agricultural Policy of the EEC[1] and in particular the drastic elimination by the EEC of the centuries old Hungarian beef and live cattle exports to the traditional Italian, German and other markets as a result of the application of safeguard measures.[2]

In the East European region Hungary is only the fourth seller but the number one customer of the Community, excluding the Soviet Union and Inner-German trade. Sales of the East European countries have developed in parallel with the exception of the latest fluctuations in Polish and Romanian exports. Some more important changes have altered the order of countries concerning imports from the EEC. In 1973 this order was: Poland, Romania, Czechoslovakia, Hungary, GDR, Bulgaria. At present it

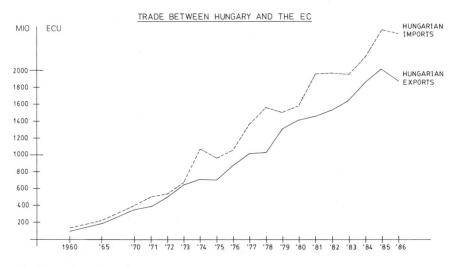

Fig. 1.
Source: Eurostat.

is: Hungary, Poland, Czechoslovakia, Bulgaria, GDR, Romania. A trend of increasing imports from the EEC can be witnessed in the case of Hungary, Czechoslovakia and the GDR (see Table 2 and Figures 2 and 3).

The commodity pattern of trade between Hungary and the EEC has its own specificities which are different from all the other CMEA countries (see Tables 5 and 6). Hungarian exports are characterised by the highest share of agricultural products (Bulgaria and Poland follow in the order). At the same time, Hungary is amongst the three most important exporters of industrial goods — including chemicals, machinery and transport equipment and other manufactured goods — into the Community (after the GDR and Czechoslovakia). As a result of these two features, Hungary is the only country in the region that bases her exports on both agricultural and manufactured industrial goods (at the same time, Hungarian exports of fuel products and raw materials — taken together — are the lowest in Eastern Europe).

As to Hungarian imports from the EEC, manufactured industrial products represent the highest percentage of them (more than 80 p.c.). The imports of food and agricultural products are the lowest in the East

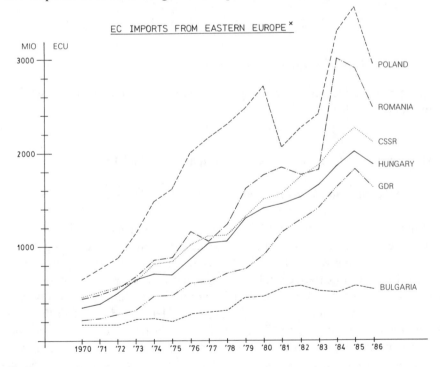

Fig. 2.

Source: Eurostat.

* Without the USSR and Inner-German Trade.

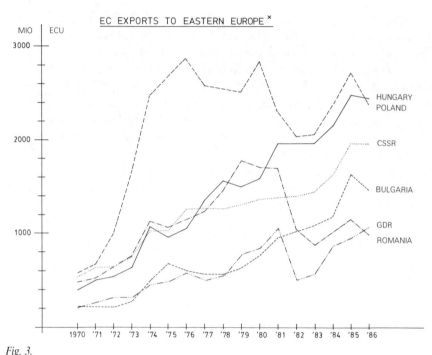

Fig. 3.
Source: Eurostat.
* Without the USSR and Inner-German Trade.

European region, Hungary being a net exporter of the same category of products herself.

II. Evolution of relations between Hungary and the EEC

A. *Technical arrangements in the field of the CAP*

Hungary, as some other CMEA countries, established the first contacts with the EEC institutions in the field of the common agricultural policy.

In accordance with a 1967 EEC Council regulation, making it possible for third countries to undertake a price-guarantee for pork meat and to be exempted from the supplementary amounts, the Hungarian Ministry of Foreign Trade undertook this guarantee in a letter addressed to the EEC Commission in June 1968. The details of the arrangement were specified between the TERIMPEX Company as sole exporter of the goods in question in Hungary and the competent services of the European Commission.[3]

Table 5. Trade between the EC and the European CMEA countries by commodity groups imports 1985 (in %)

Commodity groups	CMEA	USSR	GDR	Poland	Chechoslovakia	Hungary	Romania	Bulgaria
Total	100.0	100.0	100.0	100.0	100.0	100.0	100.0	100.0
– Food, beverages, tobacco	4.9	0.7	—	16.2	6.4	26.9	3.7	17.0
– Raw materials	6.5	2.9	4.4	13.6	13.0	9.4	3.3	7.9
– Fuel products	53.1	72.3	18.5	23.5	13.1	6.1	44.0	22.1
– Oils and fats	0.2	0.1	0.3	0.4	0.4	0.4	0.5	0.2
– Chemicals	5.5	3.5	17.2	3.9	10.7	12.0	5.3	10.2
– Machinery and transport equipment	4.7	1.5	18.3	8.8	11.5	10.1	5.3	6.0
– other manufactured goods	16.6	4.7	38.3	28.7	43.5	32.5	37.7	31.5

Source: Eurostat, External Trade No 3/1986.

Table 6. Trade between the EC and the European CMEA countries by commodity groups exports 1985.

Commodity groups	CMEA	USSR	GDR	Poland	Chechoslovakia	Hungary	Romania	Bulgaria
Total	100.0	100.0	100.0	100.0	100.0	100.0	100.0	100.0
– Food, beverages, tobacco	11.8	14.8	16.5	12.5	6.4	3.2	4.9	10.6
– Raw materials	2.8	1.7	9.4	2.2	5.7	3.7	4.7	2.8
– Fuel products	1.7	0.8	8.1	1.0	0.8	2.6	7.9	2.2
– Oils and fats	0.6	0.6	—	1.6	0.3	0.2	0.5	0.2
– Chemicals	15.8	13.3	14.8	19.7	18.7	19.7	21.1	15.8
– Machinery and transport equipment	27.2	24.8	19.7	29.7	34.1	30.4	19.2	37.0
– other manufactured goods	34.0	39.1	23.5	26.2	26.2	34.0	33.2	24.4

Source: Eurostat, External Trade No 3/1986.

In 1970 the EEC Council introduced a similar arrangement for wines: those countries guaranteeing that export prices would not be inferior to the prices of reference minus import duties, could be exempted from the countervailing charges. The Hungarian Ministry of Foreign Trade undertook this guarantee in November 1970, the details being specified between the then sole exporter MONIMPEX Company and the competent services of the EEC Commission.[4]

A third agreement was concluded for Kashkaval cheese. In accordance with a regulation of the EEC Council of 1968 Hungary undertook a price guarantee in February 1971 and the EEC Commission applied a reduced levy for this product.[5]

B. *Multilateral relations*

A turning-point in the relations between Hungary and the EEC was Hungary's accession to the GATT which came into force on the 9th of September 1973[6] (Martonyi, *infra* p. 272). In the Protocol of Accession the Contracting Parties "still maintaining prohibitions or quantitative restrictions not consistent with Article XIII of the General Agreement on imports from Hungary", i.e. including the EEC and its Member States, declared that they "shall not increase the discriminatory element in these restrictions and undertake to remove them progressively". Furthermore: "if, for exceptional reasons, any such prohibitions or restrictions are still in force as of 1 January 1975, the Working Party (of the GATT for Hungary) will examine them with a view to their elimination".[7]

A *bona fide* implementation of these provisions should have resulted, by the beginning of 1975, in only a small number of QRs being maintained "for exceptional reasons".

As a matter of fact, the EEC has not changed the import régime applied to Hungary, as one of the so-called State-trading countries,[8] i.e. it maintained all the original wide range of discriminatory QRs on imports from Hungary (let alone some slight modifications). The scope of these QRs was, without any doubt, far beyond a "hard core" that could have been justified by the "exceptional reasons" foreseen by the Protocol of Accession of Hungary to the GATT. We have to add that in parallel all the other developed industrial countries, which had previously applied discriminatory restrictions on imports from Hungary, took the necessary measures to eliminate them. The Community simply neglected the concrete and specific content of the Hungarian Protocol of Accession to the GATT. Hungary has reacted and claimed her rights within the GATT, in the consultations held by the Working Party on Trade with Hungary under the Protocol of Accession which has its regular sessions once every two years.[9]

Another multilateral relation has been established between Hungary and the EEC by the Final Act of the Conference on Security and Co-operation in Europe. At the final meeting on 1 August 1975 in Helsinki, Hungary also took note of the fact that the document was signed by the Italian Prime Minister in his capacity of President in office of the Council of the European Communities. The Final Act stipulates that the participating states "will endeavour to reduce or progressively eliminate all kinds of obstacles to the development of trade".[10] The Final Act in its general terms did not confirm or strengthen Hungary's rights in the GATT but was, according to the Hungarian view, an overall confirmation of benevolent implementation of international legal obligations concerning the elimination of obstacles to trade.

C. *The EEC's "schéma d'accord"*

By the end of 1974, Hungary, as did all the "State-trading" countries, received a proposal from the EEC to establish "bilateral"[11] links with it by concluding a trade agreement. The proposal took the form of a roughly outlined draft agreement, the famous *"schéma d'accord"*.[12] Hungary refused this proposal for the following three main reasons:

1. The *"schéma d'accord"* did not foresee any change in the discriminatory import régime of the Community for "State-trading" countries, but proposed to maintain the same — uniform — treatment with only slight improvements. By that time Hungary had already had, for more than a year, a fundamentally different international legal position in the GATT assuring the elimination of all the discriminatory QRs, most of them within a very short period. It was obvious that Hungary put the emphasis on the implementation of the latter and that she preferred a multilateral framework in order to also ensure the necessary international control.[13]

2. The *"schéma d'accord"* did not propose any effective economic advantage to Hungary. At the same time, the dialogue between the CMEA and the EEC, at least in its early stages, provided hope that using the united power of the CMEA countries, with a special regard to the weight of the Soviet Union, an agreement bringing tangible economic advantages would be possible between the two regional organisations.[14]

3. The above-mentioned safeguard clause applied by the EEC to beef and live cattle a few months before, in July 1974 had a threefold negative effect on the relations between Hungary and the EEC: first, it caused very important immediate losses to the Hungarian producers and exporters because of the sudden introduction of the import stop without any previous warning (cattle starving in wagons, unsalable quantities during the following months etc.). Secondly, this drastic measure was at the origin

of a deep transformation of the traditional commodity structure of Hungarian exports to the EEC and of a new, structural imbalance in the trade with it. Thirdly, after the first positive impressions of the functioning of the above-mentioned price guarantees in the field of the CAP of the EEC this shock created serious doubts in Hungary about the credibility of the Community as a trading and contracting partner, doubts which were confirmed later by experiences at the meetings of the Working Party on trade with Hungary under the Protocol of Accession to the GATT (already mentioned).

D. *Sectoral agreements*

By the second half of the 1970s no progress could be reached either in the "bilateral" relations between Hungary and the EEC, or in the multi-lateral fora, namely in the GATT. After 1975, the EEC gave a new and negative interpretation to its obligation concerning the elimination of the discriminatory QRs for Hungary and the dialogue between the CMEA and the EEC was discontinued. In these years sectoral links were established between the EEC and Hungary (and four other CMEA countries as well).

The first sectoral agreement was concluded in the steel sector in 1978. It took the form of an exchange of letters and it has been renewed each year since that time.[15] This arrangement has limited traditional Hungarian steel exports to the Community but assured their continuation in spite of the crisis in the same sector in Western Europe. We can consider it as a balanced solution between the exporter and the importer in a critical economic situation.

In the framework of the International Multifibre Agreement of the GATT, signed by Hungary too, the EEC and Hungary concluded a "bilateral" textile agreement which has been renewed for the following periods as well.[16] The purpose of this agreement was not the expansion of trade between the contracting parties but on the contrary, the limitation of it in order to cope with the critical situation in the textile sector.

A third sectoral agreement for goat- and sheepmeat was somewhat different from the first two, not only because it was concluded in the field of agriculture, but it was the first — and until now unique — case in the CAP of the EEC that parallel with the introduction of a market order, third countries had the opportunity to negotiate with the Community about the future conditions of their traditional exports. Hungary, as an interested third country, concluded this sectoral agreement with the EEC as well.[17]

One general advantage — or a useful by-product — of all the sectoral agreements was that they established *de facto* contacts between the Hungarian authorities and the EEC Commission and helped to increase mutual information and confidence in a rather difficult period.

E. *Normalisation of "bilateral" relations*

In the early 1980s Hungary made renewed efforts and took initiatives with the aim of finding a solution to the normalisation of its relations with the EEC. These initiatives had the form of bilateral political approaches to some EEC Member States. Hungarian politicians and officials tested the possibilities of establishing global and long-term "bilateral" contractual links between Hungary and the EEC. (We have to note that during these contacts some new ideas were raised which proved to be either unrealistic or, to some extent, in advance of their time e.g. a free trade area between Hungary and the EEC.)

After the entry of Greece into the EEC (1981) Hungary made steps in the GATT in order to be compensated for the damages caused to her exports. Hungary asked for compensation for the losses in her agricultural exports.[18] The talks which started between Hungary and the EEC in this context constituted the basis of the agricultural chapter of a comprehensive dialogue that followed.

As a result of these initiatives, at and after the 1982 November ministerial meeting of the GATT a dialogue began between Hungary and the EEC about the conclusion of a global "bilateral" trade agreement. During this dialogue, parallel with some political contacts, two important expert meetings took place in Brussels in 1983 and in 1984.[19] At these meetings the experts embarked on a deep analysis of all the conditions of a possible trade agreement between Hungary and the EEC. This dialogue was finally interrupted for the sole reason that the EEC did not in any respect move from the platform of the principles of the 1974 "*schéma d'accord*" i.e. it was not ready to meet any of Hungary's two main demands: the elimination of discrimination and the granting of substantial economic advantages.

Even if this dialogue was interrupted, its lessons were not lost but analysed and presented to the European Parliament. In 1985 Mr. Axel Zarges, member of the EP, wrote a thorough and detailed report about Hungary and the relations between this country and the EEC. The report was discussed, adopted and presented to the plenary session of the EP by the Committee for External Economic Relations. The EP took a resolution on 13 June 1986.[20] The two most important elements of this resolution were: (1) that Hungary should be treated by the EEC taking into consideration all of her specificities (and there were many of them, according to the analysis of the report); (2) that the EEC should propose to Hungary a trade *and* cooperation agreement right at the beginning of "bilateral" contractual links (as opposed to the usual way followed by the Community i.e. concluding a trade agreement first and completing it with a cooperation chapter in a second phase).

We may note that parallel with the preparation of the Zarges report on Hungary, the CMEA-EEC dialogue reached a new and promising phase. By June 1986, when the EP took its position about Hungary, a parallel dialogue had already been opened between the EEC on the one hand and the CMEA and its member countries on the other with the mutual aim to normalise relations between the two neighbouring regions.[21] One of the important conditions of this normalisation, shared by the two sides, was an individual and differentiated approach by the EEC to the particular member countries of the CMEA. Bearing in mind this wider context, the Zarges report could not encounter political opposition, but it added practical arguments and facts on an already existing political will. (We cannot exclude at the same time that the arguments of the report, during its long preparation, could influence the maturation of the political will of the EEC concerning real differentiation.)

Taking into account all the antecedents, the preparation of official negotiations between Hungary and the EEC did not take a long time.[22] On the basis of a Hungarian draft agreement the two sides agreed in October 1986 about the content and the main points of a non-discriminatory trade and cooperation agreement to be concluded betweeen Hungary and the EEC.

The Commission completed the draft mandate and submitted it to the Council in November 1986.[23] After a thorough examination and some modifications (which did not facilitate the following negotiations, e.g. one of the most crucial questions, the fixing of a final date for the elimination of the discriminatory QRs had been left open for negotiation with Hungary) the Council approved the mandate on 27 April 1987. Official negotiations started on 4 June.[24] In 1987 the first official political contacts were also established between Hungary and the EEC Commission.[25]

III. Some general problems of the negotiations

By the end of 1987 negotiations between Hungary and the EEC are still in progress. These negotiations cover the following main points:

— a non-discriminatory trade régime
— mutual tariff reductions on industrial products
— mutual concessions for agricultural products

— business facilities
— industrial and technical cooperation
— the establishment of a mixed commission
— the establishment of diplomatic relations.

During the negotiations the following problems of a general nature or of principle have occurred:

1. The Community has declared and emphasised a differentiated approach to the individual member countries of the CMEA according to their specificities. At the same time, not only at the expert level, but among politicians too, a fear can be witnessed of the "precedent" (i.e. concerning the non-discriminatory treatment of Hungary, in compliance with the specific stipulations of her Protocol of Accession to the GATT). It is obvious that the principle of differentiation and the fear of precedents are not coherent. The case of Hungary should be considered as an example, which can be of great use for both regions, i.e. the EEC and the CMEA, providing the way and the conditions for a change from discriminatory treatment towards a non-discriminatory trade régime and on that basis towards intensive economic cooperation.

2. While politicians of the EEC Member States encouraged the conclusion of an agreement with Hungary, at the expert level an unfounded fear — or even a phobia — was to be observed for an eventual and sudden increase of Hungarian exports into the Community, more precisely in connection with the elimination of the discriminatory quantitative restrictions. This fear is flattering for Hungary's export capacity, but is totally unrealistic, not only because Hungary has had a traditional and structural imbalance with the Community but also for the following reasons:

— the QRs do not cover more than 3 to 4 p.c. of the total Hungarian exports into the Community; [26]
— their elimination should take place in several stages during a transitional period;
— selective QRs do not limit imports in reality, they only divert them from one exporting country to another, not being subject to specific QRs;
— when joining the GATT, Hungary accepted a selective safeguard clause, which makes it possible to take measures only against imports from Hungary.

We can add that the basic aim of the agreement between Hungary and the EEC should be to increase trade on both sides, consequently a possible future increase of trade should not create any fear on any side.

3. One of the positive and specific characteristics of the future

agreement is that it should cover, from the very beginning, industrial cooperation as well. In the case of Hungary, cooperation has deep traditions with several EEC Member States e.g. with the FRG, Holland, the U.K., France, Greece, to name only some. However, in this context some political reservations could be observed in that some circles of the EEC seem to identify all or the most part of the cooperation activity with illegal exports of high technology under COCOM control. The experiences of industrial and technical cooperation between Hungary and the Member States of the EEC prove that out of the very narrow circle of prohibited technologies — the adaptation and utilisation of which should not be very easy in Hungary either — several possibilities of cooperation exist.[27] These forms of cooperation can promote the exchange of mutually interesting R&D achievements or widen export markets. We have to bear in mind that cooperation belongs first of all to the Member States, not only from a legal point of view, as a "mixed" external competence, but also according to economic realities. Cooperation at Community level can only complete the existing classic, inter-state cooperation or to a much larger extent "company-to-company" cooperation.

4. Hungary (as probably all third countries) faced some difficulties because of the actual stage in the evolution of the external competences of the EEC. The Commission has the task to negotiate (and has made enormous efforts to succeed) but is not allowed to give an independent interpretation to the mandate approved by the Member States. The Member States have still maintained their rights to take decisions even on the smallest details of an agreement to be concluded with a third country, but are not allowed to take the floor in the negotiations. For the negotiating third country, the main problem is that the partner which is negotiating with it is not competent to take any decisions and those who take the decisions cannot hear its arguments but learn about them only with a delay and through several intermediaries. Let us express our hopes that the Community's international negotiating techniques have not yet reached their final and most perfected stage.

5. It is obvious that "bilateral" progress was made possible, in one way or another, by the new initiative of the CMEA. The most important political condition on both sides was "parallelism". This means that "bilateral" and CMEA level progress should be parallel. In this respect two main questions can be raised. *First*, parallelism has more than two elements that ought to be "parallel":

- to end all activities of non-recognition of the EEC in international fora,
- the conclusion of "bilateral" agreements between the individual CMEA countries and the EEC,
- the establishment of "bilateral" diplomatic relations,

— the signing of a Common Declaration between the CMEA and the EEC.

Not only the realisation of these different steps requires a different time schedule, but the interests of the individual CMEA countries can be different concerning one or another element of the overall normalisation of relations between the two regions (e.g. it would be unrealistic to ask all the CMEA countries to conclude bilateral trade agreements with the EEC at the same time, etc.).

The *second* question is: how far and how deeply the different steps should be synchronised with each other. (A — positively — disturbing factor here is that in some fields reality has already displaced legal acts, e.g. *de facto* diplomatic relations exist between the EEC and all European CMEA countries.)

As far as "parallelism" was the result of a political compromise between divergent priorities, both sides should take care to maintain the global political equilibrium of the whole process. Too keen a synchronisation of the different steps in this manifold evolution could disturb the harmonious and the globally, indeed, "parallel" procedure which has been going on since May 1986.

IV. The specificities of Hungary

One of the key elements of the Hungarian position has always been that this country should be treated by the EEC as it is, without prejudice and without prefabricated and standardised patterns. This position has been shared first by the European Parliament and later on by the EEC Commission as well.

What are the main specificities that can distinguish the individual character of the Hungarian case?

1. The EEC has a relatively high market share in Hungary with nearly 20 p.c. of all Hungarian imports. The average figure of the CMEA is about 10 p.c. (see Table 7). The consolidation and an eventual increase of the Community's market share in Hungary needs support in the field of trade policy measures concerning Hungarian exports as well.

2. At present Hungary is the most important export market for the EEC in the Central Eastern European region (without the Soviet Union and Inner-German trade). She has at the same time a structural imbalance with the Community. In order to consolidate EEC exports to Hungary, Hungarian exports should be developed in a more dynamic way.

3. The commodity structure of trade between Hungary and the EEC is

Table 6. Share of the EC from the foreign trade of some CMEA countries (in %).

Country	Imports			Exports		
	1970	1975	1983	1970	1975	1983
USSR	12.4	16.8	14.4	10.7	14.4	20.2
Poland	17.0	28.0	16.6	17.3	18.6	22.3
Czechoslovakia	15.0	14.5	8.9	13.4	13.0	9.5
Hungary	18.4	16.2	19.6	18.5	13.0	15.6
Romania	27.6	25.7	9.7	24.7	23.7	23.9
Bulgaria	12.9	16.6	10.0	10.3	6.6	6.4

Source: Statistische Grundzahlen der Gemeinschaft 23. Ausgabe, p. 6.15.

unique in the region. Hungarian exports into the EEC are based on agricultural and manufactured industrial products (Hungary not being an exporter of fuel or raw materials). EEC exports to Hungary consist mainly of industrial products. Mutual trade concessions, that take into consideration the specific commodity structure on both sides, could help a harmonious increase of trade.

4. Hungary has specific international rights and obligations: her membership of GATT (1973) and the special conditions of her accession to it, her membership of the IMF and the World Bank (1982) and of a large number of international agreements and conventions on industrial property, trade marks etc. can justify a special legal content of the agreement including non-discriminatory treatment.

5. Hungary introduced about 20 years ago a special economic system, characterised by continuous reforms and a peculiar amalgam of the positive elements of planned and market economies. This economic system includes a special price, exchange rate, import tariff, credit etc. system recognised by the competent international organisations.[28] All these elements can give a special value to trade concessions offered by Hungary.

6. Hungary has an open and transparent market that is easily accessible for foreign companies and businessmen: e.g. visitors can obtain an immediate entry visa at the border; exporters can establish direct contacts with the end-users of their products; economic and business information is easily available; permanent company representations, joint ventures and mixed companies (even with a foreign majority) can be established etc. These facilities help trade and economic cooperation (see Madl, *infra* pp. 147—182).

7. Hungary is attached by traditional historical, cultural and economic links to the majority of the EEC Member States. On this basis a wide and

deeply structured network of trade and cooperation contacts has been built up. A great number of companies, small and big enterprises, scientific institutions, businessmen and officials from Hungary and the EEC Member States have established regular relations between each other. For that reason, the cooperation chapter of the agreement can include a wide range of fields and activities.

8. Hungary lies in the immediate proximity of the EEC (even if there is no common border between Hungary and any of the EEC Member States) and represents an important transit passage for the Community partly along the Danube, partly along the flat Hungarian plain for road traffic. Since Greece joined the EEC, Hungary has become an important direction for traffic within the Community as well. To the geographical position of Hungary belongs the fact that she is a disadvantaged land-locked country. At a later stage of cooperation between Hungary and the EEC these elements can be of importance.

9. The level of economic development in Hungary, according to World Bank data, is under the lowest in the Community. For that reason, in the long run, Hungary should be treated to the preferences that the EEC — more precisely the highly industrialised centre of it — grants to the peripheral countries of the European and Mediterranean region.[29]

10. Hungary has always made special efforts, in accordance with her own economic interests, to find appropriate solutions in her relations with the EEC. Hungary gave positive answers to all the EEC initiatives that offered a mutually advantageous, well-balanced solution to a problem. She has also supported the normalisation of CMEA-EEC relations, as a general framework of contacts between the two regions, but did not make any strict linkage between the development of global and "bilateral" relations.

At the moment — the end of 1987 — while negotiations, dialogues and exploratory talks at different levels are in progress between the CMEA and its member countries on the one hand and the EEC on the other, we cannot report that anything has yet been concluded, but we can end this short analysis by expressing our hope that in 1988 the first three or four global "bilateral" agreements between European CMEA countries and the EEC will be signed and the Common Declaration of the two organisations will also be finalised. 1988 should also be the year of establishing diplomatic relations between the CMEA countries and the EEC.

One of those "bilateral" agreements should be the first global agreement on trade and economic cooperation between Hungary and the EEC. This agreement should put an end to a long period of confrontation and should open a new era of cooperation which, parallel with the final elimination of the last discriminatory elements of the treatment reserved for Hungary, will gradually bring more and more benefit for both sides, resulting from the expansion of trade and industrial and technical co-operation.

Notes

1. According to the statistical service of the Hungarian Ministry of Foreign Trade, in 1960 agriculture made up 58.5 p.c. of Hungarian exports into the EEC; in the 1980s the same category of products represents about 30 p.c.
2. Regulation 442/74 of the Commission of 21 February 1974 concerning safeguard measures in the beef sector, *O.J.*, L 50/33, 1974; see also: *Eigth General Report on the Activities of the European Communities*, 1974, sec. 381.
3. On the basis of Regulation 121/67 of the Council of 13 June 1967, expert meetings took place between Hungary and the EEC Commission on 24—26 April and 24—25 June 1968. The letters of the Hungarian Ministry of Foreign Trade and the TERIMPEX Company of 25 June were confirmed by the EEC Commission on 18 July 1968; see also: *Second General Report on the Activities of the European Communities*, 1968, sec. 543.
4. On the basis of Regulation 816/70 of the Council of 28 April 1970 and an exchange of letters of 3 November 1970 between the Hungarian Ministry of Foreign Trade and the MONIMPEX Company on the one hand and the EEC Commission on the other, the arrangement — covering eight other third countries as well — was published by Regulation 2223/70 of the Commission in *O.J.*, L 241, 1970; see also: *Fourth General Report on the Activities of the European Communities*, 1970, sec. 465.
5. On the basis of Regulation 823/68 of the Council an exchange of letters between the Hungarian Ministry of Foreign Trade and the TERIMPEX Company on the one hand and the EEC Commission on the other took place on 22 February 1971; see also: *Fifth General Report on the Activities of the European Communities*, 1971, sec. 466.
6. The Community followed with great attention the negotiations on the accession of Hungary to the GATT and the representative of the EEC played an extremely active role in these negotiations according to the *Fourth General Report on the Activities of the European Communities*, 1970, sec. 472; the *Fifth General Report on the Activities of the European Communities*, 1971, sec. 502; the *Sixth General Report on the Activities of the European Communities*, 1972, sec. 474 and the *Seventh General Report on the Activities of the European Communities*, 1973, sec. 563.
7. Protocol for the Accession of Hungary to the GATT Part I, point 4 (a) and (b).
8. The category of "State-trading countries" is based mainly on political considerations, without any logical economic or geographical definition. This notion is unknown in the GATT and has no international legal or economic definition. In the import régime of the EEC, at present, the European and Asian Member States of the CMEA, China, North Korea and Albania are classified as "State-trading countries"; see e.g. Regulation 1765/82 of the Council, *O.J.*, L 196, 1982.
9. GATT doc. L/4228 of 7 October 1975, L/4633 of 28 February 1978, L/4930 of 29 January 1980, L/5303 of 18 March 1982, L/5635 of 3 April 1984 and L/5977 of 11 April 1986.
10. Conference on Security and Cooperation in Europe, Final Act, "Second Basket", 1. Commercial Exchanges.

11. In order to distinguish the classic interstate bilateral relations from the relations of the EEC with third countries, we put the word "bilateral" in inverted commas in the latter case.

12. The "*Schéma d'accord*" was a working document and has not been published officially. It can be found in: Dossier CEE-COMECON by V. Chiusano MEP, Centre européen du Kirchberg, Luxemburg, December 1985.

13. By 1974—75 Hungary could consider her contractual links with the EEC to be in perfect conformity with the external competences of the Community as far as trade policy questions were regulated by the Protocol of Accession of Hungary to the GATT, signed by the EEC Member States and the Community, and bilateral cooperation agreements concluded with the particular Member States of the EEC.

14. Following an initiative by the CMEA in 1973, the EEC Council confirmed in May 1974 the readiness of the Community to establish contacts with the CMEA. The delegation of the EEC Commission visited the CMEA Secretariat on 4—6 February 1975. In 1976 both organisations sent a draft agreement to the other and they began official negotiations in 1978. The first phase of the CMEA-EEC dialogue was interrupted in 1981 without any positive result.

15. The EEC Commission addressed a note to the Hungarian Embassy in Brussels on 3 January 1978 proposing negotiations. The representatives of Hungary and the EEC signed the exchange of letters resulting from these negotiations on 1 May 1978; see also: *Bull. EC.*, 5—1978, para. 2.2.41.

    The arrangement has not been published, see "L'Europe aujourd'hui 1982—1983" (Parlement européen, Sécrétariat général) point 6.85: "Acier: un échange de lettres couvrant les importations CECA fixe les prix et les quantités autorisées pour différents produits. Accord conclu en 1978; Reconduit annuellement."

16. The first "bilateral" textile agreement for 1978—1982 was published by Regulation 3259/81 of the Council, of 19 October 1981, *O.J.*, L 332/81, 1981. The second agreement for 1983—1986 was initialled on 11 July 1982 and signed on 12 December 1986. This agreement has not been published yet. The third agreement for 1987—1991 was initialled on 11 July 1986 and published by the Decision 87/549 of the Council of 11 December 1987 in *O.J.*, L 331, 1987.

17. Decision 81/390 of the Council of 12 May 1981, *O.J.*, L 150/81, 1981.

18. Hungary asked for consultations with the EEC on the legal basis of Article XXIV para. 6 of the GATT; at the same time she proposed a special quota for the exports of high quality beef (Hilton beef) into the Community. Meetings of the two parties took place on 17 March 1982 and 21—22 September 1982. The EEC refused both Hungarian demands.

19. The 1983 expert meeting took place in two rounds on 24—25 May and 15—16 June. The experts met again on 15—17 May 1984 in Brussels.

20. *Report on trade relations between the European Community and Hungary*, European Parliament, Working Documents, 1986—87, Doc. A 2—28/86; see also *Resolution on the possibilities for commercial relations between the European Community and Hungary*, *O.J.*, C 176/192, 1986.

21. Following the initiative of the CMEA taken at its summit meeting in Moscow in June 1984, the Secretary General of the CMEA addressed a letter to the President of the EEC Commission in 1985 proposing to adopt a Common Declaration about the cooperation of the two organisations. At the request of the EEC, the CMEA also confirmed that the establishment of contacts between the two organisations would not prevent "bilateral" relations between the EEC and the individual Member States of the CMEA.

22. As a reaction to the CMEA initiative, the EEC Commission sent letters to each of the

European member countries of the CMEA proposing the normalisation of "bilateral" relations. A letter to the Hungarian government was sent on 3 February 1986. The Hungarian government gave a positive answer on 8 May. Answering this letter, Mr. Willy De Clercq proposed, in his letter of 29 May 1986. A meeting at political meetings followed on 22 July and on 13—14 October 1986.

23. See *Twentieth General Report on the Activities of the European Communities*, 1986, sec. 847.

24. Hungary was the third CMEA country for whom the EEC Commission obtained a negotiating mandate from the Council and the second to start official negotiations.

25. In 1987, the first official visit of the Hungarian Government to the EEC Commission took place when Mr. Jozsef Marjai, Deputy Prime Minister was received by Mr. Willy De Clercq in Brussels on 9 February 1987. On his official visit to Belgium, Mr. Jànos Kàdàr, Secretary General of the Hungarian Socialist Workers Party, member of the Presidential Council had an informal meeting in Brussels with Mr. Jacques Delors and Willy De Clercq on 15 November.

26. The products concerned are e.g. shoes, handkerchiefs, matches, tiles, some chemical products and others. The annual import quotas for 1987 were published by Council Decision 87/60 of 22 December 1986, *O.J.*, L 31/1, 1987.

27. The existing contracts for cooperation, the negotiations in progress and the new proposals for cooperation are generally listed in the protocols of the bilateral mixed commissions for economic, industrial and technical cooperation between Hungary and the individual Member States of the EEC.

28. When joining the IMF and the World Bank, a detailed report was published about the Hungarian economic system: "Hungary: An Economic Survey", Occasional Paper No. 15, International Monetary Fund, Washington D.C., December 1982. Since that time some new measures have been introduced, e.g. from 1 January 1988 a value added tax system and a quasi-automatic authorisation of all Hungarian companies for doing foreign trade operations directly etc.

29. At present, these preferences take very different forms. From this point of view the countries or regions surrounding the industrialised centre of Western Europe can be categorised in three groups:

(1) Within the EEC: Ireland, the three Mediterranean Member States, South-West France and southern Italy benefit from the regional and other programmes of the Community;

(2) The non-EEC Member States of the Mediterranean region have concluded preferential agreements with the Community with a special and advantageous content;

(3) The East European CMEA countries, that for economic reasons belong to the same category as the first two groups of countries, have made only the first steps towards a non-preferential, equal MFN-treatment.

According to the "World Bank Atlas 1986" the GNP per capita was USD 2150 in Hungary and USD 2230 in Portugal (1983-figures).

General frames of EEC-CMEA economic relations from the point of view of perestroika in the USSR

ALEXANDER BYKOV

Professor, Dr. Sc. (Econ.), Section Head, Institute of Economics of the World Socialist System, USSR Academy of Sciences, Moscow

The Soviet Union is at the turning-point of its development which is connected with perestroika involving a revolutionary restructuring of all aspects of Soviet social life. The essence of this process are democratisation, profound economic reforms, new approaches to foreign policy and participation in the world division of labour.

A task of historical significance was put forward and substantiated at the 27th Congress of the CPSU, during the last Plenary Meetings of the CPSU Central Committee: acceleration of socio-economic development and all possible promotion of scientific and technological progress, overcoming negative tendencies in socialist society while enhancing its all-round improvement with a view to the fullest realisation of its vast potential. All this defines the character and direction for the socialist construction in the USSR both during the new five-year period and in the long term.

In the field of international relations mankind is faced with a choice to be made between joint survival and collective death in thermonuclear massacre. This brings about an urgent task of a new thinking and a new approach to the problems of war or peace, necessitating a reshaping of negative trends formed during recent years towards peaceful coexistence and cooperation, and a curbing of the arms race, with totally controlled disarmament. In this context, the recent peace-loving actions and initiatives of the USSR, of the socialist community, as well as Soviet-American summits are of great significance. This is illustrated by the signing of the historical agreement in Washington.

The combination of the above-mentioned factors creates a radically new situation in the sphere of trade and economic relations between East and West and opens up new opportunities for their positive development. They in turn, are superposed by an objective tendency towards a greater internationalisation of economic life and scientific and technological progress — which is considerably intensified under the conditions of the

M. Maresceau (ed.), The Political and Legal Framework of Trade Relations Between the European Community and Eastern Europe. ISBN 0–7923–0046–7.
© *1989 by Kluwer Academic Publishers, Dordrecht – Printed in the Netherlands.*

revolution in science and technology — and by an objective tendency towards the aggravation of global problems facing mankind and necessitating closer interaction at both regional and global level for their solution, including a greater interdependence of different countries and regions. One cannot but take into consideration an intimate interrelationship in the solution of mankind's military-political and socio-economic problems.

Trade and economic relations, scientific and technological exchanges, while taking on more profound and regular proportions, serve as a material foundation for peaceful coexistence and enhance the motives for constructive interaction in other areas, also weakening the intention to solve disputes and disagreements by non-peaceful means. In the West the socialist economy is depicted as continuously urging full self-sufficiency and being "closed" to the world market. The prejudiced character of such an approach is obvious. The USSR and other countries of the socialist community never adhered to the course of autarky, neither national nor regional, and have not resorted to it, unless the West forced them to do so through its discriminatory measures. Any autarky is useless, especially under present-day conditions. The emphasis of the CMEA countries on greater technical and economic invulnerability, quite understandable in the present world political and economic situation, as well as in view of the negative results of East-West interaction in recent times, should not be regarded as an artificial fencing-off from world economic relations.

As M. S. Gorbachev noted at the April (1985) Plenary Meeting of the CPSU Central Committee, that initiated the course for perestroika, it is necessary to thoroughly examine the state of our external economic relations, to have a more profound look at them in perspective. Here favourable opportunities are available, despite international tension. The approach to mutually beneficial economic relations must be more comprehensive, large-scale, and future-oriented. The top leaders of the socialist countries at their collective fora have repeatedly called for normalisation and development of international relations in economic areas, in science and technology, for the elimination of all kinds of artificial obstacles and discriminatory restrictions in this field, for measures intended to build confidence and for principles of economic security for states in trade and economic relations.

The main route for the external economic activities of the CMEA countries at the present stage consists of the ever-growing interrelationships within the framework of the integration process including the intensification of far-reaching efforts on the basis of coordinated economic scientific and technological policies, as well as large-scale long-term programmes. Among these programmes a special role is played by the *Comprehensive Programme of Scientific and Technological Progress*[1] pooling the efforts and resources of these countries in five priority areas covering about one hundred problems of a scientific-technological and production nature, in an integrated unity of both these components.

At the same time, it should be borne in mind that the socialist integration has been always regarded as an open process closely interrelated with the entire combination of world economic relations, participation of its members in their various areas among which the leading role is played by East-West trade and economic, scientific and technological relations. Moreover, there are many reasons to declare that the progress of this integration creates additional opportunities for external relations. In implementation of large-scale integrational programmes, first of all in the area of scientific and technological progress, the CMEA countries intend to make efficient use of the mutual completion of internal and external regional relations, and of the broad international scientific and technological cooperation at large.

The course for perestroika implies a profound structural rearrangement of the entire national economy, increasing the role of mechanical engineering in it as a basis for such rearrangement, a considerably fuller satisfaction of growing material and spiritual demands of people with special attention to social problems. All this is connected, in turn, with involvement of additional resources, domestic and international ones in the first place, with a radical improvement of efficiency regarding their use. At the same time, realisation of this course also requires a more effective use of sources from outside the socialist community, primarily all those that are used in exchanges and cooperation with countries of the West. This, as a matter of fact, defines the opportunities and prospects of East-West trade and economic relations already in the current five-year period and in the long run, taking into consideration the started restructuring.

In the USSR — the largest country of the socialist community whose industrial and technical potential and resources define substantially the possibilities of the community on the whole — it is intended to lift the productive forces and production relations to a qualitatively new level within the next 13 years, to radically accelerate scientific and technological progress, and to create a production potential equal to that accumulated during all the previous years. It is also planned to almost double national income within this period, to increase labour productivity by 2.3—2.5, to reduce energy-intensity by 1.4 and metal-intensity by 2, to radically improve efficiency of production facilities, to bring the quality of goods and services up to the world level or even surpass it, and to increase real incomes of the population by 1.6—1.8.

Taking into account difficulties inherited from recent times and acquired in the external economic sphere, the task of stabilisation and rationalisation of trade and economic relations with the West, an amelioration of the structure of these relations, and a better balancing of commodity and money flows in both directions will remain short-term objectives. It should be admitted that the structure of exports of the USSR and of the CMEA countries in general does not correspond to their true potentialities, or new trends in world trade. This became especially clear during the most recent period when even petroleum which used to be the best exportable commodity failed to be so due to changes in the world situation which could not but tell upon the export opportunities for the USSR and, to some extent, for other CMEA countries.

Therefore, the problem of finding new export possibilities, the alteration of the entire structure of exports shifting it towards new goods, primarily science-intensive products, commodities (raw materials included) with a deeper degree of manufacture, and towards technical and other (e.g. space-oriented) services, means that investment assistance becomes the number one problem in the external economic activity of the CMEA countries, especially in East-West relations. For this all material preconditions are available; primarily the scientific, technological and production potential of the socialist community amounting to 1/3 of the world total, as well as vast raw-material and energy sources.

The immense scientific resources of the Soviet Union on the scale and at the pace of accumulation whereby the USSR has surpassed all countries of the world is of obvious interest to the West. Today about 2/5 of the world's patent fund consists of inventions originating in the CMEA countries, to say nothing about the especially strong position of Soviet fundamental research. All this provides sound opportunities for large-scale cooperation, including cooperation within the framework of international peaceful programmes with all — primarily Western — countries, which are implemented both in the CMEA region, in Western Europe and in other areas, in the solution of problems of scientific and technological progress in the interests of the whole of mankind.

Consequently, the well-developed rationalisation of East-West trade and economic relations is not at all directed at stagnation, but, conversely, creates real conditions for a substantial expansion and a radical improvement of the structure of participation of CMEA countries in the international division of labour as well as allowing progress in strengthening their export base which, in turn, will considerably enlarge the possibilities for purchases of the required products in the West. These developments on both sides are closely interrelated, since an optimal participation of Western companies in the solution of problems of intensification and modernisation of production in the CMEA countries (for which broad opportunities are created by their respective plans) also implies their readiness to enlarge imports from these countries, including those from export facilities erected and modernised with their own participation in mining industries and especially, in manufacturing industries including the most up-to-date technology-intensive areas.

An important prerequisite for the solution of the above-mentioned two-sided problem lies in the improvement and diversification of forms of economic relations with the West. In CMEA countries much attention is paid to it. Since within the framework of traditional trade and its present structure the possibilities of growth and qualitative improvement of such relations are limited, it is necessary to find and realise new promising forms shifting the centre of gravity to cooperation links. These can be exemplified by cross-licensing which is then converted into cooperation and coproduction, including marketing, and various forms of joint enterprises which serve to optimise diverse factors of production and marketing available to the partners.

While discussing the development of cooperation forms meeting the trends of the scientific and technological revolution and growing internationalisation of economic life noted already by V. I. Lenin and realised nowadays on a both regional and global scale, we should emphasise the promising character (including in East-West relations) of the highest form of cooperation, namely joint ventures. The USSR was attracting foreign investments in various forms already during the 20s. However, it is during the current period that this form can acquire impressive proportions, taking into consideration the vast Soviet scientific resources in important areas of scientific and technological development, its raw-material, manpower and market potential and the immense potential of the socialist community as a whole.

The strategy of perestroika cannot be successfully translated into practice within the framework of the already shaped or partly modified economic mechanism; it necessitates a profound reform which is being realised at the present time. In this respect a lot of attention is paid to the reinforcement of centralised power in the elaboration and realisation of the strategy of development, simultaneously with the strengthening of the role of economic methods in realising this strategy, and to the overall management of the national economy. Special emphasis is put on the liberation of initiatives at the micro-economic level, and the widening of economic independence and responsibility of direct producers whose activity becomes interrelated with full self-support and self-financing, i.e. the necessity to earn their living on their own and to distribute incomes (both individual and collective) depending on the production performance, to carry on an expanded redevelopment including modernisation of production facilities, satisfaction of social needs, and account settlement with the budget and suppliers. Special attention is also paid to the provision of an anti-outlay mechanism, realisation of the principles of payment according to labour and social justice, stimulation of innovation and high quality, development of contractual relations and direct links, amelioration of economic norms, pricing, credit and commodity-money instruments, management staff structure, improvement of competence and qualification at all levels.

The same principles are applicable to the external economic sphere intended to serve as an important factor of acceleration of socio-economic development. In order to decisively overcome the existing gap between the production associations and enterprises and the external market, to create better incentives for these associations and enterprises, to increase output of highly effective goods for exportation as well as increase economical use of imported resources, beginning with 1987 more than 20 ministries (mainly machine-building ones) and 70 major associations and enterprises have been entitled to the right of carrying out direct export-import transactions. They incorporate foreign trade firms. Where appropriate preconditions are formed, similar rights are given to other ministries, organisations and enterprises.

At the same time, to enhance economic incentives, widen self-sufficiency of enterprises and associations in promotion of exports and modernisation of production facilities, funds of foreign exchange are created to finance export-import operations, and to purchase the required machinery and licences on foreign markets for modernisation of production. For the same purposes credits in foreign currency can be obtained in the Vnesheconom-bank[3] of the USSR. Simultaneously the material responsibility of enterprises and associations for the fulfilment of export plans is tightened, a better relationship between foreign trade- and domestic prices is provided for settlement in export-import transactions, contractual self-support relations are established between the industry and foreign trade associations. The development of new forms including scientific, technological and production cooperation, as well as the establishment of joint ventures is envisaged in trade and economic relations with Western companies. In the promotion of these new links with foreign partners, the principles of mutual benefit are observed, and the respect of the rights and interests of both sides are guaranteed with at the same time strict observance by the partners of the Soviet laws and norms. Therefore, on the Soviet Union's part everything possible is being done to intensify its external economic relations and to render the organisation of these relations as acceptable as possible for partners from countries with a different social system. Meanwhile, the development of fair and mutually advantageous East-West trade and economic relations is still hindered by many barriers erected and continuing to be erected by the West. Primarily, there is the politicisation of such relations accompanied by an outdated and hopeless policy of blockades and sanctions against socialist countries, the imposition of various discriminatory measures in respect of them,[4] the desire of the West to pursue a differentiation policy relative to these countries, and the "linkage" of trade with political events and regional conflicts, as well as their internal and external policies.[5]

The above-discussed issues are most directly related to the destinies of Europe. It is here that, on the one hand, two of the most powerful military groupings confront each other and, on the other, the unprecedented — in world practice — Helsinki process was initiated more than ten years ago. It is in Europe that the most impressive cooperation between countries with different social systems is effected. At last, it is also here where the world's most intensive integration processes coexist which are capable of a broad mutually beneficial interaction in favour of the whole of Europe, the cause of peace and cooperation all over the world.

For CMEA countries trade and economic cooperation with Western Europe has been and still remains the main area of East-West cooperation. Moreover, due to a number of reasons, the "Europeocentrism" in the latter is even enhanced. This is exemplified by the fact that Western Europe accounts for up to 80 p.c. of the turnover of the CMEA countries with the West, including 55 p.c. with the EEC countries.[6] Though the share of the CMEA countries in the trade of West European states is more modest because of a known existing asymmetry, it is nevertheless rather significant. It is especially substantial for one member of the EEC — the Federal Republic of Germany — the largest trading partner of the CMEA countries in the West.

The major portion of more than 2000 cooperation agreements of the CMEA countries with the West also relates to West European countries. This is the case for scientific and technological exchanges including transfer of technology, and other promising forms of cooperation as well. All of them originated from the process of détente of the 70s and continue to be further developed, though less intensively than during the 70s.

For this reason, it is no wonder that when neo-conservative forces in Washington started to mercilessly demolish the house of détente built with such difficulty, West European countries as the main beneficiaries of détente tried to prevent this, though not always persistently and fruitfully. As a matter of fact, with the accord and, above all, at the expense of West European countries, Washington pursued its policies of boycott and sanctions because the USA eventually lost, both politically and economically, far less than these countries. At the same time, which is of importance for the USA, the positions of their major competitors in the world market were weakening. Though the EEC did not fully agree with the USA in the organisation of joint discrimination and sanctions against the CMEA countries, it nevertheless adhered to "Atlantic solidarity", and imposed a number of such sanctions of its own, for example against the USSR and Poland. The EEC and its members also accepted the introduction of more severe restrictive terms in respect of trade with these countries, first of all, in new technologies and in credits bound by the USA through COCOM and OECD; they have been extensively using and still use a so-called differentiated approach to these countries. In addition to purely protectionist measures, the practice of applying non-tariff and other discriminations to them on the part of the EEC is worsening. All this tells negatively on trade interests of CMEA countries, especially on their exports of agricultural products and manufactured goods to EEC countries, and on imports of high-technology articles; on the whole, it substantially narrows opportunities for mutually beneficial trade and cooperation between countries of the CMEA and the EEC.

Realising the importance of the interaction of the two major integrational associations for the progress of all-European cooperation and taking into consideration the realities in Europe, the CMEA countries already in the mid-70s came out with the initiative of establishing trade relations between CMEA and EEC and brought to Brussels corresponding proposals for their normalisation. However, the EEC did not wish to conclude an agreement with the CMEA on trade policy issues on an "inter-bloc" basis, explaining this by pointing out an insufficient competence of the CMEA, a different specificity and interests of CMEA member countries in trade with the EEC Member States and, accordingly, the preferred character of settling such problems with each CMEA country on an individual basis. In fact, the aim was that of pursuing the same differentiated policy in respect of the latter countries to the detriment of the interests of the socialist community as a whole.

Then, with the deterioration of the international situation on the verge of the 80s, corresponding negotiations were stopped and renewed only recently, again on the CMEA's initiative. At the same time, to settle urgent problems of trade relations with the EEC as regards individual commodities and in general, a number of CMEA countries signed technical and other agreements with the EEC. On account of this, the CMEA has found it possible to meet the EEC position half-way and suggested the establishment of relations with the EEC in parallel with the beginning of negotiations on signing trade agreements with it by each individual CMEA country. There is also the possibility of making contacts with the EEC in the political sphere to the extent to which the latter functions as a political entity.[7]

Therefore, it may be considered that the main obstacles for normalisation of the CMEA-EEC relations have been overcome and a way is opened for legal arrangements, for carrying out exchanges in information and contacts on certain issues of all-European cooperation that are of mutual interest. At the same time, there is still an urgent problem of overcoming protectionist tendencies in the EEC market hindering normal development of cooperation between participants of the two integrational associations of Europe and especially acutely perceived by the CMEA countries; imparting a more stable and long-term character to this co-operation and propagation thereof over the area of a multilateral all-European interaction is encouraged. An advanced movement in these directions would surely contribute to its expansion and intensification to the benefit of both sides, as well as all-European cooperation in general.

As far as the legal forms the CMEA-EEC relations might take on are concerned, it is in the interest of both parts of Europe, and of the entire continent, to impart a constructive character to them and to focus them on the solutions of such common problems, as, for instance, those concerning a reliable provision of raw materials and energy, including thermonuclear energy and related safety measures; promotion of all-European cooperation in science and technology, manufacturing industry and agricultural production, peaceful use of space and the world's oceans, environment protection, creation and development of a system of communications, tourism, and large-scale all-European projects in various fields.

A combination of the CMEA countries' vast scientific and technological potential and other resources with the West-European production-technological potential, certain harmonisation of their technological programmes (e.g. the above-mentioned Comprehensive Programme in the East and EUREKA in the West) could play a great role in the acceleration of the scientific and technological progress on the continent. It could help to overcome a known lagging-behind in this area of West European countries vis-à-vis principal competitors — the USA and Japan and, to some extent, vis-à-vis other countries of South East Asia — and in turn would contribute to strengthening the technological position of Europe as a whole. Coordinated steps in this and other directions could more effectively contribute to a solution of urgent economic and social problems, including the problem of employment in the Western part of the continent, the development of the entire European civilisation and reinforcement of its generally recognised world status. This is also important due to the fact that in the West, theories of Europe's decline are rife with the shifting of the centre of world development to the Asian-

Pacific zone where a new powerful "Pacific Community" is being formed by efforts of a number of countries. All this makes the strengthening of European self-consciousness, overcoming the "inferiority complex" and the feeling of doom of an obedient pupil following in the fairway of overseas ideas and intentions (even contrary to purely European interests), e.g. in relation to the restriction and cutting-short of East-West cooperation, very urgent. The CMEA countries are far from infringing upon the European direction of East-West cooperation in favour of its other directions and *vice versa*.

At the same time, for many CMEA countries including the USSR, the world economic situation has recently deteriorated, especially with the sharp drop of oil prices. This, however, stimulates even more active measures for the amelioration and diversification of the export potential, a wider use of new forms of cooperation — which in perspective should compensate losses in oil and create new reserves and opportunities for expansion of participation in the international division of labour — and primarily in the most promising directions and forms of production-technological cooperation.

In conclusion, I should like to emphasise once more the importance of all-European cooperation for the solution of the complicated problems of our continent and to underline the positive role which should be played by the large-scale integration processes occurring in Europe which are objectively destined to promote its development by the authorities organising and monitoring such processes and by their constructive interaction, as well as to note the readiness of the USSR and other CMEA countries to make their adequate contribution to this cause which is of importance for the whole of Europe, its present and future.

Notes

1. The five priority areas of the Comprehensive Programme are: 1. computerisation and electronics; 2. atomic energy; 3. automation; 4. biotechnology; 5. new technologies and materials.
2. This anti-outlay mechanism intends to economise expenses.
3. The Vnesheconombank is a specialised Soviet bank specifically dealing with foreign trade and other foreign economic operations.
4. Some illustrations might clarify the "disturbing nature" of these barriers. Blockades and sanctions; bans on trade with Cuba; limits on trade with *inter alia* the USSR and Poland. Discrimination: first of all the non-provision of MFN-treatment.
5. The policy of differentiation tends to result in different discriminatory régimes in respect of different socialist states, mostly through "linkage" with political events (Polish case), regional conflicts (Afghanistan, Cambodia), internal policy (emigration).
6. Source: *Monthly Bulletin of Statistics*, n° 7, July 1987.
7. On CMEA-EEC relations, see contributions in this volume by M. SYCHEV, OUGAROV, and M. DE CLERCQ, BENAVIDES, MASLEN.

European Community-CMEA: institutional relations

JOHN MASLEN

Head of Division, Eastern Europe, Commission of the European Communities

In discussing the state of relations between the Community and the Council for Mutual Economic Assistance (CMEA), it may be useful to recall briefly their earlier history. With the benefit of hindsight, this can be divided into three stages. The first of these, from the creation of the Community until 1972, was marked by a hostile attitude to the Community on the part of CMEA countries. This was expressed through intensive anti-EEC propaganda, the refusal of these countries to have dealings with the Community and their efforts to impede its accession to international conventions and its participation in multilateral organisations.

The second stage opened with Mr. Brezhnev's statement of 1972, in which he spoke of the possibility of relations between the CMEA and the 'Common Market'.[1] In my view, this initiative has to be set in the context of the state of East-West relations at that time. Preparations were just beginning for the Conference on Security and Co-operation in Europe, there was a climate of détente, and the adoption of a more realistic attitude to the Community could be presented as a gesture in this direction. Economic motives also probably played a role: some of the European CMEA countries were beginning to feel the effects of Community policies — and particularly of the Common Agricultural Policy — on their trade with Western Europe, and thus finding themselves under pressure, in their own interests, to enter into arrangements with the EEC, in the first instance in the agricultural field. A further important motive for this change in policy was certainly the wish to strengthen the CMEA both internally and externally. This was a period when very ambitious integration targets had just been incorporated into the CMEA's 1971 'Complex Programme', and when the wish to see the organisation play a more prominent role on the world stage was finding expression in the negotiation of cooperation agreements with non-Communist countries, such as those with Finland, Mexico and Iraq.

M. Maresceau (ed.), The Political and Legal Framework of Trade Relations Between the European Community and Eastern Europe. ISBN 0–7923–0046–7.
© *1989 by Kluwer Academic Publishers, Dordrecht – Printed in the Netherlands.*

The first direct CMEA approaches to the Community, in 1973 and the first half of 1974, were addressed to the Governments (Danish and German respectively) which held the Presidency of the EEC Council.[2] In September 1974 the then Secretary of the CMEA, Mr. Faddeyev, wrote to the President of the Commission, Mr. Ortoli, inviting him to Moscow to discuss relations between the two organisations. Although the invitation was accepted, Mr. Ortoli's visit never took place. A meeting between officials of the EC Commission and the CMEA Secretariat was held in Moscow in February 1975, with the aim of preparing for this visit. This meeting examined and compared various activities of the two organisations and identified a number of areas in which an exchange of information could be of mutual interest but the Commission's proposal to hold a second preparatory meeting of the same kind was never taken up. Instead, the CMEA put forward, in February 1976, the draft of an agreement to be concluded between the EEC and its Member States on one side, the CMEA and its member countries on the other.

This draft agreement of 1976 showed clearly what were the aims of the CMEA side in what I have called the 'second stage' of Community relations with Eastern Europe. Besides articles on possible areas and forms of cooperation between the CMEA and the EEC as organisations, a section on trade contained substantive provisions laying down the principles on which trade between CMEA and EEC countries should be based, notably most-favoured-nation treatment and non-discrimination, together with the granting of tariff preferences to CMEA countries at 'an appropriate level of development'. Other articles made it clear that these principles were to apply not only to the EEC-CMEA agreement but to any future agreements which might be concluded between the EEC and individual CMEA member countries; furthermore, these agreements with individual countries would concern only 'certain particular concrete questions'. Finally, the draft provided for the creation of a Joint Committee, comprising representatives of the two organisations and of their member countries, which would be responsible for overseeing the application of these principles both in the implementation of the main agreement and in that of agreements with individual countries. The objectives of the draft may be summed up as follows: basic guidelines for trade policy would be laid down in the agreement between the organisations; Community agreements with individual East European countries would be limited to technical matters and subject to supervision by the CMEA and its member countries collectively.

This concept was unacceptable to the Community, as was clear from the counter-draft which the Community put forward in November 1976. This draft agreement dealt only with working relations between the two organisations, while the covering letter from the President of the Council indicated that trade questions should be dealt with in bilateral agreements between the Community and each of the CMEA countries, as proposed by the EEC in 1974. This remained the Community's position throughout the negotiations which followed, and which were based upon the two drafts.

The first formal round of negotiations took place in Moscow in May 1978, and negotiations continued until October 1980, when they were suspended by mutual consent, the positions of the two sides being irreconcilable. Basically, the CMEA side would not relinquish, and the Community would not accept, the concept of the CMEA becoming a kind of intermediary between the EEC and individual CMEA countries, with power, through the agreement between the two organisations, not only to lay down guidelines for trade policy but also to supervise the content and execution of Community agreements with the individual countries. The Community's opposition to this idea was based on both legal and political arguments. On the one hand, it wished to negotiate on trade matters with those responsible for trade policy and wielding the instruments of this policy — i.e. in practice, the Governments of CMEA countries. On the other hand, the Community did not have any particular wish to see an extension of the CMEA's powers and activities in the trade field, limited traditionally to the coordination of intra-CMEA trade plans.

We are now in what might be called the third phase of relations between the Community and Eastern Europe. While there was no movement on the EEC-CMEA front during the period 1981—3, there were already signs of changing Eastern attitudes to the Community in 1983. The year 1984 brought clear evidence of an interest on the East European side in renewing the EEC-CMEA dialogue. In the final communiqué of the CMEA summit meeting in June of that year, the CMEA countries confirmed their readiness to conclude 'an appropriate agreement' between the CMEA and the EEC, with a view to promoting trade and economic relations between member countries of the two organisations. Various soundings were also carried out by CMEA member countries both with the Commission and EEC Member States.[3]

None of these approaches in 1984, however, had given any clear indication that there might be new elements in the CMEA position. The first such signal came during the visit of the Italian Prime Minister, Mr. Craxi, to Moscow in May 1985, at a time when Italy held the Presidency of the EC Council. In a speech on 20 May, Mr. Gorbachev said that it was time "to organise mutually advantageous relations between (the CMEA and the EEC) in economic matters. To the extent that EEC countries act as a 'political entity' we are ready to seek a common language with it, too, over international problems". The new element here was not, in fact, the reference to EEC-CMEA relations, but to the 'political entity' in other words, to the European Political Cooperation (EPC). East European attitudes to the EPC had traditionally been as hostile as towards the Community if not more so. However, since the Gorbachev statement, the Soviet and other East European Governments have shown more readiness to meet and deal with the EC Presidency acting on behalf of or in concert with the Twelve.

The first formal step in the resumption of the EEC-CMEA dialogue took the form of a letter from the new Secretary of the CMEA, Mr. Sychev, which was handed to President Delors on 14 June 1985. This proposed that official relations should be established between the CMEA and the EEC by the adoption, at high level, of a joint declaration. The idea was not a new one: during the final stages of EEC-CMEA negotiations in 1980, experts from the two sides had discussed the possibility of drafting a less ambitious document than the agreement proposed by the CMEA in 1976. The fact that, in 1985, the CMEA side was ready to make this idea an official proposal seemed to indicate a more flexible approach at least over the question of form. What was less clear was whether this flexibility extended to the content of the CMEA position. Since the Polish Ambassador in Brussels, in handing over the letter on 14 June, had indicated that a draft text of a joint declaration had already been prepared by the CMEA, Mr. Willy De Clercq asked in his reply of 29 July for further details on the content of the declaration proposed by the CMEA. At the same time, he stressed that, while the Community was ready to take up again the dialogue with the CMEA, this should not be allowed to affect in any way bilateral relations between the Community and individual CMEA member countries.

With his reply dated 26 September, Mr. Sychev sent the CMEA draft of a joint declaration. This is a short text, containing provisions of a general nature, of which only two are of substance; the CMEA and the EEC, the only parties to the agreement, are to establish official relations with each other by the adoption of this declaration; in subsequent meetings, representatives of the two sides are to discuss what the forms and methods of these relations will be and what areas they are to cover. This new draft showed, therefore, that the change in the CMEA's approach went beyond the mere form of the agreement; there was no more mention of provisions on trade or of relations between the Community and CMEA member countries.[4]

The Community now had to decide how to react to the CMEA's approach. Here I must leave for a moment the theme of EEC-CMEA relations, and look at Community policy towards CMEA *countries*: the two aspects have always been closely linked. The Community's main aim has long been the normalisation of relations between the EEC and the East European countries, treating each of these individually according to its particular circumstances — the nature of its economy, its links with the Community, its legal situation (member of GATT or not) etc. There was general agreement within the Community at the end of 1985 both on this basic aim and on the notion that it should be achieved by adopting a parallel approach — i.e. by seeking to develop the Community's relations with CMEA member countries simultaneously with its relations with the CMEA as an organisation. But there was less agreement on how this parallelism should be achieved, and intensive discussion on this took place in the Commission and Council frameworks. On the one hand, simply to reject the new CMEA approach would be inconsistent with the Community's position during the years of negotiation on an agreement, as well as politically difficult to justify at a time when East-West relations were entering a period of reduced tension. On the other hand, to accept the CMEA's ideas unconditionally could lead to rapid progress in relations with the organisation without the desired development of links with its member countries. Finally, it was decided to take the bull by the horns, to explain the Community's parallel approach clearly both to the CMEA itself and to the member countries and to see what their reaction would be.

Mr. De Clercq accordingly, at the end of January and beginning of February 1986, addressed letters both to Mr. Sychev and to the Foreign Ministers of the European members of the CMEA.[5] In the letter to Mr. Sychev, he wrote that the Community shared the CMEA's aim of establishing official EEC-CMEA relations, and proposed that a meeting be held at expert level to study ways of doing this. At the same time, he added, it would be inconsistent to establish official relations between the organisations in the absence of such relations between the EEC and the CMEA member countries; he was therefore writing to the Foreign Ministers of the latter to ask for their views on normalisation. In the letters addressed to the Foreign Ministers, Mr. De Clercq explained in similar terms the Community's parallel approach and asked for each Minister's views on the possibility of normalising relations between his country and the EEC. The Commission had been informally assured by representatives of various CMEA member countries that the latter were, in fact, willing to accept the parallel approach. This was confirmed when replies came in: the Romanian Foreign Minister's reply was received in March, Mr. Sychev's in April and those of the other Foreign Ministers in May. Mr. Sychev's answer accepted the idea of the parallel approach, while indicating that each CMEA member country would decide for itself whether to conclude agreements with the Community. At the same time, he agreed to Mr. De Clercq's proposal for an expert meeting on EEC-CMEA relations. As for the replies of the Foreign Ministers, they were all basically positive, and had three points in common: the wish to see official relations established between the CMEA and the EEC; the wish, at the same time, to normalise and develop the CMEA countries' bilateral relations with the Community (thus, acceptance of the parallel approach); willingness to negotiate bilateral agreements with the Community.[6]

The situation was reexamined in the Commission and Council framework in June. The replies of Mr. Sychev and the Foreign Ministers had made it clear that individual CMEA countries were willing and able to establish formal relations with the Community and to conclude agreements with it, and that trade matters would be negotiated by each CMEA country separately. The earlier insistence on using the CMEA as an intermediary between the Community and individual East European countries had apparently been dropped. The role of CMEA-EEC relations would be cooperation between the two organisations as such, within the limits of their respective interests and competences. The idea that EEC relations with the CMEA and with its member countries should be developed in parallel had basically been accepted, although there might be differences of interpretation of the concept of parallelism. Some CMEA countries had made specific proposals for meetings to discuss the future of their bilateral relations with the Community and with a number of others exploratory conversations had already taken place.

It was, therefore, considered that sufficient progress was being made on bilateral relations with CMEA countries to enable discussions with the CMEA itself to go forward. Accordingly, Mr. De Clercq wrote to Mr. Sychev on 17 July to suggest that a first expert-level meeting between the two organisations should be held in September.

The first face-to-face meeting for six years between experts of the CMEA Secretariat and of the EC Commission was held, like earlier 1980 expert meetings, in Geneva. The discussion centred on the draft joint declaration which had been proposed by Mr. Sychev in September 1985. The Council had given the Commission only an exploratory mandate: in other words, the Commission delegation could ask questions of its opposite numbers but not make proposals. Nevertheless, the Commission was able to explain the problems the Community had with some of the wording in Mr. Sychev's draft, while making clear that both the idea of a joint declaration and the overall shape of the text proposed were acceptable to the Community.

On one point, the Commission representatives went beyond asking questions: they made clear the Community's wish to include a territorial clause in the declaration. A territorial clause, also called application clause, is included in all Community agreements with non-Community countries. It lays down that, as far as the EEC is concerned, the agreement shall apply to the territories in which the Treaty establishing the EEC is applied and under the conditions laid down in that Treaty. This covers, among many other things, the provisions annexed to the Treaty concerning the application of the latter to Berlin (West). Such clauses exist in the sectoral agreements on textiles and sheepmeat which have been concluded with a number of East European countries. Nevertheless, the CMEA side made it clear that the inclusion of a territorial clause in the joint declaration would give them great difficulty.[7]

During the autumn and winter of 1986—7, further conversations were held between the Community and various CMEA member countries, until by the end of January 1987 a series of bilateral discussions had taken place with the European CMEA members. In keeping with the principle of parallelism, the Community agreed therefore to hold a new meeting with the CMEA on 18—20 March 1987.[8] On this occasion the Commission was able to make some proposals for wording, and accept points of the CMEA draft. A number of relatively minor problems remained open, but the question of the territorial application clause was the main point that remained unsolved. It may be asked why it has taken so long to reach agreement on this simple formula, a formula which moreover has been used many times before in agreements with CMEA countries. The answer is, of course, that for both sides this is a political problem of considerable weight. On the Community side, we wish to see acknowledged by the inclusion of this clause the fact that Berlin (West) is an integral part of the Community. The CMEA side is equally insistent on the need to stress that the current status of Berlin, as laid down by the various Four-Power Agreements and particularly that of 3 September 1971, is not affected.

Various informal contacts have been taking place, various formulas have been put forward, there are signs that the two sides have moved closer together, the outlines of a solution are emerging, but it is a slow process. Nevertheless, I do not think it is too optimistic to suppose that within a few months this and the other problems will be solved, thus opening the way to normal relations not only between the two organisations but between the Community and CMEA member countries. And what then as far as EEC-CMEA relations are concerned? The draft Joint Declaration provides for meetings to be held, and I see these as an opportunity for intensive mutual study. It is curious, and perhaps unfortunate, that the numerous meetings we have had with the CMEA since 1977 have all been devoted to the discussion of texts. Only at the first meeting, in February 1975, did we get down to discussing what the two organisations might be interested in doing together. Each side described to the other its activities in a particular field, and on this basis we were able to identify a number of areas of cooperation: economic information, planning and forecasting, norms and standards, environment. These subsequently turned up in the draft agreements of 1976 as agreed areas for cooperation. Such examination will have to be done again, both to bring up to date our information on the areas we discussed long ago, and to see whether new areas of mutual interest can be identified.

Finally, a word of caution. Experience shows that the creation of the legal framework for cooperation in the Joint Declaration will not have, as some commentators seem to think, some kind of instant magic effect in stimulating cooperation, in opening up each others' economies or giving access to each other's research programmes, for instance. The adoption of the Joint Declaration will be an important event, no doubt about it, but its importance will be in the first instance largely symbolic. It will signal the end of a long period of what a newspaper headline aptly termed some years ago a "*valse hésitation*" — a hesitation based on feelings of insecurity and distrust. It will mark the beginning of a period of "getting to know one another". We are ignorant of each other — or at least, speaking for myself, I can say that I am very ignorant about the CMEA; and maybe they find things about us that are hard to understand. Only by mutual information, by the gradual development of contacts, can this ignorance and the mistrust which arises from it be overcome.

Notes

1. *Pravda*, 22 December 1972.
2. For a chronology of this stage of EC-CMEA relations, see the Annex to the *Irmer* report of the European Parliament (Doc. 1-531/82 of 28 July 1982).
3. A review of the more recent period of EC-CMEA relations, in: J. Maslen, 'The European Community's Relations with the State-Trading Countries of Europe 1984—1986', *Yearbook of European Law 1986*, pp. 338—344.
4. The text of the CMEA draft has not been published officially, but a version appeared in *Agence Europe*, 15 January 1986.
5. *Bull. EC.*, 2—1986, para. 2.2.21.
6. *Bull. EC.*, 5—1986, para. 2.2.37.
7. *Bull. EC.*, 9—1986, para. 2.2.27.
8. *Bull. EC.*, 3—1987, para. 2.2.23.

The external relations of the CMEA with specific reference to CMEA-EEC relations

SERGEY OUGAROV
Counsellor, CMEA Secretariat

I. Introduction

The Council for Mutual Economic Assistance's cooperation with other international organisations and with CMEA non-member countries has a stable and versatile nature.

This is facilitated, first, by the broad development of bilateral trade and economic relations between the CMEA member countries and other countries of the world, creating favourable conditions for the development of multilateral cooperation; secondly, by the restructuring of the mechanism of cooperation and socialist economic integration, i.e. the activities of CMEA, which is now in progress.

The Council for Mutual Economic Assistance is known to be an intergovernmental organisation whose purposes and principles are spelled out in article I of the CMEA Charter: "The Council for Mutual Economic Assistance is based on the principle of the sovereign equality of all the member countries of the Council.

Economic, scientific and technological cooperation among the member countries of the Council shall be implemented in accordance with the principles of socialist internationalism, on the basis of respect for state sovereignty, independence and national interests, non-interference in internal affairs, complete equality in rights, mutual advantage and mutual comradely assistance".

The Council for Mutual Economic Assistance is an organisation without a supranational nature. The Council manages the process of socialist economic integration on a fully voluntary basis taking into account the interests of sovereign member countries. It does not encroach on matters of internal planning or economic activity of organisations in those countries. Therefore, the mechanism of the CMEA bodies' activities makes it impossible to impose the will of any country or a group of countries on other countries.

M. Maresceau (ed.), The Political and Legal Framework of Trade Relations Between the European Community and Eastern Europe. ISBN 0–7923–0046–7.
© *1989 by Kluwer Academic Publishers, Dordrecht – Printed in the Netherlands.*

II. The legal instruments of the CMEA

Under the Charter the Council for Mutual Economic Assistance possesses extensive functions for organising the all-round economic, scientific and technological cooperation among its member countries.

More specifically, the CMEA is called to assist its member countries in drawing up, harmonising and implementing joint measures in the development of industry, agriculture, transport, trade turnover, exchange of services between CMEA member countries themselves or between them and other countries as well as in sharing scientific and technological achievements.

A. *Recommendations and decisions*

To exercise these and other functions, the CMEA is empowered to adopt recommendations and decisions, and to enter into international agreements with CMEA member countries, other countries or international organisations (para. 2, article III, CMEA Charter).

The CMEA bodies adopt *recommendations* on all questions of economic, scientific and technological cooperation. Recommendations are submitted to the CMEA member countries for consideration and, if accepted, then are implemented by decisions of the governments or other competent bodies of these countries in conformity with their legislation.

On organisational and procedural matters in the Council for Mutual Economic Assistance *decisions* are made. As a rule, decisions enter into force from the date on which the protocol of the meeting of the respective CMEA body is signed. Other dates for the decisions' entering into force may be provided for by the decisions or stem from the nature of the decisions themselves.

All CMEA recommendations and decisions are adopted only with the consent of the interested CMEA member countries and do not apply to those countries which have declared their disinterest in a particular matter.[1]

B. *Cooperation agreements*

Matters concerning the conclusion of cooperation agreements with non-member countries, with UN bodies, specialised or other international organisations are regulated by articles XI and XII of the CMEA Charter.

International agreements concluded by the CMEA may involve a vast range of cooperation matters in foreign trade, industry, agriculture, science, technology, i.e., all matters which might be the subject of multilateral cooperation carried out within the framework of the Council in accordance with the purposes and tasks provided for in the CMEA Charter.

Presently the CMEA maintains various forms of relations with more than 30 international organisations.

Such relations may be established both at the level of the organisations themselves, and at the level of their secretariats. The CMEA relations with other international organisations may be established by signing a protocol or concluding an agreement on cooperation which determines the nature and forms of cooperation. In particular, protocols on the nature and forms of cooperation have been signed by the Council with the Railways Cooperation Organisation and with the Joint Nuclear Research Institute.[2] The CMEA relations with such organisations as IAEA, UNIDO, UNEP and the Danube Commission are carried out on the basis of signed agreements. In some cases, forms of CMEA cooperation with other international organisations are established through an exchange of letters as it was the case with WHO and WIPO. In other organisations — UNCTAD, for instance, and the UN regional economic organisations — the CMEA is granted an observer status or a consultative status. Lately, the Council started also to develop relations with international organisations of the countries that are not CMEA members: in May 1987 an exchange of letters took place in Caracas on the establishment of cooperation relations between the CMEA and the LAES. It was agreed that the relations between the CMEA and the LAES will be carried out on the basis of biannual programmes of cooperation covering concrete measures of mutual interest. The first such programme for 1987—1988 was approved; it provides for joint studies and a seminar to identify the trends and forms of trade and economic cooperation among the member countries of both organisations.

The Council has also established relations with some international organisations at secretariat level by exchanging letters on cooperation. The CMEA Secretariat maintains such relations with the International Labour Office, UNESCO and FAO secretariats, International Standards Organisation and some other organisations.

External relations of the CMEA extend also to quite a number of states in various regions of our planet. A special place in these relations is occupied by Yugoslavia which, in keeping with the Agreement between the CMEA and the Government of the Socialist Federal Republic of Yugoslavia signed in 1964, participates in the work of many CMEA bodies. The Yugoslavian organisations, in particular, are widely represented among participants in the Comprehensive Programme of Scientific and Technological Progress of the CMEA Member Countries.

An important place in CMEA external relations belongs to cooperation with the countries which signed cooperation agreements with the CMEA. A total of nine such agreements have been signed to date: with Finland, Iraq, Mexico, Nicaragua, Angola, Mozambique, Ethiopia, the People's Democratic Republic of Yemen, Afghanistan.[3] Commissions for cooperation with the above countries were set up to fulfil the agreements. Within the framework of the commissions the interested CMEA member countries and their partners which are not members of the Council examine and tackle matters of mutual interest.

The CMEA agreements with these countries give rise to certain obligations for the CMEA member countries. That is why these agreements are preliminarily considered by all the CMEA member countries which officially notify the CMEA secretariat thereof. The agreement approved by the CMEA member countries and by a country that is not a CMEA member, is signed by the Secretary of the Council and by a designated representative of a country that is not a CMEA member. Subsequently, the agreement is to be approved by the Council Session and ratified by the country that is not a CMEA member and enters into force 30 days after the exchange of instruments on its ratification.

With the consent of the interested CMEA member countries and the country that is not a CMEA member, the said commissions may adopt recommendations (on questions of economic, scientific and technological cooperation) and take decisions (on organisational and procedural matters). These recommendations and decisions do not extend to the CMEA member countries that declared their disinterest. Each of these countries, however, may subsequently accede to the recommendations and decisions on agreed terms with the CMEA member countries and a country that is not a CMEA member who adopted these recommendations and decisions. Recommendations adopted by a commission are then submitted by the CMEA member countries and a country that is not a CMEA member for consideration by their competent bodies. The recommendations of a commission adopted by the said countries are implemented through the conclusion of multilateral and/or bilateral agreements between them, their bodies, organisations or through other mutually agreed procedures.

III. The cooperation agreement between the CMEA and Finland

The agreement on cooperation with Finland concluded in 1973 was the first agreement of the Council with a market-economy country.

The multilateral cooperation carried out on its basis between CMEA member countries and Finland provides a good example of interaction between countries with different social systems.

To study possibilities for cooperation between the CMEA and Finland, and to organise such cooperation, a Commission consisting of representatives of CMEA member countries and Finland, was set up.

The Commission has seven working groups in the following fields: mechanical engineering; the chemical industry; transport; scientific and technological cooperation; general matters of foreign trade; statistics and standardisation.

The main task of the Commission's working groups is to identify possibilities for cooperation between Finland and CMEA member countries on a multilateral basis, *inter alia*, in programmes being carried out within the CMEA framework. In practice this work consists of drafting proposals concerning joint projects of cooperation, the preparation of concrete programmes of work and draft agreements, and the clarification of possible participants in the cooperation effort.

Recommendations adopted by the Commission on proposals of its working bodies are then carried out by firms and organisations of the countries participating in those projects and programmes.

On the basis of the Commission's recommendations 113 agreements on cooperation were signed, an extensive exchange of information and expertise is in progress (over 160 recommendations) and working groups prepare proposals regarding lists of commodities, licences and services which are recommended for mutual exchange and involvement in trade turnover.

Work in progress within the Commission's framework contributes indirectly to the development of trade and economic cooperation. This work, which is, by the way, of an all-European importance, may include the elaboration of general terms of goods delivery, unification and simplification of foreign trade documents, harmonisation of standards on mutually delivered goods, compatibility of statistical indices, and matters of transportation of foreign trade cargoes. Concrete results have been achieved by the Commission in those areas and the experience gained is helpful in solving similar matters within the bodies of the UN Economic Commission for Europe.

In performing its tasks the Commission takes into account the activities of CMEA bodies and long-term programmes adopted by the Council. In particular, the Commission's working groups have recently prepared prospective directions of medium-term branch cooperation, which take into account the tasks arising from the Comprehensive Programme of Scientific and Technological Progress of the CMEA Member Countries up to the Year 2000.

Cooperation between the CMEA and other countries with which the CMEA has agreements follows a similar pattern.

In agreements signed between the CMEA and third countries or international organisations, the Council and its contractors act as equal parties to an international treaty. These agreements are a legal means of developing international economic, scientific and technological cooperation on a multilateral basis.

IV. Areas of cooperation between the CMEA and the EEC

In the overall complex of problems of developing trade and economic cooperation between countries with different social systems the question of relationships between the CMEA and the EEC is of special importance for it involves the two largest integration groupings that unite countries with a population of about 720 million people and account for over 50 p.c. of the world's industrial output. Europe has become cognizant that the interaction of the CMEA and the EEC is important for the all-European cooperation and normalisation of the political situation on the continent, for expanding and deepening the all-European process begun in Helsinki in 1975. This cognizance is revealed, *inter alia*, by the mutual desire of the two organisations to establish cooperation.

Pursuing a constructive dialogue with the EEC, the CMEA is directing its efforts at the legal settlement of relations between the two largest integration groupings.

We understand that we shall not manage to overcome at once negative tendencies stemming from a prolonged period of mutual misunderstanding and distrust. It is important now that both sides be prepared for a stage-by-stage approach to this problem, to begin with mutual official recognition and to determine the necessary mechanism of further contacts.

The CMEA is known to suggest establishing official relations with the EEC as a first step on this road. The Commission of the European Communities, for its part, put forward a proposal to establish relations on a bilateral basis with CMEA member countries as well. The CMEA member countries informed the Commission of their readiness to establish such bilateral relations with the EEC alongside the establishment of official relations between the CMEA and the EEC. Thus, full agreement has been achieved that the processes of establishing official relations between the CMEA and the EEC and of establishing bilateral relations between individual CMEA and EEC countries should proceed in parallel, which is taking place in practice.

For the purpose of legalising official relations between the two organisations the Council for Mutual Economic Assistance has proposed an appropriate draft Declaration. Following two working meetings of experts this draft has been practically harmonised with the exception of the provision concerning the territorial clause regarding West Berlin.[4] Presently, the two sides are taking corresponding efforts with a view to achieving a mutually acceptable solution. Information that I have about the state of affairs allows me to share Mr. De Clercq's optimism that the Declaration can finally be coordinated and signed not later than the first half of 1988.

The CMEA member countries do not link the signing of the Declaration on the Establishment of Official Relations with the specifying of possible areas of cooperation between the CMEA and the EEC. Nevertheless it can be said already now that there is certain clarity on this question. For example, the Commission of the European Communities feels that relations with the CMEA "could be useful in those areas where these two organisations are engaged in this or that kind of activity of mutual interest". With this, mention is made of economic information, statistics, environmental protection, standardisation. Therefore, the thing in point is that these areas of possible cooperation were agreed upon as a principle almost 10 years ago at expert level. However, they by no means exhaust existing potential possibilities for developing cooperation. This is all the more true now when interdependence in international economic relations is increasing, global problems are becoming more acute, the scientific and technological advance is becoming faster, and when the quest for solutions of economic, scientific, technological, social and other problems by joint efforts of all states is becoming a more pressing need.

One cannot but see that in the present-day situation in Europe it is objectively necessary to deepen the international division of labour within the confines of the entire continent irrespective of the socio-political system of the countries.

The CMEA member countries, for their part, are unfailing supporters of cooperation with Western European states and their international organisations in joint utilisation of the achievements of the scientific and technological revolution. This is of particular importance today when CMEA member countries and EEC countries are tackling similar tasks (although on different socio-economic bases) of accelerating scientific and technological progress. As is known, a certain retardation of scientific and technological development of Western European countries can be discerned in such areas as computing technology, microprocessors, robotics, biotechnology. Western European countries are drafting a number of research programmes with a view to overcoming this retardation. The CMEA member countries also have their own problems in those areas which are becoming increasingly decisive in scientific and technological progress. They are making unceasing efforts in order to solve them as soon as possible. This is what, in particular, the Comprehensive Programme of Scientific and Technological Progress of the CMEA Member Countries up to the Year 2000 is directed at.[5]

This Programme was adopted in 1985. Its basic objectives are to at least double labour productivity in the CMEA member countries by the year 2000 and sharply reduce the rate of consumption of energy and raw materials per unit of national income. To achieve these objectives, the CMEA member countries have agreed on focusing their efforts and organising multilateral cooperation in the following priority areas: electronisation of the national economy; comprehensive automation; nuclear power; new materials, and the technologies for producing and processing them; and biotechnology. The priority areas cover over 90 problems on each of which multilateral agreements and treaties have been concluded. The obligations assumed by the CMEA member countries under these treaties are incorporated into their national economic development plans for 1986—1990 and are taken into account in their annual plans. The CMEA member countries, if necessary, set up joint scientific and production associations, centres for teaching, training and advanced training of personnel with a view to implementing individual tasks of the Programme. The projects are financed by means of national funds, loans from the International Investment Bank and the International Bank for Economic Cooperation, and also out of joint funds set up by interested countries.

It is easy to notice that the Comprehensive Programme of Scientific and Technological Progress of the CMEA Member Countries and the Eureka Programme have much in common. That is why it is very important to find the points of contact in these Programmes and the possible forms of mutual participation. It would enable both sides to save time and resources and might be mutually beneficial and efficient, thus contributing to the creation of a "technological Europe", and to worldwide progress in science and technology.

I would like to point out that economic, scientific and technological cooperation between East and West in Europe is already an established reality. The matter now is to make it stable and long-lasting, to back it up with a relevant organisational structure, to impart it a truly all-European nature using already existing and new forms of cooperation covering all stages of the "research-technology-production-marketing" process.

V. The structuring of cooperation within the CMEA and the conduct of external economic activities by CMEA member countries

The process of transition towards scientific, technological and production cooperation between East and West has already begun. In a report by Mr. A. Posnik (USA) at the International Conference — "Cooperation in Europe Between the Market Economy and Planned Economy Countries" (Venice, March 1987) — it was said that in 1985—1986 about 100 agreements on production cooperation were concluded between Western firms and the CMEA member countries. New opportunities arise here that are related to the improvement of external economic activities of the CMEA member countries and the restructuring of cooperation within the Council for Mutual Economic Assistance. The decisions to that effect were adopted at the 43rd (Extraordinary) Meeting of the CMEA Session in Moscow in October 1987.

They aim at a transition to profound production cooperation of the CMEA member countries, and a wide use of economic levers of cooperation.

A new model of multilateral interaction of countries was adopted that differentiates the problems of cooperation according to the level of management. The Council for Mutual Economic Assistance is assigned the highest intergovernmental level where strategic tasks, such as the coordination of policy in economy, science and technology, the development and implementation of the Comprehensive Programme of Scientific and Technological Progress of the CMEA Member Countries up to the Year 2000, and other major long-term multilateral programmes and agreements are to be resolved. The CMEA's task will be to work out, on the basis of a profound analysis of the particular nature and trends in the improvement of national economic mechanisms of the countries, common planning, financial and legal fundamentals of cooperation that would contribute to the development of interaction of direct manufacturers of products.

The coordination of economic policy through the coordination of national economy plans in the long term is supplemented now by an elaboration of a collective concept of international socialist division of labour. Now such a concept is being drawn up for the period up to the year 2005. Its basic aim is to identify, on the basis of prospective targets and requirements of the countries, reference points of principal changes in the structure of production and capital investment, to distribute production programmes among the countries focusing these programmes on the solution of priority tasks in the sphere of scientific and technological progress. The concept will serve as a basis for the coordination of five-year period development plans for the countries; it is planned to update it every 5 years taking into account the achieved results, changing social tasks and changes in the world economy pattern.

A new element is the involvement, in the coordination of the national economy development plans, of not only branch bodies of the CMEA member countries (ministries and agencies) that will represent a second level of management, but also of enterprises, organisations and associations of the CMEA member countries that belong to the third level. The second and third levels will cover the coordination of questions on the development of sectors and their technical re-equipment, the construction of integrated projects, production, scientific and technological cooperation, etc. The cooperation at these levels will be carried out outside the CMEA bodies, on the principles of direct links between the branch national bodies of the countries and the enterprises.

Of fundamental importance is the activation of interaction of basic economic links — associations, enterprises and organisations. To this end it is intended to develop production, scientific and technological cooperation on a contractual basis through direct links, the creation of joint ventures, international associations, and research organisations.

The CMEA member countries have already enacted legislative acts that significantly expand foreign trade rights of organisations and enterprises that should contribute to the extension of their direct links.[6] Obviously, limits to the self-independence of enterprises are regulated by the legislation of each country; specific forms and methods of direct links' control vary. But already now they provide a possibility for direct cooperation of economic organisations. Practically in all European CMEA member countries, the enterprises possess the following rights: targets on international coproduction for these enterprises are not fixed "from above" and they have the right to establish links with partners on the basis of economic considerations. At the same time the enterprises themselves choose the subject of coproduction, their partner, sign contracts with it, agree on prices for parts and aggregates. They may retain currency earnings or its major share and buy necessary equipment in the CMEA member countries, and open foreign currency accounts at banks.

Substantial changes are envisaged in the CMEA monetary and financial system. They concern the expansion of monetary functions of a transferable Rouble, ensuring its convertibility into national currencies of the CMEA member countries, and in future — into freely convertible currencies. These changes will be introduced gradually and will be implemented on a stage-by-stage basis. At the initial stage some CMEA member countries have agreed to carry out an experiment by using national currencies in settlements between the enterprises maintaining direct links as well as in the settlements within joint ventures. Agreements on the procedure for settlements and accounting with respect to direct coproduction links have already been signed between the USSR and Bulgaria, and the USSR and Czechoslovakia. The measures undertaken by the CMEA create favourable prospects for cooperation with Western countries not only in the sphere of trade exchange, but in the credit and finance area as well.

The above-mentioned rights of the CMEA member countries' enterprises in the area of external economic relations extend also to the joint entrepreneurship with Western firms leading to the establishment of joint ventures that open up wide prospects for all-European cooperation.

This form allows to combine resources and theoretical groundwork of CMEA countries with the production and marketing base of West European partners, with their ability to ensure the marketing of new products and to bring them successfully on to the market.

At the same time this form of cooperation to a large degree opens up for Western partners the capacious market of CMEA member countries.

Unfortunately, one of the obstacles in the way to applying this and other forms of cooperation is the activity of COCOM resulting in the fact that a comparatively wide range of advanced technology is removed from the sphere of action of the principle of free exchange of information and benefits of research projects.

VI. Conclusion

In conclusion, assessing prospects for relations between the CMEA and the EEC, one can state with confidence the following. Neither differences in socio-economic systems nor distinctions in competence of the two groupings can hinder the development of cooperation between the CMEA and the EEC which is considered to be desirable for both sides.

This point of view is shared by scientists, businessmen, financiers, and political figures in EEC countries whom we happen to meet at various international fora where relations between the CMEA and the EEC are discussed.

The countries of the socialist community proceed from the fact that the interaction of two organisations — CMEA and EEC — would not only be conducive to creating more favourable conditions for the development of cooperation between their member countries but would also complement it substantially, and would also contribute to the improvement of the political climate in Europe.

A trend of misunderstanding and stressing distinctions in the activities of the two organisations has dominated the relations between the CMEA and the EEC for over 30 years. It becomes much more important now to look for what unites them. A real possibility has emerged now in relations between the CMEA and the EEC for mutually beneficial cooperation in the fields of production, science, technology, trade exchange and in the social sphere. The task is not to lose this chance and, as was repeatedly stressed by the CMEA member countries, to introduce the principle of peaceful coexistence of states with different social systems into the practice of such cooperation.

Notes

1. For more detailed information on the CMEA recommendations and decisions see Article IV, CMEA Charter.
2. Basic documents of the Council for Mutual Economic Assistance, CMEA Secretariat, Moscow, vol. 2, 1983, (in Russian).
3. "Economic cooperation among CMEA member countries", CMEA Secretariat, Moscow, No. 5, 1985; No. 2, 1986 (in Russian).
4. 22—24 September 1986 — Geneva; 18—20 March 1987 — Geneva.
5. "Towards Scientific and Technological Progress", Council for Mutual Economic Assistance, Secretariat, Moscow, 1986.
6. For instance, the USSR Council of Ministers Decree — "Procedure for Setting up in the Territory of the USSR and Activities of Joint Ventures, International Associations and Organizations of the USSR and other CMEA Member Countries", *Pravda*, 27 January 1987; the USSR Council of Ministers Decree — "Procedure for Setting up Joint Ventures in the Territory of the USSR with Participation of Soviet Organizations and Firms from the Developing and Capitalist Countries", *Pravda*, 27 January 1987.

The contribution of the European Parliament towards the development of the relations between Western and Eastern Europe

HANS-JOACHIM SEELER

Member of the European Parliament; Vice-President of the Commission for External Relations of the European Parliament

I. Introduction

In the last few years I have been very much involved in matters concerning EC/COMECON relations. As rapporteur for the Committee on External Economic Relations, I submitted a report on relations between the EC, COMECON and the East European member countries of COMECON, which was adopted by Parliament in January 1987 with a large majority.[1] At the moment I am preparing another report on the subject of EEC relations with the three non-European member countries of COMECON (Cuba, Mongolia and Vietnam). Moreover, as the chairman designate of the European Parliament's delegation for cooperation with the parliaments of the GDR, Poland and Czechoslovakia, I have in the last few weeks had a great deal of contact with politicians and scientists in these three states.

Things have started to move in Europe. For decades now we have been used to watching an endless interplay between the two superpowers; time and again we have seen one side reject out of hand any disarmament or peace proposal put forward by the other. Success and progress were only achieved after years, even decades, of negotiation. But now, all of a sudden, history seems to be on the move. Each side is beginning to take the other's proposals more seriously; and in Europe too people have begun talking to one another in order to tackle the practical problems that they so urgently need to settle together. What is more, cautious attempts are being made in the Soviet Union to allow more democracy and more individual responsibility. Of course, it is still early days for any great optimism, but the important thing in politics is knowing how to sit tight until history begins to move forward again and then to act decisively. Perhaps we are, without fully appreciating the fact, witnesses of a transformation which future generations will one day describe as having laid the foundations for a new and better world. Be that as it may, although we should not lose sight of the vision — I won't say Utopia — of a better world, we should all the same be careful not to lose our grip on reality.

M. Maresceau (ed.), The Political and Legal Framework of Trade Relations Between the European Community and Eastern Europe. ISBN 0–7923–0046–7.
© *1989 by Kluwer Academic Publishers, Dordrecht – Printed in the Netherlands.*

II. Relations between the European Community and COMECON

We can divide these relations into three periods. The first period, up to the beginning of the seventies, was marked by COMECON's rejection of the Community and a refusal to even acknowledge its existence. At that time COMECON viewed the EC as a short-lived phenomenon, an economic offshoot of the USA. Like imperial Russia, the Soviet Union had always favoured a foreign policy which supported independent — and hence divided — European states. The integration of Western Europe was therefore seen as an act of imperialistic policy and it was only quite late on that the realisation dawned that something like an objective process had got underway, and that a new political and international reality was emerging in Western Europe.

In the second period, in the early seventies, they began to talk of this reality and to show an interest in discussions. However, the first contacts between the two sides clearly showed that their objectives were poles apart.

And now there is the dawning of the third phase, a phase ushered in by General Secretary Gorbachev at the COMECON summit meeting in June 1984; a phase which genuinely promises to change the nature of these relations. Offical contacts are desired between COMECON and the 'economic organisations of the developed capitalist countries' to quote the Moscow declaration. Talks which had earlier been broken off by COMECON were resumed in October 1984 with the aim of establishing official relations and strengthening economic ties between the EC and COMECON member countries.

I believe COMECON has really come to understand that the European Community is on the road to a new political identity. It is also understood, as is clear from the many discussions I have had, that the EC and the United States of America do not have an identical economic policy, and that it is by no means a contradiction in terms to say that every political partnership has its economic disagreements, even if these are as frequent as we have seen in recent times.

Negotiations have not yet been concluded, but it looks as if there will shortly be an agreement on a solemn declaration. Once this is signed, the requirements will be met for mutual recognition under international law, and a start can be made not only on bilateral negotiations but also on talks between the two communities on the many problems of East-West relations.

May I now say a few words about the possible aims and content of relations between the two European organisations, as conceived by the European Parliament in its discussions and decisions on the subject. The first priority is mutual recognition, as this would allow relations to be established in international law. Diplomatic representation would be a further implication. As a rule, all accredited embassies in Belgium are automatically accredited by the institutions of the EC. I believe it is quite possible that the European Community, in its exchanges and dealings with COMECON, will establish a diplomatic representation — or a delegation, as we call it — in Moscow. But, quite apart from this formality, it would be helpful, and indeed necessary, to find joint answers to a good many individual questions which are of interest to people and population groups in both parts of Europe. And here I would include matters which were under discussion in the late seventies and early eighties, such as the adoption of the same bases for statistics and economic forecasts as well as the development of common norms and standards for industrial, technical and similar products. Protection of the environment is certainly a pressing task for the whole of Europe, for there is no such thing as communist or capitalist pollution, and national frontiers do not stop dirty rivers and increasingly polluted seas. So there are matters which, from a purely geographical point of view, require a joint European solution in the course of the next few years and decades. And I include here the development of a European transport system, the planning and development of roads and railways and the like. I am also thinking of the development of joint safety standards for nuclear reactors, for as long as such reactors are necessary. There should be no question whatsoever about the need to draw up safety standards following the Chernobyl disaster.

I would also like to include joint energy research on my list, because we really do need to develop new sources of energy together, so that we are no longer dependent on traditional sources. However, all these are long-term prospects. COMECON has a particular interest in increasing scientific/technological cooperation with the EC. One important reason why it is interested in closer links with us is because it needs Western technology. Without modern technology, it could not hope to achieve the aims of the current five-year plan which began back in 1986. Our finite supplies of energy and raw materials are becoming scarcer. Manpower reserves, particularly labour siphoned off from agriculture for economic and industrial development, are now depleted. So it is only possible to achieve the desired productivity with the help of modern, predominantly Western, technology.

III. The European Community's trade and economic relations with COMECON

It was because of differences of opinion on trade arrangements that talks first broke down at the beginning of the eighties. COMECON wanted an agreement containing provisions on reciprocal trade, despite the fact that COMECON leaves responsibility for overseas trade with its individual member countries, which have always attached great importance to maintaining their independence in this area. In the European Community responsibility for foreign trade has been transferred to the Community as a whole. So the Community has sole competence in negotiations in this area. The European Parliament has made repeated reference to this problem and stressed that the European Community should not be a party to any action that would increase Soviet influence over the trade policy of East European COMECON member countries.

For the European Community trade in goods is essential to the development of the living standard and well-being of its citizens. The volume of world trade today is one of the blessings of the 1948 GATT agreement. COMECON countries with their state-controlled economies have till now been striving to become independent — I won't say autarkical — particularly in the long term. However, the primary purpose of trade for them today is to procure much-needed technological know-how and food on the world market. The two sides have essentially conflicting aims which would not in the long term provide a good basis for close economic and trade relations between East and West. The free exchange of goods is also impeded by the pricing policy applied in the East, which is usually subject to ideological constraints. The West has market prices, the East administrative prices. Most COMECON countries are members of GATT, and thus bound by the principle of the most-favoured nation treatment, but, for ideological reasons, they are not able to pull their full weight. For example, the ban on quantitative restrictions cannot always be reconciled with the requirements of a planned economy. Customs duties cannot, therefore, be used as a corrective when prices are determined on an administrative basis. And often it is not possible to offer anything in return for reductions in duties, one of the features of GATT. So State-trading countries can only make limited, as opposed to full, use of the opportunities afforded by GATT membership.

By looking at the growth of trade and economic relations between the West and East of Europe up to the present time, we find that the volume of trade has risen significantly in the past 25 years, but it is still quite insignificant compared with the rest of the EC's foreign trade. This point emerges more clearly perhaps, when one considers that the volume of visible trade between the Federal Republic of Germany and the Netherlands is greater than all trade taking place between the EC and the East.

Recently there has been an increase in the EC's trade deficit with the Eastern Bloc states. One of the reasons for this is the all too familiar fluctuations in oil and natural gas prices on the world market, and the need for a number of COMECON member countries to pay off their heavy debts with high export surpluses.

IV. Conclusion

We should not fool ourselves. There will probably not be any appreciable increase in the volume of trade in the short term, but we should still take every opportunity to develop trade. In the medium term its growth will depend on the improved competitiveness of the COMECON countries and their performance on Western markets. So the economy needs to be freed once and for all from the shackles of bureaucratic control. Enterprises and businesses need to show more initiative. It is vital that they should be exposed to the chill wind of competition, so they can find out what their products are really worth on the world market. More individual freedom and more responsibility for the workers are what is needed. Management should show greater flexibility in order to develop precisely this sort of genuinely fair, economic competition.

During a visit to Poland some time ago, I myself saw the serious efforts being made to reform the economy in this way. I also saw how much opposition there still is to these reforms and how difficult those in positions of responsibility are finding it to accept that a restructuring of the economy has to be accompanied by a radically new economic, monetary and stabilisation policy, if the economic strength and export potential of the country are to be improved.

In the long term, the European Community has a major interest in developing trade with COMECON, as it is quite certain that there will not be much scope in the coming years for further development of trade relations with our traditional export areas in North and South America and Africa, largely because of their heavy burden of debt. Such development is only possible now in two areas, two world economic zones. The first is the Western Pacific from Korea to Japan, from China/Hong Kong to the ASEAN states, Australia and New Zealand. The other is, to my mind, the COMECON area, and since a large part of the European Community's gross domestic product comes from its overseas trade, we have a long-term interest in expanding these trade and economic relations to a quite considerable degree. Modern technological and biological development will make Europe and the world a smaller place.

If we Europeans are to survive in the world of the superpowers, we have no alternative but to adopt a joint European concept for future development. The process which has now been set in train to improve

European relations can also remove the ideological differences and overcome the deep divisions in Europe in the longer term. Economic cooperation is the first step towards better political partnership. It is time that we in Europe realised that technical and sociological development left 19th century Marxism and Liberalism behind long ago. The sooner we learn that the time has passed when national self-interest, isolationism and the principle of maximising profits were the sole aims of European countries, the sooner we will be able to guarantee a future for our children and a place in tomorrow's world for Europe. Only in this way will Europeans in the West and the East one day cease to be the junior partners of the superpowers. We are always talking about the need to break down divisive frontiers and bring about détente, and we even talk about how the Poles and Hungarians are every bit as European as the French and the Danes. By improving economic cooperation between East and West in Europe, we could be taking the first real step towards achieving this oft-avowed aim. And the hopes and prospects for success will be all the greater if we take this step in a rational and realistic spirit.

Note

1. *Report on relations between the European Community and the Council for Mutual Economic Assistance (CMEA) and the Eastern European Member States of the CMEA*, rapporteur: H.-J. Seeler, Working Documents of the European Parliament, Doc. A2 — 187/86.

PART TWO

The position of Western European companies in their trade relations with Eastern Europe

The position of Western European companies in their trade relations with Eastern Europe: general introduction

UMBERTO AGNELLI
Vice-Chairman FIAT, Turin

At this moment in time it is of great importance to find out just how far collaboration between companies in Eastern and Western Europe is possible today and in the near future, in what areas and in what forms. There are two factors to be borne in mind. First, the "general climate" is a lot more hospitable than it was, both in the East and in the EEC. Secondly, however, as we all know, business dealings between two systems so profoundly different in political, economic and legal terms are always difficult.

There is also a third factor, almost unknown to the man in the street and not always recognised by politicians, though it is well known to businessmen or anyone who works for a company. For us EEC businessmen the rules and procedures that govern our dealings with the Eastern States are now more or less uniform. This, however, is not the case in the COMECON area where each country seems to have its own legal and administrative practices which are, furthermore, often confused by frequent changes. In fact it is often hard to understand whether the new rules and organisations cancel out the previous ones or merely supplement them.

I mentioned the improved climate of relations between the EEC and COMECON and I hardly need to tell you that the attention of the Western World is focused on the process of Soviet restructuring now universally known under its Russian name of "perestroika."

In this brief introduction I would like to confine myself to highlighting the topics and problems of major interest to businessmen. However, if only in the hope of stimulating comments I would like to offer a few ideas of my own, triggered not only by what is happening in the Soviet Union but also, and above all, by my meetings with Eastern representatives of the industrial and economic sectors in Vienna, Venice and Moscow in recent months.

As an entrepreneur, and a European entrepreneur at that, I have to

M. Maresceau (ed.), The Political and Legal Framework of Trade Relations Between the European Community and Eastern Europe. ISBN 0–7923–0046–7.

admit that our initial reaction to the first changes proposed by the Gorbachev leadership was considerable scepticism or, to be honest, incredulity. However, as the new policy has been pursued, our interest has grown enormously because "perestroika" has become credible. Certainly credible at the level of political intention but also credible as the start of concrete achievements. I do not mean just economic measures because I think the new possibility for more openness in government, for debate and criticism are even more important.

As a Western businessman the increase in civil liberty is fundamental to my judgment of any country that I am thinking of doing business with: any country, east or west, north or south. Now the Soviet government's determination in pursuing its new line undoubtedly heralds new developments. In the economic sector the very complexity of the changes intended is sufficient to justify what now look like contradictions or a "stop and go" approach to the new course. What probably worries a Western businessman most is the uncertainty typical of all transitional phases that one finds in talks with our Soviet counterparts. Uncertainties that derive, partly from their awareness that certain decisions if logically pursued will lead to structural changes in the economic and financial fields, and their fear of the consequences, partly from their awareness that there will be no going back.

Apart from the uncertainty there is undeniably a problem of mentality. We cannot expect people who have been used to running economic structures on the basis of ministerial orders and government planning suddenly to turn into managers. It takes a long time to motivate people to change and the task is never easy. I feel that rather than making instant judgments about the obstacles that still remain we should be feeling a great deal of respect for the changes now taking place. We should acknowledge the successes and recognise the difficulties. After all, if there were no difficulties it would simply be a question of changing the façade which is quite definitely not the case in the Soviet Union at the moment where something very serious is certainly going on, though no one can be sure exactly where it will end.

I would like to draw your attention to three major legal developments in the USSR that have particularly interested me: the law on individual work; the law on mixed companies; the law coming into force next year that will authorise companies and consortia to operate on the basis of the cash flow principle. Obviously these new laws and the others that will follow will need further adjustments, just like the law on joint ventures that has recently been amended and extended.

We entrepreneurs need to know more about these laws. Inevitably, there will be a number of practical difficulties in the application phase. So

things may take longer than the Soviet Government itself might have envisaged originally. What we most need to know, however, is what lines the Soviet Government intends to adopt in introducing reforms and what industrial objectives it has in mind. It is the depth of change in its totality that we have to assess. There are two fundamental questions:
— will we be dealing with more "market-oriented" partners or competitors in the future?
— will we be dealing with people interested in concepts like profit, efficiency, competitiveness, quality? In the past such concepts were almost entirely ignored in the East. Maybe things will be different now. I hope they will be very different.

In this situation we should not forget the possibility of new bilateral agreements between the EEC and the Eastern European countries that could lead to increased trade for both groups.

Finally, I would like to say that it is quite possible that if "perestroika" is a success in the Soviet Union, it will spread to the other Eastern Bloc countries, though no doubt in different ways. If that happens, we shall have much closer dealings with our Eastern European neighbours, neighbours with whom we share not only borders but centuries of cultural links. At times history has drawn us together, at times it has forced us apart, but those links have never been wholly severed. Against this background we also share several aspirations: a common desire for peace, for a better quality of life and a better environment, and the commitment to tackle the challenges of an increasingly complex society.

The position of Western European companies in their trade relations with Bulgaria

ATANAS PAPARIZOV

Director General Ministry of Trade, Sofia

I. Introduction

The conditions in Bulgaria for trade and economic cooperation between Bulgarian enterprises and foreign companies, including those from the European Economic Community, are in full conformity with the principles of equal treatment, non-discrimination and mutual advantage.

No doubt a new impetus for greater utilisation of existing opportunities could be provided by a conclusion of a trade and economic cooperation agreement between Bulgaria and the EEC. Guarantees for market access and mutual confidence between business partners will be further strengthened by the accession of Bulgaria to the multilateral trading system under the GATT.

Many issues are relevant to the conditions for foreign companies for trade and economic cooperation: the general economic situation, economic and trade policies, economic cooperation and joint venture legislation, infrastructure, geographic, labour financing and other business factors. Since it is not possible to cover all these topics in a single presentation this report concentrates on the following three subjects:
— general economic conditions;
— rights and responsibilities of Bulgarian enterprises in foreign trade;
— trade policy issues and legislation on economic cooperation and joint ventures with foreign companies.

II. General economic conditions

A basic feature of the development of the Bulgarian economy in recent decades has been the active participation in the international division of labour and the growth of trade at rates higher than the country's overall economic growth. As a result the economy evolved from being virtually

M. Maresceau (ed.), The Political and Legal Framework of Trade Relations Between the European Community and Eastern Europe. ISBN 0–7923–0046–7.
© *1989 by Kluwer Academic Publishers, Dordrecht – Printed in the Netherlands.*

closed to international trade to a state of extensive involvement in the international division of labour.

In 1939 the level of foreign trade turnover relative to national income was 2.3 p.c. Industrial goods of non-agricultural origin contributed to only 0.4 p.c. of exports. After 1950, when it attained the pre-war level of 1939, foreign trade turnover increased 64 times by 1986 (at comparable prices).[1] In 1986 trade (as average of exports and imports) slightly surpassed 50 p.c. of national income in value terms, while according to GATT Secretariat estimates, the present average contribution of trade to the GDP of GATT member countries amounts to 20 p.c.[2] The structure of exports has been substantially modified, industrial goods of non-agricultural origin reaching 79.6 p.c.

At present Bulgaria takes 32nd place in world exports and 30th in imports and conducts trade with 119 countries.[3]

In an agricultural country with virtually no industrial production forty years ago, with restricted natural raw material base and small internal market only a trade-oriented strategy of development could ensure accelerated industrialisation, rising economic efficiency and constant growth of standards of living of the population. As a result Bulgaria was able to radically restructure the manufacturing and agricultural sectors of the economy.

Between 1948[4] and 1986 national income grew at an average annual rate of 7.4 p.c. The structure of national income produced changed fundamentally, with industry accounting for 60 p.c. and agriculture for 15 p.c. by 1986 while in 1939 they accounted for 15 p.c. and 65 p.c. respectively.[5] The new industrial structure of the economy has been based on markedly export-oriented industries such as electronics, machine-building, fork-lift manufacturing, chemicals and pharmaceuticals and food processing.

In geographical terms Bulgaria's foreign trade (see annex table) developed principally with the CMEA member countries. The share of trade with socialist countries (non-CMEA countries among them accounting for 1—2 p.c. of total turnover) in the whole period from 1948 to 1986 has been generally in the range of 75—80 p.c. of the total turnover.

The development of this flow of trade was a result of the prevailing economic conditions in the post-war period. Trade-policy conditions, especially in the 1950s and 1960s, also played an explicit role in this respect. The CMEA countries provided particularly favourable conditions for the development of Bulgaria's industry and for meeting its requirements of technology, machinery, equipment and raw materials, as well as assistance in overcoming constraints in payments and investment financing. Trade with most of these countries was also favoured by geographical proximity.

Trade with the CMEA countries is based on bilateral five-year trade agreements which are enhanced by a number of bilateral and multilateral economic cooperation agreements. Such agreements foster complementarity in trade through specialisation and cooperation of production, a high degree of predictability and possibilities for optimal utilisation of production capacities. By boosting Bulgaria's economic and export potential they have enabled it to develop its trade with other partners at comparable high rates.

At present the process of elaboration of trade and cooperation agreements with CMEA countries is undergoing substantial change. Increasingly such agreements represent the end result of trade and business contracts and arrangements between exporters and importers on production sharing, subcontracting, joint investments, etc. The decision-making process at the level of the business partners is based on economic land market interests.

The EEC countries are Bulgaria's major trading partners among the developed industrialised states (see annex table). They have been and will obviously remain so due to geographical proximity and established business contacts. However, the possibilities for broad economic cooperation have not been utilised. The leading trading partner of Bulgaria among EEC countries is the Federal Republic of Germany, followed by Italy, Great Britain and France, in order of value of trade in 1986.[6]

The patterns of our trade with EEC countries and in particular Bulgarian exports have not reflected the structure of the national economy. The structure of exports as well as the rate of their increase have rather been similar to those of the majority of the developing countries exporting to the EEC. The existing situation reflects both problems in the conditions of access to the EEC markets and the insufficient orientation of Bulgarian exporters to the particular requirements of these markets. It also shows the need for expanding trade based on complementarity between the business partners through more complex forms of economic cooperation, including joint investment, production and marketing.

Patterns of trade are affected also by artificial limitations on exports to Bulgaria of needed technology and equipment. Such measures diminish the country's possibilities to export some products with the quality and technical parameters fully corresponding to the market requirements in Western Europe. These measures have a clearly trade diversion effect and increase economic uncertainty between business partners.

The problems in mutual trade underline the need for increased joint efforts to normalise trade relations and to promote economic cooperation.

Bulgaria's post-war economic development was achieved through economic policies utilising mainly instruments of centralised planning. Under those policies the market instruments employed (prices, interest rates, taxes, customs tariffs, etc.) had limited effectiveness as factors for resource allocation and for influencing supply and demand conditions. However, the overriding objectives of accelerated economic and social development warranted centralised resource allocation and investment mobilisation as the most direct approach to successfully constructing new plants and infrastructure, to develop necessary raw materials and processing capacities. Advanced social benefits were implemented making for a high degree of social equity — stable full employment, equitable income distribution, free education and health care, constant growth of living standards.

By the beginning of the 80s the limits of centralised economic management became increasingly evident. Further dynamic growth and social advancement, given the level and diversity of economic and welfare systems attained by present-day Bulgaria, are feasible primarily on the basis of full implementation of efficiency criteria through competitive market conditions and the corresponding instruments. Such a reorientation of economic policy is necessitated also by the requirements of the new international economy and the globalisation of competition resulting from the revolution in science and technology.

Thus both for national economic and foreign trade reasons since the mid 80s a comprehensive programme and corresponding legislation have been adopted for transforming economic policies on the basis of efficiency criteria and market instruments.

The main legal act for the current stage of the reform with general validity for all business operations and government policy measures is embodied in the new Regulations on Economic Activity (REA) adopted by the Council of Ministers in December 1987. A number of specific legal acts were also adopted by the government stipulating the basic instruments and measures for the current implementation of the economic reform in the areas of prices, taxes, the investment process, contractual procedures and obligations for business transactions and the formation and functioning of business partnerships.

The guiding principle of the reform is economic self-management. Under this principle of the reform, enterprises have acquired broad independence in matters of operation and development as to decisions on purchases, sales and prices in the local and foreign markets, production and marketing strategies, income distribution, investment resources and decisions, financing, etc.

Enterprises assume direct responsibility for their economic state and prospects. Their operating results depend on their production costs and on the prices at which a given product or service can be realised on the market. They are free to choose their domestic and foreign suppliers. Enterprises under the new system are not limited to a given economic sector and are free to enter any line of production or trade activity (provided they satisfy consumer demand in their main sector of operation).

Accordingly, there are essential changes in the economic role of the state as well:

— increasingly government intervention is being limited to the implementation of specific welfare objectives and programmes, leaving correspondingly greater scope for market-based adjustment and incentives for growth;

— directive planning is being supplanted by a new approach to planning emphasising mainly its strategic aspects and relying basically on economic instruments;

— government measures and economic policy instruments are being applied on the basis of rules of general validity in a non-arbitrary and transparent manner and on an equal basis regarding domestic and foreign suppliers;

— competitive market conditions are being promoted through relevant legislation and economic policy measures.

The national plan for socio-economic and technological development is adopted by Parliament and sets out target levels for national income, target rates of growth in production, investment, consumption, foreign trade turnover, etc. But in the absence of directives these targets are to be achieved through economic and market policy measures and instruments. These targets, however, are no longer broken down by enterprises.

Thus the national plan acquires an indicative nature and its implementation is based on the interplay of economic interests and market factors.

In practice the combining and harmonising of the interests of the economic enterprises with the goals of the national strategy are achieved through series of discussions ("dialogues"). The rules and procedures for these discussions are spelled out in the new economic legislation. They provide for joint examination and agreement on targets, budgeting, etc. at the various levels in the economy.

In addition to the system of discussions in individual cases the interests of the enterprise and the national plan are matched through *ad hoc* measures within a legal framework for government intervention in exceptional circumstances. Such measures are implemented principally for specific welfare considerations and external economic obligations undertaken at the national level. Existing market imperfections and imbalances are also subject to similar *ad hoc* adjustment measures. However, government intervention measures are applied on an equal basis towards all producing and trading enterprises and to the sale, purchase and distribution of domestic and imported products.

III. Rights and responsibilities of Bulgarian enterprises in foreign trade

Another feature of the new economic conditions is the assumption of direct responsibility by the enterprises for their foreign trade. The export and import activities are an integral part of the business activities of any enterprise under the reform and there no longer exists separation between foreign trade and production and sales operations on the domestic market. In line with the principles of market orientation and self-financing, enterprises have been given direct access to the international markets and full possibilities to independently organise their foreign trade activities. In the new conditions enterprises will have to ensure their further growth and profitability in the first place by further enhancing their positions and competitiveness in the international market place.

The economic and foreign trade independence of enterprises is also backed up by the reform of the banking system, carried out in 1987, designed to promote, through its decentralisation and the creation of a commercial credit system, the most efficient alternative use of financial resources as well as to stimulate the most productive lines of investment through curtailing budget financing and increasing the role of enterprises and banks.

Seven commercial banks were set up as joint-stock companies with the participation of enterprises, economic corporations, banks and other organisations as shareholders. The commercial banks act as independent businesses guided by commercial considerations in attracting funds and providing loans both in local and foreign currencies. Their main criteria are the economic efficiency and creditworthiness of the individual enterprise and the relative profitability of the respective sector of the economy.

IV. Trade policy issues and legisation on economic cooperation and joint ventures with foreign companies

Under the economic reform the role of the government ministry responsible for foreign economic relations will be to secure favourable trade policy conditions and to foster rising efficiency and the restructuring of the foreign trade sector of the economy in line with the long-term requirements of the international markets. The ministry will further develop the legal framework for foreign trade and will follow the observance by the enterprises of the requirements for orderly, fair competition and marketing. This represents a direct departure from the administrative regulation of trade and from the involvement in day-to-day economic activities related to foreign trade.

In the present economic context in Bulgaria ensuring predictability and equal opportunities for Bulgarian enterprises on international markets acquires added importance. In line with this necessity the level of bilateral relations with trading partners and the steps to be taken on bilateral and multilateral bases are at present being examined.

However, even the most developed bilateral framework cannot replace the guarantees, the rights and obligations in the multilateral trading system under the General Agreement on Tariffs and Trade. Bulgaria's request for accession to the GATT presented to the Contracting Parties on 8 September 1986 is a logical outcome of the new economic conditions in the country and of the need for further harmonious development of trade and economic cooperation with foreign partners.

A competitive environment is essential to enhancing economic efficiency and furthering the development of the country's economy. However, Bulgaria needs a fair competitive environment under a clear, predictable and strict set of rules. Therefore, striving to achieve these goals, the Bulgarian authorities are interested in full and unreserved adherence to the dispositions of the General Agreement on Tariffs and Trade. In the conditions of self-management and self-financing of the enterprises, long-term trading and investment arrangements with foreign companies acquire new impetus and new importance for the purposes of mutually beneficial growth and development.

As far back as 1980, by Decree No. 535 of the State Council, the legal framework was established for joint ventures with foreign partners[7] providing for joint management and profit-sharing with the possibility of the share of the foreign partner to be above 50 p.c. No trade-related performance requirements such as export minimum requirements and local content requirements are stipulated in the Decree. On this basis eleven mixed partnerships have been set up, among them with the participation of firms such as "Fanuc", "Dow Chemicals", "APV" and "Sormel".

Meanwhile, long before 1980, the practice of concluding industrial cooperation agreements and specific contracts with Western firms was established. Today more than 70 such agreements and 200 specific contracts are being implemented. On the basis of the cooperation contracts already signed, the manufacture has been organised of new competitive products which fully meet the quality standards of the partner and are freely sold on both home and international markets under his trade mark. This makes it possible for the contribution by the foreign partner in machines, technologies and know-how to be returned under mutually advantageous conditions through the export of part of the produce obtained from cooperative manufacture. Examples in this respect are the successfully used contracts with firms such as "Romica", "Puma", "Adidas", "L'Oreal", "Rottel", "Atomic" and other manufacturers of industrial consumer goods and producers of foodstuffs, as well as with firms from other industrial sectors such as "AEG", "Siemens" and other firms.

As part of the economic reform additional legal instruments were adopted in 1987 which significantly broaden the opportunities for joint business with foreign companies. By them the rights of Bulgarian economic enterprises to engage directly in cooperation contracts, joint ventures, and other forms of economic activities with foreign investment participation are stipulated. New incentives for foreign partners to set up — with Bulgarian enterprises and organisations — partnerships and associations, for the formation of consortia, for signing contracts for the leasing of machines and installations and for other kinds of investment-type co-operation are offered.

The newly adopted legislation favours the joint utilisation of the general advantages for doing business with Bulgarian partners — the balanced and dynamic development, the availability of suitable production capacities, of skilled personnel and of a developed network of trade relations and routes for the marketing of the common product. These opportunities may now be better utilised thanks to the possibilities for mutual coordination of the interests of the partners in generating exports and obtaining higher returns from the investment made which are stipulated in the legislation:

— possibility for exemption from taxation during the first three years of activity of the mixed partnership;
— lower taxes after the third year — 20 p.c. of the annual profit and when the share of this profit is not reinvested but is taken out of the country the additional tax is only 10 p.c.;
— independent choice for reinvestment or for export of the profit, as well as the possibility for foreign investors to have their own current deposits or deposits with fixed terms in the Bulgarian banks;
— accelerated depreciation rates for newly introduced capacities;
— right to free transfer of the share of profit of the foreign participants in the partnerships, and possibilities for the purchase of goods against local currency for the realisation of the transfer;
— establishment abroad by the mixed partnerships of subsidiary firms and branches, as well as joint investments in third countries on a consortium or other basis, including through financing by international credit institutions, etc.

For the organisation and realisation of the economic activities with foreign investment-type participation, the partners can make available funds, machines, installations, raw materials and other materials, and rights over industrial property in the form of licences, know-how industrial design, firm appellations, trade marks, etc.

The property rights and interests of the foreign investors, the right to industrial property included, enjoy the protection of Bulgarian law.

Within their competences, the authorities at the national and local levels are obliged to assist and ensure the necessary conditions for the successful functioning of joint ventures with foreign partners, such as: reducing to a minimum export formalities for the products of the mixed partnerships; assistance in securing the use of buildings, premises and grounds; issuing of permits for sojourn and work by foreign citizens without undue delays or formalities, etc. Conditions promoting joint business are also being created at intergovernmental level. Recently, Bulgaria signed agreements on avoiding double taxation with eight European market-economy countries and agreements for mutual promotion and protection of investments with five European market-economy countries. Negotiations on such agreements are progressing with a number of other interested countries.

An important additional opportunity for expanding business relations with foreign partners is provided by Decree No. 2242 of the State Council of 1987 on tariff-free zones and the specific set of more detailed regulations on their functioning adopted in 1987 and 1988. In these zones foreign companies can organise production, processing, trade and other activities on their own or jointly with partners from Bulgaria. All payments within the zones are to be accomplished in convertible currencies. Imports into the zones are exempted from customs duties. Tax-relief is granted to the economic activities in such zones. Imports from and exports to zones from inside Bulgaria are effected according to the usual export-import procedures.

For the time being two tariff-free zones have been established in the areas of Vidin and Rousse (both are on the Danube).

V. Conclusion

Over the past decades Bulgaria has consistently sought to introduce new measures and instruments for dynamic growth and rising efficiency. The new stage of the economic reform is linking more closely the Bulgarian economy to the world economy in line with the new realities in today's world and the challenges of tomorrow.

At present we are witnessing historical steps by the two most powerful nations, the Soviet Union and the United States, along the road to a more secure world thanks to the common realisation that new approaches and joint efforts are needed to get out of the old stereotypes which provide no rational perspective, no real alternatives.

Nowadays attempts to think and act in line with the old concepts of unequal treatment and differentiation for non-economic reasons are becoming even less acceptable. In the emerging new international economy based on greater interdependence European countries should be able to identify significant additional opportunities for trade and economic cooperation between the East and West on the basis of complementarity of economic structures and common interest.

Notes

1. Statistical Yearbook of the People's Republic of Bulgaria, 1987.
2. The GDP/NMP ratio for Bulgaria in the early 1980s according to different estimates is 1.11 to 1.37. GATT "International trade 1986—1987", p. 157.
3. Statistical Yearbook of the People's Republic of Bulgaria, 1987.
4. 1948 — the year in which the economy basically attained its highest pre-war level of 1939.
5. National income data are based on net material product calculations. Data on the major national accounts aggregates in Bulgaria are based on the concepts and definitions of the MPS (Material Production System) and are compiled in accordance with the "Basic Principles of the Balances of the National Economy", Studies in methods, Series F, No. 17 (United Nations Publication, Sales No. E. 71. XVII. 10).
6. Statistical Yearbook of the People's Republic of Bulgaria, 1987, pp. 377-378.
7. For a detailed analysis of the legislation on joint ventures see V. Tadjer, *Joint Ventures in Bulgaria*, Bulgarian Chamber of Commerce and Industry, 1987 (in English, German and French).

Annex

Turnover, exports and imports by kind of payment and groups of countries

(mln. leva)

	1980	1981	1982	1983	1984	1985	1986
Turnover	17184.4	19818.2	21855.9	23783.5	25829.6	27805.9	27703.8
1. In non-convertible currencies,	12836.3	14320.2	16249.3	18583.6	20059.0	21405.0	22173.6
of which:							
— CMEA-countries	12509.9	13994.8	15947.2	18280.8	19722.4	21030.3	21791.7
2. In convertible currencies,	4348.1	5498.0	5606.6	5199.9	5770.6	6400.9	5530.2
of which:							
— Developed market economy countries	2833.2	3314.4	3062.3	2902.0	2950.6	3310.9	3137.3
— EEC countries	1995.0	2165.2	2051.5	1898.8	1917.5	2202.8	2055.6
— Developing countries	1514.9	2183.6	2544.3	2297.9	2820.0	3090.0	2392.9
Exports	8901.5	9860.3	10880.0	11817.5	12987.3	13739.4	13350.5
1. In non-convertible currencies,	6303.7	6811.1	7771.9	9033.1	9804.6	10578.9	11101.9
of which:							
— CMEA-countries	6127.4	6632.7	7606.7	8894.7	9643.3	10407.5	10907.2

(mln. leva) (Continued)

	1980	1981	1982	1983	1984	1985	1986
2. In convertible currencies, of which:	2597.8	3049.2	3108.1	2784.4	3182.7	3160.5	2248.6
– Developed market economy countries	1407.0	1326.1	1236.7	1234.4	1179.2	1168.9	925.8
– EEC-countries	1020.2	983.7	921.5	856.3	828.4	874.9	655.1
– Developing countries	1190.8	1723.1	1871.4	1550.0	2003.5	1991.6	1322.8
Imports	8282.9	9957.9	10975.9	11966.0	12842.3	14066.5	14353.3
1. In non-convertible currencies, of which:	6532.6	7509.1	8477.4	9550.5	10254.4	10826.1	11071.7
– CMEA-countries	6382.5	7362.1	8340.5	9386.1	10079.1	10622.8	10884.5
2. In convertible currencies, of which:	1750.3	2448.8	2498.5	2415.5	2587.9	3240.4	3281.6
– Developed market economy countries	1426.2	1988.3	1825.6	1667.6	1771.4	2142.0	2211.5
– EEC-countries	974.8	1181.5	1130.0	1042.5	1089.1	1327.9	1400.5
– Developing countries	324.1	460.5	672.9	747.9	816.5	1098.4	1070.1

Source: *Foreign Trade Statistical Yearbook of the People's Republic of Bulgaria*, 1985, p. 34; 1987, p. 34.

Some legal aspects of joint ventures in Czechoslovakia

MILAN ČERNOHUBÝ

Director General Ministry of Foreign Trade, Prague

Czechoslovakia is a country with a highly developed industrial base on the one hand, but not very rich in raw materials on the other. If, in addition to this, we take into consideration a limited domestic market as well as the fact that Czechoslovakia is a land-locked country geographically situated in the very centre of Europe, it is not surprising that it is highly dependent on foreign trade through which approximately one third of the whole national product is being transformed, and therefore maintains broad business ties with abroad. Such a situation provides favourable business opportunities for foreign companies and their operations on the Czechoslovakian market. This is important because it is firms rather than governments which make and sell goods and, whatever the economic system, it is the customer who buys them. Governments on their part can make an important contribution in developing the proper climate in which trade and economic cooperation can flourish.

The Czechoslovak government tries to encourage mutually beneficial trade and cooperation which in manufacturing can take many forms. There is the simple purchase or sale of semi-finished products, then comes the joint manufacturing programme and finally the full-scale (jointly-owned) joint venture. No particular form is intrinsically better than the other. The form is dictated by the degree of cooperation involved in satisfying the customer, who expects the highest quality, a reasonable price and prompt delivery. However, at the present level of international interdependence new and progressive forms of cooperation, such as joint production and joint ventures, are gaining ground even though traditional transactions based on contracts of sale and purchase of goods, leasing operations, licence contracts and similar forms do not lose their importance.

The Czechoslovak government plays an active role in encouraging these new trends which fully fit in with its efforts towards restructuring economic management with the objective of accomplishing structural changes leading to even greater specialisation in production and its higher

M. Maresceau (ed.), The Political and Legal Framework of Trade Relations Between the European Community and Eastern Europe. ISBN 0–7923–0046–7.
© *1989 by Kluwer Academic Publishers, Dordrecht – Printed in the Netherlands.*

efficiency. Among the new forms of cooperation a specific role is attributed to joint ventures.

The beginning of this new development dates back to August 1985, when the so-called "Principles Governing the Establishment and Activities of Joint Companies" formed between Czechoslovak corporations and companies from non-socialist countries were enacted. They embrace general, financial and economic principles setting out a framework within which such companies may be established and operated in Czechoslovak territory. So far two such joint ventures have been established: the TESSEK Association, created jointly by the Czechoslovak corporation Tesla and the Danish company Senetek in the field of manufacturing stuffs used in diagnostics and the AVEX Company, created jointly by the same Czechoslovak corporation Tesla and the Dutch multinational Philips in the field of consumer electronics.

This is a rather modest achievement which of course has its reasons. I would like to point out that, in spite of the progress reached in this field since 1985, our practical experience with joint companies is still only limited and that some key problems are still being encountered. Our situation is different compared with some other socialist countries where joint ventures have been in existence since the 1970s and more prominent since the beginning of the 1980s. We in Czechoslovakia are still at an experimental stage. Under these circumstances joint ventures are more an exception than a general rule and our companies continue giving preference to other forms of cooperation if the same objectives could be achieved through them rather than through a joint venture deal. Nevertheless, some new important projects in the field of joint ventures are under consideration. Joint ventures have become a reality in our economic life.

This brings me to the difficult point of a legal basis regulating the establishment and operation of joint companies in Czechoslovakia. In the absence of comprehensive legislation codified in a single legal instrument, individual rules and regulations which are scattered about in numerous Czechoslovak laws are applicable, such as the 1949 Act on Joint Stock Companies, the 1952 Sales Tax Act, the 1963 International Trade Code, the 1970 Foreign Control Exchange Act, the 1974 National Economy Planning Act from the same year, the 1974 Customs Act, the 1982 Act on Economic Relations with Foreign Countries and others, most of them with amendments. Particulars, regulating the activities as well as the winding-up of joint companies are to be agreed on between the partners, preferably in the memorandum and articles of incorporation. Such a legal framework has its advantages as well as its drawbacks.

The reason why Czechoslovak authorities have given preference to the present solution is based on the consideration that joint ventures present certain new elements for the Czechoslovak socialist economy and that there is no experience either in legislation or day-to-day practice. Therefore, a cautious attitude has been taken, which means that necessary experience is to be gathered first in order to avoid a possible review of newly enacted legislature.

Such a legal approach to joint ventures is characterised by a certain flexibility providing room for the contracting parties to adjust their rights and obligations through mutual consent.

On the other hand, however, some foreign companies consider the present legal framework insufficient. Misgivings mostly stem from the feeling of legal uncertainty which adversely affects the general climate for foreign investments. Such an attitude is sometimes influenced by the assumption that the "Principles" enacted in 1985 are not fully legally binding and only provide an administrative instrument for the regulation of the establishment and operation of joint companies in Czechoslovakia. This is incorrect and misleading, because the "Principles" form an integral part of the Czechoslovak legal order and with other relevant laws guarantee foreign companies full legal security.

These misgivings, however, irrespective of their correctness or incorrectness have influence on the attitude of foreign companies towards joint venture operations in Czechoslovakia. The problem is further complicated by the lack of intergovernmental agreements on the protection of capital investments which make foreign companies even more hesitant.

Here, in my view, is the explanation for the fact that, in spite of all efforts, the results in this field of international cooperation between Czechoslovak and Western companies still remain modest, with just two joint companies, TESSEK and AVEX, in existence.

Such a situation speaks in favour of the enactment of a single Joint Ventures Act comprising explicit legal rules and regulating such matters as the legal status of joint companies, the areas of their operation (industrial production, services etc.), their place in the system of Czechoslovak economy and the applicability of taxation laws, labour laws and others. The first steps in this direction have already been made and we expect that the respective law will be adopted in the course of next year. Furthermore, the Czechoslovak government has entered into negotiations with some West-European countries such as Belgium, France, the Federal Republic of Germany and others on bilateral agreements covering the promotion and protection of capital investments. We believe that the introduction of such a comprehensive legal framework will provide a momentum for efficient, mutually beneficial cooperation between Czechoslovak and Western companies also in this relatively new field in the Czechoslovak economy.

Assurance can be given that the Czechoslovak government will take all

the necessary steps to encourage any kind of mutually beneficial cooperation with Western firms, not just because increased trade and economic
cooperation is desirable in itself, but also because we believe that the
multiplicity of contacts, which trade between individuals, firms and enterprises involves, is a vital confidence-building measure.

The position of Western European companies in their trade relations with the GDR

WOLFGANG NICOLAI

Professor, Dr. Sc., Head of the Department of World Economy and International Economic Relations, Potsdam-Babelsberg

I. Introduction

The GDR, being an industrial country that relies heavily on foreign trade, with exports accounting for approximately 40 p.c. of its national income,[1] is interested in stable external economic relations on a basis of equality and mutual advantage. This holds equally true for the GDR's economic relations with the Western industrial countries which have a share of over 28 p.c. in the GDR's foreign trade turnover (1986).[2] In developing economic cooperation with Western countries, and more particularly with its Western European partners, which account for the bulk of these links, the GDR is guided both by political and economic considerations. One of the fundamental political guidelines is the maintenance and expansion of peaceful East-West cooperation.

In the nuclear and space age, where the very survival of mankind is at stake, every chance should be seized to strengthen confidence among states and make peace more secure by way of a constructive dialogue. Economic relations are well-suited to make a specific contribution of their own to ensure that political détente will regain a firm foothold in Europe, so that disarmament can move forward on a basis of increased confidence. At the same time the GDR gears its economic relations with Western industrial countries to its overall economic objectives, to the targets set forth in the five-year plan for the period from 1986 to 1990 and in its annual economic plans. From this angle, it will be of interest to every commercial partner of the GDR to get informed about the GDR's economic objectives and concepts. This shows where the GDR's interests lie as regards cooperation with Western companies and where new commercial contacts can be initiated.

M. Maresceau (ed.), The Political and Legal Framework of Trade Relations Between the European Community and Eastern Europe. ISBN 0–7923–0046–7.
© *1989 by Kluwer Academic Publishers, Dordrecht – Printed in the Netherlands.*

II. The GDR's growth-oriented economic strategy

In a speech he made in Moscow in November 1987 the General Secretary of the Central Committee of the Socialist Unity Party of Germany (SED) and Chairman of the GDR Council of State, Erich Honecker, underlined the GDR's firm determination to maintain its position as one of the world's ten top-ranking industrial countries with an annual 4 to 5 p.c. growth in national income and a 7 to 8 p.c. rise in labour productivity calculated on net output figures.[3] These ambitious targets are being pursued on the basis of the economic strategy adopted at the 11th SED Congress in April 1986 with a view to the year 2000. The principal purpose of this strategy is to effectively combine the advantages of a socialist planned economy with the scientific-technological revolution. Labour productivity is to grow at a faster pace and production growth is to be ensured with lower unit inputs of raw material, feedstock and fuel. In line with its economic conditions the GDR pursues an "Upgrading Strategy" designed to obtain both higher useful value and more added value from each kilogram of material input.

Our economic strategy includes the necessity to ensure quality levels that meet exacting international standards. Greater efforts will be made in the areas of socialist rationalisation and automation, both in terms of quantity and quality in order to raise effectiveness. This makes greater demands on investment policies, calling for a bigger share of investments for streamlining and rationalisation purposes in the processing industries. The task is to produce newly-developed high-standard consumer goods in larger and growing quantities at low cost both for domestic use and export.

On the whole, our economic strategy is geared to a sustained increase in performance since our social policy objectives, the raising of material and cultural standards of living and a system of assured social benefits require high and dynamic economic growth also in a situation where international economic processes are not without impact on the GDR's national economy. Such economic growth can be ensured only on the basis of intensive expanded reproduction.

As was underlined by Dr. Günter Mittag, Member of the Political Bureau and Secretary of the Central Committee of the SED and Deputy Chairman of the GDR State Council, in his closing words at a recent meeting with leading economic figures of the FRG in Cologne, basic guidelines for the GDR's economic development have been laid down with a long-term view, which makes them reliable. "The GDR economy is oriented toward key technologies, i.e. productivity-boosting techniques, including solutions involving flexible automating in all sectors of the national economy, toward increasing the added-value content of raw materials and their full utilisation — the term "recycling" covers this aspect — and toward the modernisation of industrial installations, also involving considerations of environmental protection. All this accounts for a heavy demand for machinery and equipment, for capital goods of all kinds. This goes for the national economy in its entire breadth."[4]

It goes without saying that East-West trade is not and must not be a one-way street for the GDR either. If emphasis has been laid here on the import interests of the GDR, it should be noted that the GDR is an exporter, too. Western European companies should take due account of these interests as well, so that trade with the GDR can move forward. In other words, the GDR is not only a promising market for Western European companies but, simultaneously, a capable supplier country with a competitive range of goods and services for export. Though not in every calender year, the GDR's external economic policy is, in its tendency, directed toward well-balanced trade with its partners. Having the economic structure of an advanced industrial country, the GDR is interested in exporting from industries like mechanical and electrical engineering, electronics, printing machinery, the chemical industry, woodwork and food-processing, the metallurgical industry, glass and ceramics, and light industry — to mention but a few. These are also the branches which offer the best prospects for longer-term industrial cooperation. In furthering and applying key technologies the GDR focuses on micro- and opto-electronics, sensor and computer technologies, optic fibre, laser and bio-technology.[5] The GDR believes that, on balance, its ambitious targets can only be reached if advantage is taken of the benefit of active participation in the international division of labour.

Against the background of complicated conditions prevailing in the Western markets in the 80s, the GDR's economic advance has benefitted from its solid economic ties with the USSR, its main partner, with a share of nearly 40 p.c. in the GDR's foreign trade turnover and from the fact that it is firmly embedded in the CMEA. In the CMEA market increasingly exacting demands are made on the technical and qualitative standards of products. This spurs economic relations with Western countries. Concrete offers from Western companies are always welcome if they represent international top standards in terms of science and technology and if they are made on the customary economic terms. Thus until September 1987, the GDR had directed inquiries about imports of capital goods valued at approximately 3.5 billion Marks to companies in the FRG and Berlin (West), while projects worth 2.4 billion Marks are already being negotiated. During the state visit of Erich Honecker to Belgium it was disclosed that from autumn 1986 till October 1987 the GDR purchased goods to the tune of 13 billion Bfr. from Belgium and has approached Belgian companies with inquiries concerning items worth another 11 billion Bfr.[6]

The fact that annual growth rates of 20 p.c. and more are envisaged for high-technology products[7] illustrates how the GDR's industry which produces some 90 p.c. of the country's export commodities[8] is rising to the challenges of the world's markets. This is in line with the international trend. GDR micro-electronics, in 1986, registered a nearly 20 p.c. production increase on the previous year,[9] and GDR Kombinate are expected to attain product innovation rates of more than 30 p.c.[10] According to Western figures the GDR at present ranks sixth in the production and third in the export of machine tools worldwide.[11] In order to maintain this position the portion of machine tools equipped with microelectronic controls will rise from 30 p.c. in 1985 to 70 p.c. in 1990.

III. The role of the Kombinate in the economy of the GDR[12]

Kombinate represent the bulk of the country's industrial and civil engineering potential. Their establishment in these and in other sectors has proved an effective form of organising socialist property to meet current needs. Without these efficient economic units, which enjoy a high degree of autonomy, the implementation of our economic strategy would be unthinkable. Under the conditions of the planned economy Kombinate allow the linking of all elements of the cycle of reproduction and, consequently, control of that cycle by a single managerial body. The Kombinate are an appropriate form of managing socialist property because their science and research as well as foreign trade are under the same management and are intimately connected with the production process. What matters most in this context is no doubt the establishment of a direct link between science and production. Today, the Kombinate and their member companies decide autonomously on approximately 90 p.c. of their research and development projects and about 80 p.c. of their funds. Some 70 p.c. of scientists and technologists get their work assigned by companies.[13] The question of the commitment of companies on external markets is not of secondary importance. That is why the four main economic indicators of enterprise performance include export, in addition to net output, gains as well as consumer goods and services. The Kombinate are fully in charge of their imports and exports. This reflects the increasing significance of close and direct links with foreign markets. Twenty-two out of the current total of 45 foreign trade enterprises are directly affiliated to the Kombinate. Another 20 have been subordinated to industrial ministries, with the remaining three being directly answerable to the Ministry of Foreign Trade. In addition, all foreign trade enterprises are at the same time subordinate to the Ministry of Foreign Trade for purposes of proper balancing.

Let me use the example of the Carl Zeiss Jena Kombinat to illustrate how efficient the GDR's Kombinate are as economic partners of Western European companies. In terms of product range and scope of scientific and technological topics dealt with in basic and applied research VEB Carl Zeiss is one of the world's leading enterprises in precision engineering and opto-electronics. The product range comprises approximately 800 major items grouped in 30 major product units. Most prominent among them are micro-electronics, optical-fibre communication, computer-aided design and production preparation and highly automated manufacturing units. The 24 member companies of the Kombinat, most of them in Jena and Dresden, have a workforce of 69,000, with staff figures per company ranging from 300 to 7,000. The member companies include 13 final producers, five suppliers, two engineering firms for rationalisation equipment, three research centres and one foreign trade enterprise. The Kombinat produces goods worth more than 4.5 billion Marks each year. It is represented in some 40 countries by its own marketing and purchasing agency. In another 40 countries products of Kombinat VEB Carl Zeiss Jena are offered by marketing firms. It is part and parcel of the strategy of the Kombinat to deepen economic, scientific and technical relations, also with western companies.

IV. Development of the GDR's economic relations with western industrialised countries

Since the signing of the CSCE Final Act in 1975 up to the end of 1986, the GDR concluded 196 intergovernmental treaties and agreements with 21 western participating states, which virtually cover all areas dealt with in "basket two" of the Final Act, i.e. cooperation in the economic, scientific and technological fields as well as in matters of environmental protection.[14] In this context, it can be noted that apart from long-term agreements on economic, industrial and scientific-technological cooperation, more and more interdepartmental and special agreements have been concluded, *inter alia* on cooperation in science and technology, environmental protection matters, and in third markets. Generally, such agreements incorporate new forms of East-West economic relations, such as industrial cooperation, joint activities in third markets, specialisation of production, mutual participation in investment activities, and streamlining projects.

The fact that intergovernmental agreements and activities, notably at high or top level, stimulate the exchange of goods is borne out by the figures of the GDR's foreign trade turnover with Western industrialised countries. From 1975 till 1986, these figures more than doubled, eventually reaching a volume of 51.4 billion exchange Marks.[15] Over the same period, the goods exchange with Austria quadrupled while trebling with Switzerland and Liechtenstein and almost doubling with Finland, France, Great Britain, Italy, and other countries. The GDR's foreign trade turnover with western industrialised States, naturally, depends on many factors. Adverse trends of price development in the Western markets, accompanied by negative effects on the terms of trade, excessive exchange rate fluctuations of the Dollar and other Western currencies, keener rivalry in the Western markets, adverse consequences of structural crises, persistent and unabated protectionism, and especially the COCOM restrictions — all these phenomena in the final analysis have a bearing on the trade relations, which is surely not of a stimulating nature. Against this backdrop, it is understandable why the GDR's foreign trade turnover with Western industrialised countries was more or less stagnant in the years between 1985—1986.[16]

The GDR is not interested in a continuation of this situation. The Law on the Five-Year Plan for the period from 1986 to 1990 states in this regard that the Kombinate will have to make every effort to increase the output of profitable high technology products in order to strengthen the market positions presently held.[17]

During the state visit of Erich Honecker to Belgium in October 1987, it became particularly clear that contacts at intergovernmental level can give a major impetus to cooperation at company level and that both levels are closely linked with one another. The GDR and Belgium, for instance, have agreed the following measures for the year 1988:

— to establish priorities for the participation of Belgian firms in projects for the expansion and streamlining of industrial enterprises in the GDR;

— to send an economic delegation from Belgium's industry to the GDR in the first half of 1988;

— to hold discussions in the Joint Commission on economic, scientific-technological and industrial cooperation;

— to organise Belgian symposia in the GDR, *inter alia*, on the subjects of power production and transmission, and communication;

— to secure the participation of Belgian companies in the Leipzig Fairs with larger displays than in the past;

— to identify further areas and projects, and take concrete measures for strengthening and expanding cooperation in third countries.[18]

Favourable conclusions have been drawn from mutual symposia and demonstrations of technical products, such as Belgian symposia in the GDR on textile machines, machine tools, food-processing and packaging machines as well as the Third Technical Days of the GDR which were held in Brussels and Liège from 5 to 10 October 1987.

The long-term programme signed during the state visit to Belgium for the development of the economic, industrial and technical cooperation between the GDR and the Belgian-Luxembourg Economic Union envisages the conclusion of long-term agreements on mutually beneficial cooperation particularly in the fields of mechanical engineering, construction of plants, equipment and other components, environmental protection, agricultural and food-processing equipment, as well as apparatus for the chemical and petrochemical industries.

Moreover, the Governments of the GDR, Belgium and Luxembourg will see to it that due attention and consideration is given to offers from foreign trade enterprises or companies of the respective partners whenever there is a demand for corresponding industrial equipment and machines.

Article 4 of the above-mentioned programme stipulates that both sides will promote cooperation in third markets, especially in such fields as the construction of cement mills, metallurgical installations and equipment, rail vehicles, power stations, the establishment of chemical and petrochemical plants, supply of hospital equipment and installations and of plants and equipment for agriculture and food-processing. At the same time, these fields, with certain variations, indicate where to look for possibilities of cooperation with other Western European countries and companies in third markets. Scientific-technological cooperation should be pursued in future-oriented areas such as chemistry, biotechnology, metallurgy, efficient power production and consumption, electronics and information technologies.[19]

The holding of Technical Days of the GDR in western industrialised countries, and *vice versa,* has proved its worth as a means to promote trade and commerce. From 1975 to 1986, 33 of such Technical Days of the GDR were held in 16 western CSCE participating States while eight of the latter organised 14 such events in the GDR (see Annex 1). In addition, every year some 300 companies from western CSCE participating States present their product ranges and service offers in exhibitions, symposia and special lectures held in the GDR. The participation of a great number of Western European firms in the Leipzig Fairs bears witness to the significance western economic partners attach to these events in view of the possibilities they provide for developing economic relations. The Leipzig Autumn Fair of 1987, for instance, was attended, among others, by 62 exhibitors from the Netherlands, some forty from Belgium, and about seventy from France.

Since 1975, the GDR has provided twice as much information on commercial and economic matters to Western European companies and economic journalists as before. Let me mention here only the weekly publication "Dokumentationen zur Außenwirtschaft", the information sheet series "Theorie und Praxis des Außenhandels", the economic information bulletin of the GDR Chamber of Foreign Trade, foreign-language comments on important legal regulations having an impact on foreign trade relations, the annual publication of the directory of foreign trade enterprises and their product ranges, the statutes of the foreign trade enterprises, including information on their assets, set-up, product ranges and service offers, the publications of the Leipzig Fairs Bureau, promotional material of individual foreign trade enterprises as well as the GDR's Statistical Yearbook.

V. Agreements between companies

The foreign trade enterprises of the GDR seek to develop their cooperative relations with large-scale enterprises, small and medium-size companies of western countries on a long-term contractual basis in accordance with the principles of mutual benefit and equal rights. In this context, underwriting contracts with large-scale companies have proved their worth as one form of pursuing cooperation with them. Such contracts, which run up to the year 1990, were concluded by GDR foreign trade enterprises, *inter alia*, with Montedison (Italy), Rhône-Poulenc (France), AKZO (Netherlands), Ciba-Geigy (Switzerland) as well as the Johnson Group of Sweden. They set out targets to be pursued in export and import dealings, in scientific-technological cooperation and in joint activities in third markets, in the organisation of marketing through the sales network of the partner, as well as in other fields. This form of cooperation also provides a framework for new ways of cooperation in the industrial sector. GDR foreign trade enterprises are working together on a long-term basis also with the Belgian Cockerill (metallurgical plants) and ACEC (products of electrical engineering) companies.

Mindful of the significance which the presence in international markets has assumed, the GDR's foreign trade enterprises[20] have established 158 and the Deutsche Aussenhandelsbank (German Foreign Trade Bank) 3 representations in 16 western CSCE participating States. At present, there are 95 companies and 5 banks from 15 Western CSCE participating States represented in the GDR. They opened office in the GDR, enjoying the favourable conditions envisaged in the Helsinki Final Act. These conditions include exemption from custom duties, long-term residence permits, material and technical assistance in appointing offices, recruitment of GDR staff etc. (See Annex 2).

In an exemplary way, the GDR is following the recommendation of the Helsinki Final Act that smaller and medium-size companies be accepted as partners in economic, scientific and technological cooperation. About two thirds of the GDR's foreign trade with western countries is done with small and medium-size companies. Forty p.c. of the more than 2,500 Austrian concerns involved in goods exchanges with the GDR are medium or small-size, and in trade with Italy, such companies account for more than 70 p.c. In the FRG every year some 6,000 to 7,000 small and medium-size enterprises conclude about 25,000 to 27,000 contracts with GDR companies. These contracts cover about 40 p.c. of the total goods exchanges between the two countries, while some 150 large-scale companies account for the remaining 60 p.c. Major investment projects under the 1986—1990 Five-Year Plan and modernisation or reconstruction schemes in various economic branches in the GDR offer wide-ranging opportunities to highly-specialised small and medium-size enterprises of Western countries for the establishment or broadening of commercial relations with GDR foreign trade enterprises, especially when it comes to capital goods, rationalisation equipment, environmental protection equipment, software, and so-called custom-made projects. The GDR facilitates the participation of small and medium-size enterprises also by offering them the possibility to exhibit their products on joint stands at the Leipzig Fairs (e.g., Italy, France, Belgium, Great Britain, Switzerland, Greece, FRG).

In his earlier mentioned statement in Cologne Dr. G. Mittag also underlined the constructive attitude of the GDR's Kombinate and foreign trade enterprises towards new forms of East-West economic cooperation. There he noted, *inter alia*: "We are prepared to retain proven methods and forms of trade such as cooperation in third markets or counterpurchase deals, but we are also looking for new forms of cooperation. The German Democratic Republic will examine any proposal likely to benefit both sides and make a favourable impact on the balance sheets of the business partners involved."[21] The decisive criterion for the choice of a certain form of economic relations is the cost-profit ratio. There is never a definite form "as such". If at the lowest possible cost and smallest risk, the greatest possible effect is produced for both sides, the form of commercial relations chosen is the right one.

So far GDR enterprises have collected only little experience with regard to those forms of cooperation with western companies that go beyond pure export or import deals. However, some conclusions may nevertheless be drawn, also from experience gathered by other countries in their East-West cooperation.[22] The gradual development of industrial cooperation has proved to be a useful principle. Such an approach makes it easier for the partners to get to know each other and reduces the initial risk. As a first stage of such cooperation, semi-finished or finished products could be exchanged to supplement existing product ranges or to complement finished products. After that attention could be focused on the joint improvement of existing products and development of new ones. Another experience is that the repetitive aspects of different projects tend to enhance efficiency of cooperation.

Successful industrial cooperation presupposes the existence of capacities that interest the trading partners. This also goes for the capacity for scientific and technological achievements. It should be possible to maintain a flow of technologies in both directions. This is a guideline for the GDR. There can be no question of making the GDR into an "extended workbench" for Western European corporations. When planning for industrial cooperation involving the exchange of technologies care must be taken to exclude any potential interference factor as far as possible. Embargo provisions in the framework of COCOM must be regarded as such an interference factor because not only do they have an impact on the products that are on the COCOM list but beyond that, they also have a snowball effect in that they give rise to uncertainty among business partners in all fields related to high technology in one way or another. After all, nobody knows today what items will appear tomorrow on the COCOM list. Hence, business partners in East and West urgently require greater predictability and reliability in these matters. The best way to achieve this would be to reduce the COCOM lists, to keep them from mushrooming the way they do. As progress is made between East and West in the disarmament field and as acceptable verification procedures are found, institutions like COCOM should become extinct.

Moreover, trade obstacles such as tariffs, quotas, so-called self-restraint agreements and technical trade impediments do not allow the advantages of industrial cooperation over traditional export-import transactions to become fully effective.

VI. Conclusion

Finally, attention should be drawn to a document presented by the Greek Government for an ECE symposium at Thessaloniki which contains the following five conclusions that may serve as general guidelines for present-day forms of East-West cooperation:

— cooperation must be based on correct information and hard and fast rules valid for longer periods;
— common interests and mutual advantages must be identified;
— the elimination of red tape and greater flexibility of economic life to enhance the effectiveness of such cooperation;
— cooperation must be pursued in accordance with the legal and other regulations in force in the countries concerned, i.e. regulations which determine the economic conduct of the partners, thus furthering structural and technological innovations;
— decisive importance must be attached to enhancing mutual confidence.[23]

Notes

1. According to *Statistisches Taschenbuch der DDR 1987*, Staatsverlag der DDR, Berlin 1987, p. 25 and p. 102.
2. *Ibid.*, p. 102.
3. Speech by Erich Honecker at the festive meeting in the Kremlin Congress Palace, in: *Neues Deutschland*, 3 November 1987.
4. Concluding words of Dr. Günter Mittag, Member of the Politbureau and Secretary of the SED Central Committee, Deputy Chairman of the Council of State of the GDR, at the meeting with leading economic figures of the FRG in Cologne, in: *Ein Erfolg der Politik der Vernunft und des Realismus*, Offizieller Besuch des Generalsekretärs des ZK der SED und Vorsitzenden des Staatsrates der DDR, Erich Honecker, in der BRD vom 7. — 11. September 1987, p. 29.
5. *Directives of the 11th SED Congress for the Five-Year Plan for the GDR's National Economic Development 1986–1990*, Dietz Verlag, Berlin 1986, pp. 48–52.
6. *Neues Deutschland*, 15 October 1987.
7. Act on the Five-Year Plan for the GDR's National Economic Development 1986–1990, in *Neues Deutschland*, 28 November 1986.
8. Estimated value based on data of *Statistisches Taschenbuch der DDR 1987, loc cit.*, p. 101.
9. Communication of the Directorate of Statistics on the Carrying-through of the National Economic Plan 1986, in: *Neues Deutschland*, 19 January 1987.
10. Act on the Five-Year Plan . . . , *loc. cit.*
11. *Neues Deutschland*, 12 November 1987.
12. For further information on the position of the Kombinate in the GDR's national economy see, *inter alia*:
    — Verordnung über die volkseigenen Kombinate, Kombinatsbetriebe und volkseigenen Betriebe vom 8. 11. 1979, *Gesetzblatt der DDR*, Teil I, Nr. 38/1979, p. 355.
    — G. Friedrich, "Kombinate — Rückgrat sozialistischer Plan-wirtschaft", *Neues Deutschland*, 18 June 1987,

- *Sozialistische Außenwirtschaft, Lehrbuch,* Verlag Die Wirtschaft, Berlin 1984, pp. 42—46 and pp. 309—322,
- W. Biermann, *Kombinate als Hauptträger des wissenschaftlich-technischen Fortschritts,* Einheit (Berlin), 7/1987, pp. 610—613,
- R. Weidauer, "Zur Organisation der Leitung von Kombinaten", *Wissenschaftliche Zeitschrift der Technischen Universität,* Dresden 6/1986, pp. 77—82.

13. See H. Koziolek/O. Reinhold, *Über die schöpferische theoretische Arbeit in der politischen Ökonomie bei der Gestaltung des entwickelten Sozialismus in der DDR,* Einheit (Berlin), 3/1987, p. 216.

14. O. Fischer, *Der sozialistische deutsche Staat im Kampf um die Sicherung des Friedens,* Einheit (Berlin), 10—11/1987, p. 930.

15. *Statistisches Taschenbuch der DDR 1987, loc. cit.,* p. 102.

16. *Ibid.,*

17. Act on the Five-Year Plan for the GDR's National Economic Development 1986— 1990, in: *Neues Deutschland,* 28 November 1986.

18. *Neues Deutschland,* 15 October 1987.

19. *Neues Deutschland,* 16 October 1987.

20. Nationally-owned foreign trade enterprises (German abbr.: AHB) are economically and legally independent basic units of the GDR economy implementing state tasks and plan targets of foreign trade within the framework of a programme of goods and services approved by the Minister of Foreign Trade. The AHB, predominantly, is the marketing organ of one or more Kombinate and the delivery organ for their balancing scope. The AHB is a corporate body, assumes obligations in its own name, and is severally liable for meeting these obligations with its capital stock. The AHB has a statute and is run by a director general on the principle of individual management. The representations established by the defined AHB in western countries are technical-commercial offices which, being AHB organs, help to ensure their presence on the markets.

21. Concluding words by Dr. Günter Mittag, p. 31.

22. G. Scharschmidt, Möglichkeiten und Formen der ökonomischen Beziehungen zwischen Ost und West aus der Sicht der DDR, lecture at the 20th International East-West Seminar in Bad Ischl, Austria, April 1987.

23. "Modern forms of stable economic cooperation between East and West", Document transmitted by the Government of Greece, *ECE Symposium on East-West-Business Opportunities and Trade Prospects,* Thessaloniki, Greece, 8—11 September 1986, TRADE/SEM./R. 30, p. 9.

Annex 1

"Technical Days" held by the GDR in western CSCE participating States from 1975 to 1986

1. France	4
2. Austria	3
3. Netherlands	3
4. Switzerland	2
5. Belgium	2
6. Greece	2
7. Italy	2
8. Spain	3
9. Great Britain	2
10. Finland	1
11. Canada	2
12. Denmark	1
13. USA	1
14. Portugal	1
15. Sweden	2
16. Norway	2
16 States	33 "Technical Days"

"Technical Days" held by western CSCE participating States in the GDR from 1975 to 1986

1. France	3
2. Netherlands	3
3. Austria	2
4. Italy	1
5. Great Britain	2
6. Belgium	1
7. Denmark	1
8. Switzerland	1
8 States	14 "Technical Days"

Annex 2

Representations of GDR foreign trade enterprises in western CSCE participating States: (by 31 December 1986)

	Representations	Including bank representations
1. France	22	1
2. Austria	16	—
3. Belgium	9	—
4. Netherlands	7	—
5. Great Britain	15	1
6. Italy	16	1
7. Spain	6	—
8. Sweden	16	—
9. Finland	6	—
10. Denmark	1	—
11. Greece	8	—
12. USA	5	—
13. FRG	26	—
14. Turkey	2	—
15. Switzerland	2	—
16. Norway	1	—
	158	3

Representations of companies of western CSCE participating States in the GDR: (by 31 December 1986)

	Representations	Including bank representations
1. France	12	3
2. Austria	7	—
3. Belgium	7	—
4. Finland	2	—
5. Norway	2	—
6. Sweden	7	—
7. Netherlands	4	—
8. Spain	3	—
9. Greece	1	—
10. Italy	9	1
11. Switzerland	25	1
12. Liechtenstein	3	—
13. Great Britain	9	—
14. USA	3	—
15. Denmark	1	—
	95	5

The position of Western European countries in their trade relations with Hungary

FERENC MÁDL

Professor, Faculty of Laws, University of Budapest

I. Introduction

A. *Business and investment climate*

In this paper, we will mainly deal with the business and investment positions of foreign companies in Hungary on the one hand, and with the scope of the Hungarian trading partners on the other. Of course, it would be tempting to go over to basic theoretical economic considerations and general foreign trade theories also as regards East-West economic co-operation. This paper, however, is aimed more at the practice-oriented legal issues of the questions concerned. As to general principles, let me refer only to the fact that Smith, Ricardo and Mill, as well as Marx, would be amazed to see the huge dimensions of present-day international economic relations, both in the magnitude and the differentiation of international trade as a result of the new industrial revolution in the second half of the twentieth century. This picture today is characterised by a relative unity of a world market on whose stage the developed free-market economies, the socialist countries and the third world are present and perform their activity adjusted to their mutual interests. What we witness is an unprecedented intensity of international division of labour.

1. *Business climate.* Business and investment are identical and comple-mentary phenomena respectively. Business in its traditional sense means trading in the well-known traditional forms (sale, delivery, barter, lease, transport, commission, banker's activity, payment transactions, contrac-tor's contracts, etc.). That Hungary is a good partner in this field follows from its high per capita foreign trade turnover. It goes without saying that Hungarian firms are availing themselves also of new forms of doing business in this "traditional" field such as leasing, counter trading, com-

M. Maresceau (ed.), The Political and Legal Framework of Trade Relations Between the European Community and Eastern Europe. ISBN 0–7923–0046–7.
© *1989 by Kluwer Academic Publishers, Dordrecht – Printed in the Netherlands.*

pensation deals and various forms of insurance. In fact, this includes all possible forms of contracts in all possible fields of foreign trade. These contracts may be entered into abroad or in Hungary by a foreign firm and a Hungarian partner.

However, what is of interest here are the following questions:

(1) first, who are the possible Hungarian trading partners (as we will see, we can witness a new opening-up development); (2) what are those legal forms by which foreigners perform economic activity in Hungary in their capacity as legal entities with some kind of lasting presence in Hungary? These forms are roughly the following: (a) long-term cooperation contracts; (b) trade representations; (c) foreign companies and subsidiaries; (d) joint venture companies. The latter are channelling new forms of doing business in Hungary, creating investment activity in their various guises. While commercial representation may serve both "traditional" trading and investment strategies, contractual joint ventures and equity (corporate) joint ventures are of special interest here.

2. *Investment climate.* As to the investment activities, let us start with this very pragmatic approach: what are the considerations by which joint ventures can be expected to be good ventures? No question, *a favourable investment climate* is surely needed for a more sizable development in this field. As for Hungary, this can be seen, *inter alia*, in the following facts and considerations.

Looked at from the position of foreign investors: new markets and resources; a trained and less expensive labour force; a transferable profit; a direct presence and efficient direct participation in the management of the invested capital; favourable tax laws; closeness (especially for European investors); access to the greater CMEA market; a fairly good telecommunication system with improving connections to all countries (telex, direct dialling long distance telephone system, ect.); liberal travel and visa facilities; a fairly modern company law system. All these tend to result in comparatively higher profits and other advantages for foreign investors.

Looked at from the Hungarian side: strong commitment both politically and economically to East-West trade; the need for modern technology, management and marketing skill for a more efficient growth of the economy; relatively fast and efficient accommodation of advanced investment goods and strategies; the commitment and expectation to expand the market for the joint venture productions in joint efforts also in third countries. Moreover, joint venture investments are also devices for acquiring more capital needed by the economy and the enterprises, which is otherwise (through credit) often hard to come by.

B. *Other considerations for doing business and investments*

Other general considerations, which could also encourage Western companies to do business and to invest in Hungary, include their general policy to proliferate their formerly predominantly non-socialist market and investment strategy; the admission of the fact that they too need this side of the world market for their expansion; the recognition of the market-oriented economic reforms in the socialist countries as facilitating investment and other cooperation processes; and the gradually improving international political climate strengthening the confidence in lasting East-West cooperation efforts.

To be more specific, we should refer to some additional facts and considerations demonstrating Hungary's strong commitment to be active in this field. Most of them are facts of pressing objective necessity. One of them is that Hungary is a highly foreign trade-oriented country. This is largely due to the fact that Hungary has limited resources in raw materials (except for agricultural production), energy and domestic market potentials. Consequently, it is forced to live on what is called a transforming economy: buying raw materials and energy, transforming these into manufactured goods for consumption and for sale on foreign markets to earn the import costs. Roughly 50 p.c. of the GNP comes and goes through international economic processes. In other words, an efficient national economy depends heavily on the efficiency of the external economy. Efficient external economy requires openness, good instrumental channels to the world market on the one hand and, on the other, a domestic economic management system by which the economic entities have flexible autonomy and the inner efficiency-oriented pressure to act successfully on the world market. The main elements substantiating these requirements and efforts include the following:

(i) Besides CMEA as the main international economic and legal scheme representing ca 50 p.c. of the country's foreign trade turnover, Hungary — performing 50 p.c. of its foreign trade turnover with the developed Western (40 p.c.) and the developing (10 p.c.) countries — acceded to the GATT, the International Monetary Fund and the World Bank, as the major global institutions of the world economy. Hungary maintains trade agreements, industrial cooperation agreements and other intergovernmental treaties with many countries. These instruments are meant to serve and facilitate economic intercourse. A number of arrangements with the EEC are aimed at improving mutual relations, while a general trade agreement seems to be forthcoming.

(ii) The economic reforms — the new economic mechanism (NEM) — developed a strong autonomy, self-reliance and an independent strategy-position for the economic entities (enterprises, companies, banks, cooperatives, etc.) while the State moved to more general macro-economic strategy positions. Besides general state regulatory schemes, market incentives (profit-orientedness) have been built into the strategy of the economic entities (technology-development, production and marketing). Part of these reforms included drastic moves to establish direct organic interaction of hundreds of enterprises and companies with virtually thousands of foreign partners; the monopoly of a few big foreign trade enterprises has been largely removed, and today rapidly extended foreign trade authorisations have opened hundreds of gates to the world market, while more progressive steps are to come.

(iii) On the civil or commercial law level — the sphere of the international transactions and investment operations — Hungary acceded to all major conventions channelling such international economic activity (conventions on sale, forwarding carriage, bill of exchange, cheque, commercial arbitration, etc.). Hungary is contributing to such international legislative activities as the Unification of Rules concerning leasing, documentary credit and other usages practised in international economic cooperation.

II. Direct trading rights (the Hungarian partners in the external economy)

We do not intend to discuss here the theoretical issues concerning the general external economic structure nor the drastic metamorphosis or fading away of the one time "classic" foreign trade monopoly. These issues comprise among others how the said metamorphosis of the State monopoly came about, how it became so flexible as demonstrated by recent developments, and subordinated to a more pragmatic external economic policy of the State, how the State's economic external policy was adapted to the general conditions of present-day international economic cooperation, what special legal intergovernmental schemes are being shaped, adopted or acceded to in the various relationships of cooperation within the CMEA and as regards the developed and developing countries, how the State was removed as a direct actor and manager of international economic transactions, giving real autonomy and a management role to the enterprises and, finally how the whole internal organisational structure of the external economy has been made more enterprise-oriented. These and other general issues have been analysed elsewhere (see Bibliography,

Annex 2, MADL-VEKAS, *The Law of Conflicts and Foreign Trade*, Chapter on "The State as architect of international economic relations — foreign trade monopoly in metamorphosis", pp. 119—148).

What is of basic interest for Western companies in this context, is the scope of economic entities with foreign trade authorisation, i.e. the possible partners in East-West trade and other economic relationships. If we focus on the vast field of economic activities at international level, more particularly on the actors of this activity, we may start with some general propositions.

An important goal of the economic reform was, in addition to creating enterprise autonomy, to reinforce the play of real market forces and the operation of the sets of governing laws by reshaping the concept of central planning. The pursuit of this goal in the commercial sector led to the endeavour, as formulated in Decision No. 1 of 1967 of the Government's Economic Commission, that "the basic idea in transforming the foreign trade mechanism introduced on January 1, 1968 shall be to establish an economic linkage between production and foreign trade, a goal to be achieved primarily by economic methods, through the common interests of enterprises in economic gains. In justified cases an organisational link shall also be forged between foreign trade and production or domestic trade". Seen from the standpoint of practical feasibility, the substance of this goal lies in creating an *organisational unity of and a strong interaction between production and foreign trade processes, external market and domestic economic trends.* This concept should be particularly stressed because, as it is known, under the previous external economic mechanism the relevant world market demands and challenges were only indirectly felt by the domestic economy, particularly by production industries. Such an organisational unity was enhanced by numerous measures of the economic reform: on the one hand the establishment of enterprise autonomy, modification of foreign exchange and customs regulations, regulation of price formation and income and, on the other, the restructuring of the foreign trade organisations at enterprise level, the extension of foreign trade rights to a widening range of economic organisations, and the elaboration of legal formulae to assign to enterprises not enjoying foreign trade rights a more active role in the conclusion of foreign trade contracts.

We will refer to the legislative modification of foreign trade contracts to forge a closer link between domestic producers or buyers and foreign partners and afterwards we will discuss the changes with regard to organisation and contracts and the prevailing structural pattern established in conformity with the Foreign Trade Act, which provides that "in establishing the system of foreign trade organisation, measures shall be taken to ensure the organisational conditions for efficient operations on foreign markets" (para. 2 of Art. 7).

A. *Organisational changes*

Under the given organisational pattern of enterprises with foreign trade rights, we should refer primarily to the group of enterprises established specifically for the purpose of conducting foreign trade operations. Specialising in external trade, these foreign trade companies used to be geared to a close division of work among themselves on the basis of a "product-line monopoly", which meant that the operations of each foreign trade company were limited to the exportation and/or importation of a product group specified in the deed of foundation, but the company had exclusive rights to conduct foreign trade talks and to conclude foreign trade contracts in respect of its line of output. Accordingly, domestic production and commercial enterprises had to do business only through the foreign trade company which was authorised to conduct foreign market operations in respect of the products they sought to buy or sell. The realisation of the disadvantages inherent to monopoly power prompted the Economic Commission as early as 1967 to press for changes (i—xi).

(i) One of the first steps was the right of choice between foreign trade companies, as expressed in law in the Foreign Trade Act of 1974, providing that, subject to the conditions specified by law, production, commercial and servicing organisations may choose to deal with the enterprise possessing foreign trade rights through which they wish to effect foreign trade transactions (Art. 14). In order to facilitate the utilisation of this possibility and to promote the spread of such practice, Decree No. 1/1978 (I. 14) of the Minister of Foreign Trade (as amended) provided that the Minister of Foreign Trade was empowered to designate, at the request of a domestic enterprise, another enterprise authorised to carry out foreign trade activity instead of, or in addition to, the one which was hitherto competent by its sphere of activity to conclude contracts.

(ii) Another step in the system of foreign trade organisation was the introduction of the institution of "parallel foreign trade rights" concerning the exportation of certain products, particularly manufactured items and machinery, to non-socialist markets. Under this scheme several economic organisations otherwise vested with foreign trade rights are entitled to trade in products or services of the same type (Ordinance N. 10/1981. Kk. E. 10 of the Minister of Foreign Trade). The introduction of this institution was part of the effort to widen the choice of partners by production enterprises on the one hand, and to reduce the negative effects of monopoly power and to strengthen competition with regard to foreign trade companies on the other. However, the law provided that in case of parallel foreign trade rights destructive competition shall be avoided; care must be taken that the interests of the national economy are protected; favourable conditions for exportation to and importation from foreign markets are maintained; and that the exercise of such rights does not disturb the market, prejudice the interest of domestic production or supply, nor deteriorate the conditions for efficient operations on foreign markets (Art. 4).

The foundation of foreign trade enterprises with a 'general product-mix' (e.g. *Generalimpex*) was a particular and more than just a symbolic action to help the above ideas to materialise.

(iii) A particularly important development consisted in that a growing number of production and servicing enterprises and cooperatives were granted independent foreign trade rights in an effort to institutionalise the advantages of direct operations on foreign markets. Foreign trade rights could be granted "if such authorisation was in accord with the foreign trade interests of the national economy and the particular economic organisation has the necessary economic, organisational and personnel conditions, or such conditions could be created, for successful foreign trade activity" (Art. 7, para. 1 of the Foreign Trade Act). The rather vague formulation of this clause gave strong discretionary power to the authorising (foreign trade) ministry.

(iv) New trends called for a more normative system. No question, the granting of independent foreign trade authorisation to more than 300 economic units, mostly in the reform years, was already a substantial step ahead but more was needed. A normative system was called for. It was expected that through this new system the number of economic entities with direct access to the world market would increase rapidly. Normativism in the new regulation meant that — concerning convertible currency deals — authorisations, as a rule, had to be issued in 45 days to all economic units which wanted to be their own masters with regard to their own products and own needs on foreign markets. This was the message of the Decree No. 7 of 1985 of the Minister of Foreign Trade on the authorisation of foreign trade. But this still required "authorisation" by the ministry and this still meant discretionary power and procedures. The next step was Decree No. 1 of 1987 pursuant to which foreign trade activity involving convertible currency deals (with some specified exceptions) only requires *registration*. This made the previous centralised and discretionary authorisation regulations legal history; so, for example, the "parallel foreign trade rights" and other similar devices as described above also became obsolete and were therefore abrogated. By the said Decrees No. 7 of 1985 and No. 1 of 1987, as regards Western markets, the branch monopoly has been totally eliminated.

(v) Enterprise autonomy is widened by the provision of law which enabled and still enables (in fact encourages) production and servicing enterprises to establish, separately as well as together, foreign trading corporations to handle their foreign trade operations (*Videoton Ltd* and *Budavox Ltd* are examples of this).

(vi) A significant role was played by the institution of *ad hoc* foreign trade rights, under which an enterprise otherwise not vested with foreign trade rights was authorised to directly effect large transactions. This was and still is the case especially in the various industrial and other long-term cooperation contracts. After the introduction of the normative system as described above, the institution of *ad hoc* foreign trade rights preserved its function in the non-convertible currency sphere as well as regards some specified commodities (Sec. 2 of the Decree No. 1 of 1987). In these latter fields a more "traditional" authorisation procedure has been maintained (Sec. 1, para. 3 of the cited Decree).

(vii) The Foreign Trade Act seeks to ensure that economic entities non-registered or non-authorised to international trade in any of the above forms are also actively involved in the operations of the enterprises concluding foreign trade contracts in or on their behalf, that they participate in the contracting process, and that, in general, the linkage between production and trade, between the domestic and the foreign market should be closer in this respect as well. This objective is served by the provision of Art. 15 that "contractual relations between the enterprises vested with foreign trade rights and the production, commercial or servicing ones shall be adjusted to national economic interests. With this end in view measures shall be adopted to bring about cooperation between these economic organisations and to accommodate their economic interests, as well as to ensure transmission of world market effects to production, commercial and servicing organisations". A form by which to translate this general theoretical tenet into practice is likewise prescribed by the Act stating that in the case of transactions concerning cooperation or specialisation in production the economic organisation concerned may, without possessing foreign trade company rights, participate in the preparation and conclusion of contracts, but it shall also be bound by the provision of law governing foreign trade (Art. 9). Moreover, the Foreign

Trade Act allows foreign trade companies to commission economic organisations or natural persons on an *ad hoc* basis to carry out certain foreign trade tasks falling within their sphere of activity, such as conducting negotiations requiring technical or other special knowledge (Art. 10).

(viii) When looking at the organisational structure of foreign trade, the economic and legal entities of foreign investments should also be mentioned. Economic associations — a fairly recent phenomenon — that operate with mixed or, in exceptional cases, entirely foreign capital in the national territory and are subject to Hungarian law by reason of their place of business may similarly acquire various foreign trade rights under equal conditions with Hungarian enterprises. Special mention of them is justified for two additional reasons. First, they form part, in their origin, of international commercial processes and hence of the enterprise structure of the external economy. Secondly, the multinational companies or joint ventures in customs-free territories have unlimited foreign trade possibilities, including exemption from domestic law governing foreign trade (for a detailed analysis of international investments or joint ventures in Hungary, see *infra* VI).

(ix) While the possibility for cooperative organisations to acquire independent foreign trade rights is decades old, a more sizable role of natural persons (private undertakings) is a recent development. It started with the Decision of 1974, No. 1053 of the Council of Ministers (sec. 3) according to which natural persons, too, may be granted foreign trade rights to perform tasks of a complementary nature. The more recent step is the Decree No. 1 of 1987 of the Minister of Trade, pursuant to which private entrepreneurs and their economic associations (partnerships), patent-holders and artists included, may act directly on foreign trade markets with the permit of the Ministry thereto (sec. 8).

(x) A closer linkage between international and domestic economic processes, between foreign trade and production is facilitated by the possibility and inducement for foreign trade companies to be involved more directly in the development programmes of export-oriented domestic enterprises, namely to form foreign trade associations for the efficient execution of joint investment projects by pooling uncommitted financial resources, establishing joint ventures for that purpose (e.g. *Interinvest*) and affording to domestic producing enterprises external economy-oriented incentives through foreign trade associations as well.

(xi) An essential element of the organisational structure of foreign trade at the enterprise level, as also of the development of their organic unity referred to above, is the foreign-market organisation of enterprises vested with foreign trade rights, namely the fact that such enterprises have enterprises, economic interests and representations abroad (Art. 13 of the Foreign Trade Act; Joint Decree No. 4, 1975 of the Minister of Foreign Trade and the Minister of Finance on Economic Undertakings Abroad).

B. *The contribution of contract law*

In addition to the said organisational solutions, a better accommodation of production and foreign trading considerations is being served by the system of contract law under which foreign trade-related domestic contracts of enterprises with foreign trade rights, and those of other domestic companies are currently carried into effect. It should be kept in mind that all non-registered or non-authorised economic entities for foreign trade must perform their imports and exports through entities with the said registration or authorisation, and this via contractual channels.

The legal regulation currently in force enables foreign trade companies and production or commercial enterprises to choose the contract form of their domestic but foreign trade-related commercial transactions. The relevant legislation (Government Decree No. 32/1967 IX. 23, as amended by Decree No. 54/1978 of the Council of Ministers) puts notable emphasis on foreign trade commission contracts and foreign trade association contracts. These two types of contract are best suited to accommodate the interests of production and commerce and thus serve the interests of both parties on foreign markets, while transmitting most directly the effects and demands of foreign markets to the sphere of domestic production. A noteworthy element of both contract types is the material interest of foreign trade companies in entering into and executing transactions under favourable conditions, whereas the risk factors of foreign trade transactions are not concentrated on the side of foreign trade companies alone, as for example is the case for contracts of delivery on own account, but are divided between the commercial (foreign-trading) and production enterprises.

In the sphere of foreign trade, commission contracts are followed in importance by association contracts, which play a growing role especially in exports.

It deserves a short separate subsection to emphasise that, as a result of the above development, the *ownership basis* of foreign trading activity also changed drastically. Whereas in the traditional concept of the foreign trade monopoly of the state, foreign trade was claimed to be based on state ownership, now we have a totally comprehensive ownership structure. This relies on all types of property, including, besides state property, also cooperative, foreign and domestic private property which is surely a challenging new phenomenon.

C. *The role of the Hungarian Chamber of Commerce*

Besides the different economic units at the enterprise level, an important institution of the enterprises, namely the Hungarian Chamber of Commerce, recently called, the Hungarian Economic Chamber, should also be mentioned. There are also other similar social organisations (e.g. those of the cooperatives, the private small-scale business, etc.), which have a role in promoting foreign trade. The most important one, however, is the Economic Chamber. As a representative, informative and consultative organ of enterprises the Chamber of Commerce has a large membership and exercises wide powers in foreign trade organisation (Sec. 12 of the Decision of the Council of Ministers; Law Decree No. 11/1985 on the Hungarian Chamber of Commerce). In addition to representing the interests of its members, the most important function of the Chamber of Commerce is to promote the attainment of the national economic plan targets and the foreign trade policy objectives and to lend effective support to the production and external economic activities of enterprises. In doing so, the Chamber of Commerce contributes towards deeper relations, constant and mutual information and exchange of views between production, utilising, commercial enterprises and foreign trade companies on the one hand, and between its members and the economic management organs of the State, on the other.

The Chamber maintains wide-ranging international relations; carries out an intense international activity; represents the interests of its members in similar international organisations; cooperates in exploring and procuring new markets and finding new partners; and organises Hungarian economic days with exhibitions and displays to promote the Hungarian economy.

The Chamber may initiate legislation and express its views on bills or other drafts in the preparation of which its experience can be relied upon. With a view to international commercial dispute settlement, it provides facilities for a standing court of arbitration functioning under its auspices, elects and removes its arbitrators, and establishes rules of procedure.

In order to facilitate the legal and technical handling of foreign trade the Chamber publishes in foreign languages the principal Hungarian laws and regulations on foreign trade and prepares compilations of the Hungarian versions of the major international agreements.

As an organ of information the Chamber keeps the Hungarian economic organisations posted on the long-term and current economic development objectives and tasks, on foreign and domestic markets, well-informed on the fundamental laws and regulations affecting the possibilities of enterprises. It also issues publications in Hungarian and foreign languages on topical issues of international economic relations.

III. Commercial representation

The commercial representation is by definition a sign and form of a lasting and commercially substantial presence of a foreign company. It is common knowledge that to be efficient in a market, the intensive and responsible presence of the company is needed. This may take the form of commercial representation which is possible in Hungary to a wide extent.

The Hungarian law on commercial representation of foreign firms rests on two different types of regulation. One of them is the bilateral governmental trade or industrial cooperation agreement. Such an agreement may emphasise the importance of commercial representation and imposes the obligation on the respective governments to enable and facilitate its operation (e.g. US-Hungarian Trade Agreement of 1978, Article II; the Hungarian Industrial Cooperation Agreements with Italy of 1974, Articles 1 and 8; with France of 1974, Articles 1, 2 and 7; with Austria of 1968, Articles 1 and 4). The other type of regulation is based on domestic law (Article 25 of the Foreign Trade Act, Decree Number 8 of 1974 of the Minister of Foreign Trade on the general commercial representation of foreigners and Decree Number 1 of 1977 of the Minister of Finance on the representation of foreign banking institutions).

A. *Legal forms*

The legal forms of general commercial representation determined by Hungarian regulation are the following:

1. The foreigner may have his business interests represented by a specialised Hungarian representation agency within the framework of a commercial contract, requiring no specific permission;

2. Similarly, no specific permission is needed if the foreigner stays only temporarily in Hungary to discharge its representation activity. However, a licence of the Ministry of Foreign Trade is needed for the three forms of representation mentioned under (3) to (5);

3. The foreigner may establish his own trade office within the framework of the Hungarian agency mentioned above under (1);

4. The foreigner may enter an economic association for trade representation with such agencies or with other Hungarian economic entities;

5. The foreigner may establish his own independent, direct commercial representation.

B. *Sphere of activities*

The sphere of activities of the foreigner's commercial representation operating with Hungarian participation or that of direct representation may cover the following:

1. Negotiating contracts between the foreigner, represented by the representation and the domestic organisation entitled to foreign trade activity and the preparation and conclusion of such contracts.

2. Operation of a stock on commission, customer service, and servicing for goods delivered by the foreigner or for services rendered by him.

3. Commercial information and promotional activities and arranging the foreigner's participation in exhibitions, fairs, shows, professional lectures and similar events.

The representation of foreign banking institutions is meant to serve the interest and enlargement of international financial and banking relations. Such representation may do business in the sphere defined in the licence issued by the Minister of Finance. The agent performs his activity in the name of the foreign banking institutions, observing the provisions of the existing statutes.

IV. Investment activities in Hungary by cooperation contracts (contractual joint ventures)

A. *General legal forms of investment activity*

To perform economic activities as a legal entity in Hungary means to be in the country either through commercial representation or through a subsidiary, branch office, or through a joint venture company. Whatever the form, legal personality is required which is normally established by company law and the rules on commercial representation. The institutions described in company law are the general legal forms of investment activity.

B. *Long-term cooperation contracts*

However, there are other forms by which investments with foreign contributors materialise, by which foreign investment, goods, technology and know-how are transferred to Hungary and transformed into a turn-key modern plant. One such possible form is the long-term cooperation contract which provides for the transfer of goods, know-how and technology. Examples are the Hyatt and Forum hotels in Budapest built by Austrian constructors, a plant producing truck and bus components built by French and German firms, and the Hungarian-owned Hilton Hotel. These have been realised by investment contracts of substantial magnitude without direct company law involvement. They were big transactions accomplished by foreign companies from abroad without joint ownership implications and without complicated company establishment procedures.

Hungary exploits this form of economic cooperation with Western firms to the mutual benefit of the partners for long periods stipulated by the contract, often creating a pseudo-company relationship. According to statistics the number of such cooperation contracts goes into several hundreds. Their real economic magnitude is, as against joint venture companies, outstanding; it also represents a high percentage in the whole foreign trade turnover. It has proven to be a good and flexible form of cooperation. Its advantages are flexibility, exclusion of ownership implications and establishment procedures, a better taxation situation, more independence of the partners, less risk as compared to investing in company shares, and the possibility of less but more certain profit. Its disadvantages may be the lack of direct control and management of the joint business by the foreign partner, the possible harm of a changing economic situation, and no real presence in the domestic market.

There are legal rules on cooperation contracts. One of them requires specific licences for long-term cooperation contracts. It is not a classical export or import licence issued by the Ministry of Foreign Trade but a licence for a long-term cooperation agreement which will be issued by the licensing authority. It is therefore subject to somewhat more intensive scrutiny. It should be emphasised, however, that this licence also has to be arranged by the Hungarian party, and the foreign partner does not need permission to perform its contractual obligations in Hungary.

The other rule to be mentioned seems to be in contradiction with what has just been stated. In particular cases the foreign partner may be considered as being a legal entity residing in Hungary. There is no doubt, that most of the cooperation contracts are fulfilled without any lasting presence or working site of the foreign partner in Hungary, but some of them may require a lasting presence of the representatives of the foreign company, and others may require a working site operated by the foreign partner. If the foreigner is present to fulfil its performance under the cooperation contract, he will not need any permission or licence for this presence (Article 25 of the Foreign Trade Act, 1974). However, if he maintains a working site and stays beyond a certain period of time, he will come under taxation rules, e.g. foreigners who stay in Hungary as legal entities established in Hungary.

Cooperation contracts are considered very essential also by intergovernmental trade or industrial cooperation agreements. Not only do they emphasise their importance, but also they specify the fields or industries in which the contracting parties would prefer to promote this form of economic cooperation. In addition, the governments assume different obligations to facilitate the increasing practice of cooperation contracts.

Hungarian regulation of the commercial law elements of cooperation contracts is very flexible. As it is well known, in Hungarian law there is no specific type of contract for cooperation contracts — as opposed to sale, barter, licensing or other types of contract —, but the Hungarian Civil Code, as the main source of Hungarian commercial law, grants total freedom of contract. They may draft contracts which have elements of different contract types. The whole contract will then come under the general rules of contract (Civil Code, Sec. 198 *et seq.*).

Where a cooperation contract comes under Hungarian law, the Hungarian commercial law rules pertaining to contracts will apply. The parties are also totally free to stipulate any law to govern their contract.

Elements which, according to Hungarian contractual practice, are usually part of cooperation contracts are the following:

1. The subject-matter of the contract is defined by the nature of the economic transaction. It covers or may include feasibility studies, design, and provisions for carrying out civil engineering, erection of a project, installation of equipment and machines supplied by the seller, the stipulated technology, the stipulated per quantum output, test-runs, necessary tooling, and joint-marketing of the commodities to be produced;

2. Licence and know-how transfer conditions;

3. Technical assistance and training;

4. Conditions on the site (energy, telephone, water, living quarters or accommodation for the seller's staff, sanitary measures, etc.);

5. Supply of spare parts;

6. Timing of performance;

7. Warranty provisions;

8. Quality investigation, acceptance and certificates;

9. Insurance scheme;

10. Price and payment procedures and eventual buy-back or barter elements;

11. Resolution of legal disputes including applicable law, jurisdiction and *force majeure* clauses.

V. Foreign-owned companies and subsidiaries

To be the exclusive owner of a company or to run a subsidiary is not very common in Hungary due to the socialist character of the economy. After World War II, private capital was nationalised and private companies were transformed into state-owned enterprises. Ever since then, the economy has been expanding on the foundation of social ownership. This transformation also affected foreign companies.

Those foreign companies (e.g. IBM, a registered company in Hungary) which have not been nationalised, are mostly agency companies for their parent company. They operate according to the rule of commercial companies, as regulated by the relevant provisions of the Hungarian Commercial Code 1875 and by Act Number V of 1930 (as subsequently amended).

There is no new regulation either on the admission or on the operation of the exclusively foreign-owned companies. This indicates that, although many forms of foreign business are welcome in Hungary, exclusively foreign-controlled capital was not meant to expand substantially. This does not mean that this channel is closed altogether. Article 25 of the Foreign Trade Act provides a viable method for this form to be used. Foreigners need to obtain permission for their business activity if it exceeds the scope of usual foreign trade contracts. The growing awareness of the need for licences for cooperation contracts, commercial representations and joint ventures as prescribed by the above mentioned Article 25 has encouraged a new detailed regulation in that area of the law. The exclusively foreign-owned economic unit will have to start and conduct its business activity according to the conditions defined by the licence. This licence will probably be more detailed than in the case of the preferred business forms. This will be, at least in part, a *ius speciale* for such an undertaking as against the *ius generale* of the normal regulations for the other forms. The future will show whether and to what extent this method will become more widely used.

VI. Corporate joint ventures in Hungary

A. *The investment laws (joint venture legislation) and legal writing*

1. *Joint venture legislation.* Hungary was second — after Yugoslavia — in opening up the economy for international investments in corporate form. Beginning with the early seventies when in 1970 the fundamental and in 1972 more specific regulations were enacted, foreign investments by joint venture companies became most welcome.

Other socialist countries, such as Bulgaria, Romania, Poland, Yugoslavia, China and recently the Soviet Union have also provided the opportunity for joint ventures. This is additional evidence that the considerations and the guarantees by the relevant law discussed below should convince the foreign investors that these new forms are not transient or accidental efforts only to cure some ephemeral or marginal problems.

The basic sources of law for joint ventures are the Law-Decree No. 19 of 1970 on domestic economic associations (amended by Law-Decree No. 4 of 1978), Article 31 admitting foreign participants, and the Decree No. 28 of 1972 of the Minister of Finance — as the general regulation of this institution — on the economic associations with foreign participation in joint ventures. Additionally, amending regulations of the Ministry of Finance were passed, *inter alia*: Decree No. 7 of 1977, No. 35 of 1978, No. 63 of 1982, and Order No. 5 of 1979 of the Minister of Finance as amended by Order No. 110 of 1985 on the same issue (For a more complete list of the relevant enactments see Annex No. 1).

These are the main regulations of the new socialist company law in Hungary regarding joint ventures (while the legal rulings on the joint ventures in customs-free territories will be discussed separately below). They contain the new strategic rules, such as the guarantees for foreign investors, equity ratio of the foreigners, admission procedures, taxation, decision-making, etc.

At the same time, these sources rely on the Commercial Code of 1875 and Act Number 5 of 1930 for the company forms and company law rules of joint venture companies. In case of contradiction the new regulations supersede the old. The former source (the Commercial Code) regulates the joint stock or publicly held company (*Aktiengesellschaft*) while the latter applies to the limited liability or closed company (*GmbH*); it goes without saying that today both operate in their amended-modernised form.

2. *Legal writing — theoretical considerations.* Ever since joint venture or investment codes have been introduced in Hungary (and in other socialist countries), intensive attention has been paid to this phenomenon both by economists and lawyers, resulting in a growing output in the professional media (see Annex No. 2 which gives a list of the main Hungarian publications).

a. *The joint venture ownership-issue.* While legal writing covers almost all theoretical issues and the relevant questions of practice in this field, we will focus here on one problem only. This — a question of principle — is to face the ownership-implication of joint ventures. In other words: how, by which theoretical and other considerations, could socialist legal thinking accommodate foreign private equity (property) presence in a country where this is (or should be) *prima facie* contrary to the socialist ownership system? The main element of justifying a positive answer can be seen in the following considerations.

The main problem is the ratio of non-socialist holdings. As long as this is within the limits beyond which the socialist character of the ownership starts to become questionable, foreign investments can be accommodated without prejudice to the ownership structure as a whole. The question of where this limit would be has not yet really been raised. Surely, because the actual magnitude of foreign investments seems to be far from the desired level. Much more is expected and encouraged.

b. *The private property-issue.* The other problem of principle is the presence and protection of private property, its presence besides state, cooperative and other social and personal (individual) property. While personal property, in socialist terminology, covers means serving the personal needs of individuals (housing, holiday homes and all kinds of movables for personal use), means of production operated by others than state-owned, cooperative and other social entities, i.e. by individuals (both nationals and foreigners) and foreign companies come under the legal category of private property. In some host countries then, the answer to the foreign equity position is the non-exclusion of private property. This is the case, e.g. in Poland and Hungary, where private property is limited but not excluded. Both the Constitution and Civil Code of Hungary recognise the socially useful complementary activity of private property. There are two limits: it must not prejudice public interest on the one hand, and on the other, it cannot operate goods declared by law to be exclusively state property (which is a definite and limited category); thus, there is no technical property law hindrance in accommodating foreign private holdings. In other countries (such as Bulgaria, China and Romania) joint investment laws specifically admit and protect foreign property with regard to joint venture investments. The Constitution of 1982 of the People's Republic of China states that foreign investment is encouraged and that the law of the People's Republic protects the lawful rights and interests of investors. The Yugoslav answer to the issues in question is its special concept of joint ventures: the channelling of foreign investment benefits (management control and profits) by a special contract law mechanism rather than by equity holdings, whereby ownership implications are largely eliminated.

The very positive considerations mentioned above on the one hand and, on the other, these property law approaches, surely outweigh the mostly ideological reservations which emerged in the first years.

Furthermore, there are the different special legal guarantees offered by the capital importing countries, expressing thereby their commitments to the reasonable activity of foreign investors in joint ventures (see *infra* VI, B, c.1).

Finally, there is the opinion that the ownership element should not be overemphasised. Modern corporation law and business practice is less interested in abstractions of ownership. It is really the rights, power and benefits both parties may derive or retain that count. Since this can be substantiated both in the Yugoslavian model and in the other, the theoretical difficulties, so it is thought, should not be overexposed and they need not concern the foreign investor too much. The socialist theory and new practice in question, as indicated above, could justify its move in this area. And the foreign investor can see, as will be shown hereafter, that in these countries he may negotiate his rights such as to take a share in the profits, in management, transfer or sell his interest, remit profit share abroad on payment of any withholding tax, to repatriate profit or the value of his share of the assets in case of termination (for citations and sources of the above analysis, see the author's study in Annex No. 2 "Special Rules . . .", section 39/3).

B. *Major elements of the legal structure of joint venture companies in Hungary*

1. *Formation requirements.* Formation includes first some general preconditions and, secondly, more detailed formation requirements. The major rules on the general preconditions are set forth in the new joint venture legislation (in the investment code, basically in the Decree No. 28 of 1972 referred to above), whereas the formation rules *stricto sensu* come, as a rule, under the general company law (the mentioned Commercial Code, etc., see *supra* VI, B, a.).

a. *General preconditions.* The more important general preconditions relate to the following questions:

(i) Who may be a party to (or who may form) joint ventures? With regard to foreign partners the regulations do not differentiate between a one-man firm, a company or any other economic organisation. Any of these entities may associate with a Hungarian economic organisation. The only requirement is that the foreign partner should be a solid, trustworthy, competent and well-known firm in the field of planned joint undertakings. Hungarian partners must be economic organisations and legal persons active in the economy.

(ii) For what kind of activity can joint ventures be formed? What is their admitted subject-matter? The subject-matter may extend — on the basis of the members' mutual interest — to activities in production, trade and servicing in order to develop the technical and economic level. All activities are considered as promoting development of the technical and economic levels in Hungary including adaptation of high technologies, the attainment of more up-to-date production and organisational techniques, the extension of existing market-networks, the increase of exports, and other advantages in foreign exchange policy.

(iii) The possible company forms are the next issue. There are five company forms offered by the new regulation. There is the commercial partnership (*Offene Handelsgesellschaft, OHG* in German terminology), the publicly held or joint stock company (*Aktiengesellschaft*) and the closed or limited liability company (*Gesellschaft mit beschränkter Haftung, GmbH*). In addition, two new company forms have been introduced by the new Hungarian company law (Law Decree No. 4 of 1978). One of them, called joint enterprise, is, with some simplification, a new version of the commercial partnership; the other could qualify as a limited liability company. Both are legal persons with detailed regulations.

The joint venture companies established so far have taken either the form of the traditional joint stock company or that of the limited liability company. It is very likely that these will be the company forms used in the future simply because they are well-known company law institutions. Foreign partners should anticipate using these two forms under these names, for they offer a modern system for cooperation.

(iv) Members shall fix their contributions according to the rules governing the actual formation of the association. The total amount of contributed capital by the foreign member generally may not exceed 49 p.c. but the

Minister of Finance may grant exceptions to this requirement. For example, this was the case with the International Investment Bank established in Budapest with a 66 p.c. foreign share, i.e. French, Italian, West German and Japanese, and a 34 p.c. Hungarian share. The contribution of the members is to be carried out by conveyance of the cash or kind to the joint venture as fixed in the memorandum of association.

(v) As far as the formation process is concerned, let us refer to the approval and incorporation rules of the mentioned Decree No. 28 of 1972. As a rule, the procedure of establishing a joint venture starts with a corresponding initial common understanding of the future partners. This will be transcribed in mutual commitments resulting in the memorandum and articles of the planned joint venture. The memorandum and articles of association, as well as any amendments to them, are effective with the approval of the Minister of Finance. The application for approval shall contain all data from which it can be judged whether the realisation of the purposes indicated above can be expected to be carried out by association.

The Minister of Finance will pass his resolution after hearing the opinion of an Interdepartemental Expert Committee. This pre-registration review is performed by professionals who have necessary expertise and competence. Finally, to come into existence it is required that the association be entered in the Commercial Register, administered by the Municipal Court of Budapest.

General company law has very detailed and specific rules on the whole formation process.

b. *The rules on joint stock or publicly held companies.* As to the joint stock or publicly held company (*Aktiengesellschaft*), the short survey *infra* shows that the rules of the Commercial Code (as amended and operating today) meet the requirements of modern company law in general.

The publicly held or joint stock company may be founded with capital consisting of shares determined by the number and nominal value and held by the shareholders of the company. The shareholders are liable for the debts of the company only to the extent of their shares. A condition for the establishment of the company is the entering of the company in the trade register. The securing of the capital is carried out by subscription. The memorandum of association contains the amount of the capital, the number and nominal value of the shares and possibly the subject and value of the investment in kind. At subscription 10 p.c. of the nominal value of each share subscribed has to be paid in cash. The company promoters must invite the subscribers to the statutory meeting within two months of closing subscriptions. A quorum exists if at least seven subscribers are present who represent at least one third of the capital. It is the task of the subscribers attending the statutory meeting to determine the value of the investment in kind although they are not empowered to increase the value determined in the memorandum of association. Moreover, it is the task of the subscribers at the statutory meeting to decide on the acceptance of the articles of association, and the election of the governing organs (Managing Board and Board of Supervision). The articles of association determine, among other things, the name of the firm, seat, purpose and duration of the company, the voting system, the amount of the capital, the number and nominal value of the shares, the method of paying for such shares, and the quality of the shares as negotiable instruments. When the articles of association are entered in the trade register, it has to be certified that the whole capital is secured by subscription and that at least 30 p.c. of the capital is paid. The company is, as a rule, prohibited to buy its own shares.

c. *The rules on closed or limited liability companies.* The main rules of the closed or limited liability company concerning formation as laid down in the Act No. V of 1930 (and amended to its present form) show corresponding similarity with the relevant regulations of modern legislation in other countries. It is a company established with a capital consisting of contributions of determined value. The members of the company are only liable for the debts of the company to the extent of their contributions in cash or kind, fixed in the memorandum of association. The number of members may not be less than two. The company may be established for an indefinite or a definite period. There are three basic conditions for the formation of a closed or limited liability company (similar to those of the joint stock company): drafting the memorandum of association, providing the capital, and entering the company in the trade register. This type of company may be established for any economic purpose. The establishment procedure differs from the joint stock company, *inter alia*, in that the members have to pay their whole contributions prior to registering the incorporation. The memorandum of association includes the purpose of the company, the voting mechanism, the extent of the contributions of the members and the end sum of such contributions. The cash contributions have to amount at least to 30 p.c. of the stock capital. The Act does not fix the proportion of the individual contributions to the capital. There is another deviation from the regulation of the joint stock company, namely the share of capital does not determine the company rights nor is it a negotiable instrument, and securities are generally not issued for the contributions.

2. *Organisation of management.* As far as management is concerned, ultimately it comes down to the investors' power over their undertaking. On this issue the new joint venture legislation relies on the general principles and rules as laid down by the Commercial Code of 1875 (concerning the joint stock company) and the Act No. V of 1930 (concerning the limited liability company), i.e. on the general company law. To anticipate the main rules concerning the investors' power, the following propositions can be made. The decision-making, i.e. the internal power structure of the joint venture as a rule follows the classical principle: the voting power of the partners corresponds to their ratio in the capital. However, they are free to deviate from this general principle: in the memorandum, articles or by-laws they may decide their most appropriate power and voting structure; they may define the rights and obligations of the members concerning management and control of the joint venture, the organs of the company and their power, the method of decision-making and a list of questions on which the members can decide by unanimous decision only.

Besides the means and ways of protecting minority shareholders (similar to those known generally in company law), the former flexibility of the decision-making process is of special importance. In fact, a general minority-protecting arrangement. It was, however, necessary to balance out the general rule that foreigners, as a rule, cannot go beyond the 49 p.c. limit, i.e. they are almost per definition in minority. By the said flexibility, as demonstrated by the practice of the past years, this "handicap" has so far been mastered. This does not mean that a more generous limit would not be more attractive. A more intensive growth of capital flow calls objectively for such an opening.

If we go closer to the organisation of management, the said laws and their recent practice provide this organisation and competence structure of the joint stock and limited liability company as the two main forms of joint venture.

a. *Management structure of joint stock or publicly held companies.* The joint stock or publicly held company should be mentioned first. In Hungarian the name of the company shall use the complement "Részvény-társaság, Rt"; in the case of a joint venture this translates to *Aktiengesellschaft, AG* in German and *Société anonyme, S.A.* in French, and this should be defined in the memorandum, in so far as used by the company in subsequent operations.

The organisational structure follows the classical continental pattern of three organs: it consists of the Shareholders' Meeting or General Assembly, the Board of Directors and the Supervisory Board. It goes without saying that the law regulates thoroughly the composition, convocation, venue and other questions of these organs (basically along the lines of modern company law principles). What we should focus on here is the competence or decision-making power as practiced by these organs.

The *General Assembly*'s main prerogatives include, *inter alia*, the following competences: election and recall of the members of the Board of Directors and the Supervisory Board; statement of the annual balance and distribution of the profit; merger with another company; raising or reducing the capital stock; the winding-up of the company; amendments of the by-laws; (decisions on the latter four items require the permission of the Minister of Finance and the corresponding amendment of the by-laws (to be entered also into the register at the corresponding court); the shareholders have the right to also refer other matters to the competency of the General Assembly.

Since the law has no explicit rule on the quorum and the necessary majority, these issues come under the rulings of the by-laws and the shareholders' decisions. The same applies to the voting mechanism as referred to above. Proxy voting is allowed.

The *Board of Directors*' competency includes, besides acting as operative body of the company (managing the actual day-to-day activity of the company, representing the company towards authorities and third persons, i.e. exercising the so-called general powers, which, however, may be limited either by laws or by General Assembly decisions), the completion of the accounts and the annual balance, preparation and convocation of the General Assembly, keeping the company's books, notification of the Court of Registration of acts and facts determined by law (e.g. the balance sheet, amendment of by-laws, protocols of the shareholders' meeting, etc.).

The Board of Directors consists — according to the law — of one or more persons, who are elected for a definite or indefinite period as defined by the by-laws. In Hungarian practice the Managing Director or General Manager (usually a member of the board of Directors) attends to the day-to-day business, while the Board passes the major operative decisions in accordance with the General Assembly's strategic rulings.

The *Supervisory Board* consists of three or more persons; its establishment is mandatory. Its function extends to the control of the company's activity. Accordingly, it has the right to look into the company's books, files and cash at any time, to request information from the actually managing bodies on the state of affairs. What comes under the mandatory competency of the Board is the review of the balance sheet and the proposed division of profit before these are submitted to the General Assembly; furthermore it has to convoke the General Assembly in the case of any measure violating the law or by-laws by the operative managing organs and persons, or any misuse against the company's interests.

b. *Management structure of limited liability or closed companies.* The limited liability or closed company's organisation of management — organs and their competency — as regulated by the said Act No. V of 1930 reflects in its present day formulation (namely pursuant to the intervening amendments) a modern company law pattern.

The limited liability company (*"Korlátolt felelósségú társaság, Kft"* in Hungarian, a complement to be used in the name of the company, this translates — in the case of joint ventures — to *Gesellschaft mit beschränkter Haftung, GmbH* in German and *Société à responsabilité limitée, S.a.r.l.* in French, to be incorporated into the memorandum, in so far as used by the company), as should be generally anticipated, is somewhat restricted in its possible scope of activity. According to the said Act No. V of 1930, it cannot engage in underwriting of insurances, in regular banking or money-changing business, the acceptance of saving deposits or the issue of debentures or bonds with negotiable character.

The governing bodies of the company are the Shareholders' Meeting, the Managing Director, the Supervisory Board (mandatory only beyond a certain size of prime capital, otherwise optional), and the Chartered Auditor (the latter may be opted for instead of or besides the Supervisory Board, according to the memorandum which, however, must have a definite provision thereto).

The main competences of the *Shareholders' Meeting* — with a fairly strong freedom of the founders to contract their company structure according to their interests (*Satzungsautonomie*) — include quite a long list of exclusive jurisdiction issues, while others may be referred into this scope by the memorandum. These are, *inter alia*: appointment and recall of the Managing Director and the members of the Supervisory Board, annual balance and profit (division) statement, remuneration of the Managing Director, measures concerning the auditing of the company transactions, claims for damages against the founding members, against the managing members ·and supervisors, conclusion of contracts whose value exceed one fifth of the prime capital, conclusion of transactions between the company and its own members, division and recall of venture shares, merger and liquidation, etc.

The quorum is a memorandum competency. The generally needed majority in normal cases is the simple majority of the value of all shares. Where a qualified majority is required, the memorandum may not deviate from that. The Memorandum may require qualified majority or unanimity also in cases where the law would not do so. While this may extend strong guarantees to all minority members on the one hand, on the other it also may make the company management strongly inflexible if practised in a too strict and rigid way. In the case of joint ventures, where the participation of the foreign partner occasionally may be difficult, the rule can be taken advantage of, which also allows (if so foreseen by the memorandum) the decision-making without the Shareholders' Meeting, i.e. by correspondence, in this case with the accord of all members.

The *Managing Director* or managing member (who may also be a foreign citizen) is responsible for the day-to-day management of the company, for the enforcement of the decisions of the Shareholders' Meeting and for the protection of the company's interests; he represents the company before courts, and towards other authorities or third persons. If more managing directors are appointed (either by the memorandum or subsequently by the Shareholders' Meeting), their joint or sole management responsibilities should be defined; in absence of such disposition joint acting is required by law. The responsibilities and competences of the Managing Director(s), are roughly similar to those of the Board of Directors of the joint stock company indicated above; nevertheless, the list responsibilities and competences may also include additional detailed dispositions according to the preference of the investors defined in the memorandum. It goes without saying that in absence of such agreement, the relevant company law rules apply.

As to the *Supervisory Board*, its functions are similar to those of the joint stock company (supra B/b). With one difference however: by virtue of the memorandum's corresponding dispositions the Supervisory Board may discharge, besides controlling activity, also managing functions in issues not coming under the exclusive jurisdiction of the Shareholders' meeting.

The *Chartered Auditor* is an integral part of the company law constitution in Hungarian law, although optional; nevertheless the memorandum must be explicit on this issue. This function extends to the control of the management, especially accounting (the Hungarian term refers to this by the denomination "hiteles könyvvizsgáló" translating to "chartered (accredited) accountant"). Since foreign investors are mostly not very familiar with the Hungarian accounting system, their preference to also have auditors besides the Supervisory Board seems justified.

3. *Other elements (legal status) of joint ventures*

a. *Guarantees.* An essential element is the rule by which the foreign partner may claim a bank guarantee from the Hungarian National Bank for the possibility that his contributed capital may suffer any damage or loss because of any Hungarian state action. The bank guarantee needs no special requirement (it must be applied for when the memorandum of the joint venture is submitted for approval, it will cover losses up to the amount of the foreign contribution, as according to § 11 of the Decree No. 28 of 1972). Under damaging state action one could imagine, e.g. unlawful discrimination as regards the domestic economic environment (raw-material procurement, marketing, energy supply, taxation, etc.), or a very extreme and unlikely act of expropriation.

The National Bank of Hungary shall transfer abroad the profit and other income due to foreign members in a currency defined in the memorandum of association.

The association's employees of foreign citizenship may transfer from the association 50 p.c. of their income in whatever form of currency as defined in the memorandum of the association.

There are also other guarantees the foreign partner may rely on against theoretical possibilities, fears or materialising of non-commercial risks (damaging state action or nationalisation), although those are surely not envisaged. One of them is the institution of insurance: to buy insurance policies also against political risks. This is a well-known and well-developed practice all over the world (e.g. the OPIC insurance scheme in the US, political insurance policies of the Hungarian insurance companies). The other institutions protecting foreign investments are the bilateral invest-ment-protecting treaties. Their mission is to protect foreign investment against depriving-damaging state actions, recognising such acts as being in the public interest but accompanied by just compensation. Hungary is in the process of developing such treaties with a number of interested countries (recently such agreements have been concluded with the Netherlands, Belgium, Luxemburg, the Federal Republic of Germany, Sweden and Italy).

One should add concludingly that normal state intervention in the activity of a joint venture does not occur more often than is normal in Western countries. The Minister of Finance may order the winding-up of the joint venture if it becomes bankrupt, its debts exceed its assets (lasting insolvency, accordingly if rightful claims against the joint venture cannot be enforced). Should the association conduct an activity different from that stated in the memorandum of association, the Minister of Finance may order the winding-up of the association. Should the association be required to do so for reasons determined in the memorandum of associa-tion or because of the exercise of discretion of the members, the winding-up shall be conducted under the provisions applicable to the company form in question. In the event of the winding-up of any association, the foreign share of assets remaining after the settlement of the debts may be transferred abroad tax-free in the currency defined in the memorandum of association.

In should be noted that in Hungary very recently — Law Decree No. 11 of 1986 — a general reorganisation and bankruptcy law has been introduced. This applies also to joint venture companies. According to this law, prior to the winding-up procedure (which is administered by the courts) preliminary reconciliation or settlement must be attempted aiming at a reasonable reorganisation and solvent activity of the company in question. Creditors are, of course, parties to this procedure, any settlement needing their agreement. A compromise, with similar outcome, is possible also during the court's winding-up procedure.

b. *Distribution of profit; losses.* As to the distribution of profit of the joint venture — this follows strictly the equity participation of the members — the following categories have priority: (a) The company is obliged to set aside a risk fund from its profits; at least 15 p.c. of the annual profit shall be diverted for this purpose until the fund is equal to 10—20 p.c. (as defined by the memorandum) of the capital of the joint venture. (b) The joint venture may provide in the memorandum for an employees' participation (dividend-share) fund financed from the annual profit; this is not expected to exceed 15 p.c. of the total wages paid in the year in question. (c) Of course, the company may decide to reinvest part of the profit. (d) It goes without saying that taxes also have priority before dividends are paid out.

The "distribution" of losses — charging that to the members — is per definiton excluded in all company law forms where the limited liability is a *conditio sine qua non* of the corporate entity. Accordingly, losses must be charged against the assets — the risk fund of the joint venture itself. Should the risk fund not cover the losses and the partners do not settle the losses otherwise voluntarily, the company becomes insolvent leading to the winding-up of the joint venture.

c. *Taxation.* There is only one tax charged against the profit, namely the profit tax (as called by the above said Decree No. 28 1972 of the Minister of Finance), or corporation tax (as recently termed by Decree No. 42 1985 of the Minister of Finance amending the Decree No. 45 1984 of the same Minister on corporation tax).

This tax is — as a general rule — 40 p.c. of the taxable income. Taxable income is the annual profit reduced by the sums set aside for the risk fund and the employees' participation fund.

Besides this general tax rate there are very substantial preferences (tax havens) open to joint ventures. The main ones are the following.

(i) Reinvested tax profit is privileged to various refunds. Profit derived for example from productive (production) activity or operating hotels may have 50 p.c. tax refund if the investment was as high as 50 p.c. of the taxed profits obtained in the previous years and makes at least 5 Million Forints; if the reinvestment amounts to 100 p.c. of the after tax profit and makes at least 10 Million Forints, 75 p.c. tax refund can be requested.

(ii) To encourage and facilitate the initial efforts of joint ventures especially, preferences apply to the "take-off" period. In the sphere of production and the hotel business the rate of corporation tax will be 20 p.c. for the first 5 years and 30 p.c. from the sixth year on condition that the company's share capital exceeds 25 Million Forint either at the time of establishment or during the first five subsequent years and that the share of the foreign partners exceeds 30 p.c.. Joint ventures carrying out activity of outstanding importance for the Hungarian economy, are totally exempt from taxation for the first 5 years and shall pay 20 p.c. of the taxable profit from the sixth year after establishment. The spheres of outstanding importance are listed publicly and include electronics, production of vehicle parts in cooperation, machine building units, packing technology, textile and clothing products of a high processing degree, highly processed food export technologies for material and energy saving, tourism (for the detailed list see the respective Communiqués published in accordance with the said taxation enactments: Economic Associations in Hungary with Foreign Participation — Legal Measures Effective since January, 1986, a Hungarian Foreign Trade Bank Ltd. publication).

It must be noted that the above-mentioned tax regulation must be looked at against the background of the international tax treaties if the foreign investors are actually to know what taxes or additional exemptions they may be subject to. Because of the desire for good economic and political relationships between countries and the fact that the avoidance of double taxation can be a very important factor and motive in strengthening economic and commercial relations, Hungary has signed many agreements on avoidance of double taxation. The bilateral tax treaties with Western countries and their sources in Hungarian law are: Austria, Law-Decree No. 2 of 1976; Denmark, Law-Decree No. 1 of 1976; Federal Republic of Germany, Law-Decree No. 27 of 1979; Italy, Decree No. 53 of 1980 of the Council of Ministers; Japan, Law-Decree No. 18 of 1980; the Netherlands, Act No. V of 1940; Sweden, Decree No. 53 of 1982 of the Council of Ministers; Switzerland, Act No. 6 of 1949; United

Kingdom, Law-Decree No. 15 of 1978; United States of America, Decree No. 49 of 1979 of the Council of Ministers.

d. *General economic and legal environment — national treatment.* The principle of national treatment applies to the various parts of economic environment, labour relations, contractual cooperation with other firms in the daily operation of the joint venture, access to credit and other banking services, foreign exchange rules and foreign trade activity. Joint venture companies come under the same rules as other Hungarian economic entities; except for the *exceptional* state administrative instructions which domestic enterprises may exceptionally receive (with compensation, however, if losses result therefrom); joint ventures cannot be subjected to these instructions.

e. *Special status of joint ventures in customs-free territories.* It is a more recent phenomenon that joint ventures may also be established in so-called 'customs-free territories' as regulated by the new customs rules. The economic and political consideration behind this move is first of all to promote foreign investment in Hungary. This is an advantage other joint ventures do not enjoy. Since such joint ventures in customs-free territories are considered as not residing in Hungary, they are exempt from applying the rules on foreign exchange and foreign trade; no customs duties are imposed on their investment goods in kind, neither do their transactions come under Hungarian customs duties. It is hoped that by these preferences foreign investment capacity will increase in Hungary.

The new sources of law are the joint Decree No. 62 of 1982 of the Minister of Finance and the Minister of Foreign Trade "on the economic associations with foreign participation operating in customs-free territories", Decree No. 63 of 1982 of the Minister of Finance "on the economic association with foreign participation" and the joint Decree No. 64 of 1982 "on the amendment of the joint Decree No. 36 of 1976 on the detailed regulation of the Hungarian law of customs and customs procedure".

As indicated, this form of joint venture is a version (mutation) of the general category of joint ventures as mentioned above. Therefore, the general conditions and rules of the above depicted relevant general regulations apply also to them, as defined by Sec. 8 of the above Decree No. 62. What is of interest here are the preferences and other deviating specialities of the new regulation, adapting the Decree No. 28 of 1972 on joint ventures to the new concept.

Joint venture companies in customs-free territories qualify as foreign companies according to the Hungarian regulations on customs, foreign exchange and foreign trade in general. The transactions of the joint venture have to be made, as a rule, in convertible currency defined by the memorandum of the association; the same applies to the books of the joint venture. The foreign exchange of the joint venture can be kept either in Hungarian or foreign banks, except the share capital must be kept in a Hungarian bank. It goes without saying that the joint venture is also free to use its means of foreign exchange to meet its obligations in Hungary, for example wages, social insurance, taxes, domestic contracts such as land leasing, energy bills, contractors' costs, etc. Hungarian currency may be bought from Hungarian banks.

Hungarian labour law rules apply to foreign employees only if the memorandum and the actual employment contracts are silent. Hungarian employees may get higher salaries and wages than set for the categories in question by domestic regulation.

Although Hungarian company law applies to these joint venture associations, it may be superseded by the above outlined rules and their rational implications. Explicitly excluded are Hungarian rules on the income, wage and price regulation of the enterprises, investment, state control, company funds, except the risk fund, the use of the financial resources and means (i.e. the above tax regulations apply), and the acquisition and use of company vehicles.

The legal supervision over joint ventures in customs-free territories rests with the Minister of Finance. It should be noted that this is really a legal control only and no authorisation to interfere with the normal activity of the company.

A very important disposition in the amendment Decree to the usual joint venture Decree No. 28 of 1972 is that joint ventures operating and having their seat outside a customs-free territory may also be accorded privileges of joint ventures of customs-free territories, namely those set out above. This does not apply to product or other commodity exporting-importing joint ventures unless they move into a customs-free territory; authorisation for this is extended by decision of the Minister of Finance, endorsing the memorandum of the association (Sec. 7 of the cited Decree No. 63).

C. *Broader vistas for further development*

As could be seen in this paper, Hungary has made considerable efforts in this field of international economic cooperation, which is part of its general international economic strategy. Still, a lot remains to be done both in general and in this field in particular. The ca 100 joint ventures established so far with about 100 million US Dollars investment capacity have by far not reached the desired and needed magnitude.

Without going into very analytic details, let us conclude with some propositions — suggested by legal writing and indicated by experiences in practice — in which further steps could contribute to further development.

1. *Need for a general normative system.* In the internal organisational structure of the external economy a general normative system should be (and is envisaged to be) introduced, pursuant to which in East-West relations all economic units could and will have direct access to the international markets, *i.e.* would and will enjoy direct foreign trading rights through a very flexible licensing or registering process by the Ministry of Foreign Trade. Western partners, accordingly, will have very easy access to economic deals and negotiations with a big number of Hungarian economic entities, practically, with all who have a sizable interest in this sphere.

2. *Need for modernisation and consolidation.* The enactments regulating joint ventures need modernisation and consolidation. As witnessed by the Annex No. 1, *infra* p. 180 the enactments are so numerous, different in their source of law ranking and in the strategies they primarily served when they came into existence as part of the general company law reform now in progress in Hungary, that the joint venture legislation has to receive modern and consolidated, high-level (i.e. legislation by parliamentary act) comprehensive regulation. This must incorporate all relevant institution (such as enterprise autonomy to form joint ventures and operate their economy without state intervention, guarantees for investors, the company law institutions, the rule of law, dispositions on public control procedures to preclude unpredictable discretionary actions, etc.). Simultaneously (or immediately after) good foreign language translations and legal information services are needed, not only on joint ventures and company law but also on such issues as patent law, contract law, bankruptcy law, foreign exchange law, etc.

3. *Structural needs of joint ventures.* Finally, to come now to the joint venture (legal) structure itself, a number of efforts are called for by professional expertise and practice, for example further liberalisation of the formation procedure; liberalisation of the 49 p.c. limit-rule; admission of exclusively foreign-operated investments in customs-free territories; acceptance of the joint ventures' production also for the domestic market instead of too strong a preference for export and foreign exchange income; and extension of foreign trade competences to the joint ventures thereby facilitating gradual access of the joint ventures to the greater CMEA market. The latter (the promise of a really sizable market) could induce sizable investments from big (eventually multinational) companies,

amounting to several hundred million US Dollars (besides the ca. 100 million US Dollars investment value of those say 100 smaller joint ventures in operation so far). This could give a real and qualitatively decisive impetus to the catching-up strategy of the Hungarian economy. It goes without saying, all Hungarian economic entities are free in their international transactions to submit themselves to foreign jurisdiction — to courts of arbitration or courts of law — and foreign substantive law. This element too should be incorporated into the new joint venture legislation, as it has been done in other countries.

4. *To conclude.* The list of propositions and efforts to be made could surely be continued. It could also be claimed that such moves do not eclipse perhaps more important factors such as a better international climate, more willingness and less restriction on the Western side, — for example the COCOM-restrictions —, the problem of the lack of convertibility of the Hungarian currency, the need for higher technology and more reliable deliveries, the desirability of a more open intra-CMEA economic enterprise-level intercourse system based on a realistic pricing system, etc. Still, these steps and efforts — e.g. the listed ones — which are within feasibility, should be pushed forward more decisively. *Moving forward* is the only way of further development in general, and of the improvement of the Hungarian domestic and external economy in particular.

Postscriptum

Since the completion of this contribution Hungary has passed Act VI of 1988 on economic associations ("company law"). This new act sets no limits on the percentage of participation of foreign companies. It even provides the possibility of 100 p.c. foreign ownership (editor's note).

Annex 1

Major domestic sources of law

1. Act No. IV of 1959 on the Civil Code of the Hungarian People's Republic as amended by Act IV of 1977.
2. Act III of 1974 on Foreign Trade.
3. Act VI of 1977 on the State enterprises as amended by Law-Decree No. 22 of 1984.
4. Law-Decree No. 13 of 1979 on private international law.
5. Commercial Code of 1875 as amended subsequently, more recently by the Law-Decree No. 11 of 1960 and No. 34 of 1986.
6. Act No. V of 1930 on the limited liability company as amended subsequently, more recently by the Law-Decrees *supra* in footnote 5.
7. Law-Decree No. 19 of 1970 — amended by No. 4 of 1978 — on economic associations.
8. Law-Decree No. 16 of 1985 of the Presidential Council of the Hungarian People's Republic on the court-administered Company Registry.
9. Law-Decree No. 11 of 1985 on the Hungarian Chamber of Commerce (Hungarian Economic Chamber).
10. Decree No. 59/1979 (XII. 24) PM on the Main Index and the Book of Signatories of enterprises, cooperatives and the territorial (or professional) federations of the latter, and of economic associations; amending Decrees: 34/1981 (X. 8) PM, 5/1982 (II. 6) PM, 25/1984 (VII. 8.) PM.
11. Decision No. 1 of 1967 of the Government's Economic Commission on the introduction of the new economic management system.
12. Resolution of the Council of Ministers No. 1053/1974 (IV. 17) Mt on the implementation of Act III of 1974; amendment: Resolution No. 1028/1974 (IV. 13) Mt, Implementing Decree No. 7/1974 (X. 17.).
13. Government Decree No. 47/1984 (XII. 21) on corporation tax and corporation super-tax.
14. Decree No. 32 of 1967 (as amended by No. 54 of 1978) of the Council of Ministers on the domestic contracts of enterprises with foreign trade authorisation.
15. Decree No. 28/1972 (X. 3.) PM of the Minister of Finance on economic associations with foreign participation, together with all subsequent amendments and completions. Amendments in chronological order: Decree 7/1977 (V. 6.) PM of the Minister of Finance; Decree 22/1978 (IX. 19) PM of the Minister of Finance; Decree 35/1978 (XII. 22.) PM of the Minister of Finance; Decree 63/1982 (XI. 16) PM of the Minister of Finance; Order 5/1979 (PK. 10) PM of the Minister of Finance; Order 110/1985 (PK. 14) PM of the Minister of Finance.
16. Decree of the Minister of Finance No. 45/1984 (XI. 21) PM as amended by Decree No. 42/1985 (XII. 22) PM on corporation tax and corporation super-tax.
17. Joint Bulletin No. 8001/1985 (Tg. É. 7.) OT-PM-KkM of the National Planning Office, the Ministry of Finance and the Ministry of Foreign Trade on the scope of outstandingly important activities for the purpose of the implementation of Decree No. 45/1984 (XII. 21) PM on corporation tax and corporation super-tax.
18. Law-Decree No. 6 of 1974 on the Regulation of Acquiring Real Estate by aliens in Hungary; implementing statute: Government Resolution No. 1025/1974 (V. 18.) Mt.
19. Joint Decree No. 62/1982 (XI. 16) PM-KkM of the Minister of Finance and the Minister of Foreign Trade on economic associations with foreign participation established in customs-free territories.
20. Joint Decree No. 64/1982 (XI. 16) PM-KkM of the Minister of Finance and the Minister of Foreign Trade on the amendment of joint Decree No. 39/1976 (XI. 10)

PM-KkM defining the detailed rules of customs law and regulating the customs procedure

21. Decree No. 6/1985 (XI. 6) IM of the Minister of Justice on the Firm Register and Entry of Firms (Incorporation).
22. Decree No. 10/1970 (X. 25) MüM of the Minister of Labour on the work permit of aliens in the territory of Hungary; amendment: Decree 20/1972 (XI. 4) MüM.
23. Decree No. 31/1980 (IV. 25) MüM of the Minister of Labour on the completion and amendment of Decree 10/1970 (X. 25) MüM on the work permit of aliens in the territory of Hungary; amendment: Decree 1/1984 (I. 1) ÁMBH
24. Decree No. 8/1980 (X. 24) MuM of the Minister of Labour on the work permit required of Hungarian nationals before entering into the employment of an alien employer in Hungary, further on some rules of the labour relationship thus established.
25. Joint Decree No. 4 of 1975 of the Minister of Foreign Trade and the Minister of Finance on economic undertakings abroad.
26. Decree No. 7/1980 (III. 25) PM of the Minister of Finance on the Service Directorate of the Central Banking Institution.
27. Decree No. 1/1978 (I. 14) KkM of the Minister of Foreign Trade on the free choice between enterprises with foreign trade authorisation.
28. Decree No. 7/1985 (XII. 31) KkM of the Minister of Foreign Trade on the system of granting foreign trading rights and its exercise
29. Decree No. 1/1987 (XII. 29) KEM of the Minister of Trade on the carrying out of foreign trade activity.
30. Decree No. 8/1974 (X. 7) KkM of the Minister of Foreign Trade on the commercial representation of aliens.
31. Joint Decree No. 41/1984 (XII. 17) PM-KkM of the Minister of Finance and of Foreign Trade on the detailed rules of the customs law and the regulation of customs clearance; amending the Joint Decree No. 39/1976 (XI. 10) PM-KkM.
32. Bulletin No. 1/1985 of the Hungarian Foreign Trade Bank Ltd. on the money transactions and crediting of economic associations with foreign participation.

Bibliography

Bán, "Erweiterte Möglichkeiten für ausländische Investitionen in Ungarn", 32 *RIW* No. 6, pp. 429—433, 1986.

Bán-Csanádi-Mádl, "Legal aspects of doing business in Hungary". In: *Legal Aspects of doing businsess in Eastern Europe and the Soviet Union*, D. Campbell (Ed.), Deventer, Kluwer.

Campbell (Ed.), *Legal Aspects of Joint Ventures in Eastern Europe*, Deventer, Kluwer, 1981.

Fekete, *Back to realities*, Budapest, 1982.

Gyertyánffy-Kis, "Magyar-amerikai egyezmény a kettős adóztatás elkerüleseről (US-Hungarian Treaty on the Avoidance of Double Taxation)", *Külgazdaság, Jogi Melléklet*, 1980, No. 3, pp. 1—9.

Káldyné Esze, *Nemzetközi kooperáció — nemzetközi vállalkozások*, (International Cooperation — International Undertakings), Budapest, 1981.

Martonyi, "Joint Ventures in Hungary", in *The Legal Structure of the Enterprise*, Madl (Ed.), Budapest, 1985, pp. 487—498.

Marer, "A működő tőke becsalogatása Magyarországra nyugati szemszögből (Attracting Foreign Equity Capital to Hungary: A Western Perspective)", *Külgazdaság*, 1987, No. 5, pp. 12—25.

Madl, "Die Neuregelung wirtschaftlicher Assoziationen mit ausländischer Beteiligung in Ungarn", *A WD*, 1975, pp. 121—129;

"Beruházások és gazdasági társulások külföldiek részvételével (Foreign Investments and Joint Ventures in Hungary)", *Állam-és Jogtudomány*, 1972, pp. 270—320;

"Special Rules of Foreign Trade and Investment in Socialist Countries", Manuscript, 1985, for the *International Encyclopedia of Comparative Law*, vol. "State and Economy";

The Commercial Laws of the World: Hungary, New York, Oceana Publications Inc. Dobbs Ferry, 1981.

Madl-Vékas, *The Law of Conflicts and Foreign Trade*, Budapest, 1987.

Messmann, *Die rechtliche Stellung ausländischer Direktinvestitionen*, Zürich, 1978.

Nagy, "Multilateral Tax Agreements", *Europe and Taxation*, 1979, pp. 379—388.

Sugar (Ed.) *Joint Ventures in Hungary*, Budapest, 1986.

Varga, "Egy vegyes vállalat története az alapítástól a kezdeti sikererkig (The Story of a Joint Venture from the Foundation to the First Success)" *Külgazdaság*, 1978, No. 5, pp. 26—36.

Vörös, "A tõkés országok vállalataival kötött nemzetközi kooperaciós szerzõdések közgazdasági és jogi problémái (Economic and Legal Problems of East-West Cooperation Contracts)", *Gazdaság — és Jogtudomány*, 1978, No. 1—2, pp. 191—254.

Recent developments in Polish law affecting economic relations with EEC partners

ANDRZEJ BURZYNSKI

Director Legal Information and Service Centre of the Polish Chamber of Foreign Trade, Warsaw

I. Introduction

For a long time trading with Poland was based — at least from the legal point of view — on a simple and quite predictable pattern.

An EEC businessman interested in the Polish market had to locate one of 20 or so Foreign Trade Enterprises set up by the Ministry of Foreign Trade to conduct import-export transactions. Each of them had a specific group of commodities, manufactured goods or services assigned to buy from or offer to a foreign businessman. He therefore had a limited choice as to the partner of a contemplated deal. He also had few possibilities with regard to the selection of a legal framework for doing business in Poland. In the absence of the appropriate legislation allowing foreigners to conduct direct operations inside the country, their links with the Polish markets were restricted to straight-forward sell/buy transactions and occasionally joint co-production proudly called "industrial cooperation".

The foreign businessman's ability to sell in Poland depended first of all on the decision of the State Planning Commission on the allocation of the foreign exchange funds available in a given year to the different branches of the national economy and, secondly, on a further distribution of these funds among the various entities within these branches. Only then the marketing efforts of the foreign exporter directed towards a Foreign Trade Enterprise could bring results.

Receiving cheap foreign exchange (due to the unrealistic currency rates) from the State, every Polish producer was interested in importing and only very few in exporting. Exportation could neither increase the producer's importing abilities, since all the proceeds in foreign currency were automatically bought by the State Bank, nor could it earn money due again to low currency rates. Buying from Poland was therefore not always an easy job.

This system of running foreign trade operations neither benefitting the

M. Maresceau (ed.), The Political and Legal Framework of Trade Relations Between the European Community and Eastern Europe. ISBN 0–7923–0046–7.
© *1989 by Kluwer Academic Publishers, Dordrecht – Printed in the Netherlands.*

national economy nor particularly gratifying foreign partners had to go and it fortunately, even though belatedly, did. Consequently, an EEC businessman revisiting Poland after a prolonged absence will find himself in a significantly different legal environment offering relatively greater freedom and incentives for doing business.

The main features of this environment as well as their possible further modifications are discussed below.

II. Whom to trade with in Poland

In February 1982 the law concerning authorisations to carry out foreign trade transactions was enacted by the Polish Parliament (Journal of Laws No 7, item 59 as amended). The law, while preserving the State monopoly of foreign trade, abolished the exclusive position enjoyed by Foreign Trade Enterprises to conduct export-import transactions. The law provided that the authorisation to participate in foreign trade may be granted to every legal or natural person who meets the conditions specified in its provisions. In that way not merely State enterprises may be granted the right to engage directly in business with foreign partners, but also cooperatives, various kinds of social organisations engaged in economic operations, and also private businessmen and the companies set up by them.

The condition for obtaining an authorisation to engage in foreign trade was initially that the enterprise (or the individual) applying for such a licence earmarked at least 25 p.c. of its sales, or sales representing a value exceeding 1 thousand million Zlotys (1 U.S. Dollar = 300 Zlotys) for export. The meeting of that condition was not required in instances in which the applicant was a party to a cooperation contract with partners abroad, or produced goods for export from materials supplied by them. The decision turning down the authorisation could be appealed against in the administrative courts. In the five years of the operation of the law 528 authorisations were granted. This figure included 328 authorisations issued to private individuals, mostly artisans. In comparison with the earlier mentioned figure of the Foreign Trade Enterprises monopolising export-import transactions in Poland before 1982, this development certainly enlarges the choice of Polish partners available to EEC business-men. The number of companies and individuals authorised to carry out foreign trade operations should soon grow even faster as a result of the most recent amendments to the discussed law. As of 23 October 1987 the requirement of 25 p.c. export sales as a prerequisite for obtaining the foreign trade authorisation by an applicant was reduced to only 5 p.c. It was announced at the same time that no authorisation will be required to import or export goods and services placed on a special list by the Minister of Foreign Economic Relations.

Not only foreign trade has become accessible to Polish producers, but also important changes were introduced into the structure and operation of former Foreign Trade Enterprises. Most of them were reorganised into companies with limited liability in which the stock was offered to the producers. Thus they have become more responsive to the needs and expectations of end-users of imported goods and manufacturers of exported products. As of 1 January 1988 they will no longer be restrained in their foreign trade operations with regard to specific goods and commodities. In practical terms this means that deprived of their monopolistic position, they will now need to compete for domestic and foreign customers.

The considerable increase of the freedom of manufacturing state enterprises in their access to international trade is accompanied by their quite independent position as regards the organisation of their own production operations. An essential element thereof is a far-reaching autonomy in the determination of their own economic plans. The interference of State administration bodies in this area has been reduced to a minimum. Those bodies can impose additional tasks on the enterprises created by them only in exceptional cases. One such instance is the necessity of meeting the State's international obligations. Indispensable, however, in such instance is the issuing by the task-imposing body of the means, required for its implementation, and the conclusion with the enterprise of an appropriate contract to the same effect. If, when implementing the decision of the supervisory body, the enterprise suffers a loss, it is able to claim compensation, and may take such a claim to court.

III. Foreign trade financing

Locating a Polish partner legally capable of engaging in a foreign trade transaction is always a necessary step towards a successful deal. However, enjoying the required legal status and having the access to adequate foreign exchange funds might be two different things. And naturally the latter quality of a Polish partner would for the EEC businessman not be less important than the former.

The changes introduced in the foreign trade financing system over the last five years mark a significant although not always smooth departure from the previously centrally-controlled allocation of foreign exchange. Beginning in 1982 all exporters in Poland were given a right to retain a part of the hard currency proceeds from export sales. The volume of retained quotas varied and in the case of State enterprises it was determined by means of an individual decision from the Minister of Foreign Trade. The Minister's decision was largely based on an assessment of the exporter's requirements for imported spare parts, raw materials and components. Scientific institutions were authorised to retain 50 p.c. of their proceeds whereas cooperatives' and craftsmen's quotas were fixed at 20 p.c. The system, however, had its weak spot. The amounts which exporters were entitled to retain were not effectively deposited on exporters' accounts, but were changed into Polish currency by the banks, while the exporters retained in fact the right to buy them back in future. Under constant demand for foreign currency and deprived of the normal credit facilities due to the Polish debt situation, the banks could not effectively operate this system. Therefore, it had to be revamped at the beginning of 1987.

Now the retained portion of the export proceeds is deposited on the interest earning foreign exchange account of the exporter in a Polish bank. The accumulated funds can be used to buy raw materials, components, spare parts, tools, machinery and equipment needed for production not only by the exporter himself but also by the producers providing him with components. The retained amounts can also be used by the exporter for credit repayment. The financing of imports from the retained export proceeds is available, however, only for those who managed to sell their products or services on hard currency markets. What about the others who although selling to domestic or CMEA markets are nevertheless in need of imports to be paid for in exchangeable currency? There are several options open for them. One of them has already been mentioned — participation in the retained quotas from the exporter of the final product. The other — open to the manufacturers of consumer goods — was to take advantage of the exchangeable currency auctioned by the Commercial Bank to the bidders offering to use it for the increased production of consumer goods.

Quite recently, a completely new possibility to obtain foreign exchange for business purposes was opened up in Poland. Those who held deposits in exchangeable currencies in their retained quotas accounts, can offer the "rights" to buy these currencies to the highest bidder on the money market organised twice a month by the Export Development Bank in Warsaw. Those manufacturers contemplating export-oriented production can also obtain credits and loans in foreign currency from the Commercial Bank and the Export Development Bank. They are however, to be repaid in the same currency.

The different possibilities to finance the foreign trade operations presented above supplement, but do not replace imports financed in Poland from centralised funds. This year this kind of financing will amount to 2,2 billion U.S. Dollars, while imports financed from amounts retained by exporters will reach 1,6—1,7 billion U.S. Dollars. The trend towards increasing the share of imports paid for from retained export proceeds of individual producers is quite strong.

For EEC businessmen, it may signify the further diversification of the Polish market. The participation in foreign trade operations on the Polish side of a greater number of the independent business entities having first to earn foreign exchange and then to spend it in a most effective way might also result in a more innovative approach towards the choice of legal instruments in their economic relations with foreign partners. The straightforward sale might thus more often be replaced by joint production, joint development or joint distribution agreements with the appropriate licensing and other arrangements.

It is indeed in the area of the legal forms available for economic cooperation between foreign and Polish partners that the most significant developments have recently taken place in Poland and these are embodied in the brand new Joint Venture law.

IV. The joint venture law

On 23 April 1986, Polish Parliament passed the Law on Companies with Foreign Capital Participation. This law paved the way for foreign investors' direct involvement in the economic activity in Poland. Until then, foreign companies and individual enterpreneurs wishing to partici- pate in Poland's economic life could do so by setting up agencies and branch offices. Beginning in 1976 they could also establish light industry firms on their own or with Polish corporate bodies and natural persons. In 1982 the scope of foreign investor activity in Poland was expanded by the Banking Law, which allowed the establishment of banks in Poland as stock companies with foreign capital participation. However, as foreign companies and their Polish partners have long been claiming, the Polish legal system lacked detailed regulations that would clearly and unequivo- cally lay down the rules which Polish and foreign entrepreneurs could follow to carry out joint economic activity on a large scale.

The 1986 Law was the long-awaited act that bridged the gap. The Law allows foreign investors to take part in virtually any sphere of Poland's economic life, provided the investment activity takes the legal form of a company with a Polish economic organisation participation. It also contains few restrictions but allows exceptions based on well-substantiated economic evidence. The Law does not require a minimum contribution by the foreign investor to the company's initial capital. But the contribution may not exceed 49 p.c. of the capital. However, exceptions may be made if there are well-substantiated economic reasons for them.

To set up such a company, the parties involved must apply for a permit, and the Minister of Foreign Economic Relations in consultation with the Finance Minister must sanction it. Both delegation of the consent to the Minister of Foreign Trade and provision for substantial income tax reductions for export production reveal the Law's underlying intent. Clearly, its framers hope that capital cooperation with foreign partners including transfer of technology, new methods of organisation, and additional financial aid from abroad will boost the export potential of the Polish economy.

The Polish economy can only reap the benefits of such a programme, if foreign investors are persuaded that their investment will be safe and profitable. For this reason, after long and penetrating discussions, Parliament embodied the principles of foreign capital participation in law. Also for this reason, the Law offers the foreign investor favourable taxation rights as well as the right to transfer his profits abroad and, upon dissolution of the company his contribution to the company's capital. To this end, the Law authorises the Polish National Bank to give guarantees to those foreign investors who fear they may incur losses because of Polish administrative decisions affecting the company's assets.

Just as the Law is liberal as to the scope of economic activity, in allowing companies with foreign capital participation, it is also very liberal as to the partners a company may select. As for foreign partners, they may be either corporate bodies, natural persons, or unincorporated companies from socialist and capitalist countries. The Law provided equal access to economic activity in Poland.

Since the Law formulates a legal framework for large-scale economic activity, it is clear that the Polish partners in the companies can only be those organisations with adequate means to carry out such an activity; for example, state enterprises, cooperatives, and, what is really very important, universities and research institutes. The latter very often have know-how and patents whose skilful implementation in production may result in significant economic achievements. In adopting a legal form for capital cooperation between Polish and foreign partners, the Law relies on the traditional international economic operations of companies structured according to the Polish Commercial Code of 1934. Thus companies with foreign capital participation will operate as either limited liability companies or joint stock companies. Both forms of company, under Polish law, enjoy corporate status, with partners liable for the company's obligations only to the extent of their assets. The partners determine company relations, membership of its authorities (board of directors, supervisory board), and decision-making procedures in the articles of incorporation. In giving the partners decision-making freedom on these matters, the Law makes only one reservation: a Polish citizen and resident must be chairman of the Board. According to the Law, one person elected by the company's employees always sits on the supervisory board, the body which controls the board of directors on behalf of the Assembly of the Partners. This last stipulation reconciles the prevailing right of employees to participate in the running of the enterprise with the specific legal situation of the company with foreign capital participation.

As for a partner's contribution to the company's initial capital, the Law, like the Commercial Code, stipulates that it can be made in cash or in kind. In the case of the foreign partner, the money contribution should be either in foreign currency or in Zlotys from documented exchange of foreign currency. The contribution in kind can consist of equipment, raw materials, or patents and other rights; machinery may be imported from or purchased in Poland for Zlotys. The volume and type of the contribution in kind should be included and determined in the company's articles of incorporation and is subject to verification by independent experts at the request of the body which granted the permission.

In its economic activity the company enjoys equal rights with all larger economic organisations in the country, that is, with state enterprises and cooperatives. Moreover, in some areas the Law of 1986 expands these rights. It allows the permission to include rules and procedures for obtaining the raw materials, machines, and so forth that are indispensable for production, as well as rules of product marketing other than are envisaged for state enterprises.

The financing of the company is subject essentially to the same rules as the financing of state enterprises, with, however, some important differences. In contrast to all economic organisations operating in Poland, which are obliged to sell to the State at least 50 p.c. of their proceeds in foreign currency, the company with foreign capital participation must sell only 15 to 25 p.c. of such proceeds. Furthermore, in some economically justified cases, the Minister of Foreign Trade in consultation with the Minister of Finance may reduce this requirement to less than 15 p.c. of the proceeds. The amount of foreign currency that must be sold to the State is established in the company's operation permit. Thus both company authorities and partners are helped to conduct a stable financial policy. The company may use the foreign currency as it thinks fit.

Companies with foreign capital participation pay 50 p.c. of their gross profit as income tax. At the same time, they enjoy a 0.4 p.c. tax reduction for each 1 p.c. of the export value of production or services sold. Thus, a company that sells all its production for export, must pay 10 p.c. of its gross profit as income tax. Besides this, the company will enjoy tax exemption for the first two years of its production or service activity. This period does not cover the time spent on organisation and investment prior to the company's actual production activity. Finally, a company with foreign capital participation is exempted from import duties on all things that constitute the in-kind contribution of the foreign partner, as well as on machines, equipment, and means of transportation used by the company.

In the less than two years of the operation of the Law of 23 April 1986, 16 permits to establish companies with foreign participation have already been issued. Among foreign investors are companies from the US, Austria, the Federal Republic of Germany and Great Britain. The total value of equity and debt financing of these companies is estimated at 200 million U.S. Dollars. The practical results of the operation of the Law on companies with foreign participation as well as comments received so far from the foreign and domestic business community are now the subject of detailed scrutiny in Poland.

The provisions of the Law will be reexamined in 1988 and depending on the outcome the necessary changes might be introduced allowing the Law to serve the needs of economic cooperation with foreign investors better.

The economic and new business environment in the Soviet market

IVAN IVANOV

Vice-President State Commission for External Economic Relations, Council of Ministers of the USSR

I. Introduction

The foreign economic relations of the USSR are nowadays undergoing a radical restructuring. They are part of the general reform of the business mechanism in the country, based on the following guidelines: cost-accounting, self-supporting, self-financing and increased freedom and responsibilities for individual enterprises. At the same time, the new channels and opportunities are now available for Soviet and foreign partners to cooperate, taking into account recent international experience.

As a result, the business environment in the Soviet market and the ways to enter it are changing and these innovations cover foreign trade planning, newcomers to foreign trade, new contractual and equity arrangements and trade policy.

II. The new approach to foreign trade planning

The USSR is and will remain a planned economy country, but new foreign trade planning is now less detailed. The plans concerned set up aggregated value indicators only and are formulated on the basis of dialogue between individual ministries and enterprises and the State Planning Commission. The State Planning Commission prepares guidelines for the ministries and enterprises which decide to what extent these will be accepted (with the possibility of a conciliation procedure which is forthcoming).

The outcome of this dialogue is usually the following: as a result the enterprise divides its production into two parts, one for the domestic market (arranged by state procurement or contractual arrangements) and another for export with the freedom to choose foreign markets, partners, prices etc.

The fulfilment of the USSR's international commitments and obliga-

M. Maresceau (ed.), The Political and Legal Framework of Trade Relations Between the European Community and Eastern Europe. ISBN 0–7923–0046–7.
© *1989 by Kluwer Academic Publishers, Dordrecht – Printed in the Netherlands.*

tions which are embodied in trade and economic cooperation treaties (programmes) are usually enforced by state orders (GOSZAKZAZ). However, these orders specify the country concerned and the volume of exports only, with other details on the commercial terms and conditions having to be settled with the parties concerned.

Enterprises are expected to be self-sufficient in foreign currency. However, this is rather a prospective goal which cannot be achieved overnight. Therefore, for a while, imports are to be financed from two sources (a) for new construction, large investment projects and mass purchasing of raw materials and consumer products: from centralised state currency funds (b) for modernisation of the enterprises and the acquiring of technology, engineering spare parts, design etc. . . .: from the currency funds managed by the enterprises themselves. For that, they are entitled to retain a part of their export proceeds. The rate of this allocation ranges from 2 to 95 p.c. depending upon the degree of processing and research intensitivity of the products under review.

III. Newcomers to foreign trade

As previously the trade in raw materials, food, foodstuffs, some machinery and other products of national importance, remains the domain of the Ministry of Foreign Economic Relations and the 25 foreign trade organisations belonging to it. However, the rest of the turnover is now in the hands of 26 industrial ministries and 90 individual enterprises (amalgamation of enterprises) entitled to operate on foreign markets directly. These newcomers, trading mainly in machinery and chemicals may set up their own foreign trade units, open and manage accounts in foreign currency etc. . . . The same rights were also delegated to the Councils of Ministers of the constituent Republics and to the Moscow and Leningrad City Councils, trading in products of local origin.

All in all these newcomers in 1987 provided 20 p.c. of the total trade turnover and 40 p.c. of machinery exports. Preference to manufacturing enterprises in this area is a part of the effort to industrialise Soviet exports and to change the existing commodity-oriented structure. Newcomers are also entitled to borrow currency from the Soviet Vresheconombank and (with the endorsement of this bank) on the international money markets.

The USSR does maintain a network of trading and servicing companies abroad (100 p.c. owned or mixed). A number of them were also transferred from the Ministry of Foreign Economic Relations to new shareholders in industry to promote domestic imports. At last, newcomers are entitled to have their share in the staff of Soviet trade representations abroad, to make foreign investments and to operate through stock exchanges. With these developments in mind, the whole previous discussion about the qualification "State-trading" or "non-State-trading" loses much of its substance. The most important thing now is not the matter of the property of those enterprises but their business behaviour. From this point of view the new Soviet foreign trade system is compatible with international systems, including the GATT.

IV. New modalities for cooperation

The Soviet internationally-operating enterprises are entitled to enter into any legitimate business transactions as well as to set up joint ventures within the USSR and abroad. By June 1988 52 joint ventures had been registered in the USSR with participation of West German, Finnish, Italian, Swiss, US, Japanese and other interests. More than 60 ventures are about to be set up and another 300 offers are under negotiation allowing foreign investment in the USSR. The Soviet side is guided by three interrelated goals: (a) to attract advanced foreign technology and managerial experience (b) to perform import substitution and (c) to develop the export sector. Joint ventures are expected to cover their foreign currency expenses with foreign currency proceeds as the State is not responsible for the operation of the joint venture and the Rouble is not convertible. Therefore, they cannot claim any currency subsidies from the State. However, legislation allows the use of residual Rouble profits to buy Soviet products of interest to foreign partners in case of non-sufficiency of currency to cover profit remittance. Legislation also provides the foreign investor with a set of guarantees and incentives. His property is protected in the USSR on the same legal basis as state property and cannot be confiscated or expropriated by administrative decisions: penalties can only be imposed by court decision.

Furthermore, the foreign partner is entitled:

— to nominate representatives in the supervisory council and the executive board;
— to receive prompt and adequate compensation in case of the liquidation of the joint venture (on the residual balance of his contributions);
— to transfer his profit abroad in foreign currency or in kind;
— to have priority in supplying construction services;
— to recruit the foreign technicians to meet the specific needs of the joint venture (the residue of the technicians' salary may also be transferred abroad in foreign currency);

— to operate freely on foreign markets under general export and import licences;
— to evaluate his contribution to the authorised capital in any currency and on the basis of world market prices;
— to settle disputes by arbitration, including international arbitration.

As incentive he has the right to two-year tax holiday (from the date of the first declared profit), to be exempted from customs duties, to use the tax-free regime for reinvestment and to claim *ad hoc* tax concessions.

The sales and purchases of the joint venture within the Soviet market are effected on the basis of contractual prices in Roubles through the respective Soviet foreign trade organisations.

V. The new conditions to tap the market

The reforms do diversify business opportunities for foreign companies to tap the Soviet market. The new régime provides direct access to end-users and export producers and simplifies the procedure for business negotiations. At the same time the Soviet market will from now on become much more competitive with enterprises paying for themselves and from their own liquid assets.

With a view to facilitating business operations the Soviet authorities are improving market information, introducing foreign trade statistics based on international classification — "Glasnost" will also be extended in this area — and liberalising visa and travelling formalities. The consultation service was set up by the Soviet Chamber of Commerce and Industry which serves both Soviet and foreign clients. Moreover, the Chamber was reorganised to make it the "collective voice" of Soviet industry. In particular it has the right to initiate legislation and will protect the interests of industry on all levels. Foreign corporations may open their offices in the USSR and a specifically set up agency (the foreign trade branch of the Moscow City Council) is ready to provide these offices with daily services. The Soviet Academy of Foreign Trade and the Academy of Economics have also inaugurated the first Soviet Business School with foreign participation.

VI. Trade policy issues

In order to ensure a positive external environment for trade, the USSR will continue "rapprochement" with the EEC and the GATT. The USSR does not claim one-sided concessions from the West and will be aiming at business reciprocity. In order to reach these aims, the USSR is preparing a new customs tariff based on the international nomenclature and a set of non-tariff regulations.

The government is ready to consider Soviet participation in international arrangements with regard to certain markets e.g. textiles, as well as entering bilateral tax agreements and agreements on mutual investment protection. The contacts with national business associations in foreign countries are widening. The USSR intends expanding her contacts with regional economic groupings, particularly in developing countries. In 1987, the USSR joined the Common Fund organised within the framework of UNCTAD with a view to stabilising the commodities markets.

VII. Pricing policy

Internal price-setting is an important part of foreign reforms. A reasonable and economically justifiable link is planned to be established between internal and external prices. This reform should solve all speculations about dumping on the basis of reliable statistical data. For the moment, however, there is no final concept of how the pricing system should be reorganised. There is only a set of ideas which are currently under controversial discussion.

As it stands, the world market prices and Soviet domestic prices are separated and due to the size of the Soviet economy will differ to some extent from that of the outside world. This is understandable since the structure of the Soviet economy differs from the world structure.

Previously, particularly taking into account the wide-ranging production costs throughout the country, prices were set according to the "cost plus" rule. However, with cost accounting supremacy this is no longer satisfying since marginal enterprises may be masters of the situation. Consequently, there are three basic understandings on how to deal with the issue: (1) Prices ought to be set on the basis of average production costs throughout the country; (2) The new proportion of internal prices should take into account the proportion of the world market prices and their dynamics. A link between the world market and the internal market ought to be the customs tariff and parity of the Rouble. In the long run the Soviet pricing system will be comparable with the international system. This does, however, not imply that the same productions ought to have the same price within and outside the country but the gap will certainly be reduced; (3) The elimination of state subsidies especially for staple foods and services. The existing prices for some of them were fixed in the twenties and have remained unchanged. The State pays annually about 60 billion Roubles to subsidise them. Therefore the efforts to reduce the production costs of these products and services are considered as a solution in combination with price adjustments making food a bit more expensive and durables less expensive, all this with a view to keeping the standard of living in general unchanged. Nevertheless, the new pricing system may soon be the subject of a national referendum.

This approach though not fully operational at this stage, is largely acknowledged by the majority of Soviet economists.

VIII. Currency policy

It is the USSR's policy to make the Rouble a convertible currency in future. However, a reliable and responsible policy has to be pursued in this particular area. Convertibility needs some prerequisites both rooted within the country and in the international field.

To sum up, the USSR is pursuing an industrious forward-looking approach in developing mature business relations with all countries interested in cooperation.

PART THREE

Specific East-West European trade issues

Eastern European enterprises in the European Community: general conditions

JAN MONKIEWICZ

Associate Professor, Institute of Economic and Social Sciences, Warsaw Technical University

I. Introduction

One of the dominant features of the present world economy is the high degree of internationalisation of economic activities both at country and company level. In the latter case the principal form of the internationalisation is direct investment abroad. Whilst still belonging to the domain of the industrialised Western economies, direct investments also become more and more important for the external expansion of developing countries. They too seem to play some role in the economies of the socialist countries. In contrast, however, to the flourishing discussion on both Western and Southern foreign investments, the issue of Eastern investments abroad is hardly touched on in existing literature. This paper attempts to throw more light on this rather neglected issue by providing available quantitative evidence and assessing its qualitative dimension.

It begins with the discussion of the current size and structure of the East European investment involvement in the West and especially in the European Community. Thereafter, principal impediments to the growth and operation of East European enterprises in the European Community come under scrutiny. Finally, possible areas of future conflict are spelled out.

II. East European enterprises in the European Community: an overview

The number of enterprises with East European participation established in developed market economies (EEes) is rather moderate. The last available data suggest that there are around 440 EEes hosted in 23 developed market economies (see Annex). The major investor amongst CMEA countries is the USSR (116 units), followed by Hungary (107 units) and Poland (106 units). The number of EEes is rising steadily, but

M. Maresceau (ed.), The Political and Legal Framework of Trade Relations Between the European Community and Eastern Europe. ISBN 0–7923–0046–7.
© *1989 by Kluwer Academic Publishers, Dordrecht – Printed in the Netherlands.*

at rather a slow pace. In 1977 there were 312 companies registered while in 1984 — ca 440. This number seems to have stabilised in recent years which apparently reflects the growing balance of payments problems of the East European countries and hence the relative lack of the convertible currency resources for new ventures. It reflects also the attempts of the socialist investors to consolidate on the rapidly growing investments of the 1970s by making them more viable ventures able to survive under harsh economic conditions. Last but not least an important reason for the deceleration of the East European investments in the West is a deteriorated political and economic climate for the overall East-West economic relations registered in the 1980s. The most active investors in the last few years have been Hungary, the GDR and Czechoslovakia — the countries with relatively good records with regard to their hard currency payments position, which may point out the relative importance of this factor among the determinants of East European investments in the West.

The EEes are by and large established in those developed market economies with which the trade, or in general, economic ties are the most intense. Thus it seems that they are used rather to keep the markets already won than to open up new ones.

The European Community currently hosts the bulk of EEes located in the West. Their number increased from 212 in 1977 to close to 300 in 1983 (see *infra* Table 1). West Germany, the United Kingdom and France are the most important host countries, hosting regularly ca twothirds of all EEes located in the Community.

The same countries belonged to Eastern Europe's most important trading partners in the European Community in the 1970s. They were also among the most important Western partners in industrial East-West cooperation arrangements.

As far as the investing countries are concerned the largest CMEA investors in the Community are the Soviet Union, Hungary and Poland which account for over 60 p.c. of all cases registered. The most reluctant actors in this respect are Czechoslovakia, the GDR and Romania (see Table 2 below).

This is undoubtedly a policy-related variable. Precisely Czechoslovakia, the GDR and Romania are among those Eastern European countries that avoid more active involvement in some relatively innovative forms of trade and commercial activities, preferring well-known old established tracks. Only since the beginning of the 1980s does there seem to be a change in the policy pursued by the said countries, demonstrated by the capital expansion of their enterprises abroad.

As far as the activities of EEes are concerned most of them are engaged in trading operations and other services. Assembly and produc-

Table 1. East European enterprises in the West according to the host countries.

Host countries	1977	1981	1983
EEC of which	212	215 (60,8)	299 (61,5)
Belgium	20	24	34
Denmark	2	5	6
France	42	39	46
W. Germany	54	63	83
Italy	24	28	31
Luxemburg	—	2	2
Portugal	0	1	1
Netherlands	14	12	14
Spain	8	13	14
UK	48	59	68
Others of which	100	158	186
Austria	27	34	44
USA	16	32	35
Total	312	403	484 [a]

[a] 48 cases no longer operational.
Source: C. H. McMillan, "The foreign investment activity of the Comecon countries: actors and strategies", *University of Reading Discussion Papers in International Investment and Business Studies*, No. 73, June 1983, p. 1a; C. H. McMillan, *Multinationals from the second world*, MacMillan Press, 1987.

Table 2. East European enterprises in the EEC, according to the investing country (number of cases).

Country	1977	1981	1983
Bulgaria	27	32	33
Czechoslovakia	21	18	29
GDR	11	17	24
Poland [a]	41	55	45
Poland [b]	41	52	48
Hungary	35	34	63
Romania	22	24	26
USSR	55	66	71
Total	212	246	291 [c]

[a] McMillan;
[b] Polish statistics;
[c] of which 48 no longer in existence
Source: as in table 1 and Ministry of Foreign Trade of Polish People's Republic.

tion as well as extraction and raw-material processing are virtually of no importance to socialist investors (same 6 p.c. and 2 p.c. respectively of all EEes in 1981), though recently a slight tendency towards an increase of both latter types of activities could be observed (see Annex). Only the Hungarian investors established a more sizable amount of enterprises in assembly and production. The GDR, Czechoslovakia and Romania on the other hand seem to favour exclusively trade and services-related investments.

These differences in approach are apparently the result of a different perception of the necessity of setting up production-oriented ventures in Western countries. Hungary — the most export-oriented economy within Eastern Europe — seems to favour the classical path of production internationalisation i.e. via internationalisation of production capital. Most other East European countries represent a vaguer policy in this area by preferring production internationalisation via internationalised distribution networks. This may however also reflect the nature of the comparative advantages enjoyed by East European investors. Deprived of techno-logical superiority over their Western competitors in the production area they may compete successfully only in the trade and services area. A more detailed breakdown of EEes by areas of activity points out that within trading companies three quarters execute ordinary export-import opera-tions geared predominantly to trade transactions between the respective home and host countries. Only the remaining quarter additionally performs marketing, retailing and servicing operations. Their importance for Eastern European trade transactions may be judged from the Polish experience. According to the available statistics around 50 p.c. of the country's export to the West is being arranged through the said companies.[1]

East European investments in services are not limited exclusively to commercial operations. They also include banking, insurance, transporta-tion, construction and engineering. For example, the Soviet Union currently owns six banks located abroad, operating in nine different countries. Poland has altogether 8 branches and affiliations in the banking sector; Hungary has majority stakes in two banks abroad and maintains five representative offices in Paris, Zürich, Frankfurt, New York and Tokyo; and Romania has joint venture-banks in Paris, London, Frankfurt and Milan. Five East European countries — Bulgaria, Hungary, Poland, Romania and USSR — have also invested in insurance operations abroad.[2]

Thus we may conclude that the distribution of the EEes according to their main economic activity seems to support the idea that the main motives for the establishment of EEes are export promotion of the socialist countries (trading companies), and necessity of direct access to the market (service companies).

The companies in question are by and large small economic entities with the average amount of authorised capital investment of ca 1,2 million Dollars as of the end of 1983. This figure however is highly misleading as over 70 p.c. of the invested capital is located in financial services, whereas only ca 16 p.c. in trading and 4.6 p.c. in assembly and manufacturing (see *infra* Table 3). Thus on the whole EEes are small, economically weak companies.

The above-recorded pattern of the EEes distribution according to their main economic activity is well-correlated with the nature of the socialist investors (see Annex). The majority of them, 64 p.c. of the total as of the end 1981, are foreign trade enterprises and associations. The production enterprises and associations were involved as investors only in 6 p.c. of the total EEes established. The important investors are also service enterprises, which participated in 30 p.c. of the total EEes established, of which the most important were transport and freight enterprises (11 p.c.) and banks (6 p.c.).

As far as the ownership structure is concerned investors from socialist countries show a relatively high propensity for retaining control functions over the established EEes (see Annex). Nearly two thirds of the established EEes (64.8 p.c. of the total) are Eastern majority-owned. Only 11.6 p.c. of the total are Eastern minority-owned, and 24.6 p.c. are fifty-fifty ventures. The relatively high propensity for majority-owned EEes is especially exhibited by investors from: the GDR (92.8 p.c. of the total companies), the USSR (83.5 p.c. of the total companies), Czechoslovakia (78.2 p.c. of the total companies), and Poland (67.3 p.c. of the total companies). Only Romania relies mostly on the fifty-fifty ventures. This ownership structure does not mean however, that the Eastern partner maintains really tight control of each of the EEes. In practice several of the EEes with Eastern majority in equity are equally or more controlled by Western partners, mainly due to the personnel policy and stronger involvement of Western partners in some key areas, as for instance finance or book-keeping.

III. Principal impediments encountered by EEes in the Community

The discussion which follows is based on three sources of information:

a. survey carried out by the author among foreign enterprises with Polish participation located in EEC;

Table 3. Estimated value of authorised capital invested in companies in the West with Soviet and East European equity participation, end-1983 (US Dollars — thousand)[a].

Principal activity	Investing country							
	Bulgaria	Czechoslovakia	GDR	Hungary	Poland	Romania	Soviet Union	Total
Import-export	2,040	2,843	5,327	6,974	12,653	2,073	7,755	39,665
Marketing, retailing	657	2,657	0	446	2,888	0	11,739	18,387
Marketing, retailing and servicing	2,757	2,489	1,541	0	2,825	419	18,345	28,376
Assembly and manufacturing	10,737	0	0	7,957	321	0	6,258	25,273
Extraction and processing of raw materials	0	0	0	0	262	0	1,092	1,354
Financial services	73	4,175	0	22,450	31,207	29,085	299,137	386,127
Transport services	152	15	108	1,241	646	193	18,385	20,740
Technical services	430	0	0	165	1,130	367	25,675	27,767
Consumer services	87	0	84	37	84	202	0	494
Total	16,933	12,179	7,060	39,270	52,016	32,339	388,386	548,183

[a] Estimated value of capital invested in 434 companies operative at end-1983.

Source: C. H. McMillan, *Multinationals from the second world*, MacMillan Press, London, 1987, p. 44.

b. inventory of obstacles among ECE countries prepared by ECE Secretariat in its document TRADE/R. 390/Rev. 2 released in 1986;[3]
c. communications submitted to GATT in connection with the current round of multilateral trade negotiations.[4]

All different types of obstacles registered by EEes in the Community were divided into two distinct groups:

— trade-related obstacles;
— movement of people and employment-related obstacles.

In what follows we shall take them one by one.

A. *Trade-related obstacles*

Since, as pointed out before, most of EEes so far are engaged principally in trading (export, import) operations trade-related obstacles therefore constitute important determinants of their successful operation. The list of these obstacles is very long, though most of them may be subdivided into the three following groups:

— licensing procedures and related practices;
— standards and technical regulations;
— packaging and labelling requirements.

Licensing procedures and related practices seem to constitute the backbone of trade-related obstacles. They include such elements as special requirements for imports from CMEA countries, quotas, import deposits, etc. The intensity of their appearance may be judged from the number of notifications submitted by the governments of the individual CMEA countries to the ECE inventory of obstacles which totalled 55. By introducing an element of uncertainty and instability for Eastern European trading companies the licensing system is regarded as a particularly unpleasant component of their operational environment. An especially troublesome situation exists in France, Spain and the Benelux countries.

Standards and technical regulations constitute the second group of trade-related obstacles (see *infra* Table 4). Their severity for EEes however is far below the first group discussed before. They include such elements as prolonged application procedures, severe testing and certification procedures, inspection requirements, etc.

Table 4. Trade-related obstacles encountered by EEs in the Community.

	No. of notifications	Specific problems	Complaining country	Country concerned
1. Licensing procedures and related practices	48	1. Special requirements for granting permissions for imports from Eastern countries including quotas, payment of import deposits, self-restraint measures, etc.	Bulgaria	EEC
			GDR	EEC
			Hungary	EEC
			Poland	EEC
			Romania	EEC
			USSR	EEC
			Czechoslovakia	EEC
		2. Absence of information about allocation of quotas	Czechoslovakia	Benelux, Spain
	3	3. Delays in publications of quotas	—	EEC
		4. Late delivery of licences	Hungary	France, Spain
	4	5. Subdivisions of quotas by periods	Czechoslovakia	EEC
		6. Subdivisions of quotas between importing firms	Hungary	EEC
			Czechoslovakia	Benelux

Table 4. (Continued)

	No. of notifications	Specific problems	Complaining country	Country concerned
Sub-total	55			
2. Standards and technical regulations	7	1. Differences in national standards resulting in the prolonged application procedures	Hungary Poland Romania USSR	FRG France, Italy EEC EEC, FRG
	3	2. Testing and certification procedures	Hungary Czechoslovakia	FRG, France Italy
	1	3. Inspection of goods on production sites	—	Italy
Sub-total	11			
3. Packaging and labelling requirement	5	Severe national requirements with respect to labelling, marking etc.	Bulgaria Romania Hungary	EEC EEC EEC
Sub-total	5			
Total	71	x	x	x

Source: *Consolidated Inventory of All Kind of Obstacles to the Development of Trade*, TRADE/R. 390/Rev. 2.

Packaging and labelling requirements are the least important barrier to trade flows, although they too create some problems for some CMEA countries.

B. *Movement of people and employment-related obstacles*

The running of a business abroad requires the constant movement of people, from the motherland both for business purposes, inspection, training or work. Therefore, all impediments which negatively influence the freedom of such movements, cause unpredictable delays, restrict the choice of personnel for particular duties and must be considered as serious obstacles to a successful operation. This is especially true with respect to relatively small EEes in which case success or failure depends frequently on individual persons in view of limited employment abroad.

Precisely here, however, EEes are faced in the Community with a number of obstacles, which put them clearly in a disadvantageous position not only vis-à-vis Community-based companies but also vis-à-vis companies from third countries.[5] The list of these obstacles is very long and includes time-consuming visa procedures, the short-term validity of visas, difficulties in obtaining residence permits, difficulties in obtaining work permits, limitations on labour permits, etc. (see *infra* Table 5).

To quote just a few concrete examples. In Belgium, for instance, work permits are issued by the interministerial committee. Documents are frequently sent back due to some informalities and the waiting time is unspecified. In practice, the first work permit is issued after a period of up to 6 months. The said work permit has to be renewed each year during the first five years. Only thereafter is it renewed automatically. One application submitted by a Polish company in April 1987 was still unanswered by mid November 1987. In the United Kingdom work permits are issued only after the provision of substantial justification by EEes and the time requirement is ca 3 months. Residence visas are to be renewed every year and so-called re-entry visas are renewed every half year. It creates substantial problems in view of necessary business trips abroad. In Italy the worst problems are encountered with respect to work permits. For example, a new set up Polish company has been waiting for the issue of a work permit for its four employees since 28 March 1987. By the end of November 1987 it was still unresolved. In France employment of new foreign personnel has to be planned a year in advance, spelling out exactly the posts to be filled and names of employees. Any departures from the plan cause significant delays and face cumbersome procedures. A *carte de séjour* has to be renewed annually during the first three years. To renew it

Table 5. Movement of people and employment-related obstacles encountered by EEes in the Community.

Type of obstacles	No of notifications in force	Specific problems concerned	Compaining country	Countries concerned
1. Visa formalities	8	1. Time consuming visas procedures	GDR, Poland, Czechoslovakia	EEC, specially Italy, UK and France
	1	2. Refusal to issue visas for long stays to Soviet officials of joint companies	USSR	Netherlands
	21	3. Difficulties in obtaining entry visas	Czechoslovakia	UK
	2	4. Delays in granting entry visas for service engineers and technicians	Bulgaria	
	3	5. Short time validity of resident's visas for joint-venture personnel and troublesome extension procedures	Poland Bulgaria GDR	EEC
Sub-total	15			
2. Working permissions and related issues	2	1. Restrictions on the number of staff employed outside the trade and economic departments of embassies	Bulgaria GDR	EEC
	6	2. Sluggish procedures for granting work permits for joint companies and difficulties in obtaining them	GDR	Belgium, France, Italy, GDR
	1	3. Limitations on labour permits	Poland	Italy
Sub-total	9			
Total	24			

Source: as in table 4.

each time 3 visits to the local prefecture are necessary. Business visas to France are issued after a 3-week waiting period and urgent cases are handled with severe problems. In the Federal Republic of Germany basic problems have been encountered with regard to the work permits for executing servicing contracts. The procedures are complicated and time-consuming. Since 1984 the duration of a work permit for such contracts cannot be extended beyond two years. In some localities no entry visas for workers with previous working experience in the Federal Republic are granted.

IV. Final remarks

The list of obstacles encountered by EEes in their operations in the Community is obviously much larger than indicated in the foregoing discussion. It includes for example the question of professional diploma recognition, specific solvency requirements in the case of financial companies,[6] export control measures, both national and multilateral (COCOM), etc. In the paper special attention was given to those which substantially disturb the day-to-day operation of the existing companies. At first glance they might appear marginal. The significance however should be viewed in the context of the largely small-scale nature of the current EEes which means that even theoretically secondary problems become a matter of their existence. Thus in a company with a total employment of say 15 persons visa disturbances and the delay or rejection of work permits may effectively hamper its operation. The same is true with regard to solvency requirements if they are to be met by a small financial company, with limited assets.

One should perhaps be aware of the fact that current areas of conflict may undergo substantial changes in the years to come. This conviction is based on the directions of economic reforms currently under way in most of the CMEA countries. They basically include the growing role of market mechanisms and instruments, the growing role and dramatically increased autonomy of industrial enterprises, the demonopolisation of foreign trade operations, the easing of existing currency regulations, and the like. It may be argued that these changes will affect both the size, structure and the strategy of EEes in the Community and elsewhere in the West.

Firstly, an increased autonomy of national enterprises, coupled with the demonopolisation processes in the sphere of foreign trade will find its articulation, *inter alia*, in the growing volume of outward direct investments. The national companies will have to intensify their presence abroad, including the setting-up of new outlets abroad. Some signs of this new approach can already be detected in Poland.

After a long period of stagnation with respect to the size of Polish investments in the West, last year witnessed a handful of new proposals which are currently under consideration within the Ministry of Foreign Economic Cooperation. Investment processes would be undoubtedly facilitated by the opening-up of East European economies for the direct penetration of Western companies. Capital linkages created in this way may finally result in the intertwining of Eastern and Western equity ventures and the back-flow of investment capital to the Western companies. The mixing of investment capital in joint projects will thus become some sort of a natural phenomenon and not an extraordinary activity subject to severe scrutiny and cumbersome procedures. So far there are already over 900 companies in Eastern European countries with some Western participation and their number in recent years has been increasing rapidly. The very existence of the said companies provides an intense mutual learning process both for Eastern as well as Western companies which may lead to a more offensive attitude in setting up some equity joint ventures in other parts of the world. Increased propensity towards direct investments abroad will include not only traditional actors i.e. large state enterprises but also cooperatives and finally private companies, whose role should not be underestimated, at least in some CMEA countries. Already in 1987 the first equity investment of a Polish private company in the West took place.

Secondly, the growth in volume will apparently be associated with changes in the structure of investments. Traditional trading companies will be supplemented more and more by marketing enterprises, after-sale units and last but not least by production ventures. This last element will give rise to completely new problems whereby the traditional hindrances spelled out before will be of far smaller importance. The nature of these problems will be associated not so much with trade-related and personnel-related areas but with the setting-up of production outlets, buying out existing companies, getting authorisation for the production of certain goods, participation in national or regional production or development projects and the like. Last but not least the new scenario may include a departure from the thus far classical way of setting up new ventures towards the purchasing of shares in the existing Western companies and the use of their trade network, brand name or technology. This might create a substantially new situation for EEes within the Community.

Notes

1. See J. Monkiewicz, G. Monkiewicz, "East-South capital cooperation. An unexploited possibility", in: B. H. Schultz, W. W. Hansen (Eds) *The Soviet Bloc and the Third World: The political economy of East-South relations*, Westview Press, 1988 (not yet published).
2. C. H. McMillan, "Multinationals from the second world . . .", *op. cit.*, pp. 95—96.
3. *Consolidated Inventory of All Kinds of Obstacles to the Development of Trade*, Trade/ R. 390/Rev. 2, UN ECOSOC, ECE, CDT, Geneva, 1 October 1986.
4. See for example GATT, MTN. GNS/W/14.
5. See M. Maresceau, "The free movement of persons and nationals, from third countries", College of Europe, Bruges, Colloquium 1986, *External relations of the European Community and internal market: legal and functional aspects*, (mimeo).
6. Non EEC financial firms are required to meet solvency requirements on the bases of assets in each member state. EEC firms are entitled to use assets in any Member State for this purpose (see MTN. GNS/W/14).

Bibliography

1. J. Cieślik, *Zarys teorii internacjonalizacji przedsiębiorstwa*, SGPiS, Monografie i Opracowania No. 229, Warszawa, 1987.
2. *Consolidated Inventory of All Kinds of Obstacles to the Development of Trade*, Trade/ R. 390/Rev. 2, UN ECOSOC, ECE, CDT, Geneva 1 October 1986.
3. M. Łebkowski, J. Monkiewicz, *CMEA investments abroad*, World Economy Research Institute, Warsaw, 1987 (forthcoming).
4. M. Łebkowski, J. Monkiewicz, "CMEA direct investments in the Western countries: the case of Poland", *J. W.T.L.*, 1987, pp. 27—38.
5. M. Maresceau, The free movement of persons and nationals from third countries, College of Europe, Bruges, Colloquium 1986, *External relations of the European Community and internal market: legal and functional aspects*, (mimeo).
6. C. H. McMillan, *Multinationals from the second world*, London, MacMillan Press, 1987.
7. C. H. McMillan, "The foreign investment activity of the Comecon countries: actors and strategies", *University of Reading Discussion Papers in International Investments and Business Studies*, No. 73, June 1983.
8. J. Monkiewicz, G. Monkiewicz, "East-South capital cooperation. An unexploited opportunity", Paper presented at the VIth General Conference of EADI, Amsterdam 1—5 September 1987.
9. *Novyj etap ekonomitsheskogo sotrudnitchestva SSSR s razvitymi kapitalistitcheskimi stranami*, Izd. Nauka, Moskwa, 1978.
10. N. N. Vozniesenskaya, *Smieschannyje predpriyatya kak forma miezhdunarodnogo ekonomitcheskogo sotrudnitchestva*, Nauka, Moskwa, 1986.
11. N. N. Vozniesenskaya, "Utchastije sovietskich vnieschnietorgovych predprijatij v smieschannych obschkcnestvach", *Sovietskoje gosudarstwo i pravo*, 1977, pp. 89—96.

Annex I

Table 6. EEes by host and home country, 1977[a], 1978, 1981 (Number).

Host country	Home country Bulgaria			Czechoslovakia			GDR			Poland			Hungary			Romania			USSR			Total		
	77	78	81	77	78	81	77	78	81	77	78	81	77	78	81	77	78	81	77	78	81	77	78	81
Australia	0	0	0	0	1	1	0	0	0	0	3	3	0	0	0	0	0	0	0	4	4	0	8	8
Austria	2	2	2	0	1	1	3	3	3	4	7	8	13	14	16	2	2	1	3	4	5	27	33	34
Belgium	1	2	2	2	2	2	1	2	2	6	6	7	0	1	1	0	0	0	10	11	10	20	24	24
Denmark	0	0	0	0	0	0	0	1	1	1	1	1	1	2	1	0	0	0	0	1	2	2	5	5
Finland	0	0	0	0	0	0	0	0	1	1	1	1	1	1	1	0	0	0	7	7	8	9	9	11
France	3	3	5	5	5	3	4	3	3	7	7	8	5	2	3	6	6	5	12	12	12	42	38	39
Greece	0	1	2	0	0	0	0	0	0	0	1	1	0	1	1	0	2	2	0	0	2	0	5	8
Spain	1	1	1	0	0	0	0	0	0	2	2	2	2	2	2	0	1	1	3	3	6	8	9	13
Netherlands	1	0	1	1	1	1	1	2	2	3	3	3	3	2	3	1	1	0	4	3	2	14	13	12
Ireland	0	0	1	0	0	0	0	0	0	0	0	0	0	0	1	0	0	0	0	0	0	0	0	2
Japan	2	1	2	0	1	1	0	0	0	1	1	1	1	1	1	0	0	0	1	1	1	5	5	6
Liechtenstein	0	0	0	0	0	0	0	0	0	0	0	0	0	1	1	0	0	0	0	0	0	0	1	1
Luxembourg	0	0	0	0	0	0	0	0	0	0	0	0	0	0	1	0	0	0	0	0	1	0	0	2

Table 6. (Continued)

Host country	Home country																							
	Bulgaria			Czechoslovakia			GDR			Poland			Hungary			Romania			USSR			Total		
	77	78	81	77	78	81	77	78	81	77	78	81	77	78	81	77	78	81	77	78	81	77	78	81
Canada	1	1	1	2	4	5	0	0	0	2	2	3	1	1	1	2	2	1	5	5	5	13	15	16
New Zealand	0	0	0	0	0	0	0	0	0	0	0	1	0	0	0	0	0	0	0	0	3	0	0	4
Norway	0	1	2	0	0	0	0	0	0	2	1	1	0	0	0	0	0	0	3	3	3	5	5	6
Portugal	0	0	0	0	0	0	0	0	0	0	1	0	0	0	0	0	0	0	0	0	0	0	1	1
FRG	11	10	12	1	2	1	0	1	0	0	15	16	13	15	15	7	7	7	10	11	12	54	61	63
United States	0	0	0	0	0	2	0	0	1	7	15	13	2	3	7	2	1	2	5	5	5	16	24	32
Sweden	1	1	0	3	3	3	1	2	1	5	5	5	3	2	2	1	0	0	4	3	4	17	16	15
Switzerland	2	2	2	0	0	1	0	0	0	2	3	3	2	1	2	1	2	1	1	1	4	8	9	14
U.K.	4	3	6	10[b]	10	9	5[b]	6	8	8	12	15	8	6	5	3	4	5	10	10	14	48	51	59
Italy	6	6	5	2	2	2	0	1	1	2	2	3	3	3	3	5	5	6	6	8	8	24	27	28
Total	35	35	44	26	32	32	15	21	23	65	88	96	58	58	68	29	83	32	84	92	111	312	359	403

[a] including banks and financial institutions.
[b] including EEes established jointy by partners from Czechoslovakia and the GDR.
0 = data not available or no EEes established.

Source: *Transnational Corporations in World Development. A Re-Examination.* UN CTC, New York 1978, p. 283; C. H. McMillan, "Growth of External Investments by the Comecon Countries," *The World Economy*, 1979, p. 365; C. H. McMillan, "The Foreign Investment Activity of the Comecon Countries: Actors and Strategies", *University of Reading Discussion Papers in International Investments and Business Studies*, No. 73, June 1983, p. 1a.

Annex II

Table 7. Geographic distribution of CMEA investments in the West, end 1983 (number of instances).

Host country	Investing country							
	Bulgaria	Czechoslovakia	GDR	Hungary	Poland	Romania	Soviet Union	Total[a]
Australia	0	1	0	0	4	0	4	9
Austria	2	1	3	23	8	3	4	44
Belgium	2	3	7	1	8	0	13	34
Canada	2	5	0	1	4	2	5	19
Denmark	0	0	1	2	1	0	2	6
Finland	0	0	1	2	1	0	9	13
France	4	5	3	7	8	7	12	46
FRG	13	6	1	28	17	7	11	83
Greece	2	0	0	1	1	2	2	8
Ireland	1	0	0	1	0	0	0	2
Italy	6	3	1	6	2	5	8	31
Japan	3	1	0	1	1	0	1	7
Liechtenstein	0	0	0	1	0	0	0	1

Table 7. (Continued)

Host country	Investing country							
	Bulgaria	Czechoslovakia	GDR	Hungary	Poland	Romania	Soviet Union	Total[a]
Luxembourg	0	0	0	1	0	0	1	2
Netherlands	1	1	2	3	3	1	3	14
New Zealand	0	0	0	0	1	0	3	4
Norway	2	0	0	1	1	0	3	7
Portugal	0	0	0	0	1	0	0	1
Spain	1	1	2	3	2	1	6	14
Sweden	1	3	0	3	7	0	5	21
Switzerland	2	2	0	2	3	2	4	15
U.K.	6	10	9	10	13	5	15	68
United States	0	2	1	10	16	1	5	35
Total	48	44	31	107	102	36	116	484[b]

[a] Row totals indicate numbers of companies with CMEA equity participation in designated Western countries. Row sums may exceed these figures because of equity participation by several CMEA countries in some individual companies.
[b] Of these 484 cases, 48 were known to be no longer operational as of end-1983.
Source: C. H. McMillan, *Multinationals from the second world*, London, MacMillan Press, 1987, p. 34.

Annex III

Table 8. EEes hosted in DMEs, by principal activity and home country, 1977, 1981 and 1983 (Number).

Principal activity	Home country																							
	Bulgaria			Czechoslovakia			GDR			Poland			Hungary			Romania			USSR			Total		
	77	81	83	77	81	83	77	81	83	77	81	83	77	81	83	77	81	83	77	81	83	77	81	83
Trade	26	30	35	22	29	40	12	20	26	52	76	80	41	43	68	20	21	28	41	62	60	215	280	337
Assembly and production	1	5	4	1	1	0	0	0	0	0	3	3	3	13	14	1	0	0	2	2	6	8	24	27
Extraction and raw material processing	0	0	0	0	0	0	0	0	0	1	2	2	0	1	0	1	1	0	3	5	5	5	9	7
Services	8	9	9	3	2	4	3	12	5	12	15	17	13	12	25	7	10	8	38	42	45	84	90	113
Total	35	44	48	26	32	44	15	32	31	65	96	102	58	69	107	29	32	36	84	111	116	359	403	484[a]

[a] including 42 companies no longer active.

Source: Own computations based on: *Transnational Corporations in World Development: a re-examination*, UNCTC, New York 1978, p. 284; C. H. McMillan: "Growth of External Investments by the Commecon Countries", *The World Economy*, 1979, p. 368; C. H. McMillan, "The Foreign Investment Activity of the Comecon Countries: Actors and Strategies." *University of Reading Discussion Papers in International Investments and Business Studies*, No. 73, June 1983, p. 16; C. H. McMillan, *Multinationals from the second world*, London, MacMillan Press, 1987, pp. 38—39.

Annex IV

Table 9. Share of East European partners in EEes equity, by home countries, 1981[a] (Percentages).

Share of Eastern partner in equity	Bulgaria	Czechoslovakia	GDR	Poland	Hungary	Romania	USSR	Total
0—49	26,3	8,7	7,1	19,2	10,3	3,6	8,9	11,6
50	10,5	13,0	0,0	13,5	48,3	85,7	6,6	24,6
51—99	26,3	13,0	21,4	38,5	17,2	3,6	55,6	32,4
100	36,8	65,2	71,4	28,8	24,1	7,1	28,9	31,4
Total[b]	100,0	100,0	100,0	100,0	100,0	100,0	100,0	100,0

Source: C. H. McMillan, "The Foreign Investment Activity of the Comecon Countries: Actors and Strategies," *University of Reading Discussion Papers in International Investment and Business Studies*, No. 73, June 1983, p. 2a.
[a] sample of over a half of registered EEes
[b] because of roundings sum may not add up to total

Annex V

Table 10. Type of East European partners in EEes, by home country, end-1981 Numbers.

Type	Bulgaria	Czechoslovakia	GDR	Hungary	Poland	Romania	USSR	Total
Foreign trade enterprises and associations	10	8	8	14	31	16	37	124 /64%/
Production enterprises and associations	1	1	1	5	4	–	–	12 /6%/
Banks	–	1	–	4	2	1	4	12 /6%/
Insurance companies	1	1	–	1	1	1	1	6 /3%/
Transport and freight enterprises	2	1	1	1	6	2	9	22 /11%/
Engineering and construction organizations	2	–	–	1	–	–	–	3 /2%/
Tourist agencies	1	–	1	1	1	–	–	4 /2%/
Other[a]	2	–	–	4	2	2	2	12 /6%/
Total	19	12	11	31	47	22	53	195 /100%/

Source: C. H. McMillan, "The Foreign Investment Activity of the Comecon Countries: Actors and Strategies," *University of Reading Discussion Paper in International Investments and Business Studies*, No. 73, June 1983, p. 6A.

[a] Research and design institutes, publishing houses, hotel and catering firms, etc.

Annex VI

Table 11. Distribution of CMEA investments in the West by activity, end-1983 (number of instances).

	Investing country							
	Bulgaria	Czechoslovakia	GDR	Hungary	Poland	Romania	Soviet Union	Total[a]
Commerce								
Import-export operations and some related marketing functions	25	24	19	63	59	27	23	240
Marketing, including retailing	1	2	0	5	13	0	13	34
Marketing, retailing and servicing	9	14	7	0	8	1	24	63
Material production								
Extraction and processing of raw materials	0	0	0	0	2	0	5	7
Assembly and manufacturing	4	0	0	14	3	0	6	27
Other services								
Financial services	1	1	0	5	4	5	12	28
Transport services	5	1	3	5	10	1	26	51
Technical services	1	1	0	7	1	1	6	17
Consumer services	2	1	2	8	2	1	1	17
Totals	48	44	31	107	102	36	116	484[c]

[a] Row totals indicate numbers of companies with CMEA equity participation in designated Western countries. Row sums may exceed these figures because of equity participation by several CMEA countries in some individual companies.

[b] Including product modification in some cases.

[c] Including 42 companies no longer active.

Source: C. H. McMillan, *Multinationals from the second world*, London, MacMillan Press, 1987, pp. 38—39.

Financial cooperation and countertrade

JACQUES GROOTHAERT
Chairman of the Board of Directors, Generale Bank, Brussels
With the cooperation of: P. Praet, Chief economist, Generale Bank; D. A. De Haan, Senior Area Manager, Generale Bank; P. Jacques, Head of Forfaiting and Project Financing Group, Generale Bank; Y. De Cock, Senior Trade Finance Manager, Generale Bank; F. Philips, Country Risk Analyst, Generale Bank; P. Van Leeuw, Advisor, Gechem; A. Goyens, Managing Director, Eurolease Ltd.

I. Introduction

Historically, the development of financial instruments played a crucial role in the expansion of trade in general, domestic and international. There are two main reasons for this:
— Financial instruments establish a "bridge" in time between the income and spending activities of individual economic agents. Since there is usually no coincidence *in time* between both, the existence of financial instruments which can be used as stores of value for future payments or of credit instruments will permit economic transactions to occur.
— Financial instruments also facilitate the multilateralisation of transactions. In a pure barter economy, transactions occur only under very specific circumstances of double coincidence, not only in time but also in the demands of both parties. This involves high transaction or search costs, lacks transparency, which in turn affects competition and thus economic efficiency.
While it is widely recognised that financial instruments are trade-creating it is also clear that they imply the acceptance of specific risks. Under uncertainty and imperfect information, dealing with *time* and *multilateralism* generates risks which do not exist in a pure barter system of exchanges (solvency, liquidity). For economic transactions which occur within the boundaries of a country, these risks are considered as minor compared with the gains in terms of economic efficiency (although, as economic history shows there is no risk-free monetary economy). In international trade, sources of uncertainty are much more important, due notably to lower degrees of inter-country homogeneity (political, economical, technological, institutional, legal . . .) compared with domestic conditions. The risks associated with a multilateral system of exchanges based on internationally transferable payment or credit instruments are

M. Maresceau (ed.), The Political and Legal Framework of Trade Relations Between the European Community and Eastern Europe. ISBN 0–7923–0046–7.

thus much greater. This tends to explain why some countries choose forms of trade which are closer to barter than other countries, even if they imply additional transaction costs.

In Western economies, the growing complexity of financial instruments in international trade results in great part from the demand of economic agents for hedging against the risks inherent to a worldwide monetary economy in which capital transactions play a dominant role. This has led over time to a mix of financial innovation and regulation. Thus financial intermediaries not only produce instruments which facilitate transactions, but also provide insurance services against some of the risks related to an uncertain international environment. The costs of such services are generally small thanks to the specialisation of financial intermediaries which permits the diversification of risk and the concentration of expertise. In some countries, monetary authorities have acquired a great regulatory (or supervisory) authority; at the international level however the collective surveillance of the working of the financial system is still in its infancy.

On the other hand, countries like those belonging to the CMEA have been reluctant to extend their domestic system of exchanges which is based — as in all countries — on principles of trade multilateralism confined to the limits of their borders, to international transactions like Western countries did. But here also, innovation — under the impulse of banks — has been active, aiming at reducing the transaction costs of a system of exchanges traditionally based on "balanced bilateralism". Pure barter is now *quasi* inexistent in trade relations. Modern forms of countertrade involve:

— no simultaneity in transactions, thus introducing flexibility in time;
— some multilateralism, thus introducing flexibility in space (through, for example, clearing operations).

Specific financial instruments have been designed for these purposes and countertrade now requires expertise in financial engineering.[1] Banks' services in countertrade include opening letters of credit and escrow accounts, giving general advice, finding traders willing to take the counter-traded goods. It is, however, not clear to what extent modern forms of countertrade have been trade-creating at the *world level*. It is true that for individual countries the possibility to conduct countertrade operations has often been a *sine qua non* condition for transactions to take place; but if a country's poor trade performance results from a lack of world demand for the goods it produces, then a successful countertrade arrangement will be made at the expense of other exporting countries. There may thus be cases of *trade diversion* (see for example countertrade involving commodities in periods of excess supply). Lack of transparency,[2] the difficulty of making the demands coincide, costs related to the necessity of building long-term relations with customers, ... may give "non-price" advantage to some traders at the expense of others.

Alternatively, one can argue that, due to the risks involved in multi-lateral conventional trade (balance of payments problems), the level of world trade would be lower in the absence of countertrade. In addition, the establishment of long-term relations between partners which is present in some countertrade arrangements may also contribute to an improve-ment of product quality, a better transfer of technology, a better marketing of products. The question, however, remains if the free market cannot provide — at lower cost? — such improvements.

In the following section we present a general typology of the various financial instruments which are related to international trade. Then we discuss the role of countertrade in East-West relations, placing the accent on recent developments. The following section considers the experience with more traditional western-type financial instruments in East-West relations. We start with a lesser trade-related financial instrument, the euro-loan, before focusing on three product-related financial instruments: forfaiting, factoring and leasing. We conclude with some thoughts on the potential for a deepening of East-West financial cooperation.

II. Typology of trade-creating financial instruments

Table 1 give a list of available trade-creating financial instruments, qualify-ing the degree of utilisation by CMEA countries.

With regard to *bank lending* to CMEA countries, preference is being given to operations concerning *trade* transactions in which the life of the loan takes the economic value of the goods in question into consideration. However, generally banks can only effect such transactions in the medium-term if the transfer risk is covered by a credit insurance organisation. Should such cover be lacking, only a short-term loan will be envisaged.

A purely *financial* loan may be granted, providing:
— the country in question has a high level of solvency. This is linked both to the structure and the dimensions of the convertible currency foreign debt;
— the loan is used to implement a healthy investment policy;
— the loan is mainly used to re-schedule existing debts;
— the loan is *not* solely used to finance a chronic balance of payments deficit.

Certain *forms of credit* — more or less sophisticated — such as factoring

Table 1. Available export creating instruments on CMEA countries.

	Use	Payment or credit
1. Bank transfers	L	P
2. Cheques in BEF	S	P
other currencies	S	P
3. Drafts	M	P
4. Promissory notes	M	P
5. Book receivables	S	Ca
6. Documentary remittances	M	P
7. Bankers acceptances	S	P
8. L/C * at sight confirmed or not	L	Cs + P
* back to back credits	S	Cs + P
9. L/C Refinancing	L	Ca
10. Factoring	S	P or Ca
11. Export prefinancing	S	Ca
12. Suppliers credits	L	Ca
13. Forfaiting * short term		
(consumer goods)	L	Ca
* medium and long term	M	Ca
(capital goods)		
14. Buyers credit	M	Ca
15. General purpose lines of credit	L	Ca
16. Bank to bank credits		
* short term	L	Ca
* medium and long term	M	Ca
17. Countertrade — Buy back . . .	M	Ca
18. Leasing	S	Ca
19. Euroloans	S	Ca
20. Stand-by lines	S	Ca

P = payment; C = credit; Ca = with cash disbursement; Cs = without cash disbursement.
    Use: L = large; M = medium; S = small or inexistant.

and leasing, are still not widely used (see section IV,C and IV,D respectively). The banks will propose the *payment methods* which minimise the transfer risk for the seller (confirmed L/C) and which may make financing possible (idem + discounting without recourse).

Countertrade arrangements are of growing importance in East-West trade. A number of banks have set up countertrade departments and some are actively involved in trading. This is witnessed by an increase in the demand for the traditional forms of countertrade (counterpurchase, advance purchase, compensation) because of the scarcity of foreign currency in many Eastern European countries. This goes hand in hand with the lack of sufficient countertrade goods and the difficulty of arranging linkage between the various Foreign Trade Organisations. Similarly, there is increased application of more modern countertrade techniques such as buyback agreements (concluded either separately or as part of cooperation agreements such as Joint Ventures) as a means of implementing the new economic and industrial policy in the long term. Recent developments in countertrade are examined in the next section.

III. Recent developments in countertrade with CMEA countries

Countertrade has played an important role in East-West trade since 1945. No accurate statistics are available but the OECD countries estimate that some 30 p.c. of their trade with Eastern Bloc countries takes the form of countertrade. A study made by Dr Liliane Van Hoof shows that the figure for BLEU was between 10 and 13 p.c. in 1982.[3] The importance of countertrade in East-West trade is a corollary of the policy of bilateralism which the Eastern Bloc countries have always applied to international trade.

The reader is reminded briefly that there are various ideological and practical reasons for this bilateralism: deficient international marketing, a refusal to take positions in Western currencies, adjustment of annual trade agreements to economic plans and the fear of West Germany playing a dominant role in East-West trade.

In practice, countertrade was used until recently by Eastern European countries with insufficient foreign currency as a *means of payment* for their imports of Western products. It still functions as a means of payment, especially since the external debt situation is not very bright in a number of the countries involved. But there is more to it than that. In most Eastern Bloc countries countertrade is now being mobilised in overall industrial and economic policy with two fundamental trends towards:

(a) greater autonomy for enterprises, and

(b) technological renewal.

We shall examine these developments in more detail.

A. *Countertrade as a means of payment; increased pressure on Western exporters to accept countertrade in payment*

Contacts with exporters and the commerical press have shown that Eastern European countries are increasingly making import contracts subject to the acceptance of countertrade proposals. This is indeed the case in countries with large foreign currency problems such as Poland and

Romania where countertrade is often the only means of payment that the seller can propose. In such cases, countertrade usually represents 100 p.c. or more of the export contract. The other Eastern Bloc countries are also short of foreign currency — although to a lesser extent — so that, there too, a trend towards countertrade is being identified. A significant increase has been recorded in Czechoslovakia (countertrade percentages ranging from 20 to 120 p.c. of the value of an import transaction depending on the priority of the relevant import), the USSR (ranging from 10 to 20 p.c. for imports of finished goods and from 100 to 130 p.c. for turnkey projects) and Bulgaria (countertrade was not previously much in demand but now almost always represents 30 to 50 p.c. of the value of imported capital goods, rising to 100 p.c. for large projects).

Availability of the goods that the Eastern European importer is supposed to supply is a problem in many cases. It must be remembered that the increase in projects proposing countertrade in payment is not followed by a proportional increase in production, to say nothing of the problem of finding further outlets for countertrade products.

An additional problem is the fact that the products offered are mostly limited to the product range of the Eastern European importer. This is because other Foreign Trade Organisations (FTO) want to keep their products which could be used for countertrade to pay for their own imports. This linkage between one FTO's imports and payment with another FTO's exports now seems to be very difficult to arrange in Poland Romania, Bulgaria and Czechoslovakia.

B. *Countertrade as an instrument of new industrial and economic policy*

The attempts being made in most Eastern European countries to introduce a policy decentralisation and renewal of the economy has repercussions on the role of countertrade. We shall discuss this in the context of two major trends:
(1) greater autonomy of individual enterprises, and
(2) technological renewal.

1. *Greater autonomy of individual enterprises.* Since 1 January 1987, 21 ministries and about 70 enterprises and industrial groups in the USSR have been authorised to set up import and export contracts directly with foreigners. Until that date all contracts were arranged via the Foreign Trade Ministry and the associated FTOs.

The various business sectors and the enterprises under their umbrella are regarded as profit centres with the result that these individual units are also responsible for generating the foreign currency for their own imports instead of being allocated foreign currency by central government. The same marked swing towards decentralisation can also be felt in Bulgaria.

This policy of giving enterprises greater individual responsibility, which is a positive move in Western terms, has a number of important side-effects on countertrade.

First, there is increased pressure on Western exporters to offer counter-trade. This is because the Eastern European enterprises to which they want to export are increasingly urging acceptance of goods in countertrade in order to get hold of enough foreign currency to pay for their imports.

Secondly, the range of goods offered in countertrade is shrinking. It is against the interests of an FTO which is responsible for its own foreign currency requirements to make the goods it produces available to pay for the imports of another FTO since it would thereby lose a potential source of foreign currency income. For instance, while it used to be possible in Bulgaria to get countertrade goods from several FTOs for large export contracts to a single FTO, this is now virtually impossible. Take the example of a project in which Generale Bank is involved to supply equipment to the Bulgarian brewery sector where the Bulgarian FTO offers only the beer it makes itself in spite of a Belgian request for the range of countertrade goods to be widened in order to make it easier to cope with the substantial countertrade requirement (between 35 and 50 p.c. for the separate tranches of the project). This experience has been mirrored in Poland with two projects in the metal and agricultural industries respectively.

2. *Technological renewal.* The second important trend in Eastern European economic policy is towards technological renewal. A major method for bringing about this renewal consists in attracting Western technologies not only by purchasing Western equipment but also by arranging industrial cooperation between Eastern European and Western enterprises. This cooperation can take a number of forms such as technology transfer, licensing agreements, buyback agreements, coproduction agreements and — last but not least — joint ventures (JV).

The latter extreme form of industrial cooperation in particular has been in the news recently because of the enactment of laws in Poland (April 1986) and the USSR (January 1987) to promote the setting-up of such JVs, while the concept has existed much longer in Yugoslavia (law originally enacted in 1967 and much relaxed in 1984) and Hungary (law of 1972 relaxed several times with a coordinated text published in 1985). The setting-up of such JVs is promoted not only to provide the local market with more and better products but also, and principally, to sell the products on export markets and thereby generate income in hard currencies. The promoters of such JVs in the USSR and Poland state quite frankly that their main aim is to gain new export markets which is often at odds with the interests of the Western enterprises which want JVs in order to penetrate local markets and not to invite competition on their traditional home and export markets.

The link with countertrade is clear: the Eastern European governments oblige the Western partner in a JV to buy a substantial proportion of the JV's production, a process known in countertrade as the buyback technique (the supplier, the Western partner in a JV in this case, brings machinery, knowhow, etc., into the JV and buys back the goods they are used to produce). Clearly, countertrade is here being used in a very different way from the traditional forms of countertrade where, say, the import of machines is paid for with raw materials.

This pressure to generate foreign currency income is intensified by the fact that the JVs have to be self-supporting because of the trend towards greater autonomy of enterprises described in point III, A above. Thus, Soviet legislation stipulates that JVs must assume complete responsibility for their foreign currency requirements, i.e. all expenditure in foreign currency — such as purchases of machinery abroad, remuneration of expatriate staff, repatriation of dividends, etc. — must be covered by the income from exports.

IV. Experience with "Western-type" instruments

A. *Euro-loans*

Before 1970 trade between the EEC countries and Eastern Europe represented a relatively small share of largely balanced trade flows. However, there were a number of important changes to this pattern in the early 1970s: Eastern European leaders decided in favour of more "intensive" development (i.e. more efficient use of labour and capital) and Western European governments proved willing to stimulate government credits in the wake of the internationalisation of banking operations.

Although financial activities between East and West initially remained relatively concentrated both geographically (continental Europe) and in terms of the type of transaction (short-term financing such as letters of credit and acceptances), this new market became a growing success for international bankers. The profitability of the credits, the scope for portfolio diversification, confidence in the clout of centralised economies in the event of an economic crisis and belief in the umbrella theory (whereby the Soviet Union would use its surplus resources to support the other Comecon countries with financial problems) led to more credit being granted between 1970 and 1975. After 1975, however, Eastern Europe had to come to terms not only with growing competition from NICs but also with slower economic growth in the industrial countries, deteriorating terms of trade and a sharp increase in real interest rates. With the resulting deficits on the balance of trade and the current account balance, the countries of Eastern Europe saw their debts leap: some sources estimate that the gross external debt of the seven countries quadrupled between 1974 and 1981 from 20.1 billion Dollars to 87 billion Dollars with the BIS banks, share remaining relatively stable at 70 p.c. During this period, and especially towards the end of the decade, the Eastern European countries began to show an interest in syndicated loans via the Euromarkets: borrowings reached a peak of almost 5 billion Dollars in 1979 (medium and long-term). At the same time, and under the pressure of competition between lenders, there were increases in the average maturity (from 5.6 years in 1976 to 8.25 years in 1979) and in the non-call period; margins also fell from 134 base points above LIBOR in 1975 to 70 in 1979. This trend finally led to a crisis of confidence in the region: initially limited to Poland (1980—1981) and Romania (1981—1982), it spread to cover the entire CMEA area in the period 1982—1983. In addition to the economic imbalances just described, there were information and institutional problems not experienced in other debtor countries: most of the Eastern Bloc countries hid themselves in a veil of secrecy and were unable to request the assistance of the International Monetary Fund.

Following the onset of the international debt crisis in 1982, the changed stance of bankers led to a sharp reduction in the granting of discretionary credit (i.e. medium-term commercial paper and in particular syndicated loans): the volume of credit made available by banks to Eastern Europe fell by more than 20 p.c. between the first quarter of 1982 and the third quarter of 1983 (which can also the explained in part by the appreciation of the dollar). In 1982—1983 a number of Eastern European countries could only obtain commercial credits for 2—3 years with a yield of 1 to 1.5 p.c. In addition, since the banks eliminated their short-term lines the countries of this region were forced to turn to their reserves: deposits with the BIS fell by 2 billion Dollars (approximately 28 p.c.) in the first three quarters of 1982. Consequently, the suspension of traditional bank credits compelled the CMEA countries to use less conventional sources of credit: IMF and World Bank (for Hungary and Romania), BIS (for Hungary), supplier credits, intra-German trade lines and countertrade. However, there was very little financial cooperation in hard currencies within the area itself. In addition, they also implemented a painful but successful policy for recovery: imports, in particular of invest-ment goods, were cut back sharply. This enabled them to turn the deficit on the current account balance from the 1970s into a surplus from 1982 onwards, and to reduce net external debt from 78.1 billion Dollars at the end of 1981 to 59.4 million Dollars at the end of 1984.

Scarcely 2 1/2 years after the beginning of the crisis Eastern Europe succeeded in creating sufficient confidence in the financial world to once more become fully active on the international capital markets (5.2 billion Dollars in 1985 and 4.1 billion Dollars in 1986) under favourable condi-tions (an average of 26 base points above LIBOR and maturity of 7.4 years). Clearly, this new development went hand in hand with the limited scope for traditional commercial banking outside the region in question. After all, most countries that are very active on the international capital markets have a growing interest in the securitisation process currently under way.

Governments are also showing a steady interest in the countries of the Eastern Bloc: substantial official secured export credits are being granted with a view to stimulating exports to this region. Thus, OECD figures for 1985 show that 37 p.c. of the gross external debt of the seven Eastern European countries consisted of secured official credits and 43 p.c. of unsecured bank loans. While it is true that the great need for fresh money that became particularly apparent in the statistics since 1985 is connected with the deteriorating current account balance, the restructuring of external debt (with a view to lower financing costs and a less vulnerable financial position in the medium term) played a role in that year as did the topping-up of foreign currency reserves (Bulgaria, GDR and Hungary) and unused commitments (Hungary, GDR and Czechoslovakia).

Although this general trend continued in 1986 and 1987, there were nevertheless clear differences between the various countries: Bulgaria and the GDR had significantly less recourse to the international capital markets, Czechoslovakia had more whereas Hungary and the USSR maintained their high level. The last two countries also borrowed more in currencies other than the US Dollar and used other financial instruments such as bond issues, bankers' acceptance facilities and floating rate notes. Lastly, Poland and Romania have remained on the sidelines of the credit market.

In overall terms, it can be stated that the international financial position of Eastern Europe has weakened again since 1985: its net position with respect to the banks of the BIS zone has never before been so much in deficit (47 billion dollars as against 44 billion dollars at the height of the last crisis in 1980). It is consequently highly unlikely that the recent increase in debt will be able to continue in the medium term. This will work against the objectives of the new 1986—1990 five years plans unless alternatives such as joint ventures are found. While it should not be the normal function of banks to provide balance of payments financing, which implies sovereign risk, banks have an important role to play in identifying investment opportunities and in financing "self-debt liquidation" projects.

B. *Forfaiting with CMEA countries*

Forfaiting, that can be defined as the discounting of drafts or receivables without recourse to the exporter, has recently known an increasing popularity with most of the world's "bankable" borrowers (a "bankable"

Table 2. Eastern Europe's foreign trade (in USD billion).

	1965	1970	1975	1980	1985	1986
CMEA imports						
— total	19.7	30.3	88.1	154.3	165.2	176.7
— from EEC (10 countries)	2.4	4.7	15.2	27.0	17.1	18.5
— total[a]	7.4	11.9	43.7	77.8	74.9	71.9
CMEA exports						
— total	20.0	31.0	78.3	156.5	174.8	187.6
— to EEC (10 countries)	2.5	4.4	10.8	31.7	24.5	21.5
— total[a]	7.5	12.6	33.9	79.1	83.1	82.3

Source: *UNO — Monthly Bulletin of Statistics.*
[a] excluding intra — CMEA trade.

Table 3. External position of Eastern European region with banks of BIS zone * (USD billion, year-end figures).

	1974	1980	1984	1985	1986	June 87
Assets	6.7	15.7	22.1	27.0	29.5	28.4
Liabilities	14.1	59.8	48.2	60.7	72.1	75.4
Net position	−7.4	−44.1	−26.1	−33.7	−42.6	−47.0
Undisbursed credit commitments	4.1[a]	9.6	5.2	9.1	8.2	
Non-bank trade-related credits	N.A.	18.1[b]	16.5	16.6	22.4	

Source: *Bank for International Settlements.*
* The figures are not completely consistent for the relevant years because of changes in the BIS zone.
[a] 1978
[b] 1982

Table 4. Funds raised on the international capital markets (USD billion).

	1982	1983	1984	1985	1986	1987 (Jan/Sep)
Total of which by	179.1	157.8	228.8	279.1	321.4	215.4
Eastern Europe:	0.7	1.1	3.4	5.3	3.9	2.7
· Bond issues	—	—	0.1	0.5	0.3	0.5
· Loans	0.7	1.1	3.3	4.8	3.6	2.2
of which: (IMLBL)[a]	(0.6)	(0.9)	(2.7)	(4.3)	(2.5)	(1.8)
Terms on syndicated credits						(Jan/Mar)
· average margin (base points over Libor)	103	112	88	55	26	23
· average maturity	4/9	4/5	5/11	7/5	7/5	7/6

Source: *OECD, Monthly Financial Statistics.*
[a] International medium and long-term bank loans.

borrower is a borrower with whom banks are happy to deal: this definition offers large prospects). Generally, the forfaiting transactions involve a bank aval or guarantee (aval on the notes or guarantee by separate commitment).

With most of the Eastern European countries, forfaiting has always been an adequate financing technique. It is indeed well-designed to finance a regular flow of specific equipment deliveries, each of these being financed on a short- or medium-term basis, with the terms of payment materialised by drafts drawn by the exporter on the buyer/borrower (in certain cases, book receivables have been used as a substitute for drafts).

Current goods are usually financed for a 6-months term, while the financing of capital or equipment goods is normally required for a 5-year term, with half-yearly repayments.

Historically, forfaiting out of Belgium has been developed by the commercial banks (with G Bank covering more than 50 p.c. of the transactions), together with the Belgian Authorities for export promotion, namely Ducroire, the Belgian public credit insurer. We named this type of forfaiting, the "Garantie Forfaitaire de Paiement/Forfaitaire Betalingswaarborg". This technique is satisfactory as long as the financing relates to Belgian goods, to 85 p.c. of the contract price (with 15 p.c. as a down-payment), and exporters which have a "global arrangement" with Ducroire which means that the exporter has to insure all his export receivables with this institution (according to the general principle by which "the good risks pay for the bad ones"). This technique also enabled the Bank, having shared the risks with the insurer, to increase its financing capabilities. Progressively, however, our bank developed the concept of forfaiting beyond the Belgian framework, especially each time:

— the contract was to be 100 p.c. (and not 85 p.c.) financed for 100 p.c. (and not 85 p.c.); and/or

— the delivered goods were not produced in Belgium, but the bank wanted to support its customer;

— and obviously each time the borrower and its aval are considered as a bankable partner.

This "enlarged" concept of forfaiting applies to several Eastern European countries.

This is where we stand today. A specialised unit has been created within G. Bank to manage forfaiting. It works closely together with our domestic network, which originates most of the deals, our Treasury and Forex department, which provides us with the adequate funding and our correspondent banking division, whose close contacts with Eastern European countries enables us to assess and price each transaction. Our presence in Moscow is obviously a key element as far as forfaiting with the Soviet Union is concerned.

C. *Factoring*

The factor purchases the invoices issued by his client; he covers debtors' insolvency and may advance funds corresponding to a fraction of the amount of the invoices he has purchased. The special implications of factoring for East-West trade relations are such that it is essential for certain Eastern Bloc exporters.

1. *Exporters in a planned economy.* When a company from a country with a planned economy wishes to export, it must abide by 4 plans, as for its domestic market:

— the production plan
— the finance and investment plan
— the invoicing plan
— the collection schedule.

The first three plans depend solely on the exporting company's organisation. The fourth plan — collection — depends on the debtors.

2. *Debtors in a market economy.* With regard to debtors in a market economy, the invoice payment programme has three possible outcomes:

— either the debtor pays on the agreed date, in which case the exporter's payment plan is met;

— or, he pays late, in which case the plan is not complied with and the exporter will have problems;

— or, which is quite impossible in a planned economy, the Western debtor may go bankrupt, in which case the exporter will be faced with a very serious problem. The factor can provide a solution.

3. *A solution to the exporter's problem.* The exporter from the planned economy draws up a contract with a factor containing, in addition to the usual clauses, the following: the contracts signed by the exporter with his debtors must provide for payment to the factor. The contracts must also provide for late interest in the case of delayed payment, or in the case of the statutory documents required by the debtor's national authorities not being remitted to the factor on time, by fault of the debtor. Provision is made for an arbitration clause in the contract between the factor and exporter. The Paris Court of Arbitration is frequently referred to and the Vienna Court even more so for contracts with Eastern Bloc countries.

4. *Diagram showing trading procedure.* As can be seen on this diagram (see *infra* p. 235) 3 parties are involved:
— on the left, we have the exporter
— on the right, the importer, for example, a Belgian debtor, and below the factor (symbolised by H.G.F.)
The exporter sends the goods to his debtor. Prior to this, he sends his factor a "credit line" application for each of his debtors, and the factor either accepts it without reservation, accepts subject to special conditions or refuses.

Our experience has shown that in relations between Eastern Bloc exporters and Western debtors, well over 90 p.c. of credit lines are granted without limitation. The exporter sends his original invoice and copies to the factor. The factor then sends the original to the debtor; prior to sending, it is specified on the original that payment can only be made to the factor.

As we have seen, the debtor may make his payment on time, late, or fail to do so altogether. All statutory documents for obtaining the payment transfer may fail to arrive on time. This, however, is of little importance to the exporter, as the factor undertakes to transfer the monies owed when the invoices fall due. He can do so because on the one hand he covers his debtors' insolvency, and on the other, as a result of the contract linking the importer to the exporter, he can, if appropriate, claim late interest from the importer. A possible variant is even to advance the total amount of the invoices when they are issued, i.e. several weeks, sometimes several months before they fall due. All that is required is for the factor to be

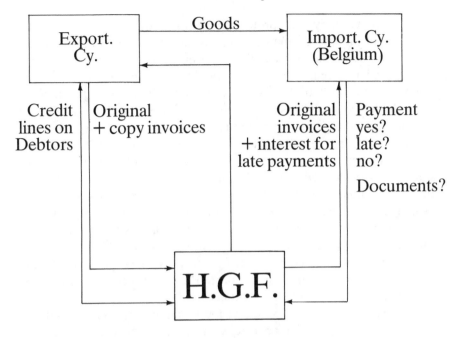

Payment on the due date
or financing if desired

100% possible in case of recourse
on a known Bank

granted surety by a bank in the exporter's country, covering any possible failure by the exporter, for example, erroneous invoices or bad delivery.

Let us conclude by stating that, to our knowledge, an Eastern Bloc exporter has never made these mistakes. Our experience with these exporters is excellent.

D. *Leasing, as a tool to boost trade between East and West*

In general terms, leasing can be defined as rental of equipment, material, or immovables, for professional purposes, specially purchased by firms which retain ownership of the goods leased, but which give the user the option to purchase the goods at the end of the contract at a price which has been previously fixed. The original and essential character of leasing lies in the fact that the hire contract is irrevocable while the obligation to buy at the end of the contract is optional.

However, besides this definition, we must add that the legal environment, and particularly the protection of the owner's rights and the organisation of the lessee's rights, as well as the equilibrium of the contract concluded between the parties, gives leasing an economic scope which may vary widely from one case to another. As an example we may mention that the investment risks are shared differently depending on whether the lessee has or has not completely reimbursed the total amount of capital invested together with the financial costs, to the lessor when the contract expires. In the case of full-pay-out-leasing, it is only the lessee who bears the economic investment risk. However, with non-full-pay-out-leasing, this risk is divided between lessor and lessee.

In our opinion, the *flexibility* of leasing, as a means of financing investments is its main contribution to the development of trade. As one of the complementary examples of this flexibility, we would like to mention that leasing, particularly leasing of movables, makes it very easy

- to set up a transaction involving successive lessees, in which the right to the lease may be transferred if the parties agree to it, this facilitates the investment decision;
- to organise, within the scope of the initial leasing contract, supplementary financing for an extension of the original investment, to allow for the development of the project or upgrading due to subsequent technological developments.

Leasing also means that the lessor is involved in the legal relationships between lessee and supplier. The lessor stipulates the "obligation to deliver" according to the specifications drawn up by the user and commits himself to pay the supplier the agreed price according to the terms agreed by the parties, even though the lessor will obviously prefer not to intervene in the economic reality of the decision to deliver and acquire respectively goods and services against payment of the agreed price. The fact that the lessor is involved and maintains a relationship with the supplier and the user which is more permanent and extended than the relationship between the supplier and user themselves, who may restrict their relationship to only one contract, may also favour the large scale export and import trade.

Leasing also makes it possible to:

- finance the investment at 100 p.c.;
- to associate (in an easy and easily modifiable legal arrangement) the supplier with the risks of financing the export transaction in question;
- easily identify the outflows which follow from the decision to acquire a particular asset, as the asset financing provided by leasing leads to identifying the financial charge deriving from the use of capital goods.

The advantages mentioned are not solely offered by leasing — they may also be obtained by using buyer's or supplier's credits. In leasing, however, they are obtained almost automatically. However, the more characteristic advantages of leasing are:

1. The nature itself of the essential obligation entered into by the user — as already mentioned the obligation to pay the agreed rental could often make it possible as well in the East as in the West (we find this formula both in big state or state-controlled organisations and in big private firms) to take a decision about investments, based on a valid hypothesis, by charging investments to the operating budgets when investment budgets are exhausted. This advantage of leasing — which is a real advantage when the decision to invest is justified in economic terms — is without doubt irrational but no less real and concrete. A deal which has been signed recently for financing equipment for a propylene plant extension for the State Chemical Company of an East European country illustrates this aspect. In fact, the cost of the plant will probably not be included either in the national account, nor in the budget controlling expenditure of the country's current five-year plan. In the West, similar examples can be found, both in financing the building of bridges, sluices, etc. on behalf of a State (Government) as in purchasing major hardware equipment for the industrial or financial sector.

2. It is easier to finance investments by leasing than by using credit facilities (because of the difficulties in selling the goods in the event of non-payment or because of the danger of the compulsory funding of debts) because the owner's rights are legally protected and the good leased will be movable (or removable without dismantling and repatriation costs

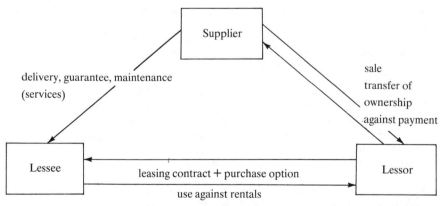

In comparison with the classical relationship represented by a commercial purchase contract coupled with a corresponding finance facility (Financier $\xrightarrow{\text{Credits}}$ Investor $\xrightarrow{\text{Purchase}}$ Supplier) it shows just how important the measures are to protect ownership.

absorbing too large a part of the replacement value) and will maintain their value on the secondhand market. This advantage of leasing will apply both to Western private investors who do not have the financial resources required, and to institutions in developing countries with for example, balance of payments problems. The above-mentioned list obviously does not give an exhaustive image of the advantages of leasing because a lot of them depend on the inventiveness of the parties concerned. To conclude, we would like to add that "project financing" and "buy-back" techniques can also be integrated in leasing transactions. This financing method is really of particular interest and important, owing to the advantages which are derived from the triangular relationship between the supplier, buyer and lessor by virtue of the leasing arrangement.

Notes

1. See for example L. G. B. WELT (1985).
2. Which, of course, can also exist in the more traditional forms of exchanges.
3. L. Van Hoof "La compensation dans les échanges Est-Ouest. Analyse théorique et vérification empirique en union économique Belgo-Luxembourgeoise" — doctoral thesis. Université de paris I Panthéon — Sorbonne, 1983.

Bibliography

M. Cabrillac, "La reconnaissance en droit international privé de sûretés réelles sans dépossession constituées à l'étranger", Rapport présenté au Xe Congrès international de droit comparé, Budapest, 23—30 August 1978: *Revue Critique de droit international privé* 1979, pp. 487—505.
J. B. Damer, "Leasing in Europe", *The Banker*, 1977, pp. 127—131.
F. J. De Cuyper, "Leasing — Stand der europäischen Harmonisierung", *SHZ*, 1977, No. 8, p. 21.
D. Fairlamb, "Eastern Europe comes in from the cold", *The Banker*, 1987, pp. 48—50.
C. Gavalda and Bey (El Mokhtar). "Problématique juridique du leasing international", *Gaz. Pal.*, 1979, I, doct., 25—26 March, pp. 143—149.
GROUP OF THIRTY, *Countertrade in World Economy*, New York, 1985.
"Ausländer wollen Leasing mit der UDSSR ausdehnen", Handelsblatt, 19 July, 1979.
F.-E. Klein "La reconnaissance en droit international privé des sûretés réelles sans dépossession constituées à l'étranger", Rapport présenté au Xe Congrès international de droit comparé, Budapest, 23—30 August, 1978: *Revue critique de droit international privé*, 1979, pp. 507—536.
A. Lelarge, *Le troc. Une nouvelle technique de commerce international*, ADETEX, Paris, 1985.
R. Monaco, Le contrat de crédit-bail international (Rapport sur les travaux d'Unidroit): *Les petites affiches*, Paris, 3 August, 1979—20 August, 1979, Nos. 92—97.
G. Nockles, "If you want to sell, you sometimes have to buy first", in *Euromoney Trade Finance Report*, February 1986.

O.C.D.E., *Echanges compensés. Pratique des pays en développement*, Paris, 1985.

OECD, *Financial Market Trends*, several issues.

OECD, *Monthy Financial Statistics*.

I. G. Park, "Countertrade Requirements in East-West Transactions", in *Journal of Comparative Business and Capital Market Law*, 1983.

TASS, News agency of the Soviet Union: "Leasing, promising form of crediting", *Economic and Commercial News Weekly*, Europe Edition, Moscow/Basle, 11 June, 1979.

UNIDROIT, Institut international pour l'unification du droit privé: Résumé des discussions du groupe de travail invité à se prononcer sur la possibilité d'élaborer des règles internationales uniformes en matière de contrat de "leasing" ou "crédit-bail", C.D. 54 — Doc. 4/1, Rome, April 1975.

J. Vanous, "A review of developments in Soviet and East European Hard-Currency trade, balance of payments, debt and assets, 1980—86", *Plan Econ. Report*, 17 September, 1987.

P. Verzariu, *Countertrade, Barter and Offsets*, New York, McGraw Hill, 1984.

Export controls: general framework

GIUSEPPE SCHIAVONE

Professor University of Catania and Institute of European Studies "Alcide de Gasperi", Rome

I. Introduction

Physical controls on the exportation of goods, whether made effective through prohibitions, quotas or licenses, have been mainly practised, in this century, in case of war (including 'cold war') or in emergencies in order to prevent critical shortages or to secure the enforcement of marketing schemes.

In the East-West framework, export controls may be considered an aspect of foreign economic policy involving a wide range of issues, from commercial policy to national security, to global foreign policy options and objectives.[1] As a matter of fact, export controls may serve a variety of purposes from the safeguard of essential supplies for domestic producers and consumers to the denial of goods and equipment of strategic import-ance to an adversary, be it extant or potential, to the enforcement of international law through economic and other non-military 'sanctions' intended to implement a policy of retaliation or 'punishment'.

It need not be stressed that any discussion about export controls, within the general framework of trade relations between the European Com-munity (EC) on one side and the Soviet Union and Eastern Europe[2] on the other, must inevitably come to terms with the realities of these late 1980s.

The multinational power-sharing experiment carried out within the EC is still fragile, despite the efforts currently being carried out to establish a single internal market by 1992. Moreover, the commercial and financial self-interest of individual member countries often makes it hard to formulate and implement a consistent foreign economic and trade policy, even on the basis of the lowest common denominator of the 12 member countries.

In the Soviet Union, Gorbachev's 'new thinking' and the consequent efforts at *perestroika*, or restructuring, are intended, *inter alia*, to bring

M. Maresceau (ed.), The Political and Legal Framework of Trade Relations Between the European Community and Eastern Europe. ISBN 0–7923–0046–7.
© *1989 by Kluwer Academic Publishers, Dordrecht – Printed in the Netherlands.*

about a decentralisation of the economic decision-making power[3] and to favour the expansion of trade and industrial cooperation, notably joint ventures, with Western countries.[4] The greater autonomy of Soviet enterprises will have important effects on trade flows and practices, including countertrade arrangements.

Attempts to introduce a policy of decentralisation and restructuring of the economy are also being made in a number of East European countries. It should be pointed out, in this regard, that the traditional view of Eastern Europe as a basically homogeneous unit within the Soviet 'sphere of influence', as carved out by Yalta negotiators in February 1945, no longer holds. Despite their allegiance to a common ideology and their ultimate dependence upon Soviet power for external protection, the countries of Eastern Europe actively pursue their own national interests and concerns, in a regional context where traditional historical rivalries are far from extinguished. This results in increasingly differentiating policies and rules in the foreign trade sector.

While discussing the general framework of export controls, however, it is not possible to confine the analysis to the EC, the Soviet Union and Eastern Europe. It is obviously necessary to take into serious consideration the attitudes and policies of the United States and the strains which characterise what is now called the West-West relationship. The differences between West European countries and the United States over a number of economic, political, and even security issues, make a broad consensus on the West's overall strategy vis-à-vis the Soviet Union and Eastern Europe difficult to achieve. Moreover, the focus of American interest has been steadily shifting away from Europe, no longer a major area of contention between the two superpowers, to the Asian-Pacific region where the United States now faces unprecedented economic challenges from long-standing allies along with growing diplomatic activity on the part of the Soviets.

II. Sanctions under the United Nations Charter

The application of measures of economic coercion against nations perceived as a threat to international peace and security, has been envisaged on a world scale by both the Covenant of the League of Nations and the Charter of the United Nations (UN). These measures usually include restrictions on exports so as to withhold vital supplies from the offending country and to isolate it economically.

The imposition of economic sanctions (such as trade embargoes, export controls, blocking of assets and credit restraints)[5] obviously carries an implication of legal or social pressure and with it a strong connotation of condemnation or disapproval.

Sanctions were considered an economic weapon by Article 16 of the League Covenant which provided for the 'severance of all trade and financial relations' with the League member going to war unlawfully.[6]

The 'complete or partial interruption of economic relations' is currently envisaged by Article 41 of the UN Charter among the measures, not involving the use of armed force, to be employed to give effect to the decisions of the Security Council.

With a view to ensuring South Africa's compliance with UN decisions for the dismantling of *apartheid*, the General Assembly and the Security Council have repeatedly asked member countries to boycott South African goods and to refrain from all exports to South Africa. In November 1977, the Security Council made the previously voluntary arms embargo against South Africa mandatory.[7] Further international action — including the imposition of economic sanctions — to isolate South Africa was requested by the International Conference on Sanctions against South Africa held in Paris in May 1981. An 11-member Group to monitor the supply and shipping of oil to South Africa was set up by the General Assembly in 1986 in order to verify and publicise violations of the oil embargo.

However, the lack of political will on the part of important trading partners of South Africa has made the generalised adoption of truly comprehensive and mandatory economic measures near to impossible. The efficacy and wisdom of such measures are also called into question in Western circles because of the harmful consequences of sanctions on the economies of the 'frontline states' which depend, to a greater or lesser degree, on South Africa. The problem may therefore arise of sanctions causing damage not only to the country to be 'punished' and, almost inevitably, to the 'sanctionist' country, but also to 'innocent' neighbouring states for whom some form of compensation ought to be eventually envisaged.[8]

The adoption of a UN embargo on arms sales to Iran has been considered by some members of the Security Council in order to favour the cessation of hostilities between Iran and Iraq. Serious doubts are raised, however, about the effectiveness and consequences of the proposed embargo.

Repeated Western — and particularly U.S. — efforts for the condemnation of the Soviet Union by the UN General Assembly and Security Council for alleged violations of international law have never materialised in the adoption of sanctions. The events in Hungary in 1956 and in Czechoslovakia in 1968 caused international protest but no specific measures were adopted within the UN or other multilateral fora.

The Soviet intervention in Afghanistan, which took place late in 1979, was strongly deplored by the General Assembly meeting in emergency special session in January 1980.[9] The Assembly called for the immediate withdrawal of foreign troops from Afghanistan and appealed to all states and organisations to extend humanitarian relief assistance to Afghan refugees. The inability to reach multilateral agreement on any kind of punitive action led the United States to adopt, *inter alia*, a unilateral grain embargo against the Soviet Union which, however, had very limited effects.

On the whole, failure to develop a coordinated approach to sanctions has severely reduced the impact of unilateral policies of embargo and trade controls ultimately making such policies unenforceable.

III. The rationale of economic sanctions

The very complex matter of export controls involves economic-financial-political issues whose manifold implications and interactions are unlikely to be fully grasped in the initial stage of the 'sanctionist' exercise.

In Western-type democracies, debates on the imposition of sanctions are seldom conducted within a framework of settled policies and strategies. Emotional factors may play a disproportionate role, without any serious attempt being made to assess the expected consequences for the economy of the 'sanctionist' country. Public pressure for prompt punitive action against a country whose behaviour offends some basic principles, either domestically (such as human rights violations) or internationally (such as the sponsorship of terrorist activities), may heavily influence the decision-making process. This may lead, at a later stage, to a softening of the restrictive measures in order to reduce the negative impact on domestic business.

In other words, sanctions may be adopted for mainly 'internal' use, that is for domestic policy considerations in order to meet the demands of specific groups or lobbies, rather than for 'external' use, that is really to hamper a foreign country's development through economic warfare.

Sanctions are normally viewed as a temporary measure to be dismantled when a positive change occurs in the offending country's conduct. The rationale of economic sanctions, in fact, transcends the purely punitive aspect to include the expectation of a return to 'correct' standards of behaviour.

The attempt to force change by economic pressure may even materialise in the offer of economic inducements with a view to encouraging a politically desirable conduct on the part of a given country. This has been, *inter alia*, the case of the Federal Republic of Germany which — on the assumption of 'change by trade' (Wandel durch Handel) — has relied on economic means to influence developments in line with its own interests in overall German relations.[10]

The use of economic relations either to punish (through sanctions) or to reward (through incentives) inevitably leads to link purely trade and financial matters to broader political and foreign policy issues. Even when they are adopted by a single country against another country as the result of a unilateral decision, sanctions and incentives may have repercussions extending far beyond the relationship between the two countries involved. Moreover, measures and countermeasures implemented on a strictly national plane may appear anachronistic in a world where multinational firms often enjoy greater mobility than national authorities.

Export controls are applied, in a number of cases, to sales of highly sensitive products and technologies having direct or indirect military applications and therefore likely to strengthen the offensive potential of a given country perceived as a 'threat'.

In the East-West context, Western export controls may therefore be described as non-military approaches to the containment of soviet 'expansionism'. The perceptions of the magnitude of the Soviet threat, however, differ markedly among Western countries and especially the United States on the one side and the West European countries on the other. Different perceptions about the dangers and benefits of dealings with the Soviet Union and Eastern Europe make the adoption of a Western common foreign policy stance extremely hard to reach.

IV. Western attitudes toward export controls

Besides the historical tendency of some countries — above all the United States — to boycott adversaries on moral grounds, Western attitudes toward export controls result from a combination of several factors involving peculiar and occasionally conflicting interests and goals on either side of the Atlantic and within Western Europe itself. It is a well-known fact that the U.S. view generally holds trade to be a greater benefit to the Soviet Union and its East European allies than to the West. Moreover, the sale of products embodying high technology is likely to narrow the West's lead over the Soviets in military technology, thereby jeopardising the successful defence of Western Europe and the United States.

The guidelines of the West European approach to the East-West relationship rest less on a basis of ideological, and national and global security implications than on economic and financial reasons. Commercial considerations and hard-currency liquidity are likely to shape West European policies toward the Soviet Union to a far greater extent than political commitments. As a matter of fact, the evolution of trade and industrial cooperation between the two halves of Europe over the past decades, only partly reflected the ups-and-downs of the political relationship.

It remains an open question whether the benefits gained by West European public and private firms from economic and financial deals with their Eastern counterparts can always be balanced against the longer-term consideration of the West's overall security objectives.

Despite recurring disagreements and clashes on specific issues between the United States and Western Europe, there are ample opportunities for compromises that take into account the different perceptions of the costs and benefits of trade and cooperation with the Soviet Union and Eastern Europe.[11]

Within this context, the central issue is whether economic warfare should be regarded by Western countries as an essential policy tool in international — or, at least, East-West — relations or whether it should be rejected as the negation of the very principles according to which market economies are supposed to behave. Of course, economic warfare is no novelty on the world scene and has been applied in several circumstances in the past to put pressure on governments.

The nations of Western Europe are basically willing to cooperate between themselves and with the United States in order to establish a common approach to the East-West economic relationship but, unlike the United States, generally object to considering export controls and credit restrictions as foreign policy instruments.

Governments in Western Europe have always been reluctant to impose economic sanctions within the framework of 'linkage' or 'leverage' policies whose basic assumptions rest on questionable moral grounds. Not only do West European governments have serious doubts about the moral justification for punishment but also call in question the practicability of economic countermeasures whose effective application is ultimately left to the direction of individual countries.

On the U.S. side, over the past two decades, permissive trade and credit policies have alternated with restrictions and embargoes, thus giving more often than not an impression of uncertainty in Western Europe and elsewhere.[12] It should also be emphasised that some restrictive practices of the United States have caused severe strains on Western solidarity, without any crippling effect on the Soviet economy.[13] This is particularly the case for retroactivity (the prohibition of the export of goods or technology even after a contract has been signed) and extra-territoriality (the control of the re-export of goods once they have left the national territory).[14]

V. The role of Western summits and international organisations

A more determined effort to coordinate Western policies on export controls should be undertaken within the framework of a number of intergovernmental fora whose activities have a direct or indirect impact on East-West economic relations.

Since the mid-1970s, economic summits of Western countries have contributed, *inter alia*, to shape common attitudes toward the Soviet Union and Eastern Europe on trade and financial matters.[15] As regards East-West relations, summit declarations have concentrated on two main issues: export controls on strategic goods and the limitation of export credits, with a view to avoiding a harmful race among Western countries.

As the meeting in the Château de Rambouillet, in November 1975, the Heads of state and government of the participating countries,[16] expressed their interest in an 'orderly and fruitful increase' in economic relations with the Eastern European countries and their willingness to intensify efforts for the 'prompt conclusion of the negotiations concerning export credits'.[17] The adoption of 'converging guidelines with regard to export credits' was highlighted by participants[18] in the San Juan (Puerto Rico) meeting of June 1976 and the hope was expressed that other countries might soon be able to join in such adoption.

A review of East-West economic relations was again undertaken at the Ottawa summit (July 1981). Participants[19] recognised the 'complex balance of political and economic interests and risks' inherent in such relations and stressed the need for a coordinated approach safeguarding political and security objectives. More precisely, participants decided to consult with a view to improving the 'present system of controls on trade in strategic goods and related technology with the USSR'.

The issues of strategic export controls, at both the international and the national levels, and of export credits were once more discussed at the Versailles summit of June 1982. The security and other implications of economic relations with Eastern countries have been dealt with in subsequent Western summits.

While economic summits may provide broad orientations on export controls and credits, it is obviously necessary to investigate and negotiate in detail in the appropriate multilateral institutions. Summit declarations, especially in the 1980s, have made explicit references to this end. Participants at the Versailles meeting indicated their willingness to 'exchange information' in the Organisation for Economic Cooperation and Development (OECD), on all aspects of economic, commercial and financial relations with the Soviet Union and Eastern Europe. At the summit held at Williamsburg (Virginia) in May 1983, mention was made of the 'work of the multilateral organisations' which had analysed and drawn conclusions regarding the key aspects of East-West economic relations. The need to continue work on the subject 'in the appropriate organisations' was again emphasised at the London meeting of June 1984.

Within the OECD framework,[20] trade and financing policies toward the Soviet Union and Eastern Europe are investigated and discussed with a view to strengthening Western solidarity. Significant progress in this direction has been made, since the early 1980s, as regards interest rates on long-term loans granted to importers in the Third World but also to the Soviet Union. In the 1970s, the Soviet Union had access to credit on highly favourable terms from several West European countries competing among themselves for Eastern markets. According to the gentlemen's agreement currently in force, reached within the OECD framework, 'consensus rates' must reflect the evolution of market interest rates, without any undue preferential treatment being granted to the Soviets.[21] As for East-West technology transfer, its manifold aspects and implications have been thoroughly analysed within the OECD.[22]

The problems arising from the dependence of Western countries on non-OECD (including Soviet) energy supplies and the necessity to rely on secure and diversified sources are debated by the International Energy Agency (IEA), an operating body created, at U.S. initiative, by the OECD Council as a response of the industrialised countries to the first oil shock.[23] For its part, the North Atlantic Treaty Organisation (NATO) provides a multilateral framework for the definition of concerted policies on issues of crucial importance from the standpoint of their security implications.

VI. The export controls administered by COCOM

The acquisition of advanced technology from Western countries is another facet of the East-West relationship that is of paramount importance to the Soviet Union and Eastern Europe.

Surveillance and control over Western exports to the Soviet Union and its Warsaw Pact allies have been carried out, over the past four decades, within the framework of an informal body, the Paris-based Coordinating

Committee for Multilateral Export Controls, generally known by the acronym COCOM.[24] Among COCOM's main tasks there is, at present, the control of technology transfers with special regard to the industrial techniques for the production of advanced weapons and strategic equipment.

Conflicts have periodically arisen among members (which include all NATO countries, with the exception of Iceland, plus Japan) over the inclusion of specific items in the lists administered by COCOM and over the national enforcement of the restrictive measures.[25]

Since the early 1980s, several steps have been taken to strengthen the COCOM system by improving its effectiveness, updating and refining lists and tightening national licensing and endorsement procedures.

The United States has consistently aimed, over the years, for the broadest possible coverage of high-technology items, while its COCOM partners have usually taken a more trade-minded stance. The West European countries, while basically recognising that a more effective control system within an improved institutional framework is of crucial importance, are afraid that stricter politically-motivated rules such as those proposed by the United States may adversely affect their trade interests and interfere in their domestic affairs.

As stated before, COCOM finds its *raison d'être* in the establishment and updating of the precise technical definitions of militarily relevant products and technologies that should be controlled. These are grouped into three lists: military; atomic energy; and 'dual use' for goods with both commercial and military applications.[26] The organisation reviews individual members' requests to permit shipment of specific embargoed items to proscribed countries when the risk of diversion to military use is sufficiently small. The COCOM member countries coordinate their export control administration and enforcement activities.

The organisational mechanism and the activities of COCOM are, at least in principle, surrounded by secrecy and therefore it is not possible to go into much detail about its structure, tasks, policy guidelines and decisions on specific issues. Secrecy appears to be motivated not only by obvious security reasons but also by the need to protect West European governments from possible domestic opposition to economic and trade measures against Eastern countries. This is the case of West European countries with strong pro-Communist groups.

Critical to any effort within the COCOM framework, is the necessity to reconcile the legitimate rights of exporters and their importance to the economy with the more or less pressing demands of national security. Further difficulties arise from the requirement, in conformity with COCOM's basic rules, to secure agreement on all issues under consideration by all member countries. Unanimity is necessary, in fact, to include an item in the lists as well as to take it off.

The joint system of controls over the export of commodities and technologies supporting Warsaw Pact defence priority industries — such as micro-electronics, aerospace, machine building, metallurgy, chemicals, heavy vehicles, and shipbuilding — must be adapted continually to developments in technology and equipment. Work is therefore done on a very broad front to both update and improve coverage and description of the various items, with a view to maintaining the West's substantial leads in manufacturing know-how and other areas of technology innovation.

Another serious problem faced by COCOM is represented by the pressing need to involve in the Western system of controls other partners, including a number of neutral and non-aligned countries. This applies to countries in Europe, such as Austria, Finland, Sweden and Switzerland, as well as in Asia, such as Singapore, which may serve as 'clearing houses' for the transshipment of high-technology items with military applications to unauthorised (and actually proscribed) end-users in Warsaw Pact nations.

VII. West European responses in a time of *Glasnost*

The countries of the EC and of Western Europe in general take care in avoiding highly confrontational postures with Warsaw Pact members and have never regarded the extensive use of export controls as a suitable foreign policy tool for putting pressure on the Soviet Union and Eastern Europe.

As a matter of fact, the basic systemic constraints involved in dealing with centrally-planned economies shape the policy of the EC and its members vis-à-vis the Eastern countries to a much greater extent than the East-West overall political climate.

According to conventional wisdom, the West — and above all the EC — should carefully discriminate between the Soviet Union and East European countries. The latter should gradually be bound by the EC members into a complex web of commercial, technological and credit ties. This would contribute to make Eastern Europe more prosperous and eventually less dependent on the Soviet Union, thereby contributing to the decline of the Soviet role in controlling the political affairs of the region.[27]

Within this context, the changing features of the relationship between the Soviet Union and individual East European countries deserve special attention. East European leaders — although they share fundamental policy interests with the Soviet leadership — appear to be willing to take into more adequate consideration the long-term advantage of their own countries. Essentially the challenge faced by East European policy-makers seems to be that of implementing much-needed reforms in the economic sphere without setting off an extensive and irreversible process of social change. The attitudes, interests and policies of Western nations may have a real influence on Eastern Europe through improved economic and trade relations.

While it is generally recognised that no EC initiative is likely, by itself, to alter in the short run the basic relationship between Eastern Europe and the Soviet Union and that over the past decades major attempts to reform have been brought about by domestic rather than foreign (non-Soviet) influence, an articulated policy of small steps toward the region on the part of the EC could encourage progress in the sense of greater autonomy and diversity. What should occur on the part of the EC is not an attempt to exacerbate existing imbalances or to exploit intellectual dissent and popular discontent in Eastern Europe but the gradual building of a more pragmatic and potentially lucrative relationship through increased commercial and other contracts — when these are not damaging the West's security interests — and the steady use of bargaining linkages to foster liberalisation and pluralism.

Whenever possible, preferential treatment ought to be granted to East European countries introducing or developing market-oriented structures. Moreover, financial ties between the two halves of Europe should be maintained and possibly extended, paying due regard to the important differences in the level of indebtedness and economic performance of the various East European countries. More frequent cultural and scientific contacts, within the context of a realistic technology-transfer policy, could help Western values penetrate in East European societies which, for their part, are showing a renewed interest in their own national heritage and culture.

A significant step toward establishing a more stable and predictable pattern for economic relations between the two halves of Europe would doubtless be taken with the long-overdue conclusion of a framework agreement between the EC and the Council for Mutual Economic Assistance (CMEA), in keeping with the goals set forth in the 1985 Final Act of the Conference on Security and Cooperation in Europe (CSCE). Guidelines could also be envisaged for the development of common action in the fields of tripartite (East-West-South) industrial cooperation and joint ventures between partners from Western and Eastern Europe in third countries.

The overall settlement reached at the inter-institutional level should be followed by bilateral negotiations over detailed agreements between the EC on the one side and each CMEA member country on the other with a view to effectively promoting the exchange of goods and services and gradually reducing the existing barriers and controls. Obviously, these agreements should by no means prevent further action by individual EC member countries aimed at strengthening bilateral ties with CMEA members and thereby furthering change and encouraging diversity in Eastern Europe.

It should also be recalled that the EC may play a substantial role in bridging gaps in understanding between East and West in a variety of multilateral fora. Growing participation by countries of Eastern Europe and eventually the Soviet Union itself in the General Agreement on Tariffs and Trade (GATT), the International Monetary Fund (IMF) and the World Bank raise the possibility of a qualitatively new level of East-West economic contacts and may offer the EC member countries a good chance to strengthen links with the Eastern half of the continent within a multilateral structure.

Notes

1. This paper concentrates on *Western* controls on exports to the socialist countries, leaving aside any question about Eastern 'counter-embargoes'. For some details on this last issue see F. Pryor, *The Communist Foreign Trade System*, London, 1963.
2. The term Eastern Europe refers to the six European allies of the Soviet Union, that is Bulgaria, Czechoslovakia, the German Democratic Republic, Hungary, Poland and Romania.
3. Although a substantial increase in enterprise autonomy is to be expected, the basic issue concerning the new division of responsibilities between central authorities and the enterprise has not yet been fully clarified. Enterprises engaged in foreign trade are allowed to keep part of the foreign exchange earned from exports.
4. The decision to end the monopoly of the Soviet Foreign Trade Ministry and the Associated Foreign Trade Organisations over imports and exports should make it easier to set up joint ventures with Western firms. A 'stage-by-stage' convertibility of the Rouble is also envisaged, initially involving only relations with other CMEA member countries.
5. Restrictions affecting the exchange of goods may be extended to cover financial and monetary transactions. This would greatly enhance the overall effectiveness and impact of trade sanctions and pave the way for full-scale economic warfare.
6. A *cause célèbre* is the Italo-Ethiopian dispute of 1935—36 and the consequent application of sanctions against Italy, under the relevant rules of the League Covenant. Sanctions, although binding on League members from October 1935, were made largely ineffective by a number of important concessions regarding oil, iron and steel, and were eventually raised in July 1936.
7. This was the first time that such an action had been taken against a UN member under Chapter VII of the Charter providing for enforcement action in cases such as threats to international peace and security. The Security Council established a committee, composed of all its members, to oversee the implementation of the arms embargo. In 1984, the Council asked all states to refrain from *importing* arms produced in South

Africa. This stance was reaffirmed in 1986 when the Council requested states to investigate violations, prevent circumventions and strengthen machinery for implementing the embargo.

8. On the mixed effects of sanctions on South Africa see M. Lipton, *Sanctions and South Africa. The Dynamics of Economic Isolation*, London, Economist Intelligence Unit, 1987. For a general assessment of international sanctions see D. Leyton-Brown (Ed), *The Utility of International Economic Sanctions*, London, Croom Helm, 1987.

9. The Security Council had met earlier in January but was obviously unable to adopt a resolution of its own because of the negative vote of the Soviet Union.

10. R. Rode, 'Summary of Western Policies', in R. Rode and H. D. Jacobsen (Eds), *Economic Warfare or Détente. An Assessment of East-West Economic Relations in the 1980s*, Boulder and London, Westview Press, 1985, p. 249.

11. P. Hanson, "Western Economic Sanctions Against the USSR: Their Nature and Effectiveness", in *NATO Economics Colloquium 1983, External Economic Relations of CMEA Countries: Their Significance and Impact in a Global Perspective*, NATO Economics and Information Directorates, 1984, pp. 69—91.

12. At present, the Export Administration Act of 1979, as amended (Export Administration Amendments Act of 1985), provides the President of the United States with the authority to control exports for national security, foreign policy and short supply reasons. The authority granted under the Act expires on 30 September, 1989.

13. R. F. Kaufman, "Changing US Attitudes Toward East-West Economic Relations", in: *NATO Economics Colloqium 1983, op. cit.*, pp. 53—67; R. Rode, *Sanktion und Geschäft. Die Ostwirtschaftspolitik der USA unter Reagan*, Frankfurt am Main, Haag und Herchen, 1986.

14. More precisely, current legislation requires that a foreign recipient of U.S. goods or technology under a validated export licence receives U.S. permission to resell or re-export the U.S.-origin good, even if it is incorporated into a foreign product.

15. On Western economic summits see C. Merlini (Ed), *Economic Summits and Western Decision-Making*, London, Croom Helm, 1984.

16. The Federal Republic of Germany, France, Italy, Japan, the United Kingdom, and the United States.

17. All quotations referring to declarations adopted at Western summits from 1975 (Rambouillet) to 1986 (Tokyo) have been taken from: *Economic Summits 1975—1986. Declarations*, Istituto Affari Internazionali (Ed), Rome on the occasion of the 1987 Venice Economic Summit.

18. This summit included Canada in addition to the six countries participating at Rambouillet.

19. Besides the seven countries already mentioned, the President of the Commission of the European Communities took part in the meeting. Actually, the President of the Commission has been participating in all Western summits since 1977.

20. For an analysis of the objectives and activities of the OECD, see M. van Meerhaeghe, *International Economic Institutions*, Dordrecht, Kluwer Academic Publishers, 1987, 5th ed. pp. 172—205. See also G. Schiavone, *International Organisations. A. Dictionary and Directory*, London, Macmillan, 1986, 2nd ed.

21. The full text of the Agreement currently in force has been published, for the first time, by the OECD, see *The Export Credit Financing Systems in OECD Member Countries*, OECD, Pairs, 1987.

22. For a comprehensive overview see E. Zaleski and H. Wienert, *Technology Transfer Between East and West*, OECD, Paris, 1980; H. Wienert and J. Slater, *East-West Technology Transfer. The Trade and Economic Aspects*, OECD, Paris, 1986.

23. It is a well-known fact that oil and gas exports have helped the Soviet Union keep a major presence in Western Europe and obtain substantial hard-currency earnings; oil,

in particular, has accounted for a very large percentage of the Soviets' hard-currency receipts over several years.

24. For an assessment of COCOM's activities see M. Lavigne, *Les relations économiques Est-Ouest*, Paris, Presses Universitaires de France, 1979, pp. 66—77; G. Schiavone, "COCOM and its Future: Strategic Controls or Economic Warfare?", in *Annali ISE*, vol. 7 (Rome: Institute of European Studies 'A. De Gasperi', 1985), pp. 295—319; P. Hanson, *Western Economic Statecraft in East-West Relations*, London, Routledge, 1987.

25. Among the most significant and recent examples of violations of security controls is the Toshiba-Kongsberg case. This involved the sale by the two firms to the Soviet Union of milling machines which were apparently used to make quieter propellers for Soviet submarines so as to escape Western naval detection.

26. An effort to streamline the 'dual use' list is currently under way, see "Cocom: A Littler List", in *The Economist*, 6 February, 1988, p. 71.

27. L. Gordon, with J. F. Brown, P. Hassner, J. Joffe, E. Moreton, *Eroding Empire: Western Relations with Eastern Europe*, Washington D.C., The Brookings Institution, 1987, R. F. Staar, *U.S.S.R. Foreign Policies After Détente*, Stanford, Hoover Institution Press, 1987.

Export controls: legal aspects

JACQUES STEENBERGEN
Member of the Bar of Brussels; Associate Professor at the Law Faculty, Catholic University of Louvain (K. U. Leuven)

I. Introduction

While in general, trade policy-makers are far more concerned with import restrictions than with export controls, export controls play a major role in the development of East-West trade.

This contribution aims at outlining the major legal aspects of export controls in the EEC. We will distinguish in doing so the general rules on export controls, the specific rules with regard to export restrictions applicable to trade in strategic goods, and economic sanctions or retaliatory measures taking the form of export controls. With regard to each of these categories, we will concentrate on aspects which are specific to EEC trade as it is not possible to discuss in the framework of this paper all legal aspects of export controls, including such issues as the general principles of public international law with respect to economic sanctions, etc.

II. General régime applicable to export controls

A. *Export controls commercial policy: the external powers of the EEC*

It may be useful to recall that under Article 113 EEC Treaty the Community has, since the end of the transitional period, exclusive powers with regard to commercial policy.[1] Article 113 uses the concept of "commercial policy" and refers explicitly to "export policy".[2] To this we can add that according to the Court of Justice the concept of "commercial policy" has the same content whether it is applied in the context of the international action of a state or of that of the Community.[3] The Court gave this ruling in an opinion given with regard to the regulation of export credits. We may therefore conclude that export controls fall, to the extent that they are an aspect of commercial policy, into the scope of the Community's exclusive powers in the field of commercial policy.

M. Maresceau (ed.), The Political and Legal Framework of Trade Relations Between the European Community and Eastern Europe. ISBN 0–7923–0046–7.
© *1989 by Kluwer Academic Publishers, Dordrecht – Printed in the Netherlands.*

It is in this respect important to point out that the Community institutions have accepted that measures can be of a mixed nature, i.e. entering partly into the scope of commercial policy while being equally closely related to other policies.[4] It remains, however, unclear when exactly a measure ceases to fall entirely into the scope of commercial policy, and therefore of the Community's exclusive external powers.

The Commission and the Council have on many occasions suggested to the Court of Justice a more precise definition of the concept of commercial policy that would help to settle a number of characterisation problems. It is the Commission's traditional view that the concept of commercial policy covers all measures that result in a change of the volume or pattern of trade, while the Council argues that only measures which aim at a change in the volume or pattern of trade can be qualified as commercial policy measures. The Court has systematically declined to settle this underlying dispute between the Commission and the Council and, rather than to give a sweeping statement, the Court has always analysed the nature of a specific measure emphasising the evolving nature of the commercial policy concept.[5]

We can therefore only conclude at present that the Community has exclusive powers with regard to all measures that are, in general state practice, considered as being commercial policy measures, as well as with regard to issues that are ancillary to trade policy measures *stricto sensu* and that do therefore not change the nature of negotiations or arguments.[6] And we must indicate from the outset that while in general export controls unquestionably enter into the scope of the Community's exclusive powers, some of the export controls discussed in this paper may either enter exclusively into the scope of the Community's external powers or fall into the category of acts where the Community and the Member States must act jointly, or may have remained within the powers of the Member States.[7]

B. *Common rules for exports in EEC law*

The Council on the basis of Article 113 EEC Treaty, on 20 December 1969 enacted Regulation 2603/69 establishing the common rules for exports.[8] This regulation contains the principle that "the exportation of products from the EEC to third countries shall be free, that is to say that they shall not be subject to any quantitative restrictions, with the exception of those which are applied in conformity with this regulation" (Art. 1).

The Regulation then provides for a number of exceptions to this principle:

1. Article 10 of Regulation 2603/69 as amended by Regulation 1934/82 lists categories of products to which the principle of the freedom of export does not apply. The list of Article 10 refers mainly to petroleum products. The Preamble to Regulation 1934/82 stipulates in this respect that it seems advisable for all Member States to exclude from the liberalisation of exports at Community level certain products of the energy sector in view of international commitments entered into by certain Member States.

2. Article 10 of Regulation 2603/69 refers also to products taken up in the Annex, but restrictions maintained in respect of such products can only be applied by the Member States indicated in the list. Thus the Regulation on common rules for exports maintains some of the national measures on export controls as do the common rules on imports with respect to national import restrictions. The list published in the Annex to Regulation 1934/82 refers mainly to French and Italian export controls concerning a somewhat surprising variety of products such as enzymes, furskins, wood, pearls, precious and semi-precious stones and precious metals, nickel as well as to some Belgian, Danish, Greek or Irish measures.

3. The common rules on exports provide further for a Community information and consultation procedure and for protective measures:

(i) Member States can ask for consulations in the Advisory Committee when they consider protective measures necessary because of an unusual development on the market (Art. 2—5, Reg. 2603/69).

(ii) When a critical situation has arisen or risks to arise on account of a shortage of essential products or when Community interests call for immediate intervention, the Commission can, acting at the request of a Member State or on its own initiative, make the export of products subject to the production of an export authorisation and determine the conditions for granting such authorisations. These measures can be taken for a period of validity not exceeding 6 weeks and the Commission must not later than 12 working days following the entry into force of the measure refer the matter to the Council with a proposal for action. The Member States can also decide to refer measures to the Council that may then decide that different action should be taken (Art. 6 Reg. 2603/69). The Council may, acting by a qualified majority on a proposal from the Commission, adopt all appropriate measures to prevent or remedy a critical situation caused by a shortage of essential products or to fulfil international undertakings entered into by the Community or all the Member States.

It should be pointed out that the comparison between Article 6 para. 1 and 7 para. 1 shows a surprising discrepancy between the cases where the Commission can impose a temporary export restriction and the cases where the Council can decide on more permanent measures. While the Commission can take measures whenever the Community interests call for immediate intervention, the Council can only adopt appropriate measures with regard to either a shortage of essential products or when export restrictions are necessary in order to allow for the fulfilment of international undertakings entered into by the Community or by all the Member States.

On the basis of these elements we can conclude that the common trade policy provides only for export controls applicable to a limited number of products (listed in Art. 10 of Regulation 1934/82 or in the Annex to that Regulation), and for specific measures of a somewhat extended period of validity provided there is either a shortage of essential products or a need to introduce export restrictions in order to fulfil international obligations entered into by the Community or by all Member States. In other instances where the Community interest might require export controls, the Commission can only take measures of a very limited period of validity.[9]

III. Specific rules applicable to trade in strategic goods

Given the special nature of the overall political relations between Western and Eastern Europe, special attention has since the Second World War always been given to trade in strategic goods or sensitive technologies.[10]

Rules on exports of such goods and technologies are a key aspect of East-West trade policy. But it cannot be said that they are only inspired by trade policy considerations. On the contrary, the main purpose of such rules is to protect national security and matters are further confused by the fact that it is not always clear whether the rules referring to national security are to be interpreted in the military strategic sense or whether they also aim at the protection of the more vague concept of national economic security.[11]

A. *Division of powers between the EEC and the Member States*

It follows from the above-mentioned rules on the division of powers between the EEC and the Member States that we must examine whether export restrictions applicable to strategic goods or sensitive technologies can be considered to be: (i) commercial policy measures; (ii) measures to be taken jointly by the EEC (because of the commercial policy aspects) and the Member States (acting with respect to other aspects); or (iii) whether such measures can only be taken by the Member States as national security policy remains within the powers of the Member States.

It is important to note in this respect that Article 223 EEC Treaty stipulates explicitly that no Member State shall be obliged to supply information when it considers the disclosure contrary to the essential interests of its security, and that Member States may take all measures they consider necessary for the protection of the essential security interests which are connected with the production of trade in arms, munitions and war material. In Article 223 EEC Treaty it is added that measures of the latter category may not adversely affect the conditions of competition in the common market regarding products which are not intended for specifically military purposes, and that the Council shall draw up a list of the products in respect of which Member States can take action under Article 223, para. 1(b) EEC Treaty.

We may conclude that under Article 223 EEC Treaty, export restrictions applicable to arms, munitions and war material in the sense of Article 223, para. 1(b) remain within the powers of the Member States.

However, the list referred to in Article 223, para. 2 was established by the Council on 15 April 1958 but has never been published.[12] We must therefore try to answer three questions: (i) how broad or narrow should we interpret the concept "war materials"; (ii) is the scope of the exceptions for national security measures provided for under Article 223 EEC Treaty extended by Article 224 EEC Treaty, or does Article 224 regulate the implementation of policies allowed for under Article 223; (iii) should measures concerning items which fall outside the scope of the concept of "war materials" and/or are concerned by measures that are not provided for under Article 224 be taken exclusively by the community or must they be taken jointly by the EEC and the Member States?

It is usually assumed that the general exception under Article 223 EEC Treaty cannot receive an extensive interpretation and that the concept of "war materials" can therefore not include all goods and technologies that might be of strategic interest.[13]

It can be argued that Member States are authorised under Article 224 EEC Treaty to take measures in the event of war, serious international tension constituting a threat of war, or in order to carry out obligations it has accepted for the purpose of maintaining peace and international security.[14] But even if it follows from Article 224 that Member States can take measures in the given circumstances, provided they consult each other with a view to prevent the functioning of the common market being affected by such measures, Article 224 does not indicate what measures Member States may take. In view of the COCOM arrangements discussed in III B it is especially relevant that Art. 224 refers to international obligations accepted for the purpose of maintaining international security. There are indications that the concept "international security" may not be interpreted as referring to the interpretation of national security interests in an international context by any given country, and that the notion only refers to security interests as determined at international level,[15] e.g. in decisions of the Security Council of the United Nations. It may also be significant that the Commission has taken a comparatively liberal attitude with respect to the range of measures that can be taken in order to protect international security as well as of the range of issues that can be held to affect international security when measures were decided by the UN Security Council in conformity with the UN Charter.[16]

And when certain matters are not covered by the exemption to the general transfer of powers as provided for under Article 223 and 224 EEC Treaty, it must be assumed that, *a contrario*, they have not remained within the exclusive powers of the Member States if they also present characteristics that can justify a Community competence. But the fact that they have not remained within the power of the Member States, does not, in the our opinion, imply that they necessarily fall within the exclusive powers of the Community. Here we face again the difficulty of determining the scope of the concept of "commercial policy". On the one hand, it can be argued that, as export restrictions of strategic goods and sensitive technologies are a characteristic of East-West policy measures, they fall into the scope of the exclusive Community powers in view of general state practice. It follows from the case-law of the Court of Justice that the fact that such export restrictions also serve other than pure trade policy purposes does not necessarily rule out such a conclusion. We may refer to the judgment of the Court of 26 March 1987 in the case *Commission v Council*. The Court ruled that the General Scheme of Preferences was part of the measures that can be said to be an inherent part of the hard core of North-South commercial policy, and that therefore other considerations may not lead to the result that the Community loses its exclusive powers in the field of commercial policy in respect of trade with developing countries. Along similar lines, it may be argued that the strategic interests served by export restrictions on some goods and technologies cannot lead to the result that the Community loses its power in the field of East-West trade policy-making when a commercial policy in respect of East-West trade is in the light of general state practice inconceivable without such measures or restrictions. This thesis is further supported by the argument that if the link between such trade and national security interests is considered to be insufficient in order to benefit from the exemption of Article 223 EEC Treaty and that if the measures are not of a sufficiently international nature in order to benefit from Article 224, it may be assumed that strategic interests take second place to general commercial policy considerations. But we should on the other hand be prudent when interpreting the judgment of 27 March 1987. The General Scheme of Preferences is not only an instrument of development policy but also of commercial policy. Export restrictions of strategic goods and sensitive technologies, however, are a characteristic of a commercial policy but cannot be said to be commercial policy instruments. Such measures do, on the contrary, impose constraints on the development of commercial relations for reasons that can, by themselves, hardly be qualified as commercial policy considerations.

We consider therefore on balance, and in the absence of a judgment by the Court of Justice, that it is prudent to consider that export restrictions on strategic goods and sensitive technologies other than arms, munitions and war materials listed in accordance with Art. 223 EEC Treaty, and that cannot be qualified as measures referred to in Article 224, fall into the category of measures to be taken jointly by the Community and the Member States.

B. *COCOM*

NATO member states and Japan have since January 1950 coordinated their controls on exports of strategic goods and sensitive technologies in COCOM. COCOM is not a Treaty or organisation but a gentleman's agreement between the afore-mentioned states whereby they promise each other to impose export bans or restrictions on the exports of specific goods to specific countries listed by COCOM.[17] The COCOM lists make a distinction between arms and military equipment *stricto sensu*, nuclear technology, and so-called dual purpose goods: civilian technology and equipment that has or may have military applications.

It follows from III, A that the implementation of restrictions on exports of military equipment *stricto sensu* falls within the exclusive power of the Member States. Exports of nuclear technology are covered not only by COCOM, but in a more enforceable way, by the Treaty on nuclear proliferation which will not be analysed in this contribution. The main problem area concerns unquestionably the dual purpose goods. The list refers to a wide range of products.[18] With respect to these goods we must analyse the legal environment for export controls in Community and national law.

C. *Export controls under EEC law*

To the extent that strategic goods and sensitive technologies do not benefit from the exemption of Article 223, para. 1(b) EEC Treaty, and measures fall outside the scope of Article 224, the EEC can only participate in the implementation of export controls in respect of goods and technologies listed in Annex to Regulation 2603/69 (as replaced by Regulation 1934/82), or when empowered to take restrictive measures under Article 7, para. 1 of Regulation 2603/69.

The main question in this respect is, apart from the uncertainty with regard to the list referred to in Article 223 para. 2, concerned with the question whether COCOM arrangements qualify as international obligations related to international security in the meaning of Article 224 EEC Treaty. If international security must be determined on a unilateral or international level as Community practice might suggest,[19] the COCOM arrangements in so far as they are concerned with dual purpose goods cannot qualify as international obligations that justify a derogation from the general rules on the division of powers between the Community and the Member States in respect of foreign trade.

And to the extent the general rules do apply, the conditions of Article 7, para. 1 of Regulation 2603/69 cause specific difficulties as the Council is only empowered to take action in order to allow for the implementation of obligations entered into by the Community or *all* of the Member States. Certainly, before the entering into force of the European Single Act, the Community could never enter into any obligation in respect of national security (whether national economic security or national security *stricto sensu*). Moreover, since the accession of Ireland to the Community, not all the Member States are party to the COCOM arrangements. COCOM obligations can therefore not be considered to be undertakings entered into by all the Member States. Thus the Council can only validly enact export controls by modifying the Annex referred to in Article 10 of Regulation 2603/82. And it is clearly apparent from the date of the last amendments to this Annex that it cannot have been made to conform with the most recent changes in the COCOM lists.[20] It should be added that, in our opinion, possible discrepancies between the lists of measures the Member States can take, and the national measures taken in implementation of COCOM arrangements, are not covered by Article 234 EEC Treaty which stipulates that the EEC Treaty does not affect obligations entered into before the entry into force of the Treaty. COCOM predates the EEC Treaty, but in view of the successive changes to the COCOM lists, the relevant COCOM undertakings have been accepted after the entry into force of the Treaty. This implies that to the extent that the participation of the Community is required in view of the division of powers between the EEC and the Member States, the conformity of Member State measures with Community law is questionable in respect of all goods that are not provided for in the said Annex unless the measures are covered by the exception of Article 224 EEC Treaty.

D. *Measures taken by the Member States*

As COCOM is not a treaty in the generally accepted sense of the term, and *a fortiori* no self-executing agreement, COCOM arrangements are only enforceable in so far as they are translated into the national law of the exporting country. National governments undertook to introduce certain export restrictions by using the appropriate techniques available under national law. Exporters must therefore seek an export authorisation in the country of exportation which should only grant such authorisation if the export operation is compatible with the COCOM arrangements. In case of doubt, or in case COCOM partners question the conformity of export licences with COCOM arrangements, the COCOM partners can or should consult with each other within the Coordinating Committee and, if necessary, discuss a modification of the COCOM lists. There are many instances where either an individual contract or a general practice became object of such discussions and in this country most people will recall in this respect the highly confusing *Pégard* file.[21]

From the exporters point of view, the legal framework is therefore exclusively determined by the domestic law of the exporting country. In Belgium's case we can refer to the Ministerial Decree of 24 September 1985 organising the requirement of an export licence for products listed in the Annex. With regard to "dual purpose goods" and COCOM we should refer more specifically to Annex 2 replaced by Ministerial Decree of 19 October 1987.[22] We should finally repeat that Ireland is not a party to COCOM, but is said to apply similar export restrictions.

E. *Extra-territorial application of national export restrictions*

Even though this paper aims primarily at analysing the legal environment in the Community in respect of export controls and trade with Eastern Europe, it should be mentioned briefly that most problems in this area in recent years were concerned with the interpretation of the COCOM arrangement between on the one hand, the USA, and on the other hand, Member States of the European Communities, and with provisions of US domestic law sanctioning US-controlled undertakings when exporting from the Communities in case such exports were deemed incompatible with COCOM by the US authorities while authorised by European authorities.

When analysed from a purely legal point of view, this problem is concerned primarily with the extra-territorial application of US domestic law.[23]

IV. Economic sanctions and retaliatory measures

Export restrictions can further be imposed as economic sanctions or retaliatory measures. Such measures may either be taken in respect of trade conflicts or as general policy measures. If taken in the context of trade conflicts, the legal environment for such actions is determined by whether the Eastern European countries involved are GATT Contracting Parties or not. With regard to GATT Contracting Parties sanctions can only be taken in accordance with article XXIII of GATT or the equivalent provisions in the relevant GATT codes.

When analysed in EEC law, it can be argued that retaliatory measures in trade conflicts should be taken by the EEC in accordance with Regulation 2641/84 (new commercial policy instrument) [24] or, at least, in accordance with the common rules on exports mentioned in part II B.

Other commercial policy instruments are concerned with import restrictions rather than export controls.

And while with regard to GATT Contracting Parties many of these measures may require the prior authorisation by the GATT Contracting Parties, such measures can be taken unilaterally with regard to other trade partners unless bilateral agreements determine otherwise.

With respect to the legal aspects of export controls used as a general foreign policy instrument we must make a distinction between the compatibility of such measures with public international law and the legal environment for the implementation of such measures in the European Community.

With regard to the compatibility of such measures with public international law, trade between the European Communities and Eastern Europe is not subject to specific rules. Within the Community, we must in respect to the taking of such measures refer again to the division of powers between the Community and the Member States. The Member States have argued for a number of years that the Community has no power in respect of trade embargoes ordered for general foreign policy reasons. But, as with regard to export controls on trade in strategic goods, it cannot be denied that such measures do have a serious commercial policy impact. To the extent that the measures are not taken in a context which is provided for under Article 223 or 224 EEC Treaty, we must therefore assume that such measures should be taken jointly by the Community institutions and the Member States. This analysis is now supported by Community practice as it has since 1982 become established practice for the Community to implement trade sanctions under Article 113 EEC Treaty as is illustrated by measures taken in the light of the Afghanistan and Falklands crises. [25]

V. Conclusions

With regard to export controls applicable to foreign trade in general or more specifically to trade between the EEC and Eastern Europe, we can conclude in view of the preceding paragraphs that:

1. the Community applies a limited number of export restrictions, mainly to petroleum products, in trade with all third countries in accordance with Article 10 of Regulation 2603/69 as amended by Regulation 1934/82;

2. the Community has authorised some Member States to apply export restrictions with regard to a limited number of products listed in Annex to Regulation 1934/82;

3. the NATO partners among the Member States (i.e. all Member States except Ireland which is said to apply similar restrictions) undertook in COCOM the obligation to restrict exports of military equipment *stricto sensu*, nuclear technology and a wide range of dual purpose goods to a list of countries including Eastern Europe.

With regard to the possibility for the Community to introduce export controls as a trade policy instrument (i.e. either to safeguard commercial policy interests of the Community in general, take retaliatory measures or impose economic sanctions in trade conflicts):

a. the Commission can, for a period of validity not exceeding 6 weeks, impose export restrictions in case of a shortage of essential products or whenever Community interests call for immediate intervention;

b. the Council can impose export restrictions in order to prevent or to remedy a critical situation caused by a shortage of essential products or to allow for the fulfilment of international undertakings entered into by the Community or by all the Member States;

c. the Council can take appropriate measures in accordance with Regulation 2641/84 (new commercial policy instrument);

d. the Member States can impose in accordance with Community law export restrictions with regard to arms, munitions and war materials as defined by the Council in accordance with Article 223 EEC Treaty;

e. the Member States are authorised to take measures in accordance with Article 224 EEC Treaty in the event of war, serious international tensions constituting a threat of war or in order to carry out obligations they accepted for the purpose of maintaining peace and international security, and Community practice seems to indicate that such international obligations must aim at the protection of international security as determined by international institutions like the United Nations.

With regard to export controls, as with regard to other aspects of trade regulation, the legal environment of trade between the EEC and Eastern Europe is inevitably characterised by the division of powers between the Community and the Member States. It follows from the preceding conclusions that there is only a limited list of Community export restrictions but that trade between the EEC and Eastern Europe is substantially affected by COCOM arrangements. The legal appreciation of national export restrictions enacted in implementation of COCOM arrangements is made difficult by uncertainties about the extent to which Member States can impose export restrictions in accordance with Community law.

To the extent that the COCOM lists refer to products also listed in accordance with Article 223 EEC Treaty, national measures taken in implementation of COCOM arrangements are certainly in conformity with Community law. To the extent that COCOM arrangements require export restrictions for a wider range of products, it seems prudent to conclude that such measures should either be taken jointly by the Community and the Member States or require a Community authorisation, except if one could establish that Article 224 EEC Treaty covers all national measures taken in implementation of COCOM arrangements. Present practice and doctrine seems to indicate, however, that the concept of international security as used in Article 224 refers to measures that have been taken in international organisations such as the United Nations in order to safeguard international security interests as determined in an international framework. We can therefore not rule out that the number of export restrictions imposed by Member States in implementation of COCOM arrangements are incompatible with the obligations of the Member States under the EEC Treaty and are therefore of questionable legal validity.

Notes

1. Art. 113 EEC applies to trade in EEC products. The Euratom Treaty contains specific rules with regard to external relations (Art. 52 (2), 64 et seq. and 101 et seq.). As far as the ECSC Treaty is concerned it is, however, generally assumed that the EEC Treaty has residuary supremacy and that the EEC Treaty therefore applies to ECSC products unless the ECSC Treaty contains specific provisions.
2. See for a recent analysis of case-law and practice: J. H. J. Bourgeois, "The Common Commercial Policy Scope and Nature of the Powers", in E. L. M. Völker (Ed.), *Protectionism and the European Community*, 1987, 2nd ed.
3. Opinion 1/75, Draft OECD understanding on export credits, [1975] *ECR* 1355.
4. See on mixed agreements: C. D. Ehlermann, "Mixed agreements. A list of problems", in D. O'Keefe and H. G. Schermers (Eds.), *Mixed agreements*, Deventer, 1983, pp. 5 et seq.
5. See, most recently, case 45/86, 26 March 1987, *Commission v. Council*, not yet published.

6. Opinion 1/78, *Natural Rubber Agreement*, [1979] *ECR* 2871.
7. With regard to the type of agreements and measures and the degree of Community participation, we should distinguish the legal nature of an agreement or measure, and the organisation of negotiations with third countries. Exclusive Community measures are frequently negotiated jointly by the Community and the Member States, if only because the nature of a measure sometimes is only apparent after consensus is reached on its substance and content, see C. D. Ehlermann, *op. cit.*, pp. 4 et seq. In the following paragraphs we will only discuss the nature of measures or agreements.
8. *O.J.*, L 324/25, 1969, amended by Reg. 1934/82 of 12 July 1982, *O.J.*, L 211/1, 1982.
9. Thus the possibilities to implement export controls (in extra-community trade) are rather more limited than the range of trade policy instruments allowing for import restrictions. Compare E. L. M. Völker, "The major instruments of the common commercial policy of the EEC", in E. L. M. Völker (Ed.), *op. cit.*, pp. 17 et seq. With regard to intra-Community trade, the Court is on the other hand more lenient when interpreting Art. 34 (export restrictions) than in respect of Art. 30 (import restrictions). Compare 8/74, *Dassonville*, [1974] *ECR* 837 and 237/82, *Jongeneel Kaas*, [1984] *ECR* 483).
10. See for historic survey e.g. G. K. Bertsch, *East-West strategic trade, COCOM and the Atlantic Alliance*, Atlantic papers No. 49, Paris 1983, pp. 31—36.
11. See on economic security e.g. F. A. M. Alting von Geusau and J. Pelkmans, *National economic security*, Tilburg 1982, p. 253.
12. See on this list Groeben, Boeckh, Thiesing and Ehlermann, *Kommentar zur EWG Vertrag*, Baden Baden 1983, 3rd ed., p. 1033 and P. J. Kuyper, "De Amerikaanse exportrestricties in een nieuw jasje: een verbetering?", *SEW* 1987, p. 20.
13. See on narrow interpretation of exceptions to the EEC's external powers, the general approach as it appears from Case 41/76, *Donckerwolcke*, [1976] *ECR* 1921, and more specifically with regard to Art. 223: Groeben, Boeckh, Thiesing and Ehlermann, *op. cit.*, p. 1032, or P. J. Kuyper, *loc. cit.*
14. See Groeben, Boeckh, Thiesing and Ehlermann, *op. cit.*, p. 1034.
15. See contrary P. J. Kuyper, "Sanctions against Rhodesia", *CMLRev.*, 1975, pp. 231 et seq.
16. Parl. Question 527/75, *O.J.*, C 89/8, 1975.
17. See e.g. G. K. Bertsch, *op. cit.*
18. See for this list e.g. the implementation in Belgium, *Moniteur Belge*, 28 October 1987, pp. 15770 et seq.
19. See Groeben, Boeckh, Thiesing and Ehlermann, *op. cit.*, p. 1035.
20. Compare P. J. Kuyper, *SEW* 1987, p. 20.
21. The Pégard contract concerned the export of advanced technology drilling equipment.
22. *Moniteur Belge*, 28 October 1987, p. 15770.
23. See P. J. Kuyper, *SEW* 1987, pp. 4 et seq.
24. *O.J.*, L 252/1, 1984.
25. Reg. Council 596/82, *O.J.*, L 72/15, 1982 and Reg. 877/82, *O.J.*, L 102/1, 1982.

Eastern European countries and the GATT

JÁNOS MARTONYI

Director General Ministry of Foreign Trade, Budapest; Associate Professor, University of Budapest

I. Historical background and developments

The relationship of Eastern European countries to GATT is, indeed, an old and at the same time a very timely subject. There is a large amount of economic and legal literature[1] dealing with a number of controversial, politically sensitive, economically important and intellectually stimulating issues all connected to the fundamental questions: how to create a better functioning and universal international trading system, how to assure and to increase the benefits of international trade for all nations wishing to have an equitable share in those benefits and how to strenghten and improve the functioning of the present world trading system as embodied in the principles and the rules of GATT.

Historically and logically there are *two different*, diametrically opposing *approaches* to the problem. One of these approaches in its most radical or extreme form is that the presence of Eastern European countries is a kind of cuckoo's egg in the nest of free-trading nations. In this view the economic and social system as well as the trade policy of these countries is fundamentally alien to and therefore cannot be reconciled with the objectives and principles of GATT, that are inspired by a free trade philosophy and destined for the restriction of state interference with international trade and for the progressive removal of all trade barriers except for tariffs.[2] Non-market economies have therefore no place in the multilateral trading system based upon the free play of market forces reflecting comparative advantages and no accommodation between two fundamentally different systems of objectives and values is conceivable. In this view the price and cost structures of socialist economies are totally insulated from the world market and genuine cost comparisons are not available. It is the central plan, ultimately the state, that decides what is to be bought or sold and in what quantities they will be exchanged. Decisions are not based on economic merit or commercial considerations but on the

M. Maresceau (ed.), The Political and Legal Framework of Trade Relations Between the European Community and Eastern Europe. ISBN 0–7923–0046–7.
© *1989 by Kluwer Academic Publishers, Dordrecht – Printed in the Netherlands.*

administrative discretion of state authorities. Since the GATT system is based upon the exchange of concessions peculiar to and having a genuine value only in market economies, a proper balance of the rights and obligations in the relationship between a free-market economy and a planned economy cannot be established in the framework of the GATT-system.[3]

The logical conclusion of this thinking is that, on the one hand, socialist countries should not be admitted to become GATT Contracting Parties and, on the other hand, GATT Contracting Parties should not be restrained by GATT disciplines in resorting to any trade policy measures whatsoever vis-à-vis the socialist countries.

The opposing view takes a different point of departure and arrives at a totally different conclusion. None of the provisions of GATT relate to the ownership of the means of production or, indeed, of enterprises. Therefore, the differences following from the social and economic system of socialist countries are irrelevant to the functioning of the General Agreement and do not interfere with the fulfilment of GATT obligations.

The statement made by the delegate from France at the initial drafting session in London in 1946 is frequently referred to in this respect. He remarked that "there does not exist, in our opinion, any necessary connection between the form of the productive régime and the internal exchanges in one nation on the one hand, and on her foreign economic policy on the other. The United States may very well continue to follow the principle, the more orthodox principle, of private initiative. France and other European countries may turn towards planned economy. The USSR may uphold and maintain the Marxist ideals of collectivism without our having to refuse to be in favour of a policy of international organisation based on liberty and equality."[4]

The second approach referring to the absence of express provisions dealing with countries having socialist economies denies the relevance of the social and economic system in respect of the application of GATT principles and rules as well as the need for special arrangements or for accommodation.[5]

While according to the first approach no accommodation is possible because irreconcilable things cannot be reconciled, the conclusion of the second approach is that accommodation is not necessary. To put it bluntly, in the first view the problem cannot be solved, while in the second view the problem does not exist. Paradoxically, the self-consistent application of any of the two conflicting concepts would have led to the same practical result: the countries having a socialist economic system would have been excluded from the multilateral trading system as embodied in GATT, and this would certainly have greatly impaired the originally intended and still not forgotten universality of the principles and rules of the General Agreement. This, however, did not happen as none of the two approaches has ever been applied in their logical extremity.

As frequently occurs, the realities of historic developments have softened, to a large extent, both concepts. One socialist country, *Czechoslovakia*, had been a founding member of GATT and remained to be a Contracting Party irrespective of the changes in its social and economicsystem. With the exception of the United States[6], the Contracting Parties continued to grant MFN treatment to Czechoslovakia and did not want to disrupt their trade relations. However, the discriminatory quantitative restrictions introduced or retained by numerous Contracting Parties against products originating from socialist countries applied to Czechoslovak products as well which was, of course, not in conformity with Art XIII.

In the late fifties and the early sixties some of the Eastern European socialist countries started to build up contacts with GATT. *Yugoslavia* established special relations with the Contracting Parties in a declaration signed in 1959 and 7 years later became a full Contracting Party. While in the 1959 declaration Yugoslavia was accorded "such treatment as will achieve an equitable balance of rights and obligations as envisaged in the General Agreement" (a reference to the conclusion that the treatment is not necessarily the same as would normally follow from the general rules) the final Protocol of Accession did not establish any special conditions or obligations and Yugoslavia became a Contracting Party *under the general terms*. It is often pointed out that in the 7-year period significant economic reforms took place in Yugoslavia and it was this *progressive development* that permitted the accession on general conditions.[7, 8]

The question of compatibility of the socialist economic system with the GATT rules arose in its full complexity in *Poland's case*. Poland applied for full accession as early as in 1959 but it was only in 1967 that it became a Contracting Party. The special terms and conditions of this accession that have been included in a separate Protocol of Accession are well known. Apart from the acceptance of a selective safeguard clause and the maintaining of some discriminatory quantitative restrictions (discriminatory QRs were only to be progressively "relaxed" and not removed and no date for the end of the transitional period was established)[9] the Polish side was obliged to accept an obligation to "increase the total value of its imports from the territories of the Contracting Parties by not less than seven per cent per annum". This was the first time that an import commitment — in the form of an undertaking to quarantee a rate of increase of imports — appeared in the GATT system. While in the first years the commitment did not raise any particular problem, it soon became clear that such a commitment, even in its redefined form (compound i.e. annual average rate for a two-year period in 1971 and 1972 and for three-year periods thereafter) is not only against the principle of a reasonable balance of mutual advantages but it is unworkable as well. Hence the formula which was premised on "effective" reciprocity turned out to be theoretically questionable and technically defective.[10]

In the case of *Romania* the formula based upon the exchange of tariff concessions for an import commitment considerably softened in the Protocol of Accession signed in 1971. Romania only expressed its "firm intention" to increase imports from the GATT Contracting Parties at a rate not smaller than the growth rate of its total imports provided for in its five-year plans.[11] The import commitment, or rather the intention was tied to the growth rate of total imports, ultimately, as some put it, to the Romanian export performance. The selective safeguard clause was included in the Protocol of Accession but in a mutually applicable version. The provision relating to the discriminatory QRs was formulated in a different way as it was the progressive removal of these QRs, without fixing, however, a target date for their final and total elimination, that was promised by the GATT Contracting Parties.[12]

The next applicant, *Hungary*, accepted very similar special terms on the "get side" (mutually applicable selective safeguard, progressive removal of discriminatory QRs without fixing a target date) but on the "give side" acceded to GATT on an entirely different basis. Instead of an import commitment — in any form whatsoever — tariff concessions were offered and accepted and thereby the effectiveness of tariffs as the primary trade policy means was admitted. The case as well as the solution found were undoubtedly special; in respect of the selective safequard and the QRs not consistent with Art. XIII the terms of accession turned out to be similar to the Romanian and — to a less extent — to the Polish "precedent"[13] while as regards the concessions given the general rule was followed as was the case with Yugoslavia.

China's GATT membership is probably the most controversial and most important issue with respect to the relationship between socialist countries and the GATT and, indeed, to the future functioning of the multilateral world trading system. Again, we are confronted with a special case, not only in terms of substantial, but also as regards procedural questions. The Chinese side points out that there is no question about an accession under Art. XXXIII, since China only wants to resume its Contracting Party status established by the signature, in 1947, of Chapter IV of the Final Act of the UN Conference on Trade and Employment generally known as the Havana Charter. Since, the validity of Taiwan's withdrawal from the General Agreement in 1950 has never been recognised by the Chinese government it can be legally argued that the Contracting Party status has never ceased to exist and after a long period of recess or suspension it now only has to be reinstated.[14] Apart from this formal issue, however, both the Contracting Parties and China essentially concur in the view that the problem of ensuring an equitable balance of mutual rights and obligations will have to be resolved and this may require special arrangements. It is precisely the nature and extent of these arrangements that are in dispute and will have to be agreed on.[15] Although it would be premature to anticipate the result of the negotiations, it seems to be clear already at this stage that China does not want to follow any of the above precedents and referring to special circumstances asserts that the Chinese case is different. Among the special circumstances attention is drawn to the fact that China is a developing country, that it does not belong to any economic bloc, that 85 p.c. of its trade is conducted with GATT Contracting Parties, that sweeping economic reforms are being realised and that no import commitment could be undertaken and implemented in view of the decentralised trade régime of the country.[16]

The announcement of the *Soviet Union's* intention to build up a closer relationship with the GATT, to obtain observer status and eventually to become a Contracting Party is undoubtedly one of the most important developments in the General Agreement's history.[17] The fundamental question to be answered is whether the GATT can fulfil its originally visualised universal vocation and if yes, under what conditions. It is clear that the Contracting Parties will be confronted again with a "special case" characterised by a number of factors peculiar to the geographic, economic, social, etc. circumstances of the applicant country.

The differences among the socialist countries that have up to now acceded to or have declared their intention to join the General Agreement render any rigid classification a futile exercise and warrant a case-by-case, a country-by-country approach. Among the numerous differences mention has to be made of the sheer geographic and economic size, including the volume of exports and imports, the economic structure, the commodity pattern of production and exports, the economic management system, the role and the legal nature of the plan, the nature and rules of ownership, the degree of the autonomy of enterprises, the degree of centralisation or decentralisation of foreign trade,[18] the price policy, the exchange rate policy, the role of tariffs, etc. Some of these differences were already reflected in the different terms of accession to GATT and the different legal terms have themselves become differentiating factors. The result is that both the economic and the legal criteria are now largely different in the case of each socialist country.

II. Main areas of dispute

The main areas of the present and future disputes in the field of finding arrangements between socialist countries and the GATT are essentially related to the fundamental theoretical question, how the principles of equal treatment and non-discrimination as universally recognised and legally binding principles of international law have to be implemented.

It must be the point of departure that these principles form the legal foundation of the world trading system and their observance is an essential condition of its functioning. There cannot be several categories of participants, a category of equals, another category of more equals, and a further category of countries that are less equal than others. As regards the relationship between the principle of equal treatment and the most-favoured nation treatment it has to be underlined that the two are not identical. The *unconditional MFN treatment* is only the principal legal device for the implementation of the principle of equal treatment. It is "an ingenious form of legal shorthand"[19] that ensures equal conditions of competition, equality among the participants of the world trading system. MFN is, however, not an exclusive device for the implementation of equal treatment. In the field of tariffs it is certainly the most appropriate means, but in certain other fields other devices are also conceivable. In the field of tariffs it is the multilateral MFN as formulated in Art. I of the GATT that ensures equal conditions of competition,[20] while in the field of quantitative restrictions it is the rule of non-discrimination as laid down in Art. XIII of the GATT that ensures equal treatment. MFN and non-discrimination cannot be identified; they are two techniques both serving the same purpose, both aiming at the same effect, i.e. equal treatment.[21]

The historic question that arose soon after the establishment of the first socialist state was, how a country having no tariffs whatsoever can reciprocate tariff concessions? The search for an answer gave rise to the theory or concept of *effective reciprocity* and to its simplest application where tariff concessions (usually MFN treatment) are exchanged for import commitments i.e. for an obligation to purchase (the word "effective" intends to convey the meaning that obligations or concessions of different nature are to be exchanged).[22]

In order to dispel some misunderstandings it has to be emphasised that the validity of reciprocity as a fundamental principle of international relations can by no means be questioned. Nor can one deny the right and possibility of any country to demand or to accept any kind of international obligation it deems appropriate.

The preoccupations caused by the concept of effective reciprocity are therefore rooted in some other factors. First, there are some legal or technical problems involved in the MFN for import commitment formula as the obligations exchanged are of different nature, the consideration offered for the tariff concession is of different legal character. The tariff concessions give only a possibility to export while the import commitment is supposed to give a guarantee as regards the result. In addition to this legal problem there is a practical one: experience shows that the implementation of the formula has not been very succesful and in some cases it turned out to be unworkable.[23]

The basic problem with the theory of effective reciprocity lies in the danger of its becoming a generalised and unconditional answer to the question of integrating a socialist country in the world trading system. It is important that the question should be answered *in concreto*, in the light of the circumstances of the case, of the particular country and not on the basis of preconceived, *a priori* ideas.

One of the most sensitive and controversial issues in connection with the trade policy treatment of socialist countries is the question of *discriminatory quantitative restrictions*. As it is well known the GATT, in line with the principle of non-discrimination, prohibits quantitative restrictions unless the restriction is applied *erga omnes*, i.e. to the like product of all third countries. There is an argument, however, that given the peculiar features of the socialist countries' economic system (decisions in the field of production and exports are made by the state, prices do not reflect actual production costs and production costs are distorted anyway) special weapons, special trade policy means are needed. The most effective special weapon is the "specific" hence discriminatory QR which excludes or restricts imports *ab initio* eliminating even the risk of an eventual market disruption. (the QRs may, and indeed, often do cover products from countries where there is no production at all of the given product).[24]

The question of these QRs was the subject of long debates when the conditions of accession of Poland, Romania and Hungary were negotiated and a compromise was eventually agreed on, the terms of which have been referred to above. The two interrelated elements of the compromise are that (a) the possibility of taking selective safeguard measures has been adopted and included in the protocols of Accession; (b) the progressive relaxation, respectively *removal* of the QRs not consistent with Art. XIII of the GATT was provided for. Hence, the essential feature of the compromise is that of the two special measures one was accepted and the other was to be progressively abolished. There was an understanding that the acceptance of a selective safeguard facilitated the early elimination of the discriminatory QRs. In Poland's and Romania's case the understanding was tacit or implied, while in Hungary's case it was expressly stated in the report of the working party.[25]

A further area of disputes is related to the application of *trade protec-tive measures*, with special regard to anti-dumping and countervailing duty procedures (trade protective measures, in general, include safeguard measures, be it *erga omnes* or selective as well as anti-dumping and countervailing duty procedures). The essential question is how to assess dumping, how to compare domestic and export prices in the case of economies where prices do not reflect production costs and, indeed, production costs themselves depend on governmental decisions (see Jacobs *infra* p. 000). Another question is how to calculate subsidies. As it is known, the US Federal Court of Appeal in the case *Georgetown Steel Corp. v. US* has recently reversed the decision of the first instance, and supporting the administration's view it stated that no countervailing duty procedure can be initiated against products originating from countries having a state-controlled economy, essentially because the amount of the subsidy cannot be established and verified.[26]

In the GATT system very little, almost nothing is said in this respect. In the Notes and Supplementary Provisions to Article VI it is recognised that in a country which has a complete or substantially complete monopoly of its trade and where all domestic prices are fixed by the State, difficulties may exist in determining price comparability.

Art. 15 of the Subsidy Code refers to this provision and provides for the possibility of the application of a special method for price comparison based upon the surrogate country approach.[27] It is to be underlined, however, that none of the above two criteria (monopoly of trade; all prices are fixed by the State) corresponds to the present economic and trade system of at least some of the socialist countries.

Again the establishment of a category of countries arbitrarily deemed to correspond to certain criteria leads to a wrong result. It may be that in some cases the general rules of the GATT Anti-dumping Code on price comparison cannot be applied and a special approach is warranted. This has to or should be examined carefully in each particular case and factors such as the role of the market forces in the exporting country as well as in the particular branch of industry, the pricing of the production factors and the transparency of the economic and legal system should be properly assessed. If on the balance of these factors, the special method is opted for, it has to be applied in a reasonable and appropriate manner.

This highly technical matter cannot be discussed here in detail. In the present context suffice it to note that the rigid application of the special method based upon the surrogate country approach, the establishment of *a priori* categories and the freezing of certain countries in a special, less favourable status does not help to resolve the problem.

III. Propositions

It is clear that the problem of finding the appropriate arrangements for the integration of socialist countries in the GATT system is a vast, complicated issue having far-reaching and multiple repercussions. To make progress a good amount of pragmatism and reasonability is desired. The approach should therefore be pragmatic rather than ideological. However, to be a good pragmatist we need the guidance of principles.

1. We *must not create rigid, a priori categories* and must not freeze countries in a predetermined status. The creation of a kind of Part V in GATT containing the derogations from the general rules i.e. the special rules applying to a certain group of countries termed as "State-trading" or otherwise, would be a serious mistake as it would introduce a kind of group system and it would probably mean the end of the multilateral trading system based on equal treatment and non-discrimination. With the establishment of different groups, different régimes would be applicable and some would be less equal, while others would be more equal than others.

In this context it is to be noted that most socialist countries have a similar level of economic development as a number of countries qualifying as developing nations. Some belong to the Group of 77, another does not belong to this Group but considers itself a developing country, and others do not consider themselves to be a developing country but have a similar level of economic development. On the other hand the economic and trade system of a large number of developing countries is characterised by features similar to those deemed to be particular to socialist countries. How then to draw a dividing line between Part IV and Part V?[28]

The establishment of Part V would not only have a serious disintegrating effect on the whole system, but it would contradict the realities of life and it would prove to be irreconcilable with the tendency of differentiation of the economic and trade system of countries included in the group in question. In any legal regulation the application of the same rules to different situations leads to different results and undercuts the credibility and the workability of the whole regulatory system.

2. The efforts have to be aimed at finding adequate *case-by-case solutions*. This "*beware of precedents*" approach is warranted by the developments of the last decades as well. Indeed, the history of the accession of some socialist countries demonstrates that the value of

precedents has been limited. As for future cases, it is already clear that the new applicants do not want to (or are not expected to) follow the solutions found in previous cases. It is, of course, impossible to forecast the outcome of the present or future negotiations but it seems to be fairly certain that the solutions will be different.

3. It is very important that we take a *dynamic and innovative approach* and we do not stick to traditional concepts that are becoming or may rapidly become obsolete. Recent developments amply demonstrate that we are not living in a static world and things are moving and changing. To find proper answers to new questions and to shape the appropriate legal devices reflecting the requirements of new situations, *we have to free ourselves from the shackles of old concepts and ideologies.*

4. It is equally important that existing *international commitments are respected* fully and in good faith. The observance of certain principles and rules is what the whole system is based upon. If some rules or commitments are "honoured in breach",[29] it is the whole system that is being eroded. The fundamental benefits of the GATT system are supposed to be the rule-of-law, predictability and confidence, in other words, a minimum standard of legal security.

When Hungary acceded to GATT it was precisely this legal security that she intended to obtain. Unfortunately the 15 years history of the implementation of the Protocol of Accession has not confirmed this expectation.

The famous para. 4. a and b of the Hungarian Protocol of Accession reads as follows:

"(a) Contracting parties still maintaining prohibitions or quantitative restrictions not consistent with Article XIII of the General Agreement on imports from Hungary shall not increase the discriminatory element in these restrictions and undertake to remove them progressively.

(b) If, for exceptional reasons, any such prohibitions or restrictions are still in force as of 1 January 1975, the Working Party provided for in paragraph 6 will examine them with a view to their elimination."

In the 15 years that have passed since the entry into force of the Protocol only a tiny share of the QRs referred to in the above text has been removed and the vast majority of them has been and is still maintained, for "exceptional reasons", by the EEC member countries.[30] The question, therefore, whether the commitment relating to the removal of the discriminatory QRs expressly undertaken in the above Protocol has been respected, cannot be responded in the affirmative. For this reason it would be most unwise to expect that Hungary could accept a bilateral agreement where the final and total elimination of all discriminatory QRs is not clearly and expressly provided for.

5. In the socialist countries *economic and legal transparency* will have to be qualitatively *improved*.

The notion of transparency includes essentially two elements: (a) that the decisions are brought in accordance with legal rules or norms instead of being brought on the basis of discretionary powers of administrative bodies (rule-of-law aspect) and (b) existing rules or norms are published so that everybody knows them (publication aspect). The interdependence between indirect macro-economic control and the reliance on market mechanisms, on the one hand, and the rule of law, on the other does not need a detailed demonstration. No market-oriented reforms can operate without duly published legal rules applied and observed by all participants, including the state itself.

The improval of transparency is therefore an indispensable condition for the succesful functioning of the market-oriented reforms of socialist countries. At the same time improving transparency would help to dispel scepticism or suspicions as regards the effectiveness and seriousness of the market-oriented reforms and also as regards the strict observance of the socialist countries' international commitments that have been undertaken up to now or will be undertaken in the future.

IV. Conclusion

The last proposition leads directly to the final conclusion to be drawn. The reform process and the international trade policy environment of socialist countries are interrelated, the speed and the success of economic reforms and the improval of trade policy treatment feed on each other to a large extent. Indeed, the close interrelationship between the realisation of market-oriented reforms and the terms and conditions of the integration of each socialist country in the multilateral world trading system is more apparent than ever. It can be generally stated that the reforms can be promoted or can be impeded by the international trade policy environment. Helping or hindering the reform process: this is a choice to be made when deciding on the trade policy treatment to be accorded to the individual socialist countries and when trying to find the appropriate arrangements for the integration of socialist countries in the GATT system.

Notes

1. See *inter alia* H. Matejka, "State Trading: Instruments of Trade Control or Barriers to Control", *J.W.T.L.*, 1974, p. 209; M. Kostecki, "Hungary and GATT", *J.W.T.L.*, 1974, p. 401; J. Reuland, "GATT and State-Trading Countries", *J.W.T.L.*, 1975, p. 318; R. Baban, "State-Trading and the GATT", *J.W.T.L.*, 1977, p. 334; M. Kostecki, *East-West and GATT*, London, Macmillan, 1979; P. Náray, "Application of the MFN Treatment in East-West Trade", *Acta Juridica Academiae Scientiarum Hungariae*, Tomus 21, 1979; Grzybowski, "Socialist Countries in GATT", *American Journal of Comparative Law*, 1980, p. 539; E. Janni, "The International Treatment of State Trading", *J.W.T.L.*, 1982, p. 480; E. Patterson, "Improving GATT Rules of Nonmarket Economies", *J.W.T.L.*, 1986, p. 185; R. Herzstein, "China and the GATT: Legal and Policy Issues Raised by China's Participation in the GATT", *Law and Policy in International Business*, 1986, p. 371; K. Kennedy, "The Accession of the Soviet Union to GATT", *J.W.T.L.*, 1987, p. 23; Chung-chou-Li, "Resumption of China's GATT Membership", *J.W.T.L.*, 1987 p. 25.

2. Trade barriers other than tariffs (non-tariff import barriers) are manifold; they include quantitative restrictions, restrictive import licensing procedures, national standards and quality control, customs formalities, etc. (see E. Mc Govern, *International trade regulation, GATT, the United States and the European Community*, Exeter, Globefield Press, 1986, pp. 204—241, as it is well known, one of the fundamental objectives of GATT was that international trade had to be regulated essentially by tariffs and the other regulatory devices inasmuch as they function as barriers to trade were to be progressively reduced, see J. Jackson, *World trade and the law of GATT. A legal analysis of the General Agreement of Tariffs and Trade*, Indianapolis, Bobs-Merrill, 1969, pp. 306—307.

3. "Since the issue of non-market economy participation in the GATT was first considered, there have been those who have argued that the GATT was, and is, intended to regulate trade between market economies and cannot apply meaningfully to centrally planned, non-market economies, and that to attempt to do so will either fail or will destroy the GATT as a meaningful regulator of trade between market economies", see E. Patterson, *op. cit.*, p. 185.

4. J. Jackson, *op. cit.*, p. 361.

5. The issue is closely related to the notion of State-trading. If State-trading is a mere form of ownership and it is not an instrument of trade control it may be or may not be a barrier to trade ("the competitive State-trading enterprise in itself, therefore, is not an instrument of trade control", H. Matejka, *op. cit.*, p. 210). "Competitive State-trading" simply because of the public ownership of enterprises does not represent a barrier to trade and may be fully compatible with the GATT principles and rules even without special arrangements. For R. Baban, *op. cit.*, p. 334, "the GATT recognises that State-trading enterprises *might be operated so as to create serious obstacles to trade* and therefore contains provisions to minimise, if not eliminate, this potential. Strictly speaking, the hypothesis of possible adverse trade effects implicit in these provisions does not relate to the public ownership of trading enterprises (indeed, the GATT contains no provisions against such ownership) but rather to the exercise of entrepreneurial decision-making by the state, an entity deemed to respond not only to commercial considerations but also to other factors". If, however, State-trading is an instrument of trade regulation and it is carried out through, *inter alia*, the system of foreign trade monopoly it becomes a formidable barrier to free trade as conceived by the drafters of the General Agreement.

6. Pursuant to a mandate from the United States Congress (Under Section 5 of the Trade Agreement Extension Act MFN status had to be withdrawn from all countries "controlled by world communism") the US government was forced to refuse the extension of tariff concessions to the socialist countries, irrespective of her obligations to Czechoslovakia under GATT. As J. Reuland remarked: "the United States maintained that events within Czechoslovakia — the nationalisation of enterprises, the confiscation of Western property and the establishment of a trade monopoly — rendered normal trade relations as understood in GATT impossible," *op. cit.*, p. 322; see also J. Jackson, *op. cit.*, p. 362.

7. See Kennedy, *op. cit.*, p. 30: "the experience of Yugoslavia serves as the paradigmatic example of how a Socialist state, can join GATT unconditionally. . . . . . . During its three years as an associated member, Yugoslavia decentralised its economy, introduced tariffs, abolished multiple exchange rates, and became multilateralist in its trade relations . . . . . . Following further decentralisation of its economy, Yugoslavia obtained full GATT membership in 1966 under the normal GATT obligations as exist among the other contracting parties".

8. See Kostecki, *op. cit.* pp. 26—27: "Yugoslavia's participation in the GATT provided empirical evidence that socialist economies could decentralise sufficiently to permit their membership of the GATT under the same conditions as Western market economies".

9. "Contracting parties which on the date of this Protocol apply to imports from Poland prohibitions or quantitative restrictions which are inconsistent with Article XIII of the General Agreement may, notwithstanding these provisions, continue to apply such prohibitions or restrictions to their imports from Poland provided that the discriminatory element in these restrictions is (a) not increased and (b) progressively relaxed as far as the quantities or values of permitted imports of Polish origin are concerned so that at the expiry of the transitional period the length of which will be determined in accordance with (c) below, any inconsistency with the provisions of Article XIII has thus been eliminated", Para. 3 (a) of the Protocol for the Accession of Poland, GATT, *B.I.S.D.*, 1966—67, pp. 47—48; check *Ibid*, Annex B, p. 52; also the Report of the Working Party on the Accession of Poland pp. 109—112.

10. On the numerous defects of the formula: the absence of a connection between export and import performance, the disregard of the possibility of chronic balance-of-payment problems and the failure to account for inflation, see Kennedy, *op. cit.*, p. 32 and M. Kostecki, *op. cit.*, p. 95.

11. Protocol for the Accession of Romania, *B.I.S.D.*, 1970—71, Annex B para. 1, p. 10.

12. "Contracting parties still maintaining prohibitions or quantitative restrictions not consistent with Article XIII of the General Agreement shall not increase the discriminatory element in these restrictions, undertake to remove them progressively and shall have as their objective to eliminate them before the end of 1974. Should this agreed objective not be achieved and, for exceptional reasons, should a limited number of restrictions still be in force as of 1 January 1975, the Working Party provided for in paragraph 5 would examine them with a view to their elimination", *B.I.S.D.*, 1970—1971 p. 6.

13. See the text in para. 4(a) of the Protocol for the Accession of Hungary, *B.I.S.D.*, 1972—73, p. 4.

14. Chung-chou-Li, *op. cit.*, pp. 25—27; R. Herzstein, *op. cit.*, pp. 402—403.

15. On the possible solutions see R. Herzstein, *op. cit.*, pp. 384—392.

16. See Chung-chou-Li, *op. cit.*, p. 37.

17. On the problems and the prospects of the Soviet Union's accession to GATT, see K. Kennedy, *op. cit.*, pp. 33—39.

18. On the relationship between the application of market methods and the decentralisation of the foreign trade system P. Náray, "Hungarian Foreign Trade Reform", *J.W.T.L.*, 1986, p. 286.

19. Schwarzenberger, *International Law*, quoted by Ustor, *Second Report on the most-favoured-nation clause*, UN, A (CN 4) 228, 1970, p. 13.

20. According to D. Vignes, "La clause de la nation la plus favorisée et sa pratique contemporaine . . .", Receuil des cours, La Hague, 1970, II, p. 214: "La clause sera un instrument d'égalisation des conditions de concurrence, elle favorisera l'égalité entre partenaires commerciaux, elle empechera que l'on discrimine un État bénéficiaire de la clause".

21. On the relationship between MFN and non-discrimination, see "International Law Commission-Most-Favored-Nation Clause", *J.W.T.L.*, 1978, p. 549, also Ustor, *op. cit.*, p. 15.

22. On the theory of effective reciprocity, see *inter alia* M. Domke and T. Hazard, "State-trading and the Most-Favoured-Nation Clause", *A.J.I.L.*, 1958, p. 50, S. Pisar, *Coexistence and Commerce*, London, Allen Lane, 1970; S. Pisar, "Trade Law and Peace: A Model Code for East-West Transactions", *The Journal of Int. Law and Economics*, 1975, No. 2—3.

23. As it has been referred to the import commitment undertaken by Poland turned out to be unworkable essentially because of the formulas being unable to meet the requirements of a complex and changing economic environment.

24. In the case of Hungary, at least 20 p.c. of the discriminatory QR's maintained by EEC Member States cover products that are not produced at all in the country (e.g. tanks and orange juice originating from Hungary are under QR in France and Italy).

25. "Representatives of countries maintaining quantitative restrictions against Hungary's exports indicated in this connexion that the inclusion of such a safeguard clause would facilitate the removal of the restrictions referred to in paragraph 8 above. The representative of Hungary could agree to the inclusion of a safeguard clause, provided it operated on a reciprocal basis. He also stated that his acceptance of such a safeguard clause was in anticipation of early elimination of quantitative restrictions maintained against imports from Hungary, inconsistently with Article XIII. Paragraph 5 of the draft Protocol has been prepared, taking into account these views," Report of the Working Party on the Accession of Hungary, *B.I.S.D.*, 1972—73, p. 35.

26. In 1984 the US Department of Commerce decided that bounties and grants, which the countervailing duty law is designed to offset, could not be found in non-market economy countries. (*Carbon Steel Wire Rod from Czechoslovakia*, 49 Fed. Reg. 19370, 1984; *Carbon Steel Wire Rod from Poland*, 49 Fed. Reg. 19374, 1984.). On appeal of the petitioners the Court of International Trade rejected the Department of Commerce's conclusion and held that countervailing duty law had to apply to NMEs as well (*Continental Steel Corp. v. United States*, 614 F. Supp. 548, 557, *Ct. Int. Trade* 1985.). On September 18 1986 the Court of Appeals for the Federal Circuit reversed the CIT decision and held that countervailing duty law does not apply to imports from countries with non-market economies, see Spak, "Georgetown Steel Corp. v. United States: Applying the countervailing duty law to imports from non-market economy countries", *Law and Policy in International Business*, 1986, pp. 313—339.

27. See Art. 15 para. 1 of the Agreement on interpretation and application of Articles VI, XVI and XXIII of the General Agreement on Tariffs and Trade. On the level of international law no criteria have been established as regards the selection of the third ("surrogate") country. In the US law, however, there is a reference to the level of economic development primarily reflected by the GNP per capita; see *Code of Federal Regulations* (*CFR*) §. 358. 8.

28. On the historical and legal background of the differential and more favourable treatment including, in particular, the System of Generalised Preferences accorded to developing countries, see *inter alia* J. Jackson, *op. cit.*, pp. 625—663; E. Mc Govern, *op. cit.*, pp. 271—283; O. Long, *Law and limitations in the GATT multilateral trade system*, Dordrecht, Martinus Nijhoff, 1985, pp. 312—324, A. Jusuf, "Differential and More Favourable Treatment: The GATT Enabling Clause", *J.W.T.L.*, 1980, p. 488, B. Balassa and C. Michalopoulos, "Liberalizing Trade Between Developed and Developing Countries", *J.W.T.L.*, 1986, p. 3.

29. J. Jackson, *op. cit.*, p.15.

30. Some quantitative restrictions inconsistent with Art. XIII of the GATT had been maintained by Sweden and Norway until the early 1980s and were then abolished. At the same time voluntary restraint agreements were made for the most sensitive products, essentially textiles. Since then it is solely the EEC and its member countries that refuse to remove discriminatory QRs.

The Uruguay Round and trade between the EEC and Eastern Europe

THIÉBAUT FLORY
Professor, Universities of Lille and Paris

I. Introduction

It is a known fact that the GATT has pioneered the elaboration of trade cooperation between East and West which has allowed a certain number of Eastern European countries[1] — almost all of them in fact — to gradually fit into the multilateral trade system. Parallel with this the EEC has attempted to conclude bilateral trade cooperation agreements with the Eastern European countries already members of the GATT. That was the case for Romania in 1980.

However, the agreement between the EEC and Romania was the only agreement of this kind during this period. Subsequently there was a break in relations between the EEC and Eastern Europe during the first part of the eighties.

At the moment a certain amount of factors have come together establishing a completely new and promising resurgence: the multilateral negotiations of the Uruguay Round (to be concluded in 1990), the realisation of a large Community internal market (by 1992) and the very recent adoption of the Joint Declaration between the EEC and CMEA.[2] The coming together of these factors should have a decisive influence on the pursuit of the liberalisation of trade between the EEC and Eastern Europe and at the same time on the redefinition of new forms of reciprocity in mutual relations.

II. The pursuit of the liberalisation of trade between the EEC and Eastern Europe

Under the influence of the three factors mentioned above, the resumption of the liberalisation of trade in goods in relations between the EEC and Eastern Europe — which has indicated the way for a certain number of

M. Maresceau (ed.), The Political and Legal Framework of Trade Relations Between the European Community and Eastern Europe. ISBN 0–7923–0046–7.
© *1989 by Kluwer Academic Publishers, Dordrecht – Printed in the Netherlands.*

years — should simultaneously result in a new process of dismantling obstacles to trade and relations based more on competition.

A.   *Dismantling obstacles to trade in goods*

The dismantling of obstacles to trade in goods between the EEC and Eastern European countries should all together be the result of the conclusion of bilateral agreements between the Community and certain Eastern European countries individually and the subsequent impact of the multilateral negotiations of the Uruguay Round.

Within the framework of bilateral relations where a freezing — really a putting on ice — of the Agreement with Romania could be ascertained a few years ago, there is now a trade cooperation agreement between the EEC and Hungary which was recently initialled in Brussels on 30 June 1988. This reciprocal agreement of progressive liberalisation between the two partners provides that, on the one hand the Twelve must abolish the quantitative restrictions which they apply to imports from Hungary according to a timetable in three stages,[3] and that on the other Hungary on her part, gradually improves access to her market for the exports of the Community. Moreover, negotiations on a trade cooperation agreement of the same type between the EEC and Czechoslovakia are close to coming to a conclusion.

Within the multilateral framework of relations, the protocols of accession of the Eastern European countries to GATT are the object of periodic examination on a biennial basis. In the GATT reports,[4] the problems which recur most often are those regarding the dismantling of discriminatory quantitative restrictions and those of the unconditional application of the most-favoured nation clause for Western European countries vis-à-vis Eastern Europe. If in the negotiations of the Uruguay Round currently in progress future reductions in customs duties decided upon between Contracting Parties will not be of much economic importance in East-West relations, the negotiations are conversely susceptible to having an impact — or at least to applying favourable pressure — on the mutual opening of systems of quotas of a non-discriminatory nature and on the increased application of the most-favoured nation clause on an unconditional basis. Moreover, the Punta del Este Declaration of 1986[5] entreats the Contracting Parties of GATT to in time abolish the Multifibre Arrangement which means that the bilateral self-restraint agreements, which the EEC has been obliged to conclude with a certain number of Eastern European countries, should in time gradually disappear.

B.   *Trade relations based on more competition*

It is obvious that the development of trade between the EEC and Eastern Europe will depend also on a greater degree of transparency in information, on the realisation of more intensive competition in external commercial operations and on public markets and private investments on all sides. The insufficiency of transparency existing at institutional level and of regulations of certain Eastern European countries, the non-convertibility of the currencies of the Eastern European countries — which inevitably induces compensation trade practices — and the price-structuring of Eastern European countries not being based on a market economy which makes comparisons difficult between the prices in the Eastern European countries and those in the Member States of the EEC (notably when the functioning of anti-dumping procedures is involved)[6] — these are all factors which still constitute obstacles to the development of trade between the EEC and Eastern European countries. However, the actual course being followed and the internal liberalisation in certain Eastern European countries are promising and are moving in the direction of the introduction of greater competition in commercial relations between Western and Eastern Europe.

III. The redefinition of new forms of reciprocity in the economic relations between the EEC and Eastern Europe

In the present and future negotiations between the EEC and Eastern European countries, either in a bilateral framework or the multilateral framework of the Uruguay Round, it is time to go beyond the stage of reciprocity relating *stricto sensu* to the liberalisation of trade in visible products and time to redefine the new forms of effective and balanced reciprocity in the economic relations in the broad sense of the expression. In this perspective, the quest for such reciprocity will have to be concentrated on new economic areas — other than the strictly commercial area — and will have to be secured by adapted institutional techniques.

A.   *The application of reciprocity in new areas*

The coming together of the Uruguay Round, the conclusion of bilateral agreements and the completion of the internal Community market should, between the EEC and Eastern European countries, stimulate the beginning of reciprocal apertures in public markets as well as the attraction of liberalisation of trade in services, notably in the road and sea transport sectors. A recent report by the Economic and Social Committee recommended in this respect that "both groups should undertake not to discriminate against each other's shipping". More precisely the report recommended that the two groupings should notably "not exclude outsiders operating on a commercial basis; not impose any restriction on bulk shipping; refrain from imposing unfair customs' penalties on each other's shipping companies; exempt each other's shipping companies from taxation; uphold the principle of freedom of navigation, with the implication of free access to ports as long as internationally agreed safety regulations are complied with". Effective reciprocity in effect demands, in the area of transport or in that of other services, mutual concessions from equal counterparts who may assume many forms.

B. *Reciprocity secured by adapted techniques*

Effective reciprocity between the partners will have to be guaranteed by adequate institutional and legal mechanisms be it within a bilateral framework or within the multilateral framework of GATT.

If the bilateral agreements on trade cooperation between the EEC and Romania and the EEC and Hungary provide a relatively complete apparatus of safeguard clauses and consultation procedures, in turn, the mechanism within the framework of GATT should be reformed at the negotiations of the Uruguay Round on three levels.

First, the criteria for the functioning of the safeguard clause laid down in Article XIX of the GATT should be made more precise, notably as regards the problem of the application — selective or non-discriminatory — of safeguard measures. Secondly, the dispute settlement procedure within the framework of Article XXIII of the GATT as well as within the framework of codes agreed upon in the Tokyo Round should be improved, notably with regard to the make-up of the panels and the entry into force of eventual countermeasures with a view to combatting disloyal commercial practices and at the same time to allow the reestablishment of balanced relations between partners.

Finally, and on a third level, surveillance mechanisms within the framework of the GATT, in liaison with other international economic institutions, should be made more efficient. In this way these different mechanisms improved to the extent possible by 1990, at the close of the Uruguay Round, should guarantee more effective reciprocity between partners.

Notes

1. Czechoslovakia was a founding member of GATT. Poland, Romania, Hungary are by virtue of protocols of accession members of the GATT. Bulgaria has observer status.
2. Joint Declaration on the establishment of official relations between the EEC and CMEA adopted at Luxembourg 25 June 1988 (*O.J.*, L 157/34 and 35, 1988). See also the Opinion of the Commission for External Economic Relations of the European Parliament, 15 June 1988, *A Series*, Document A2-0119/88/Annex and *E.P.* 124.085/def/Ann.
3. One year from now the 12 should abolish the quantitative restrictions which they apply to imports originating in Hungary for the "less sensitive" products from the 31st of December 1992 for "reasonably sensitive" products and from the 31st of December 1995 for textiles, fertilizers, polymers, glass, cement, colour televisions, wood and leather products.
4. See notably the fifth examination of the Protocol of Accession of Romania (*B.I.S.D.*, Supplement No. 32 pp. 89—95) and the sixth examination of the application of the Protocol of Accession of Hungary (*B.I.S.D.*, Supplement No. 33, pp. 149—166).
5. See the text of the Declaration in *B.I.S.D.*, Supplement No. 33, pp. 79 et seq.
6. See the *Technointorg* case which is currently pending before the Court of Justice of the European Communities (see Jacobs, *infra* p. 300).
7. Report by M. Briganti on "Relations between the European Community and European State-trading countries", *Economic and Social Committee*, 16/88, 8 April 1988, at p. 14.
8. See *Trade policies for a better future, The "Leutwiler Report, the GATT and the Uruguay Round*, Martinus Nijhoff Publishers, 1987.

Anti-dumping procedures with regard to imports from Eastern Europe

FRANCIS JACOBS

Professor, Centre of European Law, King's College, University of London

I. Introduction

Article 113(1) of the EEC Treaty establishes the exclusive competence of the Community (to the exclusion of its Member States) to adopt commercial policy measures governing trade with third countries, specifically including "measures to protect trade such as those to be taken in case of dumping or subsidies": By the terms of Article 113(2), the Commission is to submit proposals to the Council for implementing the common commercial policy.

The EEC acquired its exclusive competence in this field in 1968 and the first EEC anti-dumping legislation (Council Regulation (EEC) No. 459/68) dated from the same period. However, the development of the Community's active role in the field can be traced back to the mid-1970's following the 1973 oil crisis and the onset of recession. The first anti-dumping case (which concerned Japan) was taken to the Court of Justice in 1977 and decided in 1979.

In a nutshell, an anti-dumping proceeding is initiated by the Commission, usually in response to a complaint by the Community industry adducing evidence of dumping and of injury. Where the Commission reaches a provisional finding of dumping resulting in injury to the Community industry, it may by regulation impose provisional duty; importers are then required to lodge security in respect of the provisional duty. Alternatively, the Commission may accept price undertakings. After the completion of the Commission investigation, definitive duties may be imposed by a regulation of the Council, which may also order the definitive collection of the provisional duty. Measures of the Council or Commission may be challenged before the Court of Justice.

In the substantial increase in anti-dumping procedures which has been a feature of the EEC's commercial policy in the 1980s, a substantial role has been taken by imports from Eastern Europe. Approximately half the

M. Maresceau (ed.), The Political and Legal Framework of Trade Relations Between the European Community and Eastern Europe. ISBN 0–7923–0046–7.
© *1989 by Kluwer Academic Publishers, Dordrecht – Printed in the Netherlands.*

cases in this period involve "non-market economy countries", i.e. countries which have centrally-planned economies in which costs, prices and exchange rates are generally determined without regard to market forces, so that none of the usual criteria can be regarded as providing a reliable basis for establishing the "normal value" of imports from those countries. Most of these cases concern imports from Eastern Europe (including for the purposes of this paper the USSR); the other countries concerned are Mongolia, North Korea, Vietnam and the People's Republic of China. The expression "normal value" is that used in Article VI of the GATT and in the basic EEC anti-dumping Regulation, Council Regulation (EEC) No. 2176/84 of 23 July 1984, Article 2(2) of which provides that: "A product shall be considered to have been dumped if its export price to the Community is less than the normal value of the product." Article 2(3) provides that the normal value is normally "the comparable price actually paid or payable in the ordinary course of trade for the like product intended for consumption in the exporting country or country of origin."

No meaningful comparison between the export price and the domestic price is possible in the case of a non-market economy. Apart from the fact that costs and prices are determined without regard to market forces, the difficulties are compounded by the fact that the currencies of non-market economy countries are often non-convertible. This makes meaningless a comparison between domestic prices or costs and export prices, which are typically determined by State-trading organisations. While export prices can be determined in the same ways as those of market economy countries, domestic prices and costs cannot be determined on a basis which would permit a realistic comparison.

The difficulties of determining price-comparability were reflected in the period between the two World Wars when anti-dumping measures were taken against Soviet products by several Western countries.[1] The issue achieved a sharper focus with the international regulation of world trade under the auspices of the GATT, designed to counter protectionism and to implement a free trade régime.

GATT, reflected in this respect by Article 113 of the EEC Treaty, recognised as "measures to protect trade" the legitimacy of anti-dumping measures adopted following a finding of dumping and countervailing duties imposed in the case of subsidies. These are governed by *Article VI of the GATT*, headed "Anti-dumping and Countervailing Duties". There has also been drawn up within GATT the *Anti-dumping Code* of 30 June 1967, revised on 30 June 1979 (Agreement on implementation of Article VI of the GATT), and the *Subsidies and Countervailing Measures Code* of 12 April 1979 (Agreement on interpretation and application of Articles VI, XVI and XXII of the GATT).

In some cases there may be a choice between the use of anti-dumping and anti-subsidy measures. Article 15 of the Subsidies Code explicitly recognises the right of signatories to take either countervailing or anti-dumping action to deal with imports from a State-trading country. In general, however, for practical or even conceptual reasons, the signatories have preferred anti-dumping measures. While there are considerable difficulties in determining price-comparability for imports from such countries for anti-dumping purposes, it would be more difficult, if not impossible, to quantify the amount of subsidisation granted in a non-market economy country.

The U.S. authorities decided, in carbon steel wire rod from Czechoslovakia and Poland, that, conceptually, no subsidy can be found in a non-market economy country[2] and the view that countervailing duty law does not apply to such countries was finally upheld in the Georgetown Steel case in September 1986.[3]

The European Community's legislation provides for countervailing duties to be imposed on imports from State-trading countries and, in line with the Subsidies Code, adopts the same provisions as are used for the determination of the dumping margin in the case of imports from such countries.[4] However, there appears to be no case in which countervailing duties have been imposed on such imports. The Community has preferred to use anti-dumping measures and appears to regard such measures as providing adequate protection against imports from non-market economy countries. Anti-subsidy measures have also been used very rarely against imports from other countries.

II. Non-market economy

What is a non-market economy for the purposes of the anti-dumping legislation? The Community's approach can be expressed in two principles. First, Community legislation contains no definition of the notion of non-market economy; instead, it proceeds by reference to a list of non-market economy countries to which, "in particular", the special provisions are to apply. Secondly, all imports from such countries are subject to those special provisions, regardless of whether a particular industry in such a country might be said to be subject to market forces.

1. Article 2(5) of the basic Regulation refers to "imports from non-market economy countries and, in particular, those to which Regulations (EEC) No. 1765/82 and (EEC) No. 1766/82 apply."

The basic Regulation governing imports from State-trading countries (Council Regulation (EEC) No. 1765/82 of 30 June 1982 on common rules for imports from State-trading countries) applies to imports from Bulgaria, Czechoslovakia, the German Democratic Republic, Hungary, Poland, Romania, and the USSR; and also to imports from Mongolia, North Korea and Vietnam. Identical provisions govern imports from the People's Republic of China (Council Regulation (EEC) No. 1766/82 of 30 June 1982 on common rules for imports from the People's Republic of China). However, trade between the two Germanies is regarded as German internal trade under the Protocol on German internal trade and connected problems annexed to the EEC Treaty; accordingly anti-dumping duties cannot be levied on imports from the GDR into the Federal Republic of Germany.

The words "in particular" make it clear that the list is not exhaustive; other countries, such as Cuba (a member of COMECON), could also be regarded as a non-market economy country for the purposes of the anti-dumping legislation.[5] Subject to that point, Community legislation precludes any analysis of whether the exporting country has a non-market economy. This approach has the advantage of certainty and predictability — elements often lacking in the anti-dumping process.

2. As a corollary of the first principle, the special provisions apply to all imports from the countries in question, even if there might be said to be elements of a free economy in a particular industry; and the special provisions do not apply to other countries, even if the market in a particular industry is regulated.

As is pointed out by Beseler and Williams:[6]

"These rules apply to imports from non-market economy countries, the decisive criterion being the existence of a centrally planned economy. They would not apply to imports from a nationalised industry located in a market-economy country and which, therefore, has to base its pricing decisions on market considerations. In the same way, Community legislation excludes the possibility of market-economy criteria being applied to any particular industry within a non-market economy country, even if it is alleged that this industry is subject to market forces. This is because in a non-market economy country it is impossible to distinguish the influence of such market forces from the overall effect of state intervention in the formation of costs and prices for that industry."

III. Price-comparability

As mentioned above, the issue of the price-comparability of exports from non-market economy countries arose at an early stage within the GATT.

Czechoslovakia, an original Contracting Party to the GATT, referred to the problem in the working party on other barriers to trade[7] and this led to the adoption in 1955 of an interpretative note on the first paragraph of Article VI.[8] The note recognises in cautious terms that in the case of imports from a country which has a complete or substantially complete monopoly of its trade, and where all domestic prices are fixed by the State, special difficulties may exist in determining price-comparability for the purposes of establishing dumping; and that, in such cases, the importing parties may find it necessary to take into account the possibility that a strict comparison with the domestic price in the exporting country may not always be appropriate.

But although the interpretative note to Article VI warned of the difficulties involved in establishing dumping on the basis of the domestic price in a State-trading country, it suggested no alternative criteria. The Community's earliest legislation, in 1968, merely reflected the wording of the interpretative note. Article 3(6) of Regulation 459/68 provided merely that:

"In the case of imports from countries where trade is on a basis of near or total monopoly and where domestic prices are fixed by the State, account may be taken of the fact that an exact comparison between the export price of a product to the Community and the domestic prices in that country may not always be appropriate, since in such cases special difficulties may arise in determining the comparability of prices."

However, some of the other Code signatories began to base normal value on prices in or from a third market economy country. Thus in the United Kingdom (before its accession to the European Community), the Customs Duties (Dumping and Subsidies) Act 1969 provided by Section 4(4) that:

"If it appears to the Board of Trade that the system of trading in the country is such, as a result of government monopoly and control, that the fair market price there cannot appropriately be determined in accordance [with the other methods prescribed by the Section] then there shall be taken as representing the fair market price such price as the Board may determine by reference to any price obtained for goods of that description when exported to the United Kingdom from another country, with adjustments made to ensure comparability."

The criterion of a third country price was also adopted in the reports of the working parties on the accession of Poland, Romania and Hungary to the GATT between 1967 and 1973. These held that a contracting party could base the normal value of its imports from the State trading country either on the prices prevailing on its own market or, alternatively, on a price of a like product originating in a third country. Thus the report of the working party on the accession of Poland stated:[9]

"With regard to the implementation, where appropriate, of Article VI of the General Agreement with respect to imports from Poland, it was the understanding of the Working Party that the second Supplementary Provisions in Annex 1 to paragraph 1 of Article VI of the General Agreement . . . , would apply. In this connection it was recognised that a contracting party may use as the normal value for the product imported from Poland the prices which prevail generally in its markets for the same or like products or a value for that product constructed on the basis of the prices for the like product originating in another country, so long as the method used for determining normal value in any particular case is appropriate and not unreasonable."

These practices were ultimately codified in Article 15 of the GATT Subsidies Code of 12th April 1979 which applies to both subsidies and dumping and which allows for the comparison of the export price with

(a) the price at which a like product of a third country is sold, or

(b) the constructed value (cost of production plus a reasonable amount for administration, selling and any other costs and for profits) of a like product in a third country; or, if neither of the above tests provides an adequate basis, the price in the importing country.

The provisions of the GATT Subsidies Code were taken up in Community legislation in 1979 which contained the first detailed rules for non-market economy countries and which were substantially reenacted in the basic Regulation of 1984. Article 2(5) of Regulation 2176/84 reads as follows:

"In the case of imports from non-market economy countries and, in particular, those to which Regulations (EEC) No. 1765/82 and (EEC) No. 1766/82 apply, normal value shall be determined in an appropriate and not unreasonable manner on the basis of one of the following criteria:

(a) the price at which the like product of a market economy third country is actually sold:
    (i)   for consumption on the domestic market of that country; or
    (ii) to other countries, including the Community; or

(b) the constructed value of the like product in a market economy third country;

(c) if neither price nor constructed value as established under (a) or (b) provides an adequate basis, the price actually paid or payable in the Community for the like product, duly adjusted, if necessary, to include a reasonable profit margin."

The third method, under (c) above, although consistent with the GATT provisions, could be criticised on the ground that it would enable the

Community producers, by raising their own prices, to create or increase a dumping margin. In practice this method has not been used by the Commission. However, it will be noticed that the use of a third country analogue, although it introduces a greater degree of objectivity in the determination of normal value, still has the consequence that normal value is not based on any factors within the control of the exporting country under investigation, and that the exporter may be unable to predict the level at which it can avoid findings of dumping. That consequence is perhaps inherent in the exercise of seeking to apply anti-dumping methods to a non-market economy country when such methods are intrinsically inappropriate to such an economy.

While the use of a third country's price may operate to the detriment of the non-market economy country in that the latter cannot benefit from natural competitive advantages, particularly in access to raw materials, there may be compensation in other respects: production costs in the analogue country may be reduced by more advanced technology or by a more highly integrated production process. However, the use of the third country method, with all its consequences, is firmly established in Community practice in time with the GATT Code.

In the light of the provisions set out above, the procedure can be considered in three stages, as follows:

(1) The first stage involves the selection of the third country (a market economy country), known in Community practice as the "analogue" country, in which the price or constructed value of the like product will be assessed, and which also therefore involves a selection of the like product.

(2) The selection of the normal value test, i.e. selection of the appropriate criterion on the basis of which normal value will be calculated. This will be:

(a)   the domestic selling price, or
(b)   the export price, or
(c)   constructed value.

(3) If necessary, adjustments will be made under Article 2(9) to ensure fair comparison between the export price from the non-market economy country and the normal value as so calculated.

IV. Selection of the analogue country

Neither the GATT Code nor Community legislation gives any guidance on the selection of the analogue country.

One approach, which has been adopted by the United States,[10] is to base the normal value on the prices or costs in a market economy country at a comparable level of economic development to the State-trading country. There are, however, many objections which have been made to this approach, of which the following have considerable force: [11]

(1) It assumes that prices and costs in countries at a similar level of economic development are broadly comparable. This assumption is not borne out by the facts, and there is no rational basis for concluding that economies at a comparable stage of development also have comparable natural advantages and relative efficiencies of production.

(2) There is no reliable indicator of the level of economic development, since estimates of gross national product for market economy countries may not be comparable with those of State-trading countries.

(3) Even if they are comparable, GNP per capita does not provide a sufficient guide for the comparison of the prices or costs of specific products. Much will depend on the basis of the GNP of the countries being compared: for one country it may stem mainly from agricultural production, while for another it may be based primarily on industrial output.

In order to avoid some of these problems, an alternative approach which has been suggested [12] is to take account of the relative comparability of the development of the industry producing the same or similar goods. Once again, the underlying assumption appears to be that comparable industries have comparable costs. This need not be the case, as costs include factors other than those due to technological processes, including wages, raw materials and other inputs. Moreover, it has to be remembered that prices are a function of demand as well as of supply, and the former is not dependent on the level of development of the industry.

Because no ideal solution to the problem is readily available, the Code and Community legislation only provide that the comparison should be made in an "appropriate and not unreasonable manner."

"Consequently", according to Baseler and Williams, "the Community has not opted for a hierarchy of criteria for selecting the substitute market economy country to be used. Instead the Commission's practice is to consider any third market economy country which may be suggested in the initial stage of the investigation, thereby ensuring that no possible analogue is excluded from examination. Thus, the Community industry is free to base the allegation of dumping in the complaint on any third market economy price or cost to which it has access. Providing the comparison is considered reasonable enough to justify the opening of an investigation, the analogue suggested is published in the notice of opening of the investigation. This gives other interested parties the opportunity to make any representations, and to suggest a more appropriate choice, if one is known. If alternative analogues are proposed then these are considered by the Commission and may be accepted as being more reasonable or appropriate. In any event, whatever analogue is finally accepted, the Commission publishes notice of the fact, together with the reasons for the choice.

This pragmatic approach results in the consideration of a wide range of alternatives. Thus, for the 23 products originating in State-trading countries in which the investigation was terminated in the years 1980 to 1982, the normal value was based on prices or costs in 12 countries at all stages of economic development, from India and Yugoslavia to Sweden and the United States. During these investigations, only 11 of the 23 analogues finally chosen were those contained in the complaint, 10 being changed as a result of representations by other interested parties and 2 in the light of evidence which came to light during the investigation. The reasons given for the choice of the analogue finally selected include, similarity of the scale of production and production techniques; similarity of access to raw materials; efficient internal competition or price controls ensured that prices in the substitute country were not unreasonably high; the low level of protection afforded to the domestic industry in the country chosen; insufficiency of data available on the country originally suggested and the fact that the additional administrative burden of carrying out an investigation in a further country was not justified."[13]

V. Selection of the normal value test

The first criterion set out in Article 2(5), i.e. the price at which the like product is actually sold on the domestic market, is the criterion generally used. The domestic price of the like product in the analogue country has been used in most cases involving imports from non-market economy countries and will be disregarded only if it is for some reason considered unreliable, e.g. because of peculiarities of the domestic market or because a significant proportion of domestic production is exported.

The export price, the second criterion set out in Article 2(5), will normally be used where the domestic price cannot be used, but in some cases the Commission has refused to use the export price on the ground that it might be influenced by competition from low-cost exports originating in other countries.

The constructed value, the third criterion set out in Article 2(5), has been used in a few cases, where the domestic price in the analogue country was considered not be suitable because it did not cover all production costs or, conversely, because the domestic market of the analogue country was highly protected.[14]

A different approach to constructed value has been developed in the U.S. in cases where there is no production of a like product in an appropriate third country. This consists of quantifying the hypothetical costs of production on the basis of data obtained in the non-market economy country of export. The approach was first used in 1977 in the celebrated Polish golf car case.[15] Golf cars were produced in Poland solely for export to the U.S. There was no domestic market nor sales to any other country. There was also no other large-sale producer outside the U.S. and, in order to avoid using U.S. prices or costs for fair value, the U.S. Treasury based constructed value on the Polish producer's physical inputs, verified by the Treasury at the Polish factory, but valued at prices prevailing in Spain. Spain was found by the Treasury to be on a comparable level of economic development to Poland on the basis of a study of the Spanish economy prepared by the Polish State-trading company which was the respondent in the case. The approach was then incorporated in U.S. anti-dumping regulations in 1978.

The method has the advantage that it permits a constructed value calculation in a market economy country at a comparable level of economic development although there is no like product in that country. The disadvantage is that the process is a hypothetical one which also relies upon the relationship of price and cost as expressed in the particular combination of factors of production in a non-market economy country which may not be genuinely comparable to the situation in a market economy. It illustrates once again the artificiality in seeking to apply anti-dumping methods designed for market economies to an economy to which such methods are inherently unsuited.

In the Community, the difficulties in selecting the analogue country and the appropriate normal value test are well illustrated by three cases which have come before the Court, all concerning imports from the Soviet Union. Two of these cases, the first and the most recent, were brought by the exporters themselves. The first, the *Raznoimport* case, will be considered below; the most recent, Case 294/86 and 77/87 *Technointorg*, has not yet been decided by the Court.[15 bis] In the *Timex* case[16] the applicant was the complainant, a Community manufacturer; it sought the partial annulment of a Council Regulation imposing a definitive anti-dumping duty on mechanised wrist-watches. The Commission had chosen as the basis for determining the normal value the constructed value of wrist-watches manufactured in Hong Kong considered similar to the watches originating in the Soviet Union. That determination was made on the basis of the purchase price in Hong Kong of a selection of movements imported from France and the costs of assembling watches in Hong Kong.

One point at issue between the parties was the choice of Hong Kong as the analogue country. The other reference country suggested by the complainant, Switzerland, was rejected by the Commission on the ground that it was impossible to carry out an on-the-spot investigation there, as such investigations were not permitted by the Swiss authorities.

The arguments of Timex on the use of Hong Kong as the analogue country were summarised by Advocate General Darmon as follows:[17]

"Timex maintains that the institutions have always considered that the similarity of manufacturing processes and technology is the decisive element in determining the country comparable to the State-trading country. The choice of Hong Kong is contrary to that practice. Unlike the Soviet clock and watch industry, the Hong Kong industry does not have a complete cycle of production. The watch movements assembled there are imported from France. No country combines the advantages of advanced technology, as in France, and cheap labour, as in Hong Kong. If conditions in a single country are considered, the pay of skilled labour, needed to manufacture movements, inevitably has an effect on the level of wages paid to the non-skilled workers required to assemble them. The Commission thus reconstructed an artificial cycle of production which cannot exist in one and the same market-economy country. In short, the basis of determination chosen by the Commission results not in a normal value but in an 'optimal' value in so far as its level is determined by abnormally low costs. By determining the normal value on the basis of costs in two different countries, the Commission acted in breach of the provisions of Article 2(5) which require costs to be calculated in a single country."

The Advocate General rejected these arguments, emphasising the wide discretion which the Commission enjoys in the selection of the analogue country. The Court did not decide the point as it upheld the case of Timex on other grounds. But the case illustrates the risk of artificial construction in the use of an analogue country, and in the selection of the normal value test.

The *Raznoimport*[18] case concerned imports of unwrought nickel from the Soviet Union. The complainants suggested that the determination of the normal value should be based on the constructed value of the like product in Canada. The exporter and one dealer objected to this sugges-tion arguing that nickel was an internationally traded commodity whose price was determined by the price at which it was traded on an international terminal market (the London Metal Exchange), which should, therefore, be used for determining the normal value. The Commission rejected this suggestion on the ground that it was not in accordance with the criteria laid down in Regulation No. 3017/79 for determining normal value and that there was reason to doubt whether the London Metal Exchange quotations covered the production costs in market economy countries. Consequently, the Commission decided to determine normal value on the basis of the constructed value in Canada and, after dumping and injury were established, it imposed a provisional anti-dumping duty on imports of unwrought nickel from the Soviet Union.

The Soviet importer, Raznoimport, brought an action before the Court of Justice to quash the Regulation and at the same time it lodged an application requesting an order suspending its operation. The President of the Court considered[19] that "serious doubt surrounds the question whether, in adopting a constructed value as a basis of reference when prices are apparently determined by market mechanisms, and in calculating that constructed value on the basis of production costs in a non-member country which may itself be in the situation referred to in paragraph (4) of Article 2B, the Commission applied the criteria set out in paragraph (5) in an appropriate and reasonable manner. In the light of the explanations provided during the proceedings for the adoption of interim measures, there are also doubts concerning the circumstances which led the Commission to fix the rate of the provisional anti-dumping duty at 7%." While dismissing, on other grounds, the application for suspension of the provisional duty, the President of the Court held that "the Commission is under an obligation to monitor from day to day any changes in prices on the market of the product which is subject to the provisional duty in order to determine whether it is necessary to maintain that duty or the rate thereof".

At a later stage the case was settled and the security was released. Raznoimport requested the Commission to re-examine the situation and the latter, after extending the investigation period, terminated the proceedings and ordered the release of the security lodged in respect of the provisional duty.

The *Raznoimport* case aroused considerable interest because it was the first case taken to the Court by a Soviet entity; generally in previous anti-dumping proceedings involving the USSR, all contacts, which were at the Commission level, and were instigated by Commission proceedings, were made through the Community importer, but here a Soviet organisation, with an address in Moscow, instituted proceedings before the Court: the question was raised, e.g. in the London *Times*, whether this constituted a degree of recognition of the Community by the Soviet Union. The case also raised the important issue whether the normal value of a commodity traded on an international commodity market can be anything other than the price prevailing on that market. On the one hand, it is understandable that the Community authorities may wish to take account of the possibility that that market price may itself have been depressed by the practice of dumping. On the other hand, it is also hard to see how any exporter — whether from a non-market economy country or indeed from elsewhere — could be expected to trade at a higher price and so could avoid a finding of dumping at all. That issue, which was not resolved as the case was settled, arises again in other proceedings which are currently pending before the Commission.

The selection of the analogue country is also in issue in the *Technointorg* case,[19 bis] where Yugoslavia was taken as the analogue country for freezers exported from the Soviet Union.

VI. Adjustments

If normal value as determined under Article 2(5) and the export price are not on a comparable basis, adjustments can be made on the basis of Article 2(9). The Commission has frequently made adjustments to take account of differences in the physical characteristics of the product or differences in the conditions of sale.

On the other hand, the Commission has consistently refused to make adjustments for differences in costs or to take account of alleged comparative cost advantages of a non-market economy producer. The reasons for this attitude have been stated as follows:[20]

"In the first place, the comparative advantages are not known with certainty and they may be more than offset by other comparative advantages enjoyed by the market economy producer. An advantage resulting from access to cheaper raw materials, for example, might be out-weighed by advantages resulting from economies of scale or better production techniques in the market economy country. In addition, where the normal value is based on prices in the market economy country, rather than costs, there is the further problem that there is no way of knowing how any comparative advantage would be reflected in these prices, bearing in mind that they are determined by demand as well as supply. But the main objection to making any allowance for differences in comparative advantage lies in the fact that this would involve the need to rely on the methods and the costs of production in the State-trading country, an exercise which the use of a third market economy country analogue is designed to avoid."

Similar arguments were accepted in an English case in 1973 by Mr. Justice Ackner, in *Leopold Lazarus Limited v. Secretary of State for Trade and Industry*,[21] concerning an anti-dumping investigation involving imports of pig iron from the GDR:

> "It is of the very essence of [such a] case that the system of trading in the [State-trading] country is such, as a result of government monopoly or control, that the fair market price there cannot be determined by the process of taking the price at which identical or comparable goods are being sold in the ordinary course of trade for consumption there. It is for this reason that the Minister is obliged to look for identical or comparable goods ... from another country and then to discover the price obtained for such goods ...
>
> Once he discovers the identical or comparable goods ... [he] is not concerned with the conditions [in the State-trading country] or with their economies or mode of production, assuming contrary to the inherent probabilities that he could ever get a true or balanced picture. This is for the simple reason that such information, if available, cannot give him the fair market price of the goods. His attention is directed in search of that price to another country ... The Minister would accordingly have misdirected himself in law if he had taken into account such differences since they were irrelevant to the proper discharge of his functions."

Once again, the arguments illustrate the artificiality of applying traditional anti-dumping calculations to State-trading countries.

It must be stressed that, in the Community, the selection of the analogue country and the methods used to determine normal value and to effect adjustments for the purpose of comparability with the export price have a limited effect in practice because, under the Community legislation, the level of any anti-dumping duty imposed is limited to the amount required to eliminate the injury to the Community industry, where this is less than the margin of dumping (Article 13(3) of Regulation 2176/84). The "lesser duty rule", which is not required by the GATT Code and does not apply in the U.S., certainly mitigates the severity of the Community practice. Thus, although anti-dumping proceedings involving non-market economy countries have often resulted in high dumping margins being found, the level of duty imposed is often substantially less. However, the rule does not of course completely obviate the difficulties inherent in the use of the analogue country method, since the use of that method might result in dumping margins which on other tests might be lower than the duty actually imposed or even non-existent. It is certainly rare for an anti-dumping proceeding involving a non-market economy country to result in a finding of no dumping.

The overall effect of the lesser duty rule is to shift the emphasis from dumping to injury, with consequent advantages and disadvantages. A difficulty for exporters is that they cannot readily predict a finding of injury and so may be unable to predict at what level of prices their exports are likely to result in the imposition of anti-dumping duties. Moreover, the Commission's findings of injury will often be based on information which the Community industry affected may properly regard as confidential and which the Commission may therefore be unable to disclose to the exporter. The exporter may thus be precluded from challenging the Commission's provisional or definitive findings effectively either before the Commission or before the Court. Finally, a finding of injury is based, in accordance with Article 3 of the GATT Code and Article 4(2) of Regulation 2176/84, on a wide variety of factors of which, as is expressly provided, no single factor or combination of factors can necessarily give decisive guidance. Consequently findings of injury are by their very nature less readily quantifiable, less objective and less susceptible to review than the comparison of prices involved in a finding of dumping.

On the other hand, there are considerable advantages from the point of view of the non-market economy country in placing the emphasis on injury rather than on dumping. In the first place this is likely, as already mentioned, to result in a lower level of duty. While there may be difficulties in challenging findings of injury, it is illusory to suppose that findings of dumping could be more easily challenged since, as has been seen, such findings necessarily involve an artificial construction. It can be argued that protective measures should indeed be based, and perhaps can only be rationally based, on findings of injury.

VII. Conclusions and suggestions for reform

The problems which have arisen in applying anti-dumping rules to imports from Eastern Europe are not to be regarded as criticisms of the Community's approach which is firmly based on the GATT system. They are rather the result of the inherent unsuitability of the anti-dumping mechanism itself as applied to non-market economies. While the problems may be resolved in the longer term by the increasing liberalisation of these economies, it seems desirable to consider the possibilities of other solutions.[22]

The central issue is that of the adjustments necessary at the "interface" between the non-market economies of Eastern Europe and the free-market system of the West: some gearing mechanism is necessary if the systems are to interlock fairly and effectively. Because, compared with other trading entities which make regular use of the anti-dumping rules —

the U.S., Australia and Canada — the European Community has a far higher proportion of trade with Eastern Europe, and because of its closer geographical, historical and cultural links, the Community should be in the forefront of ideas for reform.

Such ideas can be considered here only in outline. One approach which has been much ventilated in recent years in the United States would consist in the adoption of a trigger price or "benchmark" price which might be based on various formulas, e.g. the lowest average price charged for the products by producers from free-market economies. Where the export price from a non-market economy country fell below the trigger or benchmark price, duties equal to the difference between the two prices would be imposed. A similar approach has been adopted by the European Community in other areas of commercial policy, for example in the EEC — China agreement on textiles, which takes as a criterion the price usually governing similar products sold under normal trading conditions by other exporting countries. If the relevant price were ascertained from time to time by transparent and objective methods, this approach would have the advantage of introducing an element of predictability. It still involves, however, a degree of artificiality by virtue of the use of prices in third countries.

For this reason it might be preferable to adopt a different approach which would explicitly recognise the need to focus on the injurious effects of the imports and would limit remedial action to the imposition of duties, or possibly quantitative restrictions, to the extent necessary to give protection against injury. This would be similar to the market disruption law under Section 406 of the US Trade Act of 1974, which essentially requires findings of rapidly increasing imports and of injury to the domestic industry to justify the imposition of duties. This approach has the advantage of involving no inquiry into the economy of the non-market economy country — an inquiry which is of doubtful utility; nor into the economy of a third country — an inquiry of doubtful relevance. It has the disadvantage of failing to recognise the possibility of lower prices based on a genuine competitive advantage in the non-market economy country. But since the existence of a genuine competitive advantage seems impossible to measure in a non-market economy that may be a small price to pay for the adoption of a more realistic method; and since the remedial action would be taken only in the event of market disruption, the objection presupposes a sudden change in competitive advantage, probably a rather infrequent situation.

Finally, consideration might be given to protective measures in the form of quantitative restrictions rather than duties. The latter, although in principle limited to the amount necessary to avoid injury, might have the effect of excluding the imports affected from the Community market altogether by rendering them uncompetitive; the former would limit the quantity of imports to the degree actually necessary to avoid injury to the Community industry, by preventing a substantial increase in imports above the level previously tolerated.

The introduction of more realistic methods might be expected to contribute to a greater degree of mutual confidence between the Community and the countries of Eastern Europe. This in turn is a prerequisite of other reforms which might be envisaged in the longer term: provision for consultation before the adoption of protective measures, and perhaps some machinery for joint supervision, and for the settlement of disputes. For its part, the Community's policy should be designed to encourage a greater degree of transparency in the practices and policies of non-market economies: an objective which is essential for their integration into the world trading system. As for the Community itself, its policies should also be more exposed to debate: a process to which this discussion is intended to contribute, in the belief that the Community also can benefit from Glasnost.

Notes

1. Wilczynski, "Dumping and central planning", *J.Pol. Econ.*, 1966, p. 250.
2. See U.S. Department of Commerce, final negative countervailing duty determination in respect of carbon steel wire rod from Czechoslovakia and Poland: 49 Fed. Reg. 19370 and 19374.
3. See *Georgetown Steel Corp. v. United States*, U.S. Court of Appeals for the Federal Circuit, 18 September 1986: 801 F. 2d 1308.
4. Article 3(4) (d) of Regulation 2176/84.
5. Some recognition of the possibility that Cuba might be considered as a non-market economy country may be found in the fact that, while not included in Regulations 1765/82 and 1766/82, it is specifically excluded by Article 1(1) from Council Regulation 288/82 on common rules for imports from countries other than State-trading countries.
6. Beseler and Williams, *Anti-Dumping and Anti-Subsidy Law: The European Communities*, London, Sweet and Maxwell, 1986, p. 67.
7. GATT, *B.I.S.D.*, Third supplement p. 223, para. 6, Geneva, June 1955.
8. Second supplement provision to Art. VI of the GATT.
9. Report of the Working Party on the Accession of Poland, *B.I.S.D.*, Fifteenth Supplement p. 111 Geneva, April 1968; cfr. Report of the Working Party on the Accession of Romania, *B.I.S.D*, 18th Supplement, p. 96, Geneva, April 1972; Report of the Working Party on the Accession of Hungary, *B.I.S.D.*, 20th Supplement p. 37, Geneva, January 1974.
10. Section 353.8 of the U.S. Anti-dumping Regulations of 6 February, 1980, 45 Fed. Reg. 8192 1980.
11. See especially Verril in: Interface One, *Conference Proceedings on the Application of*

U.S. *Anti-Dumping and Countervailing Duty Laws to imports from State Controlled Economies and State Owned Enterprises*, Georgetown University Law Center, Washington D.C., 1980 pp. 168 et seq. (with further references), cited in Beseler and Williams, *op. cit.*, pp. 67—68.

12. See Verril, *op. cit.*, p. 173.

13. Beseler and Williams, *op. cit.*, pp. 69—71. For a full discussion of the Community practice, see Denton, "The non-market economy rules of the European Community's anti-dumping and countervailing duties legislation",*ICLQ* 1987, p. 198; Konstantinides, The application of the EEC anti-dumping rules to State-trading countries (not yet published).

14. See, with references to the Regulations, Van Bael and Bellis, *International Trade Law and Practice of the European Community: EEC Anti-Dumping and other Trade Protection Laws*, 1985, Bicester, CCH Editions Limited, p. 47.

15. See Horlick and Shuman, "Non-market economy trade and U.S. Antidumping/Countervailing duty laws", *The International Lawyer*, 1984, p. 807.

15 bis. See note 19 bis.

16. Case 264/82, *Timex Corporation v. Council and Commission of the European Communities*, [1985] *ECR* 849.

17. at 859.

18. Case 120/83R V/O *Raznoimport v. Commission of the European Communities*, [1983] *ECR* 2573.

19. [1983] *ECR*, 2578—2579.

19 bis. After completion of this book the Court of Justice gave judgment in this case on 5 October 1988 rejecting *Technointorg* argument that Yugoslavia could not be taken as the analogue country.

20. Beseler and Williams, *op. cit.*, pp. 71—72. Similar arguments have been used by the Commission in several cases: see e.g. the cases cited by Denton, *op. cit.*, p. 233.

21. Unreported.

22. See Patterson. "Improving GATT rules for non-market economies", *J.W.T.L.*, 1986, p. 185.

PART FOUR

Concluding observations

East-West European trade: the CMEA-view

VIATCHESLAV SYCHEV

Secretary of the Council for Mutual Economic Assistance

I would like to note with satisfaction that the atmosphere of optimism has clearly prevailed at international symposia, conferences and seminars devoted to the issues of relations between East and West in Europe, the number of which has markedly increased lately. Such optimism is being shown not only by scientists and representatives of business and financial circles but also by some of the officials who, as is known, are least inclined to overestimate the situation. True, in Europe the extremely favourable conditions for expanding business-like cooperation between states with different social systems are building up now and the 1980s can well become a turning point in their mutual relations. There are important objective preconditions for that.

First and foremost, there is an understanding on our Continent of the great importance of the interaction of the said groups of countries to the all-European cooperation and normalisation of the political situation in Europe, as well as to the extending and deepening of the all-European process begun in Helsinki in 1975. This understanding manifests itself, in particular, in the mutual aspiration of CMEA and EEC to establish official relations.

Secondly, there is mutual economic interest in trade. I would like to remind you that during the years of détente commodity exchanges between countries of CMEA and EEC were the most dynamic area of world trade. Between 1970 and 1980 the foreign trade turnover between these two groups of countries increased more than 4.8-fold. Its growth retardation in recent years was due to structural barriers and financial constraints as well as to artificial restrictions used by West European countries in trade with their East European partners.

I would like to stress that the aspiration to establish official relations with the EEC logically stems from the CMEA member countries' policy of developing equal rights and mutually beneficial cooperation between states with different socio-economic systems. The preparedness to establish

M. Maresceau (ed.), The Political and Legal Framework of Trade Relations Between the European Community and Eastern Europe. ISBN 0–7923–0046–7.
© *1989 by Kluwer Academic Publishers, Dordrecht – Printed in the Netherlands.*

trade, economic, scientific and technological relations with those developed capitalist countries which display a readiness to do so, was confirmed by the Economic Summit Conference of the CMEA Member Countries. The Declaration "Maintenance of Peace and International Economic Cooperation", adopted by that Conference, stresses that in international economic relations practice demands mutually beneficial and equal cooperation between all countries. Every act of discrimination or economic diktat, such as the use or threat of embargo, boycott, or trade, credit and technological blockade, should be excluded from the practice of international relations. It is necessary in economic relations among all states to strictly observe the principles of respect for national independence, sovereignty, non-interference in internal affairs, complete equality, respect for national interests, mutual benefit, and most-favoured-nation treatment.

In our opinion, these ends should be served by a speedy establishment of official relations between CMEA and EEC taking into consideration the existing realities and the relations established between CMEA member countries and capitalist countries in Western Europe.

I can state with satisfaction that the current stage of relations between CMEA and EEC is characterised by mutual interest and consolidated understanding that peaceful coexistence of states belonging to different social systems and their economic cooperation should become one of the main principles of international relations and that the improvement of universal economic security can be achieved only through negotiations and by signing balanced agreements that can be reliably controlled. This manifests itself in a gradual approximation of the positions of the two sides on the draft Declaration on the Establishment of Official Relations between CMEA and EEC suggested by CMEA, in which, in fact, the form reflecting the West Berlin territorial clause has yet to be agreed upon. Both sides are making corresponding efforts to seek a mutually acceptable solution and to coordinate the document as soon as possible. But it can be stated already now that on the whole the main issues have been coordinated. It is fully agreed that parallel to the establishment of official relations between CMEA and EEC, individual CMEA member countries will settle their relations with the Community on a bilateral basis. In so doing, the issues of trade between CMEA member countries and the Community can be settled in a contractual way on the basis of corresponding agreements, with every CMEA member country deciding on the expediency of signing them independently. The correctness of such an approach was reconfirmed in the course of bilateral negotiations conducted between individual European CMEA member countries and the Commission of the European Communities in 1986—1987. Therefore, only good will is needed for the establishment of official relations between CMEA and EEC and the subsequent normalisation and expansion of mutually beneficial and non-discriminatory trade within the confines of the whole of Europe. The preparedness for new thinking with its human criteria and orientation to reason and openness should find its way into negotiations between the two largest international economic organisations. The future of integration processes under way in Europe largely depends on the way of formation of the relations between CMEA and EEC. So far, it is impossible to say that these processes have been conducive to its unification which is extremely important since the normalisation of international relations is unthinkable without broad internationalisation. There is no doubt that each group of states has its own interests. However, the expansion of economic relations between CMEA member countries is an objective trend. Underlying the interest of both sides in developing cooperation, are a number of long-term factors: the worldwide process of the internationalisation of economic activity and the extension of the international division of labour; the requirements of economic development in both parts of Europe; and rapid development of scientific and technological progress. All this prompts a search for such forms of mutually beneficial cooperation which would make it possible to use to the utmost the overall potential of Europe for the benefit of all European peoples.

Today more than ever before it is inadmissible to use economic relations as an instrument of political confrontation. We can and we should cooperate in all economic spheres keeping in mind that Europe is our common home and that it is our common task to strengthen the security of that home. Peaceful co-existence in the nuclear age has become a condition for the survival of the whole of mankind and we, Europeans, just have to make our contribution to this process. Today when the treaty between the USSR and the USA is being signed to become a turning point in history, it is particularly important to endeavour understanding between peoples with different political views. This is why it is so important to use every opportunity for a free exchange of opinions on relations between East and West, such as that offered by the Ghent Colloquium.

East-West European trade: the EC-view

WILLY DE CLERCQ
Member of the Commission of the European Communities responsible for External Relations and Commercial Policy

The topics analysed in this volume have covered the whole range of European Community relations with Eastern Europe and indeed gone some way beyond them. Mention has been made of the progress towards setting up a legal framework for normal relations between the Community and the East European countries as well as, in parallel, between the Community and the CMEA. Here, the picture is on the whole an encouraging one. The old atmosphere of mistrust and hostility towards the Community has gone far towards being dissipated. The current situation in which there are no official relations between the Community and Eastern Europe is widely recognised as an "anachronism". More than 130 countries in the world already regard it as perfectly normal to recognise us. But it is only recently that there has been a change in the attitude of East European countries on this point, and a very welcome change, I must say. We now find more and more willingness to recognise the Community as it is, to accept it as the rightful partner on matters such as trade, and to do business with it.

We cannot separate, to my mind, the improved atmosphere in Community-East European relations from the general improvement in the East-West climate. This was dramatically illustrated last week by the signing of the INF Treaty in Washington. A new, more pragmatic spirit is in the air: a clearer recognition of the interdependence which binds us all together. "No man is an island", it is said: in the same way no country, or group of countries, can afford to ignore what is going on in the outside world. This is true in the security field. This is true for the environment, as Chernobyl has reminded us. This is true — and how true — for our economies. The various economic crises of the recent past have affected East as well as West, North as well as South. In Europe — on this small continent, where we rub shoulders with a rich diversity of neighbours — we are particularly conscious of our interdependence in all these areas.

This brings me to the subject of the Community's trade with Eastern

M. Maresceau (ed.), The Political and Legal Framework of Trade Relations Between the European Community and Eastern Europe. ISBN 0–7923–0046–7.
© *1989 by Kluwer Academic Publishers, Dordrecht – Printed in the Netherlands.*

Europe. At present this forms only some 7 p.c. of our total external trade as compared with more than 25 p.c. for the "other" Europe, the EFTA-countries. This proportion has stayed much the same for years, and the present trend is downward, in both value and volume terms. There are several factors which tend to keep the level of East-West trade below its potential. One important factor is obviously the sharp rise in indebtedness in almost all East European countries. It is estimated that hard currency net debt will be some 100 billion Dollars at the end of this year. Indebtedness is, of course, a symptom as well as a cause of reduced trade. Indebtedness in itself is not so much of a problem — and as a Belgian, I feel qualified to comment on this! But it becomes a problem once it gets out of hand either because a country cannot reimburse at all, or because it tries to reimburse too fast, to the detriment of its economy.

Some other important factors have been mentioned. Some of those are traditional, such as the unfavourable trade structure of Eastern Europe, with its low-value-added exports, and the difficulties of access to Western markets, due to problems of quality, marketing, regularity of supply and servicing. Another problem can be the way in which export prices are determined. I will not go further into the argument here: I will just say that when a country's exports are competing on price *alone*, and not taking account of the costs of production, there are likely to be difficulties for its trading partners. Apart from the traditional systemic problems of East-West trade, there are also newer, macro-economic factors such as the decline in oil prices and the fall in the Dollar which have affected the value of Soviet and other East European exports.

After listing all these factors which adversely affect East-West trade, I should like to point to one encouraging factor which has emerged. This is the awareness, on the part of most East European countries, of the need for radical solutions. They have realised that if there is to be a lasting improvement in their economies they must change tack. The reform process in the USSR and certain other countries seeks to alter the way in which the entire economy is run. The contributions in this book have highlighted the new thinking in the foreign trade field. Eastern European countries have traditionally sought to expand their trade by such methods as borrowing heavily to finance imports, and engaging in countertrade to facilitate exports. Experience has shown that these methods have their limits. Now the trend is to encourage direct Western investment in Eastern Europe, to set up joint ventures, and to grant direct trading rights to East European enterprises. We welcome these new initiatives, but they should not be regarded as some kind of miracle solution to all our problems. Flexibility and cooperation are needed. For example, in joint ventures we know that Western investors are mainly interested in gaining access to East European markets. East European countries, on the other hand, see joint ventures as a means of obtaining new technologies and increasing exports to the West. So far, it is too early to tell how effective these new forms will be in improving trade flows. They can realistically be expected to pay off only in the medium term. But one aspect I do find particularly encouraging is the greater pragmatism in the approach of many East European countries, a willingness to learn by experience and to adapt their legislation to the exigencies of international trade. In other words they realise the need to absorb some elements of the market economy if they are to improve their situation. We hope that this trend will continue, because — and here we come to the main conclusion which I draw from the Ghent Colloquium — we stand at a crossroads, at a time of tremendous challenge for East-West trade. The challenge for Eastern Europe is to see whether these new pragmatic internal policies can be introduced in time to overcome inertia and to awaken and to renew talents and productive capacities. The challenge for the Community is to respond to the reform efforts of the East, to contribute to their industrial and technological development. This is in our mutual interest. Business is a two-way street, after all, particularly when one is trading between such different economic systems.

So how, in practice, is the Community responding to this challenge? We are seeking to normalise relations with the East European countries, and to create frameworks for action such as agreements and joint committees. This will enable us to discuss our problems, develop our cooperation, and in particular to ensure that our businessmen operating in Eastern Europe get the facilities which they need to develop East-West trade. We are ready to develop relations with each country individually, bearing in mind its own specific characteristics and interests. Interventions by Commission officials at the Ghent Colloquium have made it clear that the Community does not favour a bloc-to-bloc approach. This is an important element of our policy, which I would like to stress.

The ultimate aim, of course, is to realise the huge untapped potential in the Community's trade with Eastern Europe. Improved trade could also, in a more general way, improve the climate of relations between Eastern and Western Europe.

Some sceptics may be wondering if the Community has much to offer the outside world at the moment. The media has drawn an unfavourable contrast between the recent successful superpower summit and the unsuccessful European council. But we like to think of such meetings as an example of the mature democratic process at work. It is said that the road to hell is paved with good intentions. Well, the road to Community integration is certainly paved with good intentions, but they do not lead to hell. Nor, I must admit, do they seem to be leading to heaven. They usually lead to the next meeting. Of course we have problems, but they should not be exaggerated. We know that Eastern European countries are undertaking their own perestroika in the interests of improved economic performance. No doubt they encounter problems in this process, as the Community does in its march towards a unified market in 1992. But this is no reason for discouragement. Rome was not built in one day. Since our work in the Community is based on the treaty of *Rome*, we should understand that as well as the ancient Romans. I am confident that the Community of 1992 will offer even more opportunities to its foreign trading partners than it does now. I know that some of our Eastern European friends have criticised the EC for what they have called a "protectionist attitude". But let me in this context remind you that the Community is the most open trading bloc in the world. And if we are not — yet — a political superpower, we can certainly claim to be an economic giant. And if we are so protectionist, how is it that we have a permanent trade deficit with Eastern Europe?

So I do seriously believe that the Community has much to offer Eastern Europe, to our mutual benefit. And I see 1988 as a year of great promise. As we all know, 1988 is a leap year. So what better time could we pick for a leap forward in our relations? With goodwill on both sides, I am confident that next year should see the normalisation of our relations with all the East European countries, and with the CMEA, together with the conclusion of a clutch of commercial agreements. This will lay the foundations for a long-term development of our relations. For we must understand this development as a long-term process — we should not expect to see a sudden, enormous increase in our trade flows. Slowly but surely the race will be won. And, as we all know, this hoped-for improvement in our economic relations has a political impact as well. Economic prosperity is a powerful factor in underpinning our democratic freedoms and peaceful ideals.

ADDENDA

I

JOINT DECLARATION
on the establishment of official relations between the European Economic
Community and the Council for Mutual Economic Assistance [1]

THE EUROPEAN ECONOMIC COMMUNITY,
of the one part, and

THE COUNCIL FOR MUTUAL ECONOMIC ASSISTANCE,
of the other part,

HAVING REGARD to the acts establishing the European Economic
Community and the Council for Mutual Economic Assistance, and in
particular the Treaty of Rome,

ON THE BASIS OF the Final Act of the Conference on Security and
Cooperation in Europe, and taking account of the results of the subsequent stages of the CSCE process,

DESIROUS of contributing, by the activities they pursue within their
fields of competence, to the further development of international
economic cooperation, an important factor in economic growth and social
progress,

DECLARE AS FOLLOWS:

1. The European Economic Community and the Council for Mutual
   Economic Assistance establish official relations with each other by
   adopting this Declaration.
2. The Parties will develop cooperation in areas which fall within their

---

1. *O.J.*, L 157/35, 1988.

*M. Maresceau (ed.), The Political and Legal Framework of Trade Relations Between the
European Community and Eastern Europe. ISBN 0–7923–0046–7.*
© 1989 by Kluwer Academic Publishers, Dordrecht – Printed in the Netherlands.

respective spheres of competence and where there is a common interest.

3. The areas, forms and methods of cooperation will be determined by the Parties by means of contacts and discussions between their representatives designated for this purpose.

4. On the basis of the experience gained in developing cooperation between them, the parties will, if necessary, examine the possibility of determining new areas, forms and methods of cooperation.

5. As regards the application of this Declaration to the Community, it shall apply to the territories in which the Treaty establishing the European Economic Community is applied and under the conditions laid down in that Treaty.

6. This Declaration is drawn up in duplicate in the Bulgarian, Czech, Danish, Dutch, English, French, German, Greek, Hungarian, Italian, Mongolian, Polish, Portuguese, Romanian, Russian, Spanish and Vietnamese languages, each text being equally authentic.

Done at Luxembourg, on the twenty-fifth day of June one thousand nine hundred and eighty-eight.

II

AGREEMENT

on Trade and Commercial and Economic Cooperation between The
European Economic Community and The Hungarian People's Republic [2]

THE EUROPEAN ECONOMIC COMMUNITY

and

THE HUNGARIAN PEOPLE'S REPUBLIC,

Considering the traditional trade and economic links between the
European Economic Community, hereinafter called "the Community" and
the Hungarian People's Republic, hereinafter called "Hungary";

Taking into account the favourable implications for trade and economic
relations between the Contracting Parties of their respective economic
situations and policies;

Desirous of creating favourable conditions for the harmonious development and diversification of trade and the promotion of commercial and
economic cooperation on the basis of equality, non-discrimination, mutual
benefit and reciprocity.

Having regard to the particular importance of foreign trade for each of the
Contracting Parties and for their economic and social development;

Having regard to the importance of giving full effect to the Final Act of
the Conference on Security and Cooperation in Europe and the Concluding Document of the Madrid Meeting;

Reaffirming the international commitments of the parties, in particular
those arising from the General Agreement on Tariffs and Trade, including
the Protocol of Accession of Hungary;

Recalling Hungary's membership of the International Monetary Fund and
the World Bank;

---

2. *O.J.,* L 327/1, 1988.

Believing that the time is opportune to give further impetus to the trading and economic relationship between the Community and Hungary;

Recognizing that the Hungarian People's Republic and the European Economic Community desire to establish extensive contractual links with each other which will complement and extend the relations already existing between the two Parties:

HAVE DECIDED to conclude this Agreement and to this end have designated as their plenipotentiaries:

HAVE AGREED AS FOLLOWS:

TITLE 1

COMMERCIAL COOPERATION

Article 1

The Contracting Parties reaffirm their commitment to accord each other most-favoured nation treatment in accordance with the General Agreement on Tariffs and Trade and the Protocol of Accession of Hungary thereto.

Article 2

1. This Agreement shall apply to trade in all products originating in the European Economic Community or in Hungary with the exception of the products covered by the Treaty establishing the European Coal and Steel Community.

2. Unless otherwise specified in this Agreement trade and other commercial cooperation between the Contracting Parties shall be conducted in accordance with their respective regulations.

Article 3

1. This Agreement shall not affect the provisions of the existing Agreements concerning trade in textile products between Hungary and the Community, nor of any such agreements subsequently concluded.
   Furthermore, in the event that the Community invokes paragraph 24 of the Protocol Extending the Arrangement regarding International

Trade in Textiles of 31 July 1986, the provisions of the said Arrangement shall apply to the products in question.

Not later than six months before the expiry of the Agreements concerning trade in textile products referred to above, the Contracting Parties shall consult each other with a view to determining the arrangements to be applied to trade in textile products after the expiry of the said Agreements.

2. This Agreement shall not affect specific agreements or arrangements covering agricultural products in force between the Contracting Parties or any successor agreements or arrangements.

Article 4

1. Each Party will accord the highest degree of liberalization which they generally apply to third countries to imports of the other's products taking into account all the provisions of GATT and of the Protocol of Accession of Hungary thereto.

2. To this end the Community undertakes to abolish the quantitative restrictions referred to in Article 4(a) of the Protocol of Accession of Hungary to GATT in accordance with the provisions set out in the Protocol to this Agreement.

Article 5

The parties undertake to examine the possibility of increasing their mutual trade by the abolition, reduction or other modification of tariffs in conformity with their obligations under the GATT.

Article 6

Taking into account the importance of their trade in agricultural products and the implications of multilateral negotiations in the GATT framework, the Contracting Parties shall examine in the Joint Committee referred to in Title III of this Agreement, the possibility of granting each other reciprocal concessions on a product by product basis in the field of trade in agricultural products on the basis of Article 1 above.

Article 7

1. The Contracting Parties shall consult each other if any product is being imported in trade between the Community and Hungary in such increased quantities, or under such conditions as to cause or threaten serious injury to domestic producers of like or directly competitive products.

2. The Contracting Party requesting the consultations will supply the other Party with all the information required for a detailed examination of the situation.

3. The consultations requested pursuant to paragraph 1 will be held with due regard for the fundamental aims of the Agreement and will be completed not later than 30 days from the date of notification of the request by the Party concerned, unless the Parties agree otherwise.

4. If as a result of such consultations, it is agreed that the situation referred to in paragraph 1 exists, exports shall be limited or such other action taken, which may include action, if possible, with respect to the price at which the exports are sold, as will prevent or remedy the injury.

5. If, following action under paragraphs 1 to 4 above, agreement is not reached between the Contracting Parties, the Contracting Party which requested the consultation shall be free to restrict the imports of the products concerned to the extent and for such time as is necessary to prevent or remedy the injury. The other Contracting Party shall then be free to deviate from its obligations towards the first Party in respect of substantially equivalent trade.

6. In critical circumstances, where delay would cause damage difficult to repair, such preventive or remedial action may be taken provisionally without prior consultation, on the condition that consultation shall be effected immediately after taking such action.

7. In the selection of measures under this Article, the Contracting Parties should give priority to those which cause the least disturbance to the functioning of this agreement.

8. Where necessary, the Contracting Parties may hold consultations to determine when the measures adopted pursuant to paragraphs 4, 5 and 6 shall cease to apply.

9. Either Contracting Party may refer any disagreement arising out of the adoption of safeguard measures pursuant to this Article to the Contracting Parties of the GATT in accordance with Article 5 of the Protocol of Accession of Hungary to the GATT provided that the procedures in this Article have been fully implemented.

Article 8
The Contracting Parties will inform each other of any modification in their tariff or statistical nomenclature or any other decision concerning the classification of products covered by this Agreement.

Article 9
Within the limits of their respective powers, the Contracting Parties
— shall encourage the adoption of arbitration for the settlement of disputes arising out of commercial and cooperation transactions concluded by firms, enterprises and economic organisations of the Community and those of Hungary.
— agree that when a dispute is submitted to arbitration each party to the dispute may freely choose its own arbitrator, irrespective of his nationality, and that the presiding third arbitrator or the sole arbitrator may be a citizen of a third State.
— shall encourage recourse to the arbitration rules elaborated by the United Nations Commission on International Trade Law (UNCITRAL) and to arbitration by any centre of a State signatory to the Convention on Recognition and Enforcement of Foreign Arbitral Awards done at New York on 10th June 1958.

Article 10
1. The Contracting Parties shall make every effort to promote, expand and diversify their trade on the basis of non-discrimination and reciprocity. In the spirit of this Article, the Joint Committee established under Title III of this Agreement will attach special importance to examining ways of encouraging the reciprocal and harmonious expansion of trade.

2. To this end the Contracting Parties agree to ensure the publication of comprehensive data on commercial and financial issues including production, consumption and foreign trade statistics, and information in accordance with Article X of GATT.

3. The Contracting Parties agree that countertrade practices may create distortions in international trade and they should be regarded as temporary and exceptional.
    For this reason they agree not to impose countertrade requirements on companies established in Hungary or the Community nor to compel them to engage in such trade practices.
    Nevertheless, where firms or companies decide to resort to countertrade operations, the Contracting Parties will encourage them to furnish all relevant information to facilitate the transaction.

4. In furtherance of the aims of this Article, the Contracting Parties agree that they shall maintain and improve favourable business regulations and facilities for each other's firms or companies on their respective markets *inter alia* as indicated in the Annex.

TITLE II

ECONOMIC COOPERATION

Article 11

1. In the light of their respective economic policies and objectives, the Contracting Parties shall foster economic cooperation on as broad a base as possible in all fields deemed to be in their mutual interest.

   The objective of such cooperation shall be, *inter alia*:
   — to reinforce and diversify economic links between the Contracting Parties;
   — to contribute to the development of their respective economies and standards of living;
   — to open up new sources of supply and new markets;
   — to encourage cooperation between economic operators, with a view to promoting joint ventures, licensing agreements, and other forms of industrial cooperation to develop their respective industries;
   — to encourage scientific and technological progress.

2. In order to achieve these objectives, the Contracting Parties shall make efforts to encourage and promote economic cooperation in particular in the following sectors:
   — Industry,
   — Mining,
   — Agriculture, including agro-industries,
   — Scientific research in designated sectors in which the Contracting Parties are or may be engaged,
   — Energy, including the development of new sources of energy,
   — Transport,
   — Tourism,
   — Environmental protection and the management of natural resources.

3. To give effect to the objectives of economic cooperation and within the limits of their respective powers, the Contracting Parties shall encour-

age the adoption of measures aimed at creating favourable conditions for economic and industrial cooperation including:

— the facilitation of exchanges of commercial and economic information on all matters which would assist the development of trade and economic cooperation;
— the development of a favourable climate for investment, joint ventures and licensing arrangements notably by the extension by the Member States of the Community and Hungary of arrangements for investment promotion and protection, in particular for the transfer of profits and repatriation of invested capital, on the basis of the principles of non-discrimination and reciprocity;
— exchanges and contacts between persons and delegations representing commercial or other relevant organisations;
— the organisation of seminars, fairs, business weeks or exhibitions;
— activities involving the provision of technical expertise in appropriate areas;
— the promotion of exchange of information and contacts on scientific subjects of mutual interest in accordance with each other's laws and policies.

Article 12

Without prejudice to the relevant provisions of the Treaties establishing the European Communities, the present agreement and any action taken thereunder shall in no way affect the powers of the Member States of the Community to undertake bilateral activities with Hungary in the field of economic cooperation, and to conclude, where appropriate, new economic cooperation agreements with Hungary.

TITLE III

JOINT COMMITTEE

Article 13

1. (a) A Joint Committee shall be set up, comprising representatives of the Community, on the one hand, and representatives of Hungary on the other.
   (b) The Joint Committee shall formulate recommendations by mutual agreement between the Contracting Parties.
   (c) The Joint Committee shall, as necessary, adopt its own rules of procedure and programme of work.

(d) The Joint Committee shall meet once a year in Brussels and Budapest alternately. Special meetings may be convened by mutual agreement, at the request of either Contracting Party. The office of Chairman of the Joint Committee shall be held alternately by each of the Contracting Parties. Wherever possible, the agenda for meetings of the Joint Committee will be agreed beforehand.

(e) The Joint Committee may set up specialised sub-committees to assist it in the performance of its tasks.

2. (a) The Joint Committee shall ensure the proper functioning of this Agreement and shall devise and recommend practical measures for achieving its objectives, keeping in view the economic and social policies of the Contracting Parties.

(b) The Joint Committee shall endeavour to find ways of encouraging the development of trade and commercial and economic cooperation between the Contracting Parties. In particular, it shall:

— examine the various aspects of trade between the Parties, notably the overall pattern, rate of growth, structure and diversification, the trade balance and the various forms of trade and trade promotion;

— make recommendations on any trade or economic cooperation problem of mutual concern;

— seek appropriate means of avoiding possible difficulties in the fields of trade and cooperation and encourage various forms of commercial and economic cooperation in areas of mutual interest;

— consider measures likely to develop and diversify trade and economic cooperation, notably by improving import opportunities in the Community and in Hungary;

— exchange information on macro-economic plans and forecasts for the economies of the two Parties which have an impact on trade and cooperation and, by extension, on the scope for developing complementarity between their respective economies and also on proposed economic development programmes;

— seek methods of arranging and encouraging exchange of information and contacts in matters relating to cooperation in the economic field between the Contracting Parties on a mutually advantageous basis, and work towards the creation of favourable conditions for such cooperation;

— examine favourably ways of improving conditions for the development of direct contacts between firms established in the Community and those established in Hungary;

— formulate and submit to the authorities of both Contracting

Parties recommendations for solving any problems that arise, where appropriate by means of the conclusion of arrangements or agreements.

TITLE IV

GENERAL AND FINAL PROVISIONS

Article 14

1. This Agreement shall not affect or impair the rights and obligations of the Parties under the GATT and the Protocol of Accession of Hungary to the GATT.

2. Subject to the provisions concerning economic cooperation in Article 11, the provisions of this Agreement shall be substituted for provisions of Agreements concluded between Member States of the Community and Hungary to the extent to which the latter provisions are either incompatible with or identical to the former.

Article 15

This Agreement shall apply, on the one hand, to the territories in which the Treaty establishing the European Economic Community is applied and under the conditions laid down in that Treaty and, on the other hand, to the territory of the Hungarian People's Republic.

Article 16

This Agreement shall enter into force on the first day of the month following the date on which the Contracting Parties have notified each other that the legal procedures necessary to this end have been completed. The Agreement shall be concluded for an initial period of ten years. The Agreement shall be automatically renewed year by year provided that neither Contracting Party gives the other Party written notice of denunciation of the Agreement six months before it expires.

However, the two Contracting Parties may amend the Agreement by mutual consent in order to take account of new developments.

The Protocol and the Annex attached to this Agreement shall form an integral part thereof.

Article 17

This Agreement is drawn up in duplicate in the Danish, Dutch, English,

French, German, Greek, Italian, Portuguese, Spanish and Hungarian languages, each text being equally authentic.

Done at Brussels   For the Council of the European Communities

For the Government of the Hungarian People's Republic

Annex

Relating to Article 10 of the Agreement

The regulations and facilities referred to in Article 10 of the agreement are in Hungary inter alia the following:
— Non-discriminatory application of Hungary's import licensing system in accordance with its international commitments.
— The non-discriminatory administration of Hungary's global quota for consumer goods and the provision of all necessary information relating thereto.
— Non-discriminatory treatment by Hungary when awarding contracts for goods or services as a result of World Bank or other international competitive tenders.
— Non-discriminatory procedures for the establishment of offices in Hungary, the renting of business premises, the import of necessary equipment and furniture for operating offices or branches, the recruitment, management and salary levels of staff for such offices and the movement of staff, access to communication facilities and to the publicity media (press, radio and television) and to retail distribution networks.
— The legal protection by Hungary of intellectual property rights for both products and processes in accordance with the international conventions to which Hungary is a signatory namely, the Paris Convention for the Protection of Industrial Property, as revised at Stockholm on July 14th, 1967 and the Universal Copyright Convention of September 6th, 1952, as revised at Paris on July 24th, 1971.

Protocol on the abolition of quantitative restrictions referred to in Article 4

1. The Community undertakes to abolish within one year of the entry into

force of this agreement the quantitative restrictions on imports into the Community originating in Hungary of those products set out in Annex A to this Protocol.

2. The Community undertakes to abolish on or before 31st December 1992 the quantitative restrictions on imports originating in Hungary of those products and into those regions of the Community set out in Annex B to this Protocol.

The list of products set out in Annex B may be modified by mutual consent after consultations in the Joint Committee referred to in Title III of this Agreement to take account of changes in market conditions or regulations relating thereto either in the Community or in Hungary.

3. For restrictions referred to in Article 4 (2) of the Agreement affecting those products for which no provisions have been made in Annexes A and B, the Contracting Parties shall examine before 30th June, 1992 in the framework of the Joint Committee referred to in Title III of the Agreement, whether it can be agreed to make changes in existing import arrangements. The changes to be considered may include any of the following measures:
   — Liberalisation;
   — Liberalisation with surveillance of imports;
   — Adoption of appropriate measures by Hungary such as the issue of export licences or certificates to ensure that exports remain within specified levels;
   — Measures that may be required by the Community after 1992 to adapt existing import arrangements and taken in conformity with the Protocol of Accession of Hungary to the GATT.

4. The Community undertakes to abolish by 31st December 1995 at the latest the restrictions referred to in Article 4 (2) of the Agreement affecting imports of products into the Community originating in Hungary.

5. For the products in respect of which quantitative restrictions are abolished pursuant to paragraphs 3 or 4 the following special conditions of application of the safeguard clause contained in Article 7 of the Agreement shall apply until 31 December 1998:
   (a) If the increased level of imports for a given product, or the conditions under which it is imported, cause or threaten to cause material injury to Community products of like or competitive products, the Community may request the opening of consultations in accordance with the procedure described in Article 7 (2) and (3) of the Agreement with a view to reaching agreement on the appropriate restraint level or other appropriate action for the product concerned.
   (b) If within ten working days of the request by the Community for

consultations, the Parties are unable to reach a satisfactory solution, the Community shall have the right to introduce and maintain during the initial period of validity of the Agreement a quantitative limit at an annual level not lower than the level already achieved in the normal course of trade before the consultation.

(c) Hungary shall then not resort to Article 7 (5) of the Agreement nor otherwise have recourse to retaliation or seek compensation notwithstanding the provisions of Article 14 paragraph 1 of this Agreement.

6. The Contracting Parties recognize that difficulties may arise after 1998 and agree to avoid possible market disruption. They will hold consultations before 30th June 1998 in the framework of the Joint Committee referred to in Title III of this Agreement.

III

AGREEMENT
between the European Economic Community and the Czechoslovak
Socialist Republic on trade in industrial products[3]

THE EUROPEAN ECONOMIC COMMUNITY

and

THE CZECHOSLOVAK SOCIALIST REPUBLIC,

RESOLVED to establish favourable conditions for the harmonious development of trade in the field of industrial products between the European Economic Community and the Czechoslovak Socialist Republic,

DESIROUS of diversifying the structure of trade between the Community and Czechoslovakia,

REAFFIRMING the commitment of both Parties to the General Agreement on Tariffs and Trade,

HAVING REGARD to the importance of giving full effect to all the provisions of the Final Act of the Conference on Security and Cooperation in Europe and the Concluding Document of the Madrid meeting,

HAVE DECIDED to conclude this Agreement and to this and have designated as their plenipotentiaries:

Article 1
1. Subject to paragraph 2, this Agreement shall apply to trade in products originating in the Community or in Czechoslovakia falling within Chapters 25 to 96 of the Harmonized Commodity Description and Coding System.

2. This Agreement shall not apply:
   — to products covered by the Treaty establishing the European Coal and Steel Community,

---

3. *O.J.*, C 7/3, 1988 (at the moment of proofreading the agreement was not yet published in the L-section of the *Official Journal*).

— for the period of application of the Agreement between the Community and Czechoslovakia on trade in textile products which has been provisionally applied since 1 January 1987 including any exchange of letters and other arrangements concluded in connection therewith and any agreements on trade in textile products subsequently concluded, to textile products covered by those agreements; furthermore in the event that the Community invokes paragraph 24 of the Protocol Extending the Arrangement Regarding International Trade in Textiles of 31 July 1986, only the provisions of the said Arrangement shall apply thereto to the exclusion of all dispositions of this Agreement,

— to products listed in Annex I to this Agreement.

3. Unless otherwise specified in this Agreement, trade between the Contracting Parties shall be conducted in compliance with their respective regulations.

Article 2

1. In the framework of their respective laws and regulations, the Contracting Parties will adopt measures to ensure the harmonious development and the diversification of their mutual trade.

2. To that end, they confirm their resolve to consider in a spirit of cooperation each for its own part suggestions made by the other Party with a view to attaining these aims.

Article 3

1. The Community will accord the highest possible degree of liberalization to imports of products originating in Czechoslovakia. To this end it will ensure that during the period of validity of this Agreement substantial progress is made towards the abolition of specific quantitative restrictions which apply to Czechoslovakia.

2. Progress in liberalization shall take account of the provisions of GATT, of the development of trade between the Contracting Parties and of progress made in the implementation of the present agreement.

3. Each year the Consultation body provided for in Article 12 will assess the progress made in applying paragraph 1 by reference to all relevant factors.

Article 4

The Community undertakes to eliminate quantitative restrictions on imports into those regions of the Community and of those products listed in Annex II.

Article 5

The Community undertakes to suspend the application of quantitative restrictions on imports into the regions of the Community and of those products listed in Annex III on the terms and conditions specified therein.

Article 6

1. For each calendar year, the Community shall open import quotas for products which are of interest for Czechoslovak exports and which are subject to quantitative restrictions.

2. The two parties will hold consultations each year in the Consultation Body provided for in Article 12 to determine what increases in the quotas referred to in paragraph 1 can be made for the following year.

Article 7

Imports into the Community of products covered by this Agreement shall not be charged against the quotas referred to in Article 6 provided that they are declared as being intended for re-export and are re-exported from the Community either in the unaltered state or after inward processing, under the administrative control arrangements in force in the Community.

Article 8

The Parties will inform each other of any changes in their tariff or statistical nomenclature or of any decision taken in accordance with the procedures in force, concerning the classification of products covered by this Agreement.

Article 9

The exchange of goods between the two Contracting Parties shall be effected at market-related prices.

Article 10

1. The Contracting Parties shall consult each other if any product is being imported in trade between the Community and Czechoslovakia in such increased quantities, or under such conditions as to cause or threaten serious injury to domestic producers of like or directly competitive products.

2. The Contracting Party requesting the consultations will supply the

other Party with all the information required for a detailed examination of the situation.

3. The consultations requested pursuant to paragraph 1 will be held with due regard for the fundamental aims of the Agreement and will be completed not later than 30 days from the date of notification of the request by the Party concerned, unless the Parties agree otherwise.

4. If as a result of such consultations, it is agreed that the situation referred to in paragraph 1 exists, exports shall be limited or such other action taken, which may include action, if possible, with respect to the price at which the exports are sold, as will prevent or remedy the injury.

5. If, following action under paragraphs 1 to 4 above, agreement is not reached between the Contracting Parties, the Contracting Party which requested the consultations shall be free to restrict the imports of the products concerned to the extent and for such time as is necessary to prevent or remedy the injury. The other Contracting Party shall then be free to deviate from it obligations towards the first Party in respect of substantially equivalent trade.

6. In critical circumstances, where delay would cause damage difficult to repair, such preventive or remedial action may be taken provisionally without prior consultation, on the condition that consultation shall be effected immediately after taking such action.

7. In the selection of measures under this Article, the Contracting Parties should give priority to those which cause the least disturbance to the functioning of this Agreement.

8. Where necessary, the Contracting Parties may hold consultations to determine when the measures adopted pursuant to paragraphs 4, 5 and 6 shall cease to apply.

Article 11

Czechoslovakia will take appropriate measures to encourage imports from the Community to the Czechoslovak market.

Such measures shall be aimed *inter alia* at:

(a) supplying the Community with the appropriate information, notably with regard to:

    (i) economic development plans,

   (ii) general import arrangements and forecasts,

   (iii) import and investment intentions in the sectors of Czechoslovak industry which may be of interest to Community exporters;

(b) creating conditions facilitating the activities in Czechoslovakia of Community business operators and in particular closer contacts between representatives and experts from Community firms and those of Czechoslovak firms and end-users;

(c) encouraging and facilitating, notably by means of practical measures, trade promotion activities in Czechoslovakia, such as the organization of fairs and exhibitions;

(d) promoting visits by persons, groups and delegations involved in trade between the two Parties.

Article 12

1. A body shall be established for regular consultations, composed of representatives of the Community, on the one hand, and representatives of Czechoslovakia, on the other.

The tasks of the consultation body will be:

— to ensure the proper functioning of the Agreement,

— to examine the various aspects of the development of trade between the Parties, notably its overall trend, its rate of growth, its structure and diversification, the trade balance situation and the various forms of trade and trade promotion,

— to seek appropriate means of avoiding difficulties which might arise in connection with trade and with changes in existing trade arrangements,

— to consider measures likely to develop and diversify trade, notably by opening up new opportunities for imports into the Community and in Czechoslovakia,

— to exchange views and put forward suggestions on any problem of common interest relating to trade,

— to make recommendations likely to encourage the expansion of trade,

— to examine the possibility of negotiations being initiated, within the period of validity of this Agreement, with a view to concluding a successor Agreement.

2. The consultations shall be held once a year in Brussels and Prague alternately. Special meetings may be convened by mutual agreement, at the request of either Contracting Party. The chairmanship of the consultation meetings shall be held alternately by each of the Contracting Parties.

The agenda for consultation meetings shall be determined by mutual agreement and, wherever possible, shall be agreed beforehand.

Article 13

This Agreement shall apply, on the one hand, to the territories in which the Treaty establishing the European Economic Community is applied and under the conditions laid down in that Treaty and, on the other hand, to the territory of Czechoslovakia.

Article 14

This Agreement shall enter into force on the first day of the month following the date on which the Contracting Parties have notified each other that the legal procedures necessary to this end have been completed. The Agreement shall be concluded for a period of four years. The Agreement shall be automatically renewed year by year provided that neither Contracting Party gives the other Party written notice of denunciation of the Agreement six months before it expires.

However, the two Contracting Parties may amend the Agreement by mutual consent in order to take account of new developments.

The annexes and the exchange of letters concerning the combined nomenclature attached to this Agreement shall form an integral part thereof.

Article 15

This Agreement is drawn up in duplicate in the Danish, Dutch, English, French, German, Greek, Italian, Portuguese, Spanish and Czech Languages, each text being equally authentic.

LIST OF TABLES AND FIGURES

INDEX